The Plays of HUGH KELLY

Edited with an introduction by

LARRY CARVER

and textual notes by

MARY J. H. GROSS

GARLAND PUBLISHING, INC.
New York & London
1980

828
K29p

For a complete list of the titles in this series see the final pages of this volume.

Introduction copyright © 1980 by Larry Carver
All rights reserved

These facsimiles have been made from copies in the Yale University Library, including *The School for Wives*, which is in the Lewis Walpole Collection, and excluding *False Delicacy* and *Clementina*, which have come from the Library of the University of Texas at Austin. *The Reasonable Lover* has been transcribed from a manuscript in the Larpent Collection of the Huntington Library.

Library of Congress Cataloging in Publication Data

Kelly, Hugh, 1739–1777.
The plays of Hugh Kelly.

(Eighteenth-century English drama)
Includes bibliographical references.
CONTENTS: False delicacy. 1768—A word to the wise. 1770—Clementina. 1771—The school for wives. [etc.]
I. Series.
PR3539.K2A19 1980 822′.6 78-66653
ISBN 0-8240-3600-X

The volumes in this series are printed on acid-free, 250-year-life paper.
Printed in the United States of America

80-9147

Library of
Davidson College

EIGHTEENTH-CENTURY ENGLISH DRAMA

a comprehensive collection of over 200 representative plays, reproduced in facsimile in fifty-eight volumes with critical introductions by leading scholars

General Editor

PAULA R. BACKSCHEIDER

A GARLAND SERIES

for William B. Todd

CONTENTS

INTRODUCTION

In the London of the 1760s and 1770s he was, Arthur Murphy recalled, the "well known Mr. Hugh Kelly,"[1] and well-known he must have been. His periodical essays, *The Bablers*, which advised and amused, comforted and admonished, went into a collected edition. *Thespis* I and II, which satirized and evaluated in couplets the actors of Drury Lane and Covent Garden, raised hackles and a number of vituperative replies. His poems and theatrical criticism circulated through the city; a novel, *Memoirs of a Magdalen*, went into a second edition and was adapted for the stage;[2] and his editorials in *The Public Ledger* defended George III's government almost daily against the Wilkesites. His first play, *False Delicacy*, proved the hit of the 1767–68 season; performed eighteen times that season, it became the rave of the provincial theatres and a success in France. Three thousand copies of the play were sold on the day of publication, another ten thousand during the season. But his second play more accurately measures his fame in some quarters, his notoriety in others, for three nights of rioting drove *A Word to the Wise* from the stage, rioting directed not at the play but at the author, a friend of Robert Ladbroke, a defender of Pitt and of Lord Baltimore. Kelly wrote four more plays. He practiced law and presumably continued to write government propaganda till his death in 1777. Londoners of this period would have heard of Hugh Kelly. History, however, has all but forgotten him. As his only modern biographer, Thomas O'Leary, has put it: "While Kelly lived, he was undoubtedly a highly controversial figure in letters and politics. There doubtless were agents who checked what he wrote and what he intended to write, where he went and why. But for him, the irony of history is almost complete; the record of his life has all but vanished.[3]

His work has fared somewhat better. Only specialists now read the poetry and essays, and though the plays are never performed, they are read but until recently only in a perfunctory and careless way. The standard literary histories lump Kelly with Cumberland and consider them to be "Chief among the sentimental playwrights. . . ."[4] Studies devoted to sentimental drama or to Kelly specifically apply, with all its dreary connotations, the same stock label. Yet there is something curious in these studies. As C. J. Rawson has pointed out, no matter what their definition of the sentimental, the critics have found Kelly no perfect fit.[5] Bernbaum, with whom the modern study of sentimental drama begins, becomes rather riled at Kelly for providing evidence that contradicts his hypothesis. *False Delicacy*, he writes, "is a peculiar variation of the type [sentimental comedy], and sometimes satirizes the very tendency it is supposed to support."[6] Similar critical ambivalence can be found in Nettleton, Thorndike, Nicoll, and Shorer.[7] The incongruity between hypothesis and evidence that the critics have found uncomfortable, recorded, and left unexplained is pretty much summed up in the strained logic of Arthur Sherbo's observation that "despite certain anti-sentimental notes in it, Hugh Kelly's *False Delicacy* is considered one of the most sentimental of comedies because of this very excess of sensibility, refinement, or false delicacy" (p. 85), a statement that verges on saying that the play is sentimental because it has too much of the anti-sentimental.

The close critical agreement on Kelly over a fifty-year period arises, I think, not so much because the critics have been reading each other, but because all, save for Sherbo, have subscribed to a Cavalier model of literary history that has something like the following form: Sentimental drama, which is bad, arose in reaction to the indecencies of the Restoration stage and found its first practitioners in Cibber and Steele. Middle-class in its values, it replaced wit with sympathetic laughter and became the dominant form of comedy. The later and most popular exponents were Kelly and Cumberland. Goldsmith, though defeated at first by *False Delicacy*, overcame the sentimentalists with *She Stoops to Conquer*, and Sheridan continued the rout with *The Rivals*, *School for Scandal*, and *The Critic*. Laughter of the right sort once again held the stage, but only momentarily. Goldsmith and Sheridan were throwbacks to an earlier, wittier time. Sentimentalism, to the chagrin of those with taste, triumphed despite their efforts. Though roughly put, this is the model of dramatic history that has informed criticism for the past fifty years. Kelly has been found an anomaly, but the model has been so strongly held that the evidence has been made to conform to the model, not the model to the evidence. Kelly has remained an archetypal sentimental playwright, being at once the source for the critical model and, despite the anomalies, its sustaining evidence.

Recently this critical model has, for various reasons, begun to break down.[8] Though a new synthesis may be on the way, for now we are getting readings of individual authors. Perhaps because of this breakdown, Kelly has been receiving, what has long been his due, close and sympathetic readings that have found him to be a sentimentalist, but not in the lachrymose, disparaging sense usually associated with this classification.[9] His sentimentalism, something that his contemporaries whether they damned or praised at least understood, deals to be sure with the heart but also with the head. Though Kelly occasionally indulged in the "rich-soul'd luxury of tears,"[10] his sentimentalism has more to do with an underlying set of thoughts, notions, and opinions, that is, with sentiments, than with any desire to elicit "pity for distress and admiration for virtue" (Sherbo, p. 73). Kelly was a moralist, his intentions never far from didactic, his view of literature consistently instrumental. He used the stage, as he had his essays and novel, to put forth certain sentimental attitudes and assumptions about human nature and to defend these from sentimental excesses. To do so, he appealed to the feeling and informed heart, but often not so much through the pathetic as through a deft use of parody and satire. Tracing the reasons why Kelly has been read one way, with focus on the tearful and pathetic, and should and is beginning to be read in quite another, with focus on the ironic and humorous, gives us a fascinating glimpse at those conventions—biographical, sociological, and linguistic—by which we try to render our literary past intelligible. But more importantly, it allows us opportunity to understand and to enjoy minor, but by no means negligible, works enormously popular in their own day.

I

One of the sources for the misunderstandings surrounding Kelly's plays is the man himself. For him it would perhaps have been better had the record of his life completely disappeared. Like a number of his contemporaries—Murphy, Bickerstaffe, Jephson, and Goldsmith—Kelly was born in Ireland, probably in Dublin in 1739, the son of a father who had fallen on hard times and who had consequently become a tavern keeper. He undoubtedly received some schooling, but was apprenticed early to a staymaker. When he journeyed to London in the spring of 1760, he came with only a needle to make his living. Through whatever fortuitous circumstances, he was soon, however, writing, and Irish pluck and a nimble mind gained him some money and a share of fame. But to his contemporaries, one gathers from the satires and various comments, he always remained a staymaker, and much lower one could not go. His first occupation and his Irish background led to a Kelly conceived of as naive, not knowing very much, and certainly incapable of irony or satire. Consequently, in what remains of the record of the life, we choose to remember the Kelly kind and generous to the poor, leaping with joy at the money he received from *False Delicacy*, and weeping at the grave of Goldsmith—all of which could be looked upon with approbation but which filtered through the pejorative connotations of occupation and background become evidence for simplicity, emotional and mental weakness. It is easy to treat the work of such a man indifferently. Thus *The Oxford Companion to English Literature* mentions Kelly as the author of three plays, consigning the others to oblivion. The *CBEL*'s information concerning the editions of the plays is wrong in every case. Thorndike has Mrs. Hurley for Mrs. Harley. Shorer has Lord Winworth as Sir George, which he is not, and Mrs. Harley breaking down "in a flood of tears" (p. 393), which she does not. One could go on, the stock and careless critical responses being many.

This survivor of the critical political battles of the 1760s and 1770s was not, of course, naive. And a perusal of *Thespis* will disabuse anyone of the idea that Kelly was incapable of satire, even of ill-natured scurrility. But the stereotype of Kelly as an unsophisticated, sentimental writer is not simply a case of critics seeing what they want to see. Kelly wanted to be seen this way. The "Address" prefacing *A Word to the Wise*, in which he is defending his editorial and political stance against those who damned the play, provides a typical example of Kelly's self-presentation.

> The piece, with all it's imperfections on it's head, is now before the world; and the author hopes, if it should even set the reader fast asleep, that nothing it contains will rouze his indignation: the most careful father he thinks

> may put it into the hands of his daughter, without any fear of wounding her delicacy, or unhinging her principles.[11]

The rhetorical stance, apologetic, dismissive of merit at least as the world sees merit, is pure Kelly. He may be intellectually weak, and he may put one to sleep, but he is honest, morally and feelingly right. He appeals to the touchstones of sentimentalism, the family and the importance of benevolent motives over utilitarian results. Yet anyone who reads this address will find a most impressive argument, ethically and emotionally appealing, but also logically sound. It is little wonder that some have taken it to be Johnson's, ironically so in light of the argument we are making. Johnson had to write it; Kelly would have been incapable of such a performance. That the emotional appeal stays with us results in part because we think that is what we should see in a sentimental writer, but also in part because Kelly wanted us to see him this way in order to be accepted, in order not to offend, in order to deflect criticism.

Such is the rhetorical response that we might expect of a man from the provinces. An Irishman, he is trying to make his way in England, trying to be, without much formal training, a writer. He aspires, moreover, to wealth and has little, to breeding and gentility, but is never sure he fits in. He does belong to the Wednesday Club and consorts with Goldsmith, Edward Thompson, and Thomas King, but he does not belong to the club of Johnson, Burke, Reynolds, *et al*. Thus he is forever asserting but apologetically so, saying one thing in terms of another, belittling and laughing at himself; never sure that what he says will be accepted by others, he couches it deferentially. Thus too he falls back on values that he no doubt accepts but which are also beyond criticism.[12]

This parody and sometimes "pseudo-parody to disarm criticism," to use Empson's term,[13] becomes the dominant trope in Kelly's life and work. The process can be exemplified by looking at his numerous references to the Irish. Kelly was clearly proud of being Irish, but in the London of his day this pride could never be brought forth openly. Following Cumberland's success with Major O'Flaherty in *The West Indian*, Kelly decided to present his own sympathetic Irishman. If the Irish are typically seen as barbarously ferocious, hotheaded and ready to duel, Kelly, as he puts it in the "Preface" to *The School for Wives*, will give a "different picture of Irish manners, tho' in humble life, and flatters himself that those who are *really acquainted with the original*, will acknowledge it to be at least a tolerable resemblance" (p. viii, italics mine). The character, Connolly, is good-hearted and likeable enough, but he tips over into being a clown. Though in the right in his opposition to dueling and in his views of what constitutes real honor, he cannot express these views openly; his must be acceptance through humoring his betters. When he goes, much against his inclinations, to deliver Leeson's challenge to Belville, Connolly soliloquizes:

> As this is a challenge, I shou'dn't go without a sword; come down, little tickle-pitcher. . . . Some people may think me very conceited now; but as the dirtiest blacklegs in town can wear one without being stared at, I don't think it can suffer any disgrace by the side of an honest man. [p. 10]

We laugh at Connolly's pretentions to gentility, to the wearing of a sword, but laugh as we may, he is nevertheless an honest man, wince though we do at his open avowal of such. The original for this ingratiating but self-deprecating Irishman pretending to gentility and, despite the laughter, being both genteel and honest is of course Kelly himself. He no doubt had been laughed at for being Irish as well as for his dress of "flowing broad silver-laced waistcoat, bagwig, and sword" (*DNB*), affectations which his ambition would not forgo but which his desire to be accepted by his betters had to play down.

Following Connolly's soliloquy, Kelly employs the same rhetorical strategy, only this time in reference to a sentimental playwright, Lady Rachel Mildew, who goes around taking notes for her next comedy and is disappointed when life does not conform to her sentimental expectations. She tells Mrs. Belville, who has reacted calmly and sensibly to the discovery of her husband's passion for other ladies, that she is "really sorry . . . to see you so calm under the perfidy of your husband; you should be quite wretched—indeed you should" (p. 42). Lady Rachel, though the object of good-humored satire throughout the play, has, it turns out, many of the characteristics of Kelly and of the Kelly he thinks others see. Take, for example, her encounter with Mrs. Belville.

> *Lady Rach*. My dear, how have you done since the little eternity of my last seeing you. Mr. Torrington is come to town, I hear.
>
> *Mrs. Bel*. He is, and must be greatly flattered to find that your Ladyship has made him the hero of your new comedy.
>
> *Lady Rach*. Yes, I have drawn him as he is, an honest practitioner of the law; which is, I fancy, no very common character—
>
> *Mrs. Bel*. And it must be a vast acquisition to the Theatre.
>
> *Lady Rach*. Yet the managers of both houses have refused my play; have refused it peremptorily! tho' I offered to make them a present of it.
>
> *Mrs. Bel*. That's very surprising, when you offer'd to make them a present of it.
>
> *Lady Rach*. They alledge that the audiences are tired of

> crying at comedies; and insist that my Despairing Shepherdess is absolutely too dismal for representation.
> *Mrs. Bel.* What, tho' you have introduced a lawyer in a new light!
> *Lady Rach.* Yes, and have a boarding-school romp, that slaps her mother's face, and throws a bason of scalding water at her governess. (p. 11)

Lady Rachel's play is in part *The School for Wives*. In the "Preface" Kelly had announced his intention to present a lawyer in a favorable light. Through Lady Rachel he takes, moreover, an amiable dig at Garrick and Colman, the managers of the house, and also at Goldsmith. The charge against weeping comedies was a commonplace, but, given Kelly's sensitivity to his former friend Goldsmith, the comment is probably directed at him and his *Westminster Review* article on laughing and sentimental comedy (January 1, 1773) and at the "Prologue" to *She Stoops to Conquer* (March 15, 1773; *The School for Wives* opened December 11, 1773), which had also mocked those who deal in "sentimentals." Kelly winds up having it both ways. By laughing at Lady Rachel, he defends himself against Goldsmith's charges that he indulges in what in the "Preface" he had called the "extremes of sentimental gloom." At the same time, he criticizes those, no doubt with Goldsmith in mind, who would have comedy deal merely in "uninteresting levity" (p. v). *She Stoops to Conquer*, though hardly uninteresting and containing no romps, does have much that is farcical.[14] Through Lady Rachel Kelly defends what he is doing in his play. He asserts his own values and aesthetic and corrects what he sees as the misconception of them by others, and he does so through self-effacement and self-parody.

There is the danger here of simply making Kelly say what we want him to say by claiming that he is being ironic. In this case I do not believe the danger a real one. Kelly has always been seen as an anomaly, a sentimentalist who in some sense is not sentimental. Regarding him as an ironist and seeing this irony as growing in part from his reactions to his background help us to account for the anomalous. In addition, it will lead us, I believe, to a much more comprehensive, generous, and interesting reading of the plays than we have had. Whether it holds as a general rule that the biographical has a more privileged place in the understanding of satire and sentimental works than of tragic ones, it is true that we will not fully understand and appreciate Kelly until we take into account autobiographical passages like this from *Babler* 17. A son of a tradesman, left some money by his father, imitates his betters:

> . . . bred up to an intercourse with none but sellers of linen, and dealers in packthread, I considered every man with a laced coat and cockade as infinitely my superior; and endeavoured, with a sedulity of an uncommon nature, to imitate what I so passionately admired. Happily, my endeavours succeeded so well, that in a little time I swore, got drunk, broke windows, kicked waiters, and insulted modest women, with as good a grace as if I had been colonel of a regiment.

On the one side lay the vulgarities of the tradesmen and lower and on the other the aristocrats with their freedoms, their dueling and drinking. Kelly strove for the middle way in manners and morals but also in art, ethics and aesthetics never being far apart in his thinking. "His chief study," he wrote, "has been to steer between the extremes of sentimental gloom, and the excesses of uninteresting levity," to combine "laugh" with "lesson" (*The School for Wives*, p. v). The extremes of the purely didactic, the art of the vulgar, are to be avoided quite as much as those of aristocratic wit. And so it is with behavior: "The extremes of behaviour are what every person of sense would cautiously study to avoid; since an excess of ceremony cannot fail of subjecting us to ridicule; and a total disregard of politeness must naturally expose us to contempt . . ." (*Babler* 31). A synonym for politeness is delicacy (Johnson, definition 6), and though Kelly has, save for the bailiffs in *The School for Wives*, no genuinely low characters, he does organize the plays around normative characters, the Mrs. Harleys, Miss Walsinghams, Villars, and Zelidas; those who are overly delicate, the Lord Winworths, Sir George Hastings, and Ormsbys; and those of too little delicacy, the Sir Harry Newburgs, Jack Dormers, and Belvilles. Kelly satirizes the excesses in behavior and in art, but because he is never quite sure of the normative or that the normative will be accepted, he often couches it in parodic terms.

II

We need to understand the man; we also need to understand the man as a writer in his time. When seen in context, Kelly stands out not as a unique sentimentalist, but as a writer of typically Georgian plays. These plays draw heavily upon the works of others, intimately reflect the goings on of the day, and typically blend sentiment with humor, pathos with satire and farce. Kelly was a thoroughly conventional writer, making his way in the world of letters, like a Johnson or Goldsmith, in the tested ways. The *Babler* follows in a long line begun by the *Spectator* and the *Tatler*; like Goldsmith, Kelly wrote his novel, and he imitated Churchill's success with his own version of *The Rosciad*. He was writing to the moment, trying to provide for the day passing over him, and he turned his hand to what had been successful. As he put it in the "Prologue" to *The Romance of an Hour*: "Let critics proudly form dramatic laws / Give me, say I, what's sure to meet applause." He turned, for example, to tragedy in 1772 partially because, *A Word to the Wise* having been damned for political reasons, he wanted to cover his tracks. He brought out *Clementina*, his one tragedy, anonymously at Covent Garden, though the change in theatres may have had more to do with Garrick's desire to avoid controversy. He chose, moreover, a highly successful model to imitate. *Clementina* is a thinly veiled version of *The Mourning Bride*,[15] the fourth most popular tragedy, judging by performance figures, at Covent Garden between 1747 and 1776 and the only non-Shakespearean play in the top four.

Once you begin to look, you feel that you could gloss everything in Kelly with some analogue. *The School for Wives*, which by the way has nothing in common with the play by Molière except its title, probably comes most immediately from Murphy's popular *The Way to Keep Him* and Charles Macklin's *The Married Libertine*, in which Lady Belville bears patiently Lord Belville's libertinage. But then both of these plays are just two of the myriad based on the love's-last-shift / provoked-wife plot. Kelly drew on the century's other basic pattern for comedies, the provoked-husband plot, for the Willoughbys in *A Word to the Wise* and the Freemores in *The Man of Reason*. Miss Montagu and Miss Willoughby laughing the rake Dormer into reform has its parallel in the treatment Lovemore receives from the Widow Bellmour and Mrs. Lovemore in Act V of *The Way to Keep Him*. The sea jargon of Sir Hector Strangeways in *The Romance of an Hour* mirrors that of Captain Ironsides in Cumberland's *The Brother*. Cumberland has his West Indian, Belcour, and Kelly has his East Indian, Bussora. Goldsmith has his bailiff scene; so does Kelly, who seems ready to capitalize on a cause célèbre however minor. Not surprisingly, the popular Richardson and Fielding are omnipresent in Kelly. He based his novel on *Clarissa* but gave it a happy ending, no doubt with a view to the audience. The scene of Miss Rivers and Sir Harry in the garden in *False Delicacy* has overtones of *Clarissa* as does Jack Dormer's treatment of Miss Willoughby in *A Word to the Wise*. The Lady Winterly, Gloworm, and William imbroglio in *The Man of Reason* comes right out of Joseph's encounters with Lady Booby and Mrs. Slipslop while William, the good, and Lestock, the bad nephew, are patterned on Tom and Blifil.

In his search for "what's sure to meet applause," Kelly also trafficked in the topical. Bussora, with his "me must die with grief if her do wrong ting" (*The Romance of an Hour*, p. 8), is Kelly's bow to the contemporary interest in primitivism. Mrs. Freemore's concern about hairstyles means little until one knows that in the 1775–76 season when *The Man of Reason* appeared "Female head-dresses reached an all-time high and were duly mocked on stage . . ." (*LS*, IV, 1907–08). The reference in this play to "the suffocation of some pigeons in the air-pump" (p. 14) mirrors the contemporary fascination with Priestley's discovery of oxygen. Mr. Freemore's protest against cruelty to animals in the same episode and his wife's subsequent invitation to the company to stay for dinner also reflect the growing concern over cruelty to animals and the connection of that concern with sentimentalism. Mrs. Freemore, mocking her husband's genuine delicacy and revealing her own lack of this quality, tells her guests that "We have Nothing but a couple of chickens reared by my own hand's, which I have just order'd to be kill'd, a pig whipp'd to death, and a dish of roasted Lobsters" (cf. *Babler* 121, "On Tenderness to the Animal Creation . . ."). She exits, and Lady Winterly replies, "There's a Woman of sensibility for you" (p. 15). Kelly apparently had an abiding ethical concern about dueling, but dueling was also topical. That *The School for Wives* (December 11, 1773) should dwell on this topic more than the other plays can in part be explained by George Winchester Stone's observation that during the 1773–74 season:

> Moralists were somewhat taken aback that Garrick and Colman should both persist in putting on the *Beggar's Opera* . . . when Justice Fielding had complained of the bad effects the performances had upon delinquent youth. There was some hope, expressed in the press, however, that William Kendrick's new play at Covent Garden, *The Duellist* (20 Nov.), might have a beneficial effect upon the rational delinquents in the upper and middle classes. [*LS,* IV, 1741]

Kelly was also a moralist, and no doubt Lord Winworth speaks for him when at the end of *False Delicacy* he declares that "The stage shou'd be a school of morality" (p. 87). But in penning the line Kelly had an eye to the audience, for the morality of the stage was a lively topic debated not just in prologues but in the plays themselves. For example, in Murphy's *The School for Guardians*, Lovibond and Oldcastle, the superannuated guardians, argue over the educations of their female charges.

> *Lovibond*. Ay, and I have taught her to know right from wrong.
> *Oldcastle*. Right from wrong! You have ruined the girl—have not you indulged her in every whimsy this fertile town affords?
> *Lovibond*. I have shewn her the world—
> *Oldcastle*. Have not you carried her to plays?
> *Lovibond*.To see folly ridiculed—
> *Oldcastle*. To profligate comedies?
> *Lovibond*. The stage is the school of virtue—
> *Oldcastle*. The School of Sin and Impudence![16]

The issue is never resolved as both girls, though educated differently, manage to follow nature, outwit their guardians, and gain their lovers. Murphy's play opened January 10, 1767, *False Delicacy* on January 23, 1768. In the season of 1766–67 occurred the lively debate surrounding the publication of *The Stage the High Road to Hell*, which was quickly answered by *Theatrical Entertainments Consistent with Society, Morality, and Religion*, both pamphlets appearing anonymously. Statements on the moral purpose of the stage, for or against, may reflect the author's own opinions, as they do with Kelly, but they were also, the author hoped, good box office.

I raise the issue of Kelly's topicality and of his borrowings not to suggest that the plays be read as period pieces or that Kelly be charged with plagiarism. Though they avoid politics almost altogether, Georgian plays were topical, and they were, to use Garrick's term, "concoction[s]." Johnson, to whom Garrick was speaking when he used the word, defined "to concoct" as "to digest by the stomach so as to turn food to nutriment" and cited a passage from Watts to show its metaphorical uses: "The notions and sentiments of others judgment, as well as of our own memory makes our property: it does, as it were, *concoct* our intellectual food, and turns it into a part of ourselves."[17] Taking the notions and sentiments of others—scenes, plots, ideas, snatches of dialogue—and making them their own was what Georgian playwrights—not only Kelly—did. Lydia Languish meets her downfall in the lending library, but so does her original, Polly Honeycombe. *The Brothers* has both a provoked-wife and provoked-husband plot; moreover, it draws a good deal from *Tom Jones* as does Colman's *The Jealous Wife*. One has the feeling that *The Clandestine Marriage* should not alone bear a dual authorship, that we could be citing, among others, Garrick and Hoadly, Garrick and Murphy, Garrick and Mrs. Griffiths, and yes, Garrick and Kelly. The problem with Kelly's *The Man of Reason*, it seems to me, is that it came out in its first concoction. Garrick, busy with his plans for retiring that season, 1775–76, never got a chance to touch it, and Kelly apparently received no help from the troubled Covent Garden, that season having no fewer than five managers, where the ill-fated play finally appeared for all of one night.[18] But the typical Georgian play was a highly self-conscious work, a blend of what had been successful in the past with an eye to meet the demands of the present audience.

Kelly was all too aware of how the demands of the audience affect what an author says and how he says it. Apparently recalling Johnson's own "Prologue for the opening of Drury Lane" in which Johnson had maintained that "The drama's laws, the drama's patrons give / For we that live to please, must please to live," Kelly took Johnson to task in *Babler* 104. Johnson had a good point, Kelly writes, in criticizing Shakespeare's use of puns, but he

> should have considered, that this mode of quibbling was the literary vice of the time; and that consequently the whole area was more to be censured than any individual who gave into the absurdity. Every age has some certain species of wit to distinguish it; and this wit the ablest authors must sometimes study with attention, but none more particularly than those who write for the theatre. A popular joke has more than once turned the fortune of a piece; and in the early periods of the drama, before the taste of the people was tolerable established, it might be necessary to countenance a general foible, for the sake of securing a general approbation. A dramatic writer, unlike all others, has his fate frequently depending on the whimsey of an audience; and therefore it is sometimes dangerous to combat with received prejudices.

I quote at length here because the passage reflects, I believe, Kelly's attitude toward his own craft. There is some evidence, which we will go into shortly, that Kelly considered some of what we regard as sentimental "the literary vice" of his time just as we do today. There is also evidence that he thought the audience wanted to indulge this vice, at least sometimes, and that an author must keep his audience constantly in mind if he wanted to succeed. The "Prologue" to *The Man of Reason*, for example, begins with the writer's plight:

> Hard is his Task in this inconstant Age
> Who writes for comic laurels from the Stage,
> While public taste still changing like our Dress
> Leaves no one sure criterion of success;

"Sentiment," and this is 1776, has been "thrust out of doors" and "has ample cause for all her sobs and sorrow." But one cannot be sure that "last Winters passion / For downright laughing, still exists in fashion." Therefore this writer has tried for the middle course: "We're grave and gay—Pray heav'n we may be right."

In part Kelly's sentimentalism was a creation to satisfy what he saw as the demands of his audience. In this he was at one with his times. A typical evening at the theatre with mainpiece, interludes, and afterpiece usually presented some sentiment, but also satire, comedy, and farce, with perhaps some music and dancing tossed in. To see how complex, how self-conscious this creation of the sentimental was, we need only look at a speech by Sotherton, a strolling player in William Whitehead's satire on sentimental comedies, *A Trip to Scotland* (1770). Sotherton, who could have taken advantage of one Miss Flack but who, much to her chagrin, did not, comes forward and tells a gathered group: "So that you will perceive, Sir, at least the good company will receive, that whatever effect the late run of sentimental comedies may have had upon their audiences, they have at least made the players men of honour."[19] No doubt Sotherton's speech evoked laughter, and rightfully so. First there is the satire on the players: to think that one could turn honest. Then the audience is given its turn: obviously the stage has not reformed them. Interestingly, Whitehead also wrote *A School for Lovers*, which for Bernbaum "initiated the revival of sentimental comedy" (p. 208). That Whitehead could satirize the very genre in which he had success is one point, but the plot thickens. *A Trip to Scotland* was the scheduled afterpiece for the second night of *A Word to the Wise*, which, like seemingly every comedy of the period, has its preparations for a "scamper to Scotland." And one could go on. Colman's hilarious satire on the sentimental, *Polly Honeycombe*, was the afterpiece on the opening night of *The School for Wives*, but Colman himself was capable of the sentimental as *The English Merchant* shows. All this suggests that writers were responding to what they took to be the demands of the audience and that the audience wanted to laugh at the sentimental but have the sentimental as well, to be moral, but to be moral in a sophisticated way. The theatres had not yet expanded, so the audience, still small and intimate, would have understood the allusions and private jokes. They were also middle class enough to desire the aristocratic freedom of laughter but also the stability of moral purpose. After all, Sotherton's speech suggests that perhaps the audience should have learned something from the stage. Kelly was a divided man, but then he was writing for a divided audience, one that wanted both laughter and goodness.

Despite Goldsmith's claims, "the Comic Muse" was not sick or "a-dying" ("Prologue" to *She Stoops to Conquer*). We now know, thanks to Sherbo (pp. 159–61) and the massive efforts of George Winchester Stone (see "Introduction," *LS*, IV, clix–clxix), that sentimental plays, even if one takes a latitudinarian definition, never made up more than ten percent of the plays offered at Drury Lane and Covent Garden between 1747 and 1776. In that ten percent, which would include Kelly's works, there is, however, little evidence that "Humour" was "departing the stage." No plays, at least in England in that period, were ever written solely under the inspiration of "The Goodness of the woeful countenance / The Sentimental Muse . . ." ("Prologue" to *The Rivals*). Even those plays—and Kelly's are not among these—that most would agree come closest to the mawkish, to the *comedie larmoyante*, say, Mrs. Griffith's *The School for Rakes* or Francis Waldron's *The Maid of Kent*, have genuinely comic scenes.[20] The pronouncements of Goldsmith and Sheridan have, as Robert Hume has brilliantly shown, the flavor, simplistic rhetoric, and intention of publicity campaigns.[21] And, down through the years, Kelly has been seen through their rhetoric as a weeper among the witty.

But the critics who have followed Goldsmith's and Sheridan's view of stage history have been right for the wrong reasons. Sentimentalism did triumph but not just among the Kellys and Cumberlands. It would be hard to find a play written during that period not grounded in a belief in the essential goodness of human nature, that was not moral, or did not have a relish for eccentric and imprudent characters, acts of spontaneous good nature, the melting tear, the feeling sigh, the improbable plot—all of these and sometimes in excess. It would be hard, that is, to find a play written during the period that did not tap that partially unconscious and unexamined body of beliefs, attitudes, and assumptions involving sense, sentiment, and sensibility, what Lady Betty Lampton refers to as the "laws of delicacy" (*False Delicacy*, p. 19).[22]

The dichotomy of weeping and laughing comedy simply will not stand scrutiny. *False Delicacy*, for example, is not the "mawkish, inadequate, wire-drawn" counterpart to the "wholesome and cheery *The Good Natur'd Man*," the one triumphing because of, and the other falling victim to, Garrick's promotion and the saccharine taste of the audience.[23] They share similar themes, so much so that contemporaries suspected Kelly of plagiarism.[24] Delicacy and good nature refer to the same set of underlying beliefs; indeed, they are nearly synonymous as Walpole's letter of 1768, the year of both plays, to his friend George Montague suggests. Referring to *A Sentimental Journey*, also published in 1768, Walpole wrote, "Sterne had published two little volumes. . . . In these there is great good nature and strokes of delicacy."[25] Honeywood is clearly too good-natured just as Lady Betty, Miss Marchmont, and Lord Winworth are too delicate. Honeywood courts the woman he loves for another man just as Lady Betty courts Winworth, the man she loves, for Miss Marchmont. Honeywood's statement to Jarvis concerning Miss Richland is identical to Lady Betty's to Mrs. Harley about Miss Marchmont: "No, Jarvis, it shall be my study to serve her, even in spite of my wishes; and to serve her happiness, tho' it destroys my own" (Act I). Both are connoisseurs of distress, taking their joys in sadness, and both are satirized for this. Moreover, Sir William Honeywood's admonition to Miss Richland applies to characters in both plays: "Men who, reasoning themselves into false feelings, are more earnest in pursuit of splendid than of useful virtues" (Act III). "False feelings" is synonymous with false delicacy, and delicacy itself is a key word in Goldsmith's play. Honeywood speaks of "the most delicate friendship" (Act I); Leontine explains to Olivia about the "delicacy of my passion" (Act I) and suspects Miss Richland of "indelicacy" (Act II). The elder Honeywood says of his son: "Yet, we must touch his weakness with a delicate hand. There are some faults so nearly allied to excellence, that we can scarce weed out the vice without eradicating the virtue" (Act I). The errors of Lady Betty and friends also arise from an excess of virtue, and despite Goldsmith's later complaint about sentimental drama rewarding its characters for their vices, Honeywood gets both girl and money and thus joins company with Tom Jones, Charles Surface, and a number of Kelly's characters. Goldsmith took a swipe at the Kelly play, having Lofty say that "it can't be conceal'd madam; the man was dull, as dull as the last new comedy" (Act II). Nevertheless, he could not refrain from using the word delicate even in his preface or from later making Charles Marlow reform at the sight of tears and suffer from a crude delicacy which is really false. It would remain for Sheridan with seven years of distance to make ironic use of delicate, having only the sentimental Faulkland use the word. But the sensibilities shaping *False Delicacy* and *The Good Natur'd Man* are the same; both authors, like Sterne, gently satirize the code of sentiment only to affirm it.

That we have read Kelly as exemplifying weeping and Goldsmith laughing comedy attests to the power of Goldsmith's and of Sheridan's rhetoric, but the differences among these three has little to do with underlying assumptions, which for the most part are sentimental in each case. All treat their superannuated lovers with kindness, create men of gallantry palely imitative of the Dorimants and Horners, and evoke more the sympathetic laughter of Francis Hutcheson than Hobbes's laughter of superiority. All were writing for an audience that demanded laughter and goodness, that wanted to be morally superior to their Restoration forebears but just as knowing. In satisfying this demand there is little difference between deriding the sentimental while being sentimental and proclaiming the sentimental while deriding it. What does separate Kelly from his illustrious contemporaries is craft: he had much less of it than they did. He also built his plays on something they did not: sentiments.

III

Perhaps nothing has contributed more to the misreading of Kelly than the confusion surrounding the word most often used to describe him—sentimental. If we define sentimental comedy as that displaying a belief in the goodness of man and a concern for the moral while stressing the emotions and partaking of the improbable, then, as we have seen, little separates Kelly from his Georgian contemporaries.[26] But when the stage historian Charles Dibdin lashed Kelly, he had another definition in mind.

> Kelly . . . happened, fortunately for himself, and unluckily for the public taste, to take advantage of the rage that then prevailed for sentiment. Everything was at the time sentiment. It was the only secret of writing for success. If a man was to be hanged, or married, out came a sentiment. If a rogue triumphed, or was tossed in a blanket, what an opportunity for a sentiment! If the butler was drunk or the chambermaid impertinent, listen to a sentiment![27]

By sentiment, Dibdin meant "thought; notion; opinion," Johnson's definition, or a body of philosophic doctrine, a theory, or a set of arguments, meanings the word commonly had during the eighteenth century.[28] When Kelly used the word, he meant much the same thing. It appears five times in the "Address" prefacing *A Word to the Wise* and means in each case thought, opinion, or notion, for example: "Whatever Mr. Kelly's own sentiments might be on political affairs. . ." (p. v). *Babler* 79, however, gives us a working definition of what Kelly meant by sentiment in regard to a play.

> There is a sentiment in Mr. Colman's comedy of the Jealous Wife with which I am not a little pleased, as it is no less an indication of a benevolent heart than a sound understanding. Harriet reproaching young Oakley on account of his extraordinary attachment to the bottle; the lover, sensibly struck with the justice of reproof, exclaims, that were all the ladies alike attentive to the

> morals of their admirers, a libertine would be an uncommon character.

Colman gives us a moral thought, that is, a sentiment, and so does Kelly. When we think of him as a man of sentiment, we will be closer to the truth thinking of him as Dibdin did than as a writer having "rare scenes where he is uninterested in tears and pity" (Shorer, p. 392). Tears do make appearances in Kelly, but thoughts, notions, and opinions come in clusters.

It is easy to see, however, why modern criticism has tended to stress the feeling in Kelly and not the thought. For the word "sentiment" is inherently ambiguous. The man of sentiment is a man of sense, that is, he is physically aware, he feels, something Kelly makes redundantly concrete when he says that Oakley was "sensibly struck." But because men derive their thought from what they feel, from what they sense, he is also reasonable, that is, sensible. Being sensible, he is also morally aware, "sensible" coming to mean "having moral perception; having the quality of being affected by moral good or ill" (Johnson, definition 5) and sense meaning "moral perception" (Johnson, definition 9). A sentiment, therefore, could be an "emotional thought" (*OED*, definition 8b) or a "mental feeling" (*OED*, definition 7) and have in either case moral connotations.[29]

"Sentimental," probably coined some time in the 1740s, carries with it the ambiguities of the family of words from which it derives. Moreover, it was changing meaning during Kelly's time. Originally the word meant pertaining to sentiment, in Johnson's definition, and had favorable connotations. But as Brissenden points out, "there was a marked shift in connotation. By the 1760s—particularly by 1768 when Sterne published *A Sentimental Journey*—it had acquired a distinctly emotional and sexual colouring. It was also beginning to take on the meaning current today—'addicted to indulgence in superficial emotion; apt to be swayed by sentiment'" (*Virtue in Distress*, p. 99). It is tempting to see Kelly as defending the definition of "sentiment" from the "sentimental" connotations it was beginning to have. He uses "sentimental" rarely, and always pejoratively, as something excessive. Thus "his chief study has been to steer between the extremes of sentimental gloom, and the excesses of uninteresting levity. . ." (*The School for Wives*, p. v). In *False Delicacy*, Mrs. Harley, with Sidney in mind, refers to "those half-soul'd fellows . . . who are so sentimental, and so dull. . ." (p. 4). Later she calls Miss Marchmont "Lady Sentimental" for being one of those "grave, reflecting, moralizing damsels" (p. 75). In *A Word to the Wise* Miss Dormer criticizes Miss Montagu's observation by saying it is "a very florid winding up of a period, and very proper for an elevated thought in a sentimental Comedy" (p. 2). Her style is excessively flowery, her thought, like that of Miss Marchmont, moralistic. And the name of Kelly's sentimental playwright, Lady Rachel Mildew, is reflective of her art, sentiments in her hands having suffered from a superficial growth, that is, from sentimentalism. Whether Kelly was aware of the battle of words going on about him—and in which he himself was one of the participants—is a moot question. It is demonstrable, however, that he built his plays on two things, sentiments and a ridicule of sentimental excesses.

The purpose of *False Delicacy*, for example, is exactly what Genest said it was two hundred years ago: "to ridicule False Delicacy."[30] Lady Betty possesses "an extraordinary delicacy" (p. 1), and Miss Marchmont suffers from "an uncommon share of delicacy" (p. 2), the word in both cases meaning "politeness; gentleness of manners" as well as perhaps "tenderness; scrupulousness; mercifulness" (Johnson, definitions 6 and 8). Both characters have too much of a good thing; they, like every character in the play save Mrs. Harley and Cecil, violate the "laws of delicacy" by being too delicate and thus render themselves fit subjects for ridicule. The finest gloss on the play is *Babler* 36 which opens with the observation that

> An excess of sensibility, though nothing can be more amiable than a feeling heart, is perhaps one of the greatest misfortunes which the human mind can labour under, because there is an everlasting source of objects to interest it's tenderness, and a constant round of accidents to work upon it's fears. Happily, indeed, we are not overstocked with people who possess this quality to any extraordinary degree; but the few who do might possibly, for their own sakes, as well as the happiness of others, be much better, if they were indued with no sensibility at all.

The *Babler* goes on to cite one Catherine Nettleworth, for whom "there is scarcely a circumstance in which her sensibility is not creating her a new source of disquiet; nor a friend in the world whom she does not render unhappy with her endless apprehensions and complaints." Catherine is obviously a sentimental cousin of Lady Betty and Miss Marchmont. All three seek the unhappy and distressful simply for the sake of revealing the fineness of their sensibilities. In a comment that could apply to a Catherine or a Miss Marchmont, Mrs. Harley says of Lady Betty, "now her delicacy is willing to be miserable" (p. 58). Both the *Babler* and this play satirize the propensity of sentimentalism to tip over into the perverse, a tendency evident in a harmless form in MacKenzie's man of feeling, Harley, but in quite a destructive way in Sade's Justine.

Sooner or later, nearly all the then fashionable sentimental excesses fall victim to Kelly's ridicule. Lady Betty, for example, turns down Lord Winworth, whom she wants to marry, because a "woman of real delicacy shou'd never admit a second impression on her heart" (p. 17).[31] Mrs. Harley, who has been married twice and would not mind trying again, thinks this notion absurd. If Lord Winworth came courting her:

> I might give myself a few airs at first:—I might blush a little, and look down . . . then pulling up my head, with a toss of disdain,—desire him, if ever he spoke to me on that subject again . . . To have a licence in his pocket;—that's all.—I wou'd make sure work of it at once, and leave it to your elevated minds to deal in delicate absurdities. [p. 55]

Mrs. Harley's refreshing common sense has its counterpart in the Misses Montagu and Dormer of *A Word to the Wise* and in the spirited Miss Walsingham in *The School for Wives*. These characters, like the "lively Widow," provide running commentary on sentimental excesses. Miss Montagu knows that "good-nature and sensibility" can often be but shrewder forms of selfishness. As she warns Miss Dormer:

> —ay, 'tis this good-nature and sensibility that makes the men so intolerably vain, and renders us so frequently contemptible.—If a fellow treats us with ever so much insolence, he has only to burst into a passionate rant, and tell a gross lie with a prodigious agitation;—in proportion as he whines we become softened; till at last, bursting into tears, we bid the sweet creature rise,—tell him that our fortune is entirely at his service, and beg that he will immediately assume the power of making us compleatly miserable. . . . While he, scarcely able to stifle his laughter, retires to divert his dissolute companions with our weakness. . . . [p. 35]

Actually, she describes what the rake Dormer has done to the

Portrait of Mrs. Abington, for whom Kelly wrote the part of Miss Walsingham in *The School for Wives* (Photograph courtesy of The Harry Ransom Center, University of Texas at Austin).

naive Miss Willoughby, and it is Miss Montagu who devises the plan to make a fool of this man who has been courting both of them. While Miss Willoughby listens, Miss Montagu, in a marvelously funny scene, provides Dormer with a "true translation of all the love speeches that have been made since the commencement of the world" (pp. 79– 80), a parody that shows how stilted sentimental phrases can mask desires far from benevolent. Being put on the defensive spurs Dormer to use all the trite sentimental phrases he knows in protesting his undying love. "When he is in the meridian of all his nonsense" (p. 61), swearing eternal devotion to Miss Montagu and foreswearing any interest in Miss Willoughby, Miss Willoughby reappears, and the two women laugh the gallant off the stage (pp. 76– 81).

In a scene closely parallel, Miss Walsingham gives Belville in *The School for Wives* what no rake can stand, a dose of laughter. Belville closely resembles Dormer and Sir Harry of *False Delicacy*, and what Miss Marchmont says of Sir Harry fits all three: ". . . his understanding is a fashionable one, and pleads the knowledge of everything right to justify the practice of many things not strictly warrantable" (p. 7). The married Belville puts on such a command performance that "he's actually forcing tears into his eyes" (p. 21). But Miss Walsingham sees him for what he is, insincere, and affects to weep. Belville, seeing what he takes to be a genuine feeling, declares, "The delicious emotion—do not check the generous tide of tenderness that fills me with such extasy" (p. 22). She plays up to his version of the sentimental swain until she has drawn from him promises of devotion. Her laughter then sends him packing: "Good bye.—Don't let this accident mortify your vanity too much;—but take care, the next time you vow everlasting love, that the object is neither tender enough to sob—sob—at your distress. . ." (p. 24).

These pale Mandevilleans whose ostensible benevolence belies selfishness are not the only objects of ridicule here. Throughout his work, Kelly satirizes their elevated diction, the artificiality of the sentimental declamation. He structures *A Word to the Wise* on a series of speeches or reported speeches that call upon the characters and the audience to "distinguish between the language of sincerity, and the voice of dissimulation" (p. 53), the latter inevitably a frosted language. Sherbo warned us, and Rawson has reiterated the admonition, that "we should beware of finding deliberate ridicule where excessive sentimentalism merely 'stirs *our* sense of the ridiculous' " (Rawson, p. 13). The warning is a good one, but though Kelly often practices the very thing he attacks, the consistent pattern of high-flown speeches deflated leaves little doubt about his intention.

Moreover, another group of characters that Kelly harpoons, the sentimental fops who delight in the deliciousness of their own feelings, has also mastered the declamatory. Lord Winworth, in courting one woman and then asking that woman to help him court another who happens to be her best friend, shows that he is far more interested in the niceties of discernment than in people. Like his fellow fops, he also epitomizes the popular sentimental delusion that the refined person of high social class is capable of greater feeling and therefore of greater moral discernment. Mrs. Harley makes clear just how unfeeling and morally obtuse Winworth is as she tells Lady Betty, "He gives you a pretty proof of his tenderness, truly, when he asks your assistance to marry another woman!" (*False Delicacy*, p. 32). Winworth's language as well as his morals, one mirroring the other, is accordingly ridiculed. Cecil, who with Mrs. Harley has overheard Winworth and Lady Betty, says to the Lord, "I beg . . . that we mayn't interrupt your heroics, 'when, in the moment you are sensible of her regard,—you must give her up for ever.'—A very moving speech, Mrs. Harley!—I am sure it almost makes me cry to repeat it" (pp. 80–81).

Sir George Hastings in *A Word to the Wise* is also vain about his sentimental qualities, so much so that Miss Dormer, by playing not on his benevolence but on his pride in his benevolence, makes him break off their engagement even though it means that Sir George must quarrel with her father and risk his life. After the duel scene in which Sir George acquits himself well, he opines, "The riches of the heart are the noblest of all possessions, and I don't think that, on the present occasion, I have proved myself the poorest fellow in the kingdom. . ." (p. 75). No doubt, King, who played the part, would have struck just the right note of comic boasting here and would have made the point that Sir George is an ersatz man of sentiment. His reasons for switching from Miss Dormer to Miss Montagu are a parody of sentimental motivations: "O! 'twou'd be barbarous to let her pine—I'll give her encouragement at once, and put an end to her anxiety" (p. 89). Clearly, self-love masks as benevolence, and though Miss Montagu can see his considerable merit, she too has had enough of his elevated speech and tells him at the end: "I won't hear a syllable from you now—if you can make a tollerable bow to me do, but don't let me hear a syllable of nonsense, I beg of you" (p. 98). As the pun makes clear, one who speaks "nonsense" cannot be sensible, cannot be a man of sentiment.

Kelly pokes fun at a number of other sentimental foibles. In *False Delicacy*, Colonel Rivers is satirized for being good in order to appear superior, a moral smugness often associated with Clarissa and Steele's Bevil Junior.[32] But Kelly, while satirizing sentimental excesses, is all the while affirming sentimental values. Take tears, for example, which seemingly have become synonymous with sentimentalism. Miss Walsingham and Miss Montagu cry mock tears in order to reveal that outward behavior does not always, particularly in the company of young men, reflect intentions.

Generally for Kelly tears, like those of Cecil, Connolly, and Mr. Freemore, signal benevolence and moral acuity. When Mrs. Freemore tells us that she "never cry'd but once in all my life; and that when my mother in her last will, left her, Jewells to my youngest Sister" (p. 79), she reveals her inhumanity, something the rest of the play confirms.

Criticism of sentimental comedy itself is a central theme of *The School for Wives*, parody of the sentimental happening whenever Lady Rachel appears—and she appears a good deal. Some of the parody is genuine, directed at sentimental excesses. Lady Rachel, for example, asks the stagestruck Miss Leeson, whom she is recruiting for her comedy, whether there are "none of our comedies to your taste?" "O, yes," she replies, "some of the sentimental ones are very pretty, there's such little difference between them and tragedies" (p. 33). But the criticism elicited through Lady Rachel is not simply or always directed at sentimental absurdities. Some of it is pseudo-parody that, as I have argued, allows Kelly to protect himself and also to satisfy his bourgeois audience's demand for some, but not too much, morality. For example, Mrs. Belville, when she learns that her husband is to be in a duel, really does break down in tears. The whole scene is extremely sentimental, but not because of the tears or because virtue has entered a high state of distress. Lady Rachel's comments mitigate the effects of the tears and prevent pathos. Lady Rachel finally has a moment in which life lives up to her art; as she says of the tearful Mrs. Belville, "Now I am extremely glad to see her so, for if she wasn't greatly distress'd it wou'd be monstrously unnatural" (p. 62). But the scene is sentimental because Mrs. Belville goes on to deliver a moral essay on the disastrous effects of dueling on the family and on society in general (pp. 62–63). To be sure, Lady Rachel also serves as vehicle to parody Mrs. Belville's homily:

> *Mrs. Bel.* O, why is not some effectual method contriv'd, to prevent this horrible practice of duelling?
> *Lady Rach.* I'll expose it on the stage, since the law now-a-days kindly leaves the whole cognizance of it to the theatre. [p. 63]

We laugh, but this is parody of a different order than that at work with Miss Leeson. Mrs. Belville's case against dueling repeats, almost word for word, the one Kelly made in *Babler* 29. His concern for dueling is clear throughout his work, plays and essays, and is a concern he shared with the moral sense philosopher, Francis Hutcheson. The substitution of law for the aristocratic code of dueling, of good manners, politeness, and temperance for aristocratic freedoms, is part and parcel of sentimentalism.[33] Moreover, Kelly carries out what Lady Rachel contemplates; he gives his audience sentiments that enlighten them about dueling. Here the sentiment and the "pseudo-parody to disarm criticism" are one.

And so it is with what Kelly calls the "general moral inculcated through his piece" ("Preface," p. vii). This moral arises out of something like the following concantenation of sentimental reasoning. Women are by nature endowed with an "infinitely greater share of sensibility" (*Babler* 87). On every occasion, therefore, Kelly upholds the power that women have to tame the wildness in men, never worrying, as did Adam Smith, that "the delicate sensibility required in civilized nations sometimes destroys the masculine firmness of character."[34] But women have not only the power but the responsibility to civilize men, or, in the words of *Babler* 79, "were all the ladies alike attentive to the morals of their admirers, a libertine would be an uncommon character." Mrs. Belville exemplifies these sentiments as she first suspects her husband's waywardness:

> Yet suppose it should be actually true:—heigho! . . . I think I wou'd endeavour to keep my temper:—a frowning face never recovered a heart that was not to be fixed with a smiling one:—but women, in general, forget this grand article of the matrimonial creed entirely; the dignity of insulted virtue obliges them to play the fool, whenever their Corydons play the libertine; and poh! they must pull down the house about the traitor's ears, tho' they are themselves to be crush'd in pieces by the ruins. [pp. 10–11]

Mrs. Belville keeps her temper and acts with prudence, but her behavior is mocked throughout. Lady Rachel tells her, "I shall put you into my comedy to teach wives, that the best receipt for matrimonial happiness, is to be deaf, dumb, and blind" (p. 81). The entire subplot involving Mrs. Tempest and General Savage provides another lesson on how to keep a husband, one that Mrs. Belville herself recognizes and mocks: "Shall I take a lesson from this lady [Mrs. Tempest], Mr. Belville? Perhaps, if the women of virtue were to pluck up a little spirit, they might be soon as well treated as kept mistresses" (p. 94). Despite the mockery, Mrs. Belville tames her man; her sentiments are held up as exemplary. Sentiment and parody are again one, Kelly's complex rhetorical stance containing simultaneously a mockery of and a strong sympathy for sentimentalism.

Once we understand that rhetorical stance and begin to read Kelly in the way that Johnson instructed us to read Richardson—for his sentiments—we can account for things that the stock responses either simply avoid or label mawkish and incredible. Goldsmith complained that in sentimental comedies characters are "lavish enough of their *tin* money" ("Essay on the Theater"), and Shorer is only one of many to have repeated the charge against the seemingly unmotivated generosity of some of Kelly's characters. In *The School for Wives*, Shorer writes, Torrington "for no sound reason—except, of course, his natural generosity, which we are never allowed to forget . . . endows Leeson with a substantial fortune. . ." (p. 400). First of all, Torrington only offers money to Leeson, and Leeson turns down the offer because, with the prospect of marrying a fortune, he has no need of it. Even so, there are quite sound reasons, sentimental ones, for Torrington's offer as well as for the actual generosity of Cecil and Winworth in *False Delicacy* (p. 86). The gratuitous act of generosity is, like tears, a sign of a sensible, benevolent person, and the more disinterested the act, the greater the virtue behind it.[35] Colonel Rivers's gift of twenty thousand pounds is, on the other hand, used to satirize him as he is using money to coerce his daughter. While Shorer misses the sentiment behind such actions, Goldsmith was simply being, I believe, self-serving. For if he had been sincere, his criticism would have included not only sentimental authors but nearly every writer of the time, including himself. As Brissenden has noted, during the eighteenth century "generosity was one of the most highly admired of moral traits; and it was commonly argued that the only justification for the possession of great riches was the opportunity which wealth afforded the exercising the virtues of benevolence and charity." Brissenden goes on to quote from Richardson's *Moral and Instructive Sentiments* that "the power of doing good to worthy objects is the only enviable circumstance in the lives of people of fortune" (*Virtue in Distress*, pp. 81–82). We recall Boswell giving sixpence to the poor boy, Yorick and the "good old monk," and Johnson's dictum that "a decent provision for the poor is the true test of civilization." We recall as well the ending of *She Stoops to Conquer* with Hardcastle promising to "gather all the poor of the parish about us" (Act IV) for next day's wedding festivities. The tin money of stage embodies one of the period's widely held sentiments.

I have mentioned Hutcheson and Smith, and, though Kelly was far from being a systematic philosopher, it often seems that he has come from a fresh reading of moral sense philosophy. The satire, for example, directed at singularity in *The Man of Reason* and Miss Marchmont's fear of acting from "any ridiculous singularity of sentiment" (*False Delicacy*, p. 45) take on a good deal more meaning when seen in the context of the belief of the moral sense philosophers that man is only fully human in relationship to other men and that morality arises from sympathy with others. For them man alone is man insane. Lestock's attempt in *The Man of Reason* to have Sir James committed, motivated as it is by avarice, is clearly wrong, but Sir James's singularity has given Lestock a plausible basis for his machinations (*cf. Babler* 24, "Reflections upon the Folly of Singularity"). What propels the characters in *False Delicacy* is what the moral sense philosophers claimed motivated men: the pursuit of happiness.[36] The word happy, in various forms, appears in the play fifty-six times. By recognizing this impulse and cooperating with it, men perform their highest calling; the play satirizes those who will not, through some singularity, cooperate with this impulse, who do not, as Mrs. Harley puts it, have the "good sense" (p. 87) to recognize and to follow the chief law governing their being. Zelida in *The Romance of an Hour*, on the other hand, has the good sense, when faced with marrying a man she does not love, to run away. She refuses to become prey to the snares of a false sentimentality, or as she puts it, a "false gratitude, a false generosity, which requires us to forego our happiness. . ." (p. 11).

The most important sentiment informing Kelly's plays was widely held and debated by philosopher and layman alike. Brissenden has called it the "deepest fantasy" of the period, "the notion that the spontaneous moral responses of the individual, despite their basic subjectivity, possess some special and general authority, that one's *better* feelings are necessarily reasonable" (*Virtue in Distress*, p. 54). The man of sentiment acts on what he knows, that is, feels to be right; his is not a utilitarian ethic. He does not measure what is right by sifting alternative results; his "sentiments," those "mental feelings" and "feeling thoughts," provide him with an *a priori* certitude of what is right. Duty is not a matter of obligation, of choosing among various alternatives, but of moral perception, that is, of sensibility.[37] And to see is, if he has the means, to do. Such a man of sentiment is Villars in *A Word to the Wise* who here is helping the distressed Miss Willoughby elude Jack Dormer's rakish designs:

> *Villars*. Madam, there is something in your manner . . . that disposes me very warmly to serve you, and if you really desire to leave this house, you shall leave it instantly. . . . I do not think myself oblig'd to answer Mr. Dormer's expectations, where his demands are evidently contrary to the principles of virtue.
> *Miss Willoughby*. Sir you charm me with these sentiments.
> *Villars*. Madam, they are sentiments which should regulate the conduct of every man; for he who suffers a bad action to be committed when he has the power of preventing it, is, in my opinion, as guilty as the actual perpetrator of the crime. . . . I find, I know not how, an irresistable inclination to serve you. . . . What I have done, humanity made my duty; and the most contemptible of mankind, is he who declines the performance of a good action because he has not an expectation of being rewarded. [p. 54]

Villars acts not from utilitarian motives. He returns Dormer's grant of a commission because he scorns "profit[ing] by the generosity of any man, unless upon terms that merit my approbation" (p. 67). And like Adam Smith, he can only approve that which is done from the right intention, the result of the action itself being irrelevant.[38] Of course, he will be rewarded for his actions because he lives in a generous universe in which his sense of the right turns out after all to be the good. But he cannot know that; his is a law-bound freedom, a freedom to recognize that "irresistable inclination to serve," to follow what "humanity made my duty." And to recognize is to follow. Mrs. Harley acts on her "inclinations" (*False Delicacy*, p. 18), and Wyndam in *The Man of Reason* from "pure disinterested regard for virtue" (p. 23).

Kelly never explores why these characters acting spontaneously on their feelings turn out to be right and to perform actions socially good while a Jack Dormer or a Belville, who after all also act on their feelings, turn out to do the wrong and the bad. He seems simply to have been of Adam Smith's opinion that "none but those of the happiest mould are capable of suiting, with exact justness, their sentiments and behaviour to the smallest difference of situation, and of acting upon all occasions with the most delicate and accurate propriety. The coarse clay of which the bulk of mankind are formed, cannot be wrought up to such perfections" (pp. 162–63). Most need the instruction proffered by rules and examples, and it would seem that Kelly held another of the period's prevailing sentiments. The moral sense philosophers never maintained that men are actually virtuous but that they are capable of virtue. Moreover, for them a person once aware of the superior pleasure of virtue will naturally prefer virtue to vice. As Smith wrote: "There is scarce any man, however, who by discipline, education, and example, may not be so impressed with a regard to general rules, as to act upon almost every occasion with tolerable decency, and through the whole of life to avoid any considerable degree of blame" (p. 163). This is just what happens to Dormer; he becomes, through the example of Villars, "impressed with a regard for the general rules." About to fight Villars, Dormer throws down his sword:

> Thus, my dear Villars, let me thank you for the superiority of your principles; I am myself just awakened to a sense of true honour, and cannot, now I know the real motive of your conduct, resent, as an injury, what I must look upon with the highest admiration. [p. 69]

Even the miraculous transformations of the rake figures in Kelly do not come unmotivated, albeit the motivations are sentimental ones.

The standard for behavior in Kelly's comedies is the benevolent man of sentiment. Those who pursue some form of self-interest become the objects of amiable satire meant to restore them to their full humanity. And what Villars is to Dormer, Kelly meant the stage to be to his audience, an ideal example. In the "Epilogue" to *A Word to the Wise*, he typically parodied both, jesting that plays have become sermons and deriding the use of exemplary characters: "For Villars is a phoenix, where's his brother? / 'Twill take a hundred years to find another." But the "Epilogue" is another example of pseudo-parody that mocks plays that "are merely preaching" and such ideal characters while asserting that no time has needed them more. Like Smith, Kelly would have held that without such examples of right conduct "the man who, in all his cool hours, had the most delicate sensibility to the propriety of conduct, might often be led to act absurdly upon the most frivolous occasions, and when it was scarce possible to assign any serious motive for his behaving in this manner"

(p. 163), an observation that accurately describes what takes place in the comedies of Hugh Kelly.

IV

We can understand the thoughts, notions, and opinions that inform Kelly's view of the stage and his plays and still not like the drama that arose from them. To recuperate intelligibility is not necessarily to save the drama. But at least by understanding the sentiments we have a firmer basis from which to evaluate the weaknesses of the plays. Sherbo, for example, cites two of Colonel Rivers's long speeches banishing his daughter as egregious examples of the sentimental dramatist's use of repetition and prolongation to emphasize a feeling and thus attempt to arouse pity in the audience (Sherbo, p. 63; this ed. *False Delicacy*, pp. 65–66). But Sherbo, I think, misjudges the tone. Rivers throughout the play has been mocked for his over-adherence to principle, for what even he admits is his "romantic extravagance" (p. 66), and the plethora of highblown phrases are instrumental in that mockery. Sherbo also misses the intention. Rivers, like so many of Kelly's characters, is examining and explaining his motives; in doing so he is presenting sentiments which in this case do not have much to do with tears or pity. For Rivers, as for the moral sense philosophers, the family is the source of that original affection, analogous to gravity, which holds society together.[39] Theodora, by her attempted elopement, is in danger of throwing off "every sentiment of duty" (p. 64); she has followed a man "who has taught [her] to obliterate the sentiments of nature" (p. 66). She is about to reject the very "inclinations" and "affections" that hold society together, make it meaningful, indeed, give individuals their very being. Kelly's constant satires on dueling, toasting, and gallantry in both his essays and plays is somewhat unintelligible without understanding that what motivates the satire is the value placed on the family, that most important nexus of sentimental bonds. Rivers's attempt to use familial bonds for his own self-interest serves to affirm their value.

Even with a proper understanding of tone and intention, it would be difficult to defend Rivers's speeches, or any number of others like them, as good drama. None are meant to elicit tears, but all do express sentiments and examine motivations. Brissenden has reminded us that "novelists were initially described as sentimental for two reasons: firstly because they dealt with moral or philosophical issues . . . and secondly because they were more interested in the mental and emotional than the physical lives of their characters" (*Virtue in Distress*, p. 118). Kelly, I think, was trying to do on the stage what Richardson had done in the novel. But the long speeches that attempt to capture the inner drama of consciousness simply mar the pacing and, because they often do not arise naturally from the action, appear improbable. The same can be said of the constant presence of the aphoristic and homiletic: "a man of sense shou'd despise the ridicule of the profligate" (*A Word to the Wise*, p. 58); "to engage the confidence of the innocent on purpose to betray it, is as mean as it is inhuman" (*ibid.*, p. 17); and so on. Though often true and neatly phrased, such aphorisms rarely advance the action. Kelly had not the skill to present in action and character, the two requisites of the drama, equivalents of what interested him: the emotional and mental states of those involved in moral decisions.

The weaknesses of Kelly's plays arise not from any absurdities inherent in sentimentalism. It is just that the basis of sentimentalism, its emphasis on thought and the exploration of motivation, make it antithetical to presentation on the stage. Consequently, we often find the criticism of sentimental comedy in Kelly's own day taking a formalistic turn. William Cooke, with criticism of Kelly in mind, defined sentimental comedy as "a sort of moral essay thrown into dialogue" (Genest, V, 376), and much of the contemporary criticism takes sentimental comedy to task for being novelistic. Foote's *Piety in Pattens*, which Murphy credits with having brought the sentimental "into dispute" (*Garrick*, II, 52), has as its target the novel on the stage. Genest, commenting on Waldron's *The Duel*, says, "This is a moral, vapid C. by Waldron without any particular fault—one of those things which Foote calls novels in dialogue" (V, 358). *The London Magazine* criticized Mrs. Sheridan's *Discovery* because "the last act is rather Richardsonian narration than part of a dramatic action. . ." (Sherbo, p. 148). When Goldsmith archly observed that "those abilities that can hammer out a novel are fully sufficient for the production of a sentimental comedy," he was condemning not only his former friend Mr. Kelly but also Mrs. Sheridan, Mrs. Griffiths, and himself. There is evidence to suggest that the "sentimental" parts of plays were often "pruned in the representation" but inserted for printing so they could be read in the closet. Kelly, however, does not seem to have done this.[40] He did, however, confound genres, and it is this and not so much the sentiments themselves his contemporary critics found objectionable.

Kelly was not a first-rate playwright. To read him alongside his glittering contemporaries is simply to confirm that he had not Sheridan's gift for dialogue nor Goldsmith's feeling for action and character. But when read as a man of sentiment and as a practicing author of his time, Kelly is certainly not the master of the lachrymose one might expect from the tag "sentimental." Despite the drawbacks of the novelistic and essayistic, he is nearly always interesting, often subtle, and usually delightfully humorous. What he said of himself when looking back at his performance as an essayist may with equal accuracy and felicity be applied to his performance as a playwright: "a first-rate reputation is no less beyond his hopes, than his deserts; yet, if in the scale of honourable comparison, he rises with no capital degree of merit, he is satisfied that he cannot be the lowest in the balance of contempt" ("Preface" to the *Babler*). Because he is far from the lowest and because his plays have so much to tell us about his times, Mr. Kelly, so well-known in his own day, deserves to be better known in ours.

Larry Carver
University of Texas, Austin

Notes

1. *The Life of David Garrick, Esq.* (London, 1801), II, 52.

2. By William Kendrick. *The Widow'd Wife* opened at Drury Lane on December 5, 1767, and was a moderate success, playing fourteen times that season, though only once thereafter. Kelly had both his hit play, *False Delicacy*, and the adaptation of his novel before the London audience in the 1767–68 season.

3. "Hugh Kelly: Contributions Toward a Critical Biography," Diss. Fordham University 1967, p. 1. O'Leary's extremely thorough and accurate scholarship provides the best account we have of Kelly's life.

4. George Sherburn and Donald F. Bond, *A Literary History of England: The Restoration and Eighteenth Century (1660–1789)*, 2nd ed. (1948; rpt. New York: Crofts, 1967), III, 1041; *cf.* George H. Nettleton and Arthur Case, *British Dramatists from Dryden to Sheridan* (Boston: Houghton Mifflin, 1939), p. 713.

5. "Some Remarks on Eighteenth-Century 'Delicacy,' with a Note on Hugh Kelly's *False Delicacy* (1768)," *JEGP*, 61 (1962), 12–13.

6. Ernest Bernbaum, *The Drama of Sensibility* (1915; rpt. Glouster, Mass.: Peter Smith, 1958), pp. 226–27; *cf.* pp. 235–36 and 276.

7. In *English Drama of the Restoration and Eighteenth Century (1642–1780)* (New York: Macmillan, 1921), George Nettleton maintains that *False Delicacy* is a "comedy of cross-purposes." Though the play is "essentially a sentimental comedy, justice must recognize Kelly's partial alleviation of the distresses of sentimentality" (pp. 269–70). For Ashley H. Thorndike, *False Delicacy* is "an interesting and novel attempt not merely to intermingle but to unite the humorous and the sentimental views. . . ." *A Word to the Wise* is "even more ambiguous in its mixture of comic and sentimental interest," but *The School for Wives* "mingled them more adroitly." Nevertheless, Kelly remains a citizen in Thorndike's "sentimental world" (*English Comedy* [New York: Macmillan, 1929], pp. 447–50). Nicoll avoids the problem somewhat by classifying *The School for Wives* as a comedy of manners (*A History of Late Eighteenth-Century Drama 1750–1800* [1927; rpt. Cambridge U. Press, 1937], pp. 129–31). Even Mark Shorer, who concludes that sentimentalism "must forever damn" Kelly's plays, thinks that Kelly "differed from the typical sentimentalist not only in his comic method, which attempted to mingle pathos and mirth rather than to alternate them, but, more important, in his own awareness of the fallacies in the very tradition he employed" ("Hugh Kelly: His Place in the Sentimental School," *PQ*, 12 [1933], 401). Nearly every time that Arthur Sherbo mentions Kelly he qualifies his judgment. He observes, for example, that "unfaithful husbands in eighteenth-century sentimental comedy are usually met with a shower of tears from their much abused but still adoring spouses (A notable exception is to be found in Hugh Kelly's *The School for Wives*, III)" (*English Sentimental Drama* [East Lansing, Michigan: Michigan State U. Press, 1957], p. 136; see also pp. 8, 133, and 142–44).

8. The breakdown began, I think, with Sherbo's study, which makes sentimentalism not a particular historical phenomenon but a predisposition that can and does appear to a greater or lesser extent in all times (Sherbo, p. 15). Robert D. Hume explores the reasons for the growing dissatisfaction with this critical model in his first-rate

"Goldsmith and Sheridan and the Supposed Revolution of 'Laughing' Against 'Sentimental' Comedy," in *Studies in Change and Revolution: Aspects of English Intellectual History 1640–1800*, ed. Paul J. Korshin (Marston, England: Scholar Press, 1972), pp. 237–76.

9. Readings which begin with Rawson's most insightful article; see note 5; O'Leary (pp. 241–90) has good things to say about each of the comedies; and *False Delicacy* has received a finely intelligent reading from Joseph W. Donohue, Jr., *Dramatic Character in the English Romantic Age* (Princeton: Princeton U. Press, 1970), pp. 114–18.

10. *Thespis* in *The Works of Hugh Kelly* (London, 1778), p. 351.

11. P. xvi. All references to Kelly's work, unless otherwise noted, are to the present edition and will be cited by page number of the individual play.

12. Breeding is an omnipresent topic in the *Babler*; see, for example, Nos. 31, 64, and 67. I am using the edition of the *Babler* found in Harrison's *British Classicks* (London, 1786), VI. *Cf.* John Taylor's observation that "it seemed to be Mr. Kelly's aim, both in conversation and in his writings, to use fine words, apparently, if possible, to obliterate all traces of meaness of his origin, and of his early employments. . . . Mr. Kelly . . . was, perhaps, too lofty, pompous, and flowery in his language, but good-natured, affable, and gentlemanly in his deportment, even to an excess of elaborate courtesy" (*Records of My Life* [London, 1832], I, 97; quoted in O'Leary, p. 66).

13. William Empson, *Some Versions of Pastoral* (1950; rpt. New York: New Directions, 1968), p. 57.

14. The reference to "boarding-school romp" calls to mind Thomas Durfey's *Love for Money or, the Boarding School* (London, 1691), which features a boarding-school farce and was adapted for and played as an afterpiece entitled *The Counterfeit Heiress; or The Boarding School* on April 16, 1762. Charles Coffey had earlier adapted the play retitled *The Boarding School; or The Sham Captain* (London, 1731). Neither play nor adaptations were particularly popular in the eighteenth century and none includes a slapping or a basin of scalding water. Kelly probably has in mind Bickerstaffe's *Love in the City* (London, 1767). In the preface Bickerstaffe criticizes "sentiment" and defends his play against charges of being

"LOW" (p. ii). One of his characters, Priscilla, is a romp who "was turned out of Hackney boarding-school for beating the governess" (p. 2).

15. I owe this observation to Mary J. H. Gross. Kelly simplifies the original, cutting the Zara / Osmyn and the scheming Gonzalez plots. Gone too is the gothic horror of the "King's headless Trunk." Kelly focuses on the love story. Clementina, like Congreve's Almeria, has secretly married an enemy of her father; the husband, ostensibly dead, returns in disguise. But Kelly's Anselmo, the father, is, unlike the original, a man of sentiment; when he learns of his daughter's clandestine marriage, he forgives both daughter and son-in-law, though too late. Rinaldo, through a mix-up, dies, and Clementina stabs herself. The puzzling ambiguities of Congreve's ending in which the lovers live, though the father dies, are simplified to the banal. Just after his daughter kills herself, Anselmo makes this inappropriate response:

> I yield submissive to the dreadful stroke,
> And only ask that this unhappy story,
> To future times, may forcibly point out
> The dire effects of filial disobedience. [p. 76]

Though it played nine nights, *Clementina* is not very good. This contemporary comment pretty well sums up its virtues: "A gentleman being asked after one of the representations of this play, if he did not hiss it, replied, 'How could I? A man can't hiss and yawn at the same time' " (quoted in George Winchester Stone, Jr., *The London Stage 1600–1800* [Carbondale, Illinois: Southern Illinois U. Press, 1962], Part IV, 1495).

16. *The School for Guardians* (London, 1767), pp. 9–10.

17. See the *Life*, ed. George Birkbeck Hill and revised by L. F. Powell (Oxford: Clarendon Press, 1934), III, 259. I am indebted to Leo Hughes for pointing out this passage to me and for allowing me to draw upon our discussion of the "concocted play." He has written a forthcoming article on the topic.

18. February 9, 1776. *The Westminster Magazine* damned the play, not without justification, "for developing two confusing and parallel plots, for the acting, and for the language" (*LS*, IV, 1951).

19. *A Trip to Scotland* (London, 1770), p. 38.

20. In *The School for Rakes* (London, 1769), for example, when Mrs. Winifred says that Harriet is "in her chamber, like a distracted wretch, tearing herself to pieces," she is being only slightly hyperbolic. Harriet, having undergone a sham marriage, is in tears throughout; nevertheless, the play has its comic moments and a good comic character in Mrs. Winifred.

21. The subject of his article cited in note 8.

22. Lady Betty echoes Lord Ogleby in *The Clandestine Marriage* (London, 1766), who speaks of the "laws of sympathy, and delicacy" (p. 62). Kelly's title, by the way, seems to come from this play. Sir John Melvil in proposing to Fanny asks why she will "from a false delicacy, oppose a measure so conducive to my happiness. . ." (p. 36).

23. Austin Dobson's judgment in his introduction to *Goldsmith*, ed. George Pierce Baker (1903; rpt. New York: Hill and Wang, 1966), p. 18.

24. O'Leary notes that "This libel *The Theatrical Monitor* reported as rumor in its review of Kelly's play on January 30, 1768 (No. x, p. 6). In its review of *The Good-Natured Man* in its next issue, February 6 (No. xi, p. 3), it exonerated Kelly from such charges. Other contemporary reviews noted and dismissed the same allegation" (p. 69).

25. Quoted in R. F. Brissenden, *Virtue in Distress: Studies in the Novel of Sentiment from Richardson to Sade* (London: Macmillan, 1974), p. 113.

26. The criteria are Sherbo's (pp. 1–31). He also includes an "emphasis on pity," which I do not find in Kelly. His point about "repetition and prolongation" (pp. 32–71) is a good one, and Kelly uses both, though not for the reasons Sherbo suggests as I argue later. Sherbo's further point about the "eschewal of humor and bawdy" (pp. 72–99) does not seem to me well-taken. Everyone in the 1760s and 70s plays down the bawdy (the antics of Orson and Pillage in *The Romance of an Hour* are as close as Kelly gets), and no one is totally lacking in humor.

27. *A Complete History of the Stage* (London, 1795), V, 277.

28. R. F. Brissenden, " 'Sentiment': Some Uses of the Word in the Writings of David Hume," in *Studies in the Eighteenth Century: Papers*

Presented at the David Nichol Smith Memorial Seminar Canberra 1966, ed. R. F. Brissenden (Toronto: U. of Toronto Press, 1968), p. 90.

29. As Brissenden points out in " 'Sentiment,' " p. 95.

30. John Genest, *Some Accounts of the English Stage* (Bath, 1832), V, 163.

31. For more on second marriages and what Rawson calls the "sentimental code," see Rawson, pp. 7– 8. Second marriages come up twice in Kelly's novel, itself a study in false delicacy, but unaccompanied by ridicule (II, pp. 51 and 114– 15).

32. Donohue rightly observes that Rivers is a "man who spouts sentiments about the prostitution of young women through marriages for money but who is perversely willing to allow his daughter to elope with Sir Harry . . . so that she will have the satisfaction of putting her father in an early grave" (*Dramatic Character*, p. 115).

33. See *Collected Works of Francis Hutcheson* (George Olms, 1969), IV, 237–40 and particularly VI, 97–98.

34. *The Theory of Moral Sentiments*, ed. D. D. Raphael and A. L. Macfie (Oxford: Clarendon Press, 1976), p. 209.

35. *Cf*. Hutcheson, I, 269 and Smith, p. 25.

36. Not as individuals but as men in groups. Thus one man's desire for happiness is inextricably bound up with the happiness of all, and as he pursues the one, he fulfills the other. Smith writes: "The happiness of mankind, as well as of all other rational creatures, seems to have been the original purpose intended by the Author of nature, when he brought them into existence. No other end seems worthy of that supreme wisdom . . . by acting according to the dictates of our moral faculties, we necessarily pursue the most effectual means for promoting the happiness of mankind, and may therefore be said . . . to cooperate with the Deity. . ." (p. 166). *Cf*. Hutcheson II, 33 and VI, 226. *Babler* 2 begins: "In the variety of courses which the generality of mankind pursue for the attainment of happiness . . ."; No. 91 opens with: "As happiness is the pursuit of every body . . .", see also No. 65.

37. The moral sense, that which perceives the pleasure in contemplating and in doing good, suggests a reliance on feeling rather than on reason in judging actions. But the moral sense philosophers were

aware of problems in making ethics a matter of feeling only and tried to show the relationship between feeling and reason in ethical decisions. See, for example, Hutcheson I, 176–77; Smith, p. 137; and also David Hume, *An Inquiry Concerning the Principles of Morals*, ed. Charles W. Hendel (New York: Bobbs-Merrill, 1957). Section I and Appendix I. "Sentiment," which can be both a feeling and a thought, therefore becomes a key word for them, as Brissenden has shown for Hume.

38. At least ideally. Smith writes: "The only consequences for which [a man] can be answerable, or by which he can deserve either approbation or disapprobation of any kind, are those which were some way or other intended. . . . To the intention or affection of the heart, therefore . . . all praise or blame, all approbation or disapprobation . . . must ultimately belong. When this maxim is thus proposed, in abstract and general terms, there is nobody who does not agree to it. . . . But . . . when we come to particular cases, the actual consequences which happen to proceed from any action, have a very great effect upon our sentiments concerning its merit or demerit. . ." (p. 93). The chastened Dormer tells Villars: "A man ought to be good even from policy, if he is not so from inclination" (p. 70), a sentiment echoed by Lady Havensham, who asks Lady Blandford: "Who . . . ought not to be virtuous, even from interest? Since, if the consciousness of having performed a good action, is not a sufficient reward, we are so generally certain of finding it highly to our advantage in the end?" (*Memoirs of a Magdalen*, II, 223).

39. See Hutcheson, I, 143–47 and 195–99; Smith, pp. 219–27. The *Babler* constantly addresses familial concerns, something Kelly acknowledged with the opening of No. 48: "The good-natured readiness with which I see you insert a variety of letters upon domestic occurrences. . . ."

40. Sherbo, p. 149; see also Robert D. Hume, pp. 257–58. Hume writes that "apparently much of the sentiment and moralizing found in the printed version of Kelly's successful *School for Wives* was *omitted* in the stage presentation" (pp. 258–59), something we have not found in our perusal of the Larpent manuscript.

FALSE DELICACY

FALSE DELICACY:

A

C O M E D Y.

[Price One Shilling and Six-Pence.]

☞ *THIS Play is*, **agreeable to Act of Parliament**, *entered in the Hall Book of the Company of* Stationers, *and whoever presumes to print it will be prosecuted. — The Proprietors will reward any one who will give Information of such Proceeding.*

FALSE DELICACY:

A

COMEDY;

AS IT IS PERFORMED AT THE

THEATRE-ROYAL

IN

DRURY-LANE,

BY HIS MAJESTY'S SERVANTS.

By HUGH KELLY.

The FIFTH EDITION.

LONDON,

PRINTED FOR

R. BALDWIN, No. 47, PATER-NOSTER-ROW;
W. JOHNSTON, No 16, and G. KEARSLY,
No. 1, in LUDGATE-STREET.

MDCCLXVIII.

T O

DAVID GARRICK, Esq.

Dear SIR,

I *HAVE two motives for inscribing this piece to you, Gratitude and Vanity; Gratitude, because it's success has been greatly owing to your judicious advice; and Vanity, because I wish to acquaint the world that such a character as Mr.* Garrick *has been warmly the friend of his sincerely affectionate,*

And very much obliged,

Middle Temple,
Jan. 29, 1768.

Humble Servant,

HUGH KELLY.

PROLOGUE,

Written by DAVID GARRICK, Esq.*

Spoken by Mr. KING.

I'M *vex'd—quite vex'd—and you'll be vex'd—that's worse*
To deal with stubborn scribblers! *there's the curse!*
Write moral *plays—the blockhead!—why, good people,*
You'll soon expect this house to wear a steeple!
For our fine piece, to let you into facts,
Is quite a Sermon, *—only preach'd in* Acts.
You'll scarce believe me, 'till the proof appears,
But even I, Tom Fool, *must shed some tears:*
Do, Ladies, look upon me—nay, no simp'ring—
Think you this face was ever made for whimp'ring?
Can I, a cambrick handkerchief display,—
Thump my unfeeling breast, and roar away?
Why this is comical, *perhaps he'll say—*
Resolving this strange aukward bard to pump,
I ask'd him what he meant?—He somewhat plump,
New purs'd his belly, and his lips thus biting,
I must keep up the dignity of writing!
You may; but, if you do, Sir, I must tell ye,
You'll not keep up that dignity of belly.
Still he preach'd on.—"Bards of a former age
Held up abandon'd pictures on the stage,
Spread out their wit, with fascinating art,
And catch'd the fancy, to corrupt the heart;
But, happy change!—in these more moral days,
You cannot sport with virtue, even in plays;
On virtue's side his pen the poet draws,
And boldly asks a hearing for his cause."
Thus did he prance, and swell.—The man may prate,
And feed these whimsies in his addle pate,
That you'll protect his muse, because she's good,
A virgin, and so chaste!—O lud! O lud!
No Muse the Critic Beadle's lash escapes,
Though virtuous, if a dowdy, and a trapes:
If his *come forth, a decent likely Lass,*
You'll speak her fair, and grant the proper pass.
Or should his brain be turn'd with wild pretences;
In three hours time, you'll bring him to his senses:
And well you may, when in your power you get him,
In that short space, you blister, bleed, and sweat him.
Among the Turks, *indeed, he'd run no danger,*
They sacred hold a madman, *and a* stranger.

* Mr. Kelly originally intended the prologue to be grave, and accordingly wrote a serious one himself; but as Mr. King was to speak it, Mr. Garrick, with great propriety, thought a piece of humour would be best suited to the talents of that excellent actor, and therefore very kindly took the trouble of putting it into a form so entirely different from the first, that it cannot, with the least justice, be attributed to any other author.

Dramatis Personæ.

M E N.

Colonel Rivers,	Mr. HOLLAND.
Cecil,	Mr. KING.
Sir Harry Newburg,	Mr. J. PALMER.
Lord Winworth,	Mr. REDDISH.
Sidney,	Mr. CAUTHERLY.

Footmen, Mr. Wright, &c.

W O M E N.

Lady Betty Lambton,	Mrs. ABINGTON.
Miſs Marchmont,	Mrs. BADDELEY.
Miſs Rivers,	Mrs. JEFFERIES.
Mrs. Harley,	Mrs. DANCER.
Sally,	Miſs REYNOLDS.

SCENE, *Richmond.*

TIME, *The Time of Repreſentation.*

FALSE DELICACY.

ACT I. SCENE I.

An Apartment at Lady BETTY LAMBTON's.

Enter SIDNEY *and* WINWORTH.

SIDNEY.

STILL I can't help thinking that Lady Betty Lambton's refusal was infinitely more the result of an extraordinary delicacy, than the want of affection for your Lordship.

WINWORTH.

O, my dear cousin, you are very much mistaken; I am not one of those coxcombs who imagine a woman does'nt know her own mind; or who, because they are treated with civility by a lady who has rejected their addresses, suppose she is secretly debating in their favour: Lady Betty is a woman of sense, and must consequently despise coquetry or affectation.

SIDNEY.

Why, she always speaks of you with the greatest respect.

B WINWORTH.

WINWORTH.

Reſpect! — Why ſhe always ſpeaks of *you* with the greateſt reſpect; does it therefore follow that ſhe loves you? No, Charles — I have, for ſome time you know, ceas'd to trouble Lady Betty with my ſolicitations; and I ſee myſelf honour'd with her friendſhip, though I hav'nt been ſo happy as to merit her heart: for this reaſon, I have no doubt of her aſſiſtance on the preſent occaſion, and, I am certain, I ſhall pleaſe her by making my addreſſes to Miſs Marchmont.

SIDNEY.

Miſs Marchmont is, indeed, a very deſerving young woman.

WINWORTH.

Next to Lady Betty I never ſaw one ſo form'd to my wiſhes; beſides, during the whole period of my fruitleſs attendance, ſhe ſeemed ſo intereſted for my ſucceſs, and expreſs'd ſo hearty a concern for my diſappointment, that I have conſider'd her with an eye of more than common friendſhip ever ſince. — But what's the matter with you, Charles? you ſeem to have ſomething upon your ſpirits.

SIDNEY.

Indeed, my Lord, you are miſtaken: I am only attentive.

WINWORTH.

O, is that all! — This very day I purpoſe to requeſt Lady Betty's intereſt with Miſs Marchmont; for, unhappily circumſtanc'd as ſhe is, with regard to fortune, ſhe poſſeſſes an uncommon ſhare of delicacy, and may poſſibly think herſelf inſulted

insulted by the offer of a rejected heart: — Lady Betty, in that case, will save her the pain of a supposed disrespect, and me the mortification of a new repulse. But I beg your pardon, Charles, I am forgetting the cause of friendship, and shall now step up stairs to Colonel Rivers about your affair. — Ah, Sidney! you have no difficulties to obstruct the completion of your wishes, and a few days must make you one of the happiest men in England. [*Exit.*]

SIDNEY. [*looking after him.*]

A few days make me one of the happiest men in England! — a likely matter, truly: little does he know how passionately I admire the very woman to whom he is immediately going with an offer of his person and fortune. — The marriage with Miss Rivers I see is unavoidable; and I am almost pleased that I never obtained any encouragement from Miss Marchmont, as I should now be reduc'd to the painful alternative, either of giving up my own hopes, or of opposing the happiness of such a friend.

Enter Mrs. HARLEY *and* Miss MARCHMONT.

Mrs. HARLEY.

O here, my dear girl, is the sweet swain, in *propria persona:* — Only mind what a funeral-sermon face the creature has, notwithstanding the agreeable prospects before him. — Well, of all things in the world, defend me, I say, from a sober husband!

SIDNEY.

You are extremely welcome, Mrs. Harley, to divert yourself——

Mrs. Harley.

He ſpeaks too in as melancholy a tone as a paſſing-bell: — Lord, lord, what can Colonel Rivers ſee in the wretch, to think of him for a ſon-in-law.—Only look, Miſs Marchmont, at this love-exciting countenance; — Obſerve the Cupids that ambuſh in theſe eyes! — Theſe lips, to be ſure, are fraught with the honey of Hybla:— Go, you lifeleſs devil you, — go, try to get a little animation into this unfortunate face of yours.

Sidney.

Upon my word, my face is very much oblig'd to you.

Miſs Marchmont.

You are a mad creature, my dear; and yet I envy your ſpirits prodigiouſly.

Mrs. Harley.

And ſo you ought. — But for all that, you and Lady Betty are unaccountably fond of thoſe half-ſoul'd fellows, who are as mechanically regular as ſo many pieces of clock-work, and never ſtrike above once an hour upon a new obſervation — who are ſo ſentimental, and ſo dull—ſo wiſe, and ſo drowſy. — Why I thought Lady Betty had already a ſufficient quantity of lead in her family, without taking in this lump to increaſe the weight of it.

Miſs Marchmont.

What can ſhe poſſibly mean, Mr. Sidney?

Sidney.

'Tis impoſſible to gueſs, Madam. The lively widow will ſtill have her laugh, without ſparing any body.

Mrs.

Mrs. HARLEY.

Why ſurely, my dear, you can't forget the counter part of poor Diſmal here, that elaborate piece of dignified dulneſs, Lady Betty's couſin, Lord Hectic; who, through downright fondneſs, is continually plaguing his poor wife, and rendering her the moſt miſerable woman in the world, from an extraordinary deſire of promoting her happineſs.

Miſs MARCHMONT.

And is'nt there a great deal to ſay in extenuation of an error which proceeds from a principle of real affection?

Mrs. HARLEY.

Affection! ridiculous! but you ſhall have an inſtance of this wonderful affection:—'Tother day I din'd at his houſe; and, though the weather was intolerably warm, the table was laid in a cloſe room, with a fire large enough to roaſt an ox for a country corporation.

SIDNEY.

Well, and ſo——

Mrs. HARLEY.

In a great chair, near the fire-ſide, ſat poor Lady Hectic, wrapp'd up in as many fur-cloaks as would baffle the ſeverity of a winter in Siberia:—On my entrance I expreſs'd a proper concern for her illneſs, and aſk'd the nature of her complaint.—She told me ſhe complain'd of nothing but the weight of her dreſs, and the intolerable heat of the apartment; adding, that ſhe had been caught in a little ſhower the preceding

ceding evening, which terrified Lord Hectic out of his wits; and so, for fear she might run the chance of a slight cold, he exposed her to the hazard of absolute suffocation.

SIDNEY.

Upon my word, Miss Marchmont, she has a pretty manner of turning things.

Miss MARCHMONT.

Really, I think so.

Mrs. HARLEY.

Well — unable to bear either the tyranny of this preposterous fondness any longer, or the intolerable heat of his room, I made my escape the moment the cloth was removed; and shan't be surprised if, before the conclusion of the summer, he is brought before his peers, for having murdered his poor lady, out of downright affection.

SIDNEY.

A very uncommon death, Mrs. Harley, among people of quality.

Enter a FOOTMAN.

FOOTMAN *to* SIDNEY.

Lord Winworth, Sir, desires the favour of your company above: The person is come with the writings from the Temple—

SIDNEY.

I'll wait upon him immediately.

Mrs.

Mrs. HARLEY.

Ay, pray do, you are the fittest company in the world for each other. — If Colonel Rivers was of my mind, he'd turn you instantly adrift, and listen to the overtures of Sir Harry Newburg.

SIDNEY.

I really believe you have a fancy to me yourself, you're so constantly abusing me. [*Exit.*]

Mrs. HARLEY.

I, you odious creature!

Miss MARCHMONT.

Now you mention Sir Harry, my dear, is'nt it rather extraordinary for him to think of Miss Rivers, when he knows of the engagements between her and Mr. Sidney — especially as her father has such an objection to the wildness of his character.

Mrs. HARLEY.

What, you are still at your sober reflections, I see, and are for scrutinizing into the morals of a lover.—The women truly would have a fine time of it, if they were never to be married till they found men of unexceptionable characters.

Miss MARCHMONT.

Nay, I don't want to lessen Sir Harry's merit in the least, — he has his good qualities as well as his faults, — and is no way destitute of understanding; — but still his understanding is a fashionable one, and pleads the knowledge of every thing right to justify the practice of many things not strictly warrantable.

Mrs.

Mrs. HARLEY.

Why, I never heard any thing to his prejudice, but ſome faſhionable liberties which he has taken with the ladies.

Miſs MARCHMONT.

And, in the name of wonder, what wou'd you deſire to hear!

Mrs. HARLEY.

Come, come, Hortenſia; we women are unaccountable creatures, the greateſt number of us by much love a fellow for having a little modiſh wildneſs about him; and if we are ſuch fools as to be captivated with the vices of the men, we ought to be puniſhed for the depravity of our ſentiments.

Enter RIVERS *and* Lady BETTY.

RIVERS.

I tell you, ſiſter, they can read the parchments very well without our aſſiſtance — and I have been ſo fatigu'd with looking over papers all the morning, that I am heartily ſick of your indent ures witneſſing, your foraſmuch's, likewiſe's, alſo's, moreover's and notwithſtanding's, and I muſt take a turn in the garden to recover myſelf. [*Exit.*]

Lady BETTY.

Nay, I only ſpoke, becauſe I imagin'd our being preſent would be more agreeable to Lord Winworth. — But I wonder Sir Harry doesn't come; he promiſed to be here by ten, and I want to ſee his couſin Cecil mightily.

Miſs

Miſs MARCHMONT.

What, Lady Betty, does Mr. Cecil come with him here this morning?

Lady BETTY.

He does, my dear — he arrived at Sir Harry's laſt night, and I want to ſee if his late journey to France has any way improved the elegance of his appearance. [*ironically.*]

Mrs. HARLEY.

Well, I ſhall be glad to ſee him too; for, notwithſtanding his diſregard of dreſs, and freedom of manner — there is a ſomething right in him that pleaſes me prodigiouſly.

Miſs MARCHMONT.

A ſomething right, Mrs. Harley! — he is one of the worthieſt creatures in the world.

Lady BETTY.

O, Hortenſia, he ought to be a favourite of yours, for I don't know any body who poſſeſſes a higher place in his good opinion.

Miſs MARCHMONT.

'Twou'd be odd, indeed, if he was'nt a favourite of mine — he was my father's beſt friend; —gave him a conſiderable living, you know; and, when he died, wou'd have provided very kindly for me, if your generoſity, Lady Betty, had'nt render'd his goodneſs wholly unneceſſary.

Lady BETTY.

Poh! poh! no more of this.

Mrs. HARLEY.

I wiſh there was a poſſibility of making him dreſs like a gentleman—But I am glad he comes with Sir Harry; — for though they have a great regard for each other, they are continually wrangling, and form a contraſt which is often extremely diverting —

Enter a Footman.

Sir Harry Newburg and Mr. Cecil, Madam.

Lady BETTY.

O, here they are! Shew them in. [*Exit Footm.*

Mrs. HARLEY.

Now for it!

Miſs MARCHMONT.

Huſh, they are here.

Sir HARRY.

Ladies, your moſt obedient. —

CECIL.

Ah, Girls! — give me a kiſs each of you inſtantly. — Lady Betty, I am heartily glad to ſee you: — I have a budget full of compliments for you, from ſeveral of your friends at Paris —

Lady BETTY.

Did you meet any of them at Paris?

CECIL.

I did, — and, what was worſe, I met them in every town I paſſed through; — but the Engliſh are a great commercial nation, you know, and their fools, like their broad cloths, are exported in large quantities to all parts of Europe.

Sir

Sir HARRY.

What? and they found you a fool ſo much above the market price, that they have returned you upon the hands of your country? — Here, ladies, is a head for you, piping hot from Paris.

CECIL.

And here, ladies, is a head for you, like the Alps.

Sir HARRY.

Like the Alps, ladies! How do you make that out?

CECIL.

Why 'tis always white, and always barren; 'tis conſtantly covered with ſnow, but never produces any thing profitable.

Mrs. HARLEY.

O ſay no more upon that head, I beſeech *you.*

Lady BETTY.

Indeed, Sir Harry, I think they're too hard upon you.

Mrs. HARLEY.

Why, I think ſo too — eſpecially my friend Cecil, who, with that unfortunate ſhock of hair, has no great right to be conſider'd as a ſtandard for dreſs in this country.

CECIL.

Ah, widow, there are many heads in this country with much more extraordinary things upon them than my unfortunate ſhock of hair, as you call it: — what do you think of theſe wings, for inſtance, that cover the ears of my couſin Mercury?

Sir HARRY.

Death! don't ſpoil my hair.

CECIL.

You ſee this fellow is ſo tortur'd upon the wheel of faſhion, that a ſingle touch immediately throws him into agonies; — now, my dreſs is as eaſy as 'tis ſimple, and five minutes —

Sir HARRY.

With the help of your five fingers equips you at any time for the drawing-room, — ha! ha! ha!

CECIL.

And is'nt it better than being five hours under the paws of your hair-dreſſer?

Lady BETTY.

But cuſtom, Mr. Cecil! —

CECIL.

Men of ſenſe have nothing to do with cuſtom; and 'tis more their buſineſs to ſet wiſe examples than to follow fooliſh ones.

Mrs. HARLEY.

But don't you think the world will be apt to laugh a little, Mr. Cecil?

CECIL.

I can't help the want of underſtanding among mankind.

Sir HARRY.

The blockhead thinks there's nothing due to the general opinion of one's country.

CECIL.

And none but blockheads, like you, would mind the fooliſh opinions of any country. Lady

Lady Betty.

Well! Mr. Cecil muſt take his own way, I think : — ſo come along, ladies, — let us go into the garden, and ſend my brother to Sir Harry to ſettle the buſineſs about Theodora.

Cecil.

Theodora! — what a charming name for the romance of a circulating-library! — I wonder, Lady Betty, your brother wou'd'nt call his girl Deborah, after her grandmother? —

Mrs. Harley.

Deborah! — O I ſhould hate ſuch an old faſhion'd name abominably —

Cecil.

And I hate this new faſhion of calling our children by pompous appellations. — By and by we ſhan't have a Ralph or a Roger, a Bridget or an Alice, remaining in the kingdom. — The dregs of the people have adopted this unaccountable cuſtom, and a fellow who keeps a little alehouſe at the bottom of my avenue in the country, has no leſs than an Auguſtus Frederick, a Scipio Africanus, and a Matilda-Wilhelmina-Leonora, in his family.

Mrs. Harley.

Upon my word, a very pretty ſtring of chriſtian names.

Lady Betty.

Well, Sir Harry, you and Mr Cecil dine with us. — Come, ladies, let us go to the garden.

Mrs. Harley.

I poſitively won't go without Mr. Cecil, for I muſt have ſomebody to laugh at.

CECIL.

And ſo muſt I, widow, therefore I won't loſe this opportunity of being in your company.

[*Exeunt ladies, and followed by* CECIL, *who meets* RIVERS *entering.*]

CECIL.

Ah, Colonel, I am heartily glad to ſee you.

RIVERS.

My dear Cecil, you are welcome home again.

CECIL.

There's my wiſe kinſman wants a word with you. [*Exit.*]

Sir HARRY.

Colonel, your moſt obedient : — I am come upon the old buſineſs ; —for unleſs I am allow'd to entertain hope of Miſs Rivers, I ſhall be the moſt miſerable of human beings.

RIVERS.

Sir Harry, I have already told you by letter; and I now tell you perſonally, I cannot liſten to your propoſals.

Sir HARRY.

No, Sir ?

RIVERS.

No, Sir, — I have promiſed my daughter to Mr. Sidney ; — do you know that, Sir ?

Sir HARRY.

I do ; — but what then? Engagements of this kind, you know —

RIVERS.

So then, you do know I have promiſed her to Mr. Sidney ?

Sir

Sir HARRY.

I do; — but I alſo know, that matters are not finally ſettled between Mr. Sidney and you; and I moreover know, that his fortune is by no means equal to mine: therefore —

RIVERS.

Sir Harry, let me aſk you one queſtion, before you make your conſequence.

Sir HARRY.

A thouſand, if you pleaſe, Sir.

RIVERS.

Why then, Sir, let me aſk you, what you have ever obſerved in me, or my conduct, that you deſire me ſo familiarly to break my word? — I thought, Sir, you conſidered me as a man of honour.

Sir HARRY.

And ſo I do, Sir, a man of the niceſt honour.

RIVERS.

And yet, Sir, you aſk me to violate the ſanctity of my word; — and tell me, indirectly, that it is my intereſt to be a raſcal —

Sir HARRY.

I really don't underſtand you, Colonel: — I thought, when I was talking to you, I was talking to a man who knew the world; — and, as you have not yet ſigned —

RIVERS.

Why, this is mending matters with a witneſs! — And ſo you think, becauſe I am not legally bound, I am under no neceſſity of keeping my word! — Sir Harry, laws were never made for men of honour; — they want no bond but the rectitude

rectitude of their own sentiments, and laws are of no use but to bind the villains of society.

Sir HARRY.

Well! but my dear Colonel, if you have no regard for me, shew some little regard for your daughter.

RIVERS.

Sir Harry, I shew the greatest regard for my daughter by giving her to a man of honour; — and I must not be insulted with any farther repetition of your proposals.

Sir HARRY.

Insult you, Colonel! — is the offer of my alliance an insult? — is my readiness to make what settlements you think proper —

RIVERS.

Sir Harry, I should consider the offer of a kingdom an insult, if it was to be purchased by the violation of my word: — Besides, though my daughter shall never go a beggar to the arms of her husband, I wou'd rather see her happy than rich; and if she has enough to provide handsomely for a young family, and something to spare for the exigencies of a worthy friend, I shall think her as affluent as if she was mistress of Mexico.

Sir HARRY.

Well, Colonel, I have done; — but I believe —

RIVERS.

Well, Sir Harry, and as our conference is done, we will, if you please, retire to the ladies: — I shall be always glad of your acquaintance, though I can't receive you as a son-in-law; — for a union of interest I look upon as a union of dishonour; and consider a marriage for money, at best, but a legal prostitution. [*Exeunt.*]

END *of the* FIRST ACT.

ACT II.

SCENE, *a Garden.*

Enter Lady BETTY *and* Mrs. HARLEY.

Mrs. HARLEY.

LORD, Lord, my dear you're enough to drive one out of one's wits. — I tell you, again and again, he's as much yours as ever; and was I in your ſituation, he ſhou'd be my huſband to-morrow morning.

Lady BETTY.

Dear Emmy, you miſtake the matter ſtrangely.— Lord Winworth is no common man; nor wou'd he have continu'd his ſilence ſo long upon his favourite ſubject, if he had the leaſt inclination to renew his addreſſes. — His pride has juſtly taken the alarm at my inſenſibility; and he will not, I am ſatisfied, run the hazard of another refuſal.

Mrs. HARLEY.

Why then, in the name of wonder, if he was ſo dear to you, cou'd you prodigally trifle with your own happineſs, and repeatedly refuſe him?

Lady BETTY.

I have repeatedly told you, becauſe I was a fool, Emmy. — 'Till he withdrew his addreſſes, I knew not how much I eſteemed him; my unhappineſs in my firſt marriage, you know, made me reſolve againſt another. — And you are alſo ſenſible I have frequently argu'd, that a woman of real delicacy ſhou'd never admit a ſecond impreſſion on her heart.

Mrs. HARLEY.

Yes, and I always thought you argu'd very foolishly. — I am sure I ought to know, for I have been twice married; — and though I lov'd my first husband very sincerely, there was not a woman in England who cou'd have made the second a better wife. — Nay, for that matter, if another was to offer himself to-morrow, I am not altogether certain that I should refuse listening —

Lady BETTY.

You are a strange creature.

Mrs. HARLEY.

And are'nt you a much stranger, in declining to follow your own inclinations, when you cou'd have consulted them so highly, to the credit of your good sense, and the satisfaction of your whole family.—But it is'nt yet too late; and if you will be advis'd by me, every thing shall end as happily as you can wish.

Lady BETTY.

Well, let me hear your advice.

Mrs. HARLEY.

Why this, then: — My Lord, you know, has requested that you wou'd indulge him with half an hour's private conversation some time this morning.

Lady BETTY.

Well!

Mrs. HARLEY.

This is a liberty he has'nt taken these three months — and he must design something by it; — now as he can design nothing but to renew his addresses, I wou'd advise you to take him

him at the very firſt word, for fear your delicacy, if it has time to conſider, ſhou'd again ſhew you the ſtrange impropriety of ſecond marriages.

Lady BETTY.

But ſuppoſe this ſhould not be his buſineſs with me?

Mrs. HARLEY.

Why then we'll go another way to work: — I, as a ſanguine friend of my Lord's, can give him a diſtant hint of matters, exacting, at the ſame time, a promiſe of the moſt inviolable ſecrecy; and aſſuring him you wou'd never forgive me, if you had the leaſt idea of my having acquainted him with ſo important a ——

Lady BETTY.

And ſo you wou'd have me —

Mrs. HARLEY.

Why not? — This is the very ſtep I ſhou'd take myſelf, if I was in your ſituation.

Lady BETTY.

May be ſo: — But 'tis a ſtep which I ſhall never take. — What! wou'd you have me loſt to all feeling? Wou'd you have me meanly make uſe of chambermaid-artifices for a huſband?

Mrs. HARLEY.

I wou'd only have you happy, my dear: — And where the man of one's heart is at ſtake I don't think we ought to ſtand ſo rigidly upon trifles. —

Lady BETTY.

Trifles, Emmy! do you call the laws of delicacy trifles? — She that violates theſe ——

Mrs. HARLEY.

Poh! poh! ſhe that violates: — What a work there is with you ſentimental folks. — Why, don't I tell you that my Lord ſhall never know any thing of your concern in the deſign?

Lady BETTY.

But ſha'nt I know it myſelf, Emmy! — and how can I eſcape the juſtice of my own reflections!

Mrs. HARLEY.

Well, thank heav'n, my ſentiments are not ſufficiently refin'd to make me unhappy.

Lady BETTY.

I can't change my ſentiments, my dear Emmy, — nor wou'd I, if I cou'd: — Of this, however, be certain, that unleſs I have Lord Winworth without courting him, I ſhall never have him at all. — But be ſilent to all the world upon this matter, I conjure you; — particularly to Miſs Marchmont: for ſhe has been ſo ſtrenuous an advocate for my Lord, that the concealment of it from her might give her ſome doubts of my friendſhip; and I ſhou'd be continually uneaſy, for fear my reſerve ſhou'd be conſider'd as an indirect inſult upon her circumſtances.

Mrs. HARLEY.

Well, the devil take this delicacy; I don't know any thing it does beſides making people miſerable: — And yet ſome how, fooliſh as it is, one can't help liking it. — But yonder I ſee Sir Harry and Mr. Cecil.

Lady BETTY.

Let us withdraw then, my dear; they may detain us; and, till this interview is over, I ſhall

be

be in a continual agitation; yet I am ſtrangely apprehenſive of a diſappointment, Emmy — and if — [*going*]

Mrs. HARLEY.

Lady Betty.

Lady BETTY.

What do you ſay?

Mrs. HARLEY.

Do you ſtill think there is any thing extremely prepoſterous in ſecond marriages?

Lady BETTY.

You are intolerably provoking. — [*Exeunt.*]

Enter CECIL *and* Sir HARRY.

CECIL.

Well, did'nt I tell you the moment you open'd this affair to me, that the Colonel was a man of too much ſenſe to give his daughter to a coxcomb?

Sir HARRY.

But what if I ſhou'd tell you, that his daughter ſhall be ſtill mine, and in ſpite of his teeth?

CECIL.

Prithee explain, kinſman.

Sir HARRY.

Why ſuppoſe Miſs Rivers ſhould have no very ſtrong objection to this unfortunate figure of mine?

CECIL.

Why even your vanity can't think that a young lady of her good ſenſe can poſſibly be in love with you?

Sir

Sir HARRY.

What, you think that no likely circumſtance, I ſee?

CECIL.

I do really — Formerly indeed the women were fools enough to be caught by the frippery of externals; and ſo a fellow neither pick'd a pocket, nor put up with an affront, he was a dear toad — a ſweet creature — and a wicked devil; — nay, the wicked devil was quite an angel of a man;— and, like another Alexander, in proportion to the number of wretches which he made, he conſtantly increas'd the luſtre of his reputation: — till at laſt, having conquer'd all his worlds, he ſat down with that celebrated ruffian, and wept becauſe he cou'd commit no farther outrages upon ſociety.

Sir HARRY.

O, my good moralizing couſin, you'll find yourſelf curſedly out in your politics; and I ſhall convince you in a few hours, that a handſome ſuit on the back of a ſprightly young fellow, will ſtill do more among the women than all your ſentiment and ſlovenlineſs.

CECIL.

What, wou'd you perſuade me that Miſs Rivers will go off with you?

Sir HARRY.

You have hit the mark for once in your life, my ſweet-temper'd mouther of morality — The dear Theodora ——

CECIL.

The dear Theodora! and ſo, Harry, you imagine, that by the common maxims of faſhionable life,

life, you may appear to be a friend to the Colonel, at the very moment you are going to rob him of his daughter. — For ſhame, kinſman — for ſhame! — have ſome pride, if you have no virtue — and don't ſmile in a man's face when you want to do him the greateſt of all injuries. — don't Harry —

Sir HARRY.

Cecil, I ſcorn a baſe action as much as you, or as much as any man — but I love Miſs Rivers honourably. — I aſk nothing from her father; and as her perſon is her own, ſhe has a right to beſtow it where ſhe pleaſes.

CECIL.

I am anſwered: — her perſon is her own — and ſhe has a right to be miſerable her own way. — I acknowledge it — and will not diſcover your ſecret to her father. —

Sir HARRY.

Diſcover it to her father! — why ſure you woud'nt think of it. — Take care, Cecil — take care — I do, indeed, love you better than any man in the world — and I know you have a friendſhip, a cordial friendſhip, for me — but the happineſs of my whole life is at ſtake, and muſt not be deſtroy'd by any of your unaccountable peculiarities.

CECIL.

Harry — you know I wou'd at any time rather promote your happineſs than obſtruct it. — And you alſo know, that if I die without children — you ſhall have a principal part of my fortune; — but damn it — I wiſh you had not us'd the maſk of friendſhip to ſteal this young Lady away from her relations — 'tis hard that their good nature

muſt

muſt be turn'd againſt their peace; — and hard, becauſe her whole family treat you with regard, that you ſhou'd offer them the greateſt inſult imaginable.

Sir HARRY.

Dear Cecil, I am more to be pity'd than condemn'd in this tranſaction. — When I firſt endeavour'd to make myſelf agreeable to Miſs Rivers, I imagin'd her family wou'd readily countenance my addreſſes; and when I ſucceeded in that endeavour, I had not time to declare myſelf in form, before her father enter'd into this engagement with Sidney.—The moment I heard it mention'd, I wrote to him, offering him a *carte blanche*; and this morning a repetition of my offer was treated with contempt. — I have therefore been forc'd into the meaſure you diſapprove ſo much— but I hope my conduct, in the character of the ſon-in-law, will amply atone for any error in my behaviour as a friend.

CECIL.

Well, well, we muſt make the beſt of a bad market; — her father has no right to force her inclinations; — 'tis equally cruel and unjuſt: therefore you may depend upon my utmoſt endeavours not only to aſſiſt you in carrying her off, but in appeaſing all family-reſentments. — For, really, you are ſo often in the wrong, that one muſt ſtand by you a little when you are in the right: — ſo I ſhall be ready for you, kinſman.

Sir HARRY.

Why, Cecil, this is honeſt — this is really friendly — and you ſhall abuſe me a whole twelvemonth without my anſwering a ſyllable — but

but for the preſent I muſt leave you — yonder I ſee Miſs Rivers — we have ſome little matters to talk of — you underſtand me — and now —

[*Exit.*]

CECIL.

For a torrent of rapture and nonſenſe. — What egregious puppies does this unaccountable Love make of young fellows: Nay, for that matter, what egregious puppies does it not make of old ones? — *ecce ſignum.* — 'Tis a comfort, though, that no body knows I am a puppy in this reſpect but myſelf. — Here was I fancying that all the partiality I felt for poor Hortenſia March mont proceeded from my friendſhip for her father; — when, upon an honeſt examination into my own heart, — I find it principally ariſes from my regard for herſelf. — I was in hopes a change of objects would have driven the baggage out of my thoughts, — and I went to France; — but I am come home with a ſettled reſolution of aſking her to marry a ſlovenly raſcal of fifty, who is to be ſure a very likely ſwain for a young lady to fall in love with: — but who knows! — the moſt ſenſible women have ſometimes ſtrange taſtes; — and yet it muſt be a very ſtrange taſte, that can poſſibly approve of my overtures. — I'll go cautiouſly to work however, — and ſolicit her as for a friend of my own age and fortune; — ſo that if ſhe refuſes me, which is probable enough — I ſhan't expoſe myſelf to her contempt. — What a ridiculous figure is an old fool ſighing at the feet of a young woman! — Zounds, I wonder how the grey-headed dotards have the impudence to aſk a blooming girl of twenty to throw herſelf away upon a moving mummy, or a walking ſkeleton.

[*Exit.*]

The SCENE *changes to an Apartment in* Lady BETTY's *House.*

Enter Lady BETTY *and* Mrs. HARLEY.

Lady BETTY.

You can't think, Emmy, how my ſpirits are agitated; — I wonder what my Lord can want with me?

Mrs. HARLEY.

Well, well, try and collect yourſelf a little — he is juſt coming up, — I muſt retire. — Courage, my dear creature, this once — and the day's our own, I warrant you. [*Exit.*]

Enter WINWORTH, *bowing very low.*

Lady BETTY.

Here he is! — Bleſs me, what a flutter I am in!

WINWORTH.

Your Ladyſhip's moſt obedient.

Lady BETTY.

Won't your Lordſhip be ſeated? — He ſeems exceſſively confus'd. [*aſide.*]

WINWORTH.

I have taken the liberty, Madam — How ſhe awes me now I am alone with her! [*aſide.*]

Lady BETTY.

My Lord!

WINWORTH.

I ſay, Madam, I have taken the liberty to —

Lady

Lady BETTY.

I beg, my Lord, you won't consider an apology in the least —

WINWORTH.

Your Ladyship is extremely obliging — and yet I am fearful —

Lady BETTY.

I hope your Lordship will consider me as a friend, — and therefore lay aside this unnecessary ceremony.

WINWORTH.

I do consider you, Madam, as a friend; — as an inestimable friend — and I am this moment come to solicit you upon a subject of the utmost importance to my happiness.

Lady BETTY. [*aside.*]

Lord! what is he going to say?

WINWORTH.

Madam! —

Lady BETTY.

I say, my Lord, that you cannot speak to me on any subject of importance without engaging my greatest attention.

WINWORTH.

You honour me too much, Madam.

Lady BETTY.

Not in the least, my Lord — for there is not a person in the world who wishes your happiness with greater cordiality.

WINWORTH.

You eternally oblige me, Madam — and I can now take courage to tell you, that my happiness, in a moſt material degree, depends upon your Ladyſhip.

Lady BETTY.

On me, my Lord? — Bleſs me!

WINWORTH.

Yes, Madam, on your Ladyſhip.

Lady BETTY. [*aſide.*]

Mrs. Harley was right, and I ſhall ſink with confuſion.

WINWORTH.

'Tis on this buſineſs, Madam, I have taken the liberty of requeſting the preſent interview, — and as I find your Ladyſhip ſo generouſly ready —

Lady BETTY.

Why, my Lord, I muſt confeſs — I ſay, I muſt acknowledge, my Lord, — that if your happineſs depends upon me — I ſhould not be very much pleas'd to ſee you miſerable.

WINWORTH.

Your Ladyſhip is benignity itſelf; — but as I want words to expreſs my ſenſe of this obligation — I ſhall proceed at once to my requeſt, nor treſpaſs upon your patience by an ineffectual compliment to your generoſity.

Lady BETTY.

If you pleaſe, my Lord.

WINWORTH.

Then, Madam, my requeſt is, that I may have your conſent —

Lady

Lady BETTY.

This is ſo ſudden, my Lord! — ſo unexpected!

WINWORTH.

Why, Madam, it is ſo; — yet, if I cou'd but engage your acquieſcence — I might ſtill think of a double union on the day which makes my couſin happy—

Lady BETTY.

My Lord — I really don't know how to anſwer: — Does'nt your Lordſhip think this is rather precipitating matters?

WINWORTH.

No man, Madam, can be too ſpeedy in promoting his happineſs: — If, therefore, I might preſume to hope for your concurrence — I woud'nt altogether —

Lady BETTY.

My concurrence, my Lord! — ſince it is ſo eſſentially neceſſary to your peace, I cannot refuſe any longer. — Your great merit will juſtify ſo immediate a compliance — and I ſhall ſtand excus'd of all —

WINWORTH.

Then, Madam, I don't deſpair of the Lady's —

Lady BETTY.

My Lord?

WINWORTH.

I know your Ladyſhip can eaſily prevail upon her to overlook an immaterial punctilio; and, thereſore —

Lady BETTY.

The Lady, my Lord?

WINWORTH.

WINWORTH.

Yes, Madam: Miſs Marchmont, if ſhe finds my addreſſes ſupported by your Ladyſhip, will, in all probability, be eaſily induc'd to receive them; — and then, your Ladyſhip knows —

Lady BETTY.

Miſs Marchmont! my Lord!

WINWORTH.

Yes, Madam, Miſs Marchmont. — Since your final diſapprobation of thoſe hopes which I was once preſumptuous enough to entertain of calling your Ladyſhip mine, the anguiſh of a rejected paſſion has render'd me inconceivably wretched; and I ſee no way of mitigating the ſeverity of my ſituation, but in the eſteem of this amiable woman, who knows how tenderly I have been attach'd to you, and whoſe goodneſs will induce her, I am well convinc'd, to alleviate, as much as poſſible, the greatneſs of my diſappointment.

Lady BETTY.

Your Lordſhip is undoubtedly right in your opinion — and I am infinitely concern'd to have been the involuntary cauſe of uneaſineſs to you; — but Miſs Marchmont, my Lord — ſhe will merit your utmoſt —

WINWORTH.

I know ſhe will, Madam — and it rejoices me to ſee you ſo highly pleas'd with my intention.

Lady BETTY.

O, I am quite delighted with it!

WINWORTH.

I knew I ſhou'd pleaſe you by it. —

Lady

Lady BETTY.

You can't imagine how you have pleas'd me!

WINWORTH.

How noble is this goodneſs! — Then, Madam, I may expect your Ladyſhip will be my advocate. — The injuſtice which Fortune has done Miſs Marchmont's merit, obliges me to act with a double degree of circumſpection; — for, when Virtue is unhappily plung'd into difficulties, 'tis entitled to an aditional ſhare of veneration.

Lady BETTY. [*aſide.*]

How has my folly undone me!

WINWORTH.

I will not treſpaſs any longer upon your Ladyſhip's leiſure, than juſt to obſerve, that though I have ſolicited your friendſhip on this occaſion, I muſt, nevertheleſs, beg you will not be too much my friend. — I know Miſs Marchmont would make any ſacrifice to oblige you; — and if her gratitude ſhould appear in the leaſt concern'd, — This is a nice point, my dear Lady Betty, and I muſt not wound the peace of any perſon's boſom, to recover the tranquility of my own. [*Exit.*]

Enter Mrs. HARLEY, *who ſpeaks.*

Well, my dear, is it all over?

Lady BETTY.

It is all over indeed, Emmy.

Mrs. HARLEY.

But why that ſorrowful tone — and melancholy countenance? Muſtn't I wiſh you joy?

Lady

Lady Betty.

O, I am the moſt miſerable woman in the world! — Would you believe it? — The buſineſs of this interview was to requeſt my intereſt in his favour with Miſs Marchmont.

Mrs. Harley.

With Miſs Marchmont! — Then there is not one atom of ſincere affection in the univerſe.

Lady Betty.

As to that, I have reaſon to think his ſentiments for me are as tender as ever.

Mrs. Harley.

He gives you a pretty proof of his tenderneſs, truly, when he aſks your aſſiſtance to marry another woman!

Lady Betty.

Had you but ſeen his confuſion —

Mrs. Harley.

He might well be confus'd, when, after courting you theſe three years, he cou'd think of another; and that too at the very moment in which you were ready to oblige him.

Lady Betty.

There has been a ſort of fatality in the affair — and I am puniſh'd but too juſtly: — The woman that wants candour, where ſhe is addreſs'd by a man of merit, wants a very eſſential virtue; and ſhe who can delight in the anxiety of a worthy mind, is little to be pitied when ſhe feels the ſharpeſt ſtings of anxiety in her own.

Mrs. Harley.

But what do you intend to do with regard to this extraordinary requeſt of Lord Winworth; — will you really ſuffer him to marry Miſs Marchmont?

Lady

Lady Betty.

Why, what can I do? If it was improper for me, before I knew any thing of his design in regard to Miss Marchmont, to insinuate the least desire of hearing him again on the subject of his heart, 'tis doubly improper now, when I see he has turn'd his thoughts on another woman, and when this woman, besides, is one of my most valuable friends.

Mrs. Harley

Well, courage, Lady Betty: — we are'nt yet in a desperate situation. — Miss Marchmont loves you—as herself—and woudn't, I dare say, accept the first man in the world, if it gave you the least uneasiness. — I'll go to her, therefore, this very moment—tell her at once how the case is; — and, my life for it, her obligations to you ——

Lady Betty.

Stay, Emmy — I conjure you, stay — and, as you value my peace of mind, be for ever silent on this subject. — Miss Marchmont has no obligations to me;—since our acquaintance I have been the only person oblig'd; she has given me a power of serving the worthiest young creature in the world, and so far has laid me under the greatest obligation.

Mrs. Harley.

Why, my dear ——

Lady Betty.

But suppose I could be mean enough to think an apartment in my house, a place in my chariot, a seat at my table, and a little annuity, in case of my decease, were obligations, when I continually enjoy such a happiness as her friendship and her company; — do you think they are obligations which shou'd make a woman of her fine ſenſe, reject the moſt amiable man exiſting, eſpecially in her circumſtances, where he has the additional recommendation of an elevated rank and an affluent fortune: — This wou'd be exacting intereſt with a witneſs for trifles; and, inſtead of having any little merit to claim from my behaviour to her, I ſhou'd be the moſt inexorable of all uſurers.

Mrs. HARLEY.

Well, but ſuppoſe Miſs Marchmont ſhou'd not like my Lord?

Lady BETTY.

Not like him! — why will you ſuppoſe an impoſſibility?

Mrs. HARLEY.

But let us ſuppoſe it, for argument ſake.

Lady BETTY.

Why I cannot ſay but it wou'd pleaſe me above all things: — For ſtill, Emmy, I am a woman, and feel this unexpected misfortune with the keeneſt ſenſibility: — It kills me to think of his being another's; but if he muſt, I wou'd rather ſee him her's than any woman's in the univerſe. — But I'll talk no more upon this ſubject, 'till I acquaint her with his propoſal; and yet, Emmy, how ſevere a trial muſt I go through!

Mrs. HARLEY.

Ay, and you moſt richly deſerve it. [*Exeunt.*]

END *of the* SECOND ACT.

ACT

ACT III.

SCENE, Lady BETTY's *Garden.*

Sir HARRY, Miſs RIVERS, *and* SALLY, *croſs at the head of the ſtage*; Colonel RIVERS *obſerving them.*

RIVERS.

IN cloſe converſation with Sir Harry this half hour, at the remoteſt part of the garden! — Why, what am I to think of all this? — Doesn't ſhe know I have refus'd him? —Doesn't ſhe know herſelf engag'd to Sidney? — There's ſomething mean and pitiful in ſuſpicion: — But ſtill there is ſomething that alarms me in this affair; and who knows how far the happineſs of my child may be at ſtake?—Women, after all, are ſtrange things; — they have more ſenſe than we generally allow them — but they have alſo more vanity.— 'Tisn't for want of underſtanding they err, — but through an inſatiable love of flattery. — They know very well when they are committing a fault, but deſtruction wears ſo bewitching a form, that they rebel againſt the ſenſe of their own conviction — and never trouble themſelves about conſequences till they are actually undone.—But here they come. — I don't like this liſtening: — Yet the meanneſs of the action muſt for once be juſtified by the neceſſity.

[*Retires behind a clump of trees.*]

Enter Miſs RIVERS, Sir HARRY, *and* SALLY.

Miſs RIVERS.

Indeed, Sir Harry, you upbraid me very unjuſtly. — I feel the refuſal which my father has given you ſeverely; — nevertheleſs, I muſt not conſent to your propoſal.—An elopement wou'd, I am ſure,

 break

break his heart; — and as he is wholly ignorant of my partiality for you, — I cannot accuſe him of unkindneſs.

RIVERS, *behind.*

So! ſo! ſo! ſo!

Sir HARRY.

Why then, my dear Miſs Rivers, woudn 't you give me leave to mention the prepoſſeſſion with which you honour me, to the old Gentleman?

RIVERS.

The old Gentleman! —

Miſs RIVERS.

Becauſe I was in hopes my father wou'd have liſten'd to your application, without putting me to the painful neceſſity of acknowledging my ſentiments in your favour; and becauſe I fear'd, that unleſs the application was approv'd, on account of its intrinſic generoſity, there was nothing which cou'd poſſibly work upon the firmneſs of his temper.

RIVERS.

Well ſaid, daughter!

SALLY.

The firmneſs of your father's temper, Madam! — the obſtinacy, you ſhou'd ſay. — Sir Harry, as I live and breathe, there isn't ſo obſtinate, ſo perverſe, and ſo peeviſh an old devil in all England.

RIVERS.

Thank you, Mrs. Sally.

Miſs RIVERS.

Sally, I inſiſt that when you ſpeak of my father, you always ſpeak of him with reſpect. — 'Tisn't your knowledge of ſecrets which ſhall juſtify theſe freedoms; — for I wou'd rather every thing

thing was diſcovered this minute, than hear him mention'd with ſo impudent a familiarity by his ſervants.

SALLY.

Well, Madam, I beg pardon ;—but you know the Colonel, where he once determines, is never to be alter'd ; — ſo that call this ſteadineſs of temper by what name you pleaſe — 'tis likely to make you miſerable, unleſs you embrace the préſent opportunity, and go off, like a woman of ſpirit, with the object of your affections.

RIVERS.

What a damn'd jade it is !

Sir HARRY.

Indeed, my dear Miſs Rivers, Sally adviſes you like a true friend ; — and I am ſatisfy'd your own good ſenſe muſt ſecretly argue on her ſide the queſtion.—The only alternative you have, is to fly and be happy, — or ſtay and be miſerable.—You have yourſelf acknowledg'd, my ever adorable —

RIVERS.

O damn your adorables !

Sir HARRY.

I ſay, Madam, you have yourſelf acknowledg'd, that there is no hope whatſoever of working upon the Colonel's tenderneſs, by acquainting him with our mutual affection : — On the contrary, 'tis likely, that had he the leaſt ſuſpicion of my being honour'd with your regard, he wou'd drag you inſtantly to his favourite Sidney, who is ſo utterly inſenſible of your merit, — and who, if he has a paſſion for any body, is, I am confident, devoted to Miſs Marchmont.

RIVERS

RIVERS.

Why what a lye has the raſcal trump'd up here againſt poor Sidney?

Miſs RIVERS.

Dear Sir Harry, what wou'd you have me do?

RIVERS.

There! — Her dear Sir Harry!

Sir HARRY.

My ever adorable Miſs Rivers —

RIVERS.

No, ſhe can't ſtand theſe ever-adorables.

Sir HARRY.

This exceſs of filial affection is extremely amiable: — but it ought by no means to render you forgetful of what is due to yourſelf. — Conſider, Madam, if you have been treated with tenderneſs, you have repaid that tenderneſs with duty, and have ſo far diſcharg'd this mighty obligation.

RIVERS.

A pretty method of ſettling accounts truly!

Miſs RIVERS.

Don't, my dear Sir Harry, ſpeak in this negligent manner of my father.

RIVERS.

Kind creature!

Sir HARRY.

From what I have urg'd you muſt ſee, Madam, that though you are ſo ready to ſacrifice your peace for your father, he ſets a greater value upon a trifling promiſe than upon your happineſs: —

Judge,

Judge, therefore, whether his repoſe ſhould be dearer to you than your own; and judge too, whether to prevent the breach of his word, you ſhou'd vow eternal tenderneſs to a man you muſt eternally deteſt, and violate even your veracity to kill the object of your love?

Miſs RIVERS.

Good heav'n, what ſhall I do?

SALLY.

Do — Madam — go off, to be ſure.

RIVERS.

I'll wring that huſſey's head off.

Sir HARRY.

On my knees, Madam, let me beg you will conſult your own happineſs, and, in your own, the happineſs of your father.

RIVERS.

Ay, now he kneels, 'tis all over.

Sir HARRY.

The Colonel, Madam, has great ſenſibility, and the conſciouſneſs that he himſelf has been the cauſe of your unhappineſs, will fill him with endleſs regret: — Whereas, by eſcaping with me, the caſe will be utterly otherwiſe. — When he ſees we are inſeparably united, and hears with how unabating an aſſiduity I labour to merit the bleſſing of your hand, a little time will neceſſarily make us friends; and I have great hopes that, before the end of three months, we ſhall be the favourites of the whole family.

RIVERS.

You'll be curſedly miſtaken, though.—

Sir

Davidson College Library

Sir HARRY.

But ſpeak, my dear Miſs Rivers --- ſpeak and pronounce my fate.

Miſs RIVERS.

Sir Harry, you have convinc'd me; —

RIVERS.

Ay, I knew he wou'd. —

Miſs RIVERS.

And provided you here give me a ſolemn aſſurance, that the moment we are married you will employ every poſſible method of effecting a reconciliation —

Sir HARRY.

You conſent to go off with me the firſt opportunity. — A thouſand thanks, my Angel, for this generous condeſcenſion! — and when —

Miſs RIVERS.

There is no occaſion for profeſſions, Sir Harry; — I rely implicitly on your tenderneſs and your honour. —

SALLY.

Dear Madam, you have tranſported your poor Sally by this noble reſolution.

RIVERS.

I dare ſay ſhe has; — but I may chance to cool your tranſport in a horſe-pond. —

Miſs RIVERS.

I am oblig'd to you, Sally, for the part you take in my affairs, and I purpoſe that you ſhall be the companion of my flight.

SALLY.

Shall I, Madam! — you are too good; — and I am ſure I ſhoudn't like to live in my old maſter's houſe, when you are out of the family.

RIVERS.

RIVERS.

Don't be uneaſy on that account.

Sir HARRY.

Suffer me now, my dear Miſs Rivers, ſince you have been thus generouſly kind, to inform you, that a coach and ſix will be ready punctually at twelve, at the ſide of the little paddock, at the back of Lady Betty's garden. — There's a cloſe walk, you know, from the garden to the place, and I'll meet you at the ſpot to conduct you to the coach.

Miſs RIVERS.

Well, I am ſtrangely apprehenſive! — but I'll be there. — However, 'tis now high time for us to ſeparate; — my father's eyes are generally every where, — and I am impatient, ſince it is determined, — 'till our deſign is executed.

RIVERS.

O, I don't in the leaſt doubt it. —

Sir HARRY.

'Till twelve, then, farewel, my charmer. —

Miſs RIVERS.

You do what you will with me. —

[*Exeunt ſeparately.*]

RIVERS *comes forward.*

You do what you will with me! Why what a fool, what an idiot was I, — ever to ſuppoſe I had a daughter? — From the moment of her birth — to this curſed hour, I have labour'd, I have toil'd for her happineſs; and now, when I fancy'd myſelf ſure of her tend'reſt affection, ſhe caſts me off for ever. — By and by, — I ſhall have this fellow at my feet, entreating my forgiveneſs; and the world will think me an unfeeling monſter, if I don't give him my eſtate, as a reward for having blaſted my deareſt expectations. — The world

 will

will think it ſtrange that I ſhou'd not promote his felicity, becauſe he has utterly deſtroy'd mine; and my dutiful daughter will be ſurpriz'd, if the tender ties of nature are not ſtrictly regarded in my conduct, though ſhe has violated the moſt ſacred of them all in her own. — Death and hell! who wou'd be a father? — There is yet one way left, — and, if that fails, — why, I never had a daughter. — [*Exit.*]

The SCENE *changes to an Apartment.*

Enter Miſs MARCHMONT *and* CECIL.

Miſs MARCHMONT.

Nay, now, Sir, I muſt tax you with unkindneſs; — know ſomething that may poſſibly be of conſequence to my welfare, — and yet decline to tell me! — Is this conſiſtent with the uſual friendſhip which I have met with from Mr. Cecil?

CECIL.

Look'ye, Hortenſia, 'tis becauſe I ſet a very great value on your eſteem, that I find this unwillingneſs to explain myſelf.

Miſs MARCHMONT.

Indeed, Sir, you grow every moment more and more myſterious. —

CECIL.

Well then, Hortenſia, if I thought you woudn't be offended — I

Miſs MARCHMONT.

I am ſure, Sir, you will never ſay any thing to give me a reaſonable cauſe of offence. — I know your kindneſs for me too well, Sir.

CECIL.

Where is the need of Sirring me at every word? — I deſire you will lay aſide this ceremony, and treat

treat me with the ſame freedom you do every body elſe; — theſe Sirs are ſo cold, and ſo diſtant —

Miſs MARCHMONT.

Indeed, Sir, I can't ſo eaſily lay aſide my reſpect as you imagine, for I have long conſider'd you as a father.

CECIL.

As a father! — but that's a light in which I don't want to be conſider'd. — As a father indeed! — O ſhe's likely to think me a proper huſband for her, I can ſee that already! [*aſide.*]

Miſs MARCHMONT.

Why not, Sir? — your years, — your friendſhip for my father, and your partiality for me, ſufficiently juſtify the propriety of my epithet. —

CECIL. [*aſide,*]

My years! — Yes, I thought my years would be an invincible obſtacle.

Miſs MARCHMONT.

But pray, Sir, — to the buſineſs upon which you wanted to ſpeak with me: — You don't conſider I am all this time upon the rack of my ſex's curioſity. —

CECIL.

Why then, Hortenſia, --- I will proceed to the buſineſs --- and aſk you, in one word, --- if you have any diſinclination to be married?

Miſs MARCHMONT.

This is proceeding to buſineſs indeed, Sir: — but ha! ha! ha! pray, who have you deſign'd me as a huſband?

CECIL.

Why, what do you think of a man about my age?

Miſs MARCHMONT.

Of your age, Sir?

CECIL.

Yes, of my age. ---

Miſs MARCHMONT.

Why, Sir, what wou'd you adviſe me to think of him?

CECIL.

That isn't the queſtion, for all your arch ſignificance of manner, Madam.

Miſs MARCHMONT.

O I am ſure you wou'd never recommend him to me as a huſband, Sir!

CECIL.

--- So! --- and why not pray?

Miſs MARCHMONT.

Becauſe I am ſure you have too great a regard for me.

CECIL.

She gives me rare encouragement. [*aſide*] --- But do you imagine it impoſſible for ſuch a huſband to love you very tenderly?

Miſs MARCHMONT.

No --- Sir! --- But do you imagine it poſſible for me to love him very tenderly? --- You ſee I have caught your own frankneſs, Sir, --- and anſwer with as much eaſe as you queſtion me.

CECIL. [*aſide*]

How lucky it was that I did not open myſelf directly to her! --- O I ſhou'd have been moſt purely contemptible!

Miſs

Miſs MARCHMONT.

But pray, Sir, — have you, in reality, any meaning by theſe queſtions? — Is there actually any body who has ſpoken to you on my account?

CECIL.

Hortenſia, there is a fellow, a very fooliſh fellow, for whom I have ſome value, that entertains the ſincereſt affection for you.

Miſs MARCHMONT.

Then, indeed, Sir, I am very unhappy, — for I cannot encourage the addreſſes of any body.

CECIL.

No!

Miſs MARCHMONT.

O, Sir! I had but two friends in the world, — yourſelf and Lady Betty; — and I am, with juſtice, apprehenſive, that neither will conſider me long with any degree of regard. — Lady Betty has a propoſal from Lord Winworth of the ſame nature with yours, in which I fear ſhe will ſtrongly intereſt herſelf; — and I muſt be under the painful neceſſity of diſobliging you both, from an utter impoſſibility of liſtening to either of your recommendations.

CECIL.

I tell you, Hortenſia, not to alarm yourſelf.

Miſs MARCHMONT.

Dear Sir, I have always conſider'd you with reverence, and it would make me inconceivably wretched, if you imagin'd I was actuated upon this occaſion by any ridiculous ſingularity of ſentiment. — I wou'd do much to pleaſe you, — and I ſcarcely know what I ſhou'd refuſe to Lady Betty's requeſt;

requeſt ; — but, Sir, though it diſtreſſes me exceedingly to diſcover it, — I muſt tell you I have not a heart to diſpoſe of.

CECIL.

How's this ?

Miſs MARCHMONT.

At the ſame time, I muſt, however, tell you, that my affections are ſo plac'd as to make it wholly impoſſible for me ever to change my ſituation. — This acknowledgment of a prepoſſeſſion, Sir, may be inconſiſtent with the nice reſerve which is proper for my ſex ; — but it is neceſſary to juſtify me in a caſe where my gratitude might be reaſonably ſuſpected ; and when I recollect to whom it is made, I hope it will be doubly entitled to an excuſe.

CECIL.

Your candour, Hortenſia, needs no apology ; — but as you have truſted me thus far with your ſecret, — mayn't I know why you can have no proſpect of being united to the object of your affections ?

Miſs MARCHMONT.

Becauſe, Sir, he is engag'd to a moſt deſerving young lady, and will be married to her in a few days. — In ſhort, Mr. Sidney is the man for whom I entertain this ſecret partiality ; — you ſee, therefore, that my partiality is hopeleſs ; — but you ſee, at the ſame time, how utterly improper it would be for me to give a lifeleſs hand to another, while he is entirely maſter of my affections. — It would be a meanneſs, of which I think myſelf incapable ; and I ſhou'd be quite unworthy the honour of any deſerving hand, if, circumſtanc'd in this manner, I cou'd baſely ſtoop to accept it.

CECIL.

You intereſt me ſtrangely in your ſtory, Hortenſia! — But has Sidney any idea —

Miſs MARCHMONT.

None in the leaſt. — Before the match with Miſs Rivers was in agitation, he made addreſſes to me, though privately; and, I muſt own, his tenderneſs, join'd to his good qualities, ſoon gave me impreſſions in his favour. — But, Sir, I was a poor orphan, wholly dependant upon the generoſity of others, and he was a younger brother of family, great in his birth, but contracted in his circumſtances. — What cou'd I do? — It was not in my power to make his fortune, — and I had too much pride, or too much affection, to think of deſtroying it.

CECIL.

You are a good girl, — a very good girl; — but ſurely if Lady Betty knows any thing of this matter, there can be no danger of her recommending Lord Winworth ſo earneſtly to your attention. —

Miſs MARCHMONT.

There, Sir, is my principal misfortune. — Lady Betty is, of all perſons, the leaſt proper to be made acquainted with it. — Her heart is in the marriage between Miſs Rivers and Mr. Sidney; and had ſhe the leaſt idea of my ſentiments for him, or of his inclination for me, I am poſitive it would immediately fruſtrate the match. — On this account, Sir, I have carefully conceal'd the ſecret of my wiſhes, — and on this account I muſt ſtill continue to conceal it. — My heart ſhall break before it ſhall be worthleſs;

— and

— and I ſhou'd deteſt myſelf for ever, if I was capable of eſtabliſhing my own peace at the expence of my benefactreſs's firſt wiſh, and the deſire of her whole family.

CECIL.

Zounds, what can be the matter with my eyes! —

Miſs MARCHMONT.

My life was mark'd out early by calamity, — and the firſt light I beheld, was purchas'd with the loſs of a mother. — The grave ſnatch'd away the beſt of fathers, juſt as I came to know the value of ſuch a bleſſing; — and had not it been for the exalted goodneſs of others, I, who once experienc'd the unſpeakable pleaſure of relieving the neceſſitous, had myſelf, perhaps, felt the immediate want of bread. — And ſhall I ungratefully ſting the boſom which has thus benevolently cheriſh'd me? — Shall I baſely wound the peace of thoſe who have reſcu'd me from deſpair; — and ſtab at their tranquility, in the very moment they honour me with protection? — O, Mr. Cecil! they deſerve every ſacrifice which I can make. — May the benignant hand of Providence ſhower endleſs happineſs upon their heads; and may the ſweets of a ſtill-encreaſing felicity be their portion, whatever becomes of me!

CECIL.

Hortenſia, — I can't ſtay with you. — My eyes are exceedingly painful of late: — what the devil can be the matter with them? — But let me tell you before I go, that you ſhall be happy after all; — that you ſhall, I promiſe you. — But I ſee Lady Betty coming this way — and I cannot enter into explanations: — yet, do you hear, —

don't

don't ſuppoſe I am angry with you for refuſing my friend; — don't ſuppoſe ſuch a thing, I charge you; — for he has too much pride to force himſelf upon any woman, and too much humanity to make any woman miſerable.—He is, beſides, a very fooliſh fellow, and it doesn't ſignify — [*Exit.*]

Enter LADY BETTY.

Lady BETTY.

Well, my dear Hortenſia, I am come again to aſk you what you think of Lord Winworth. — We were interrupted before, — and I want, as ſoon as poſſible, for the reaſon I hinted, to know your real opinion of him.

Miſs MARCHMONT.

You have long known my real opinion of him, Lady Betty. — You know I always thought him a very amiable man.

Lady BETTY. [*with impatience.*]

Do you think him an amiable man?

Miſs MARCHMONT.

The whole world thinks as I do in this reſpect,— yet ——

Lady BETTY.

Ay, ſhe loves him, 'tis plain; and there is no hope after this declaration.---[*aſide.*]--- His Lordſhip merits your good opinion, I aſſure you, Miſs Marchmont.

Miſs MARCHMONT. [*aſide.*]

Yes, I ſee by this ceremony that ſhe is offended at my coolneſs to the propoſal.

Lady BETTY.

I have hinted to you, Miſs Marchmont, that my Lord requeſted I wou'd exert my little intereſt with you in his favour.

Miſs MARCHMONT.

The little intereſt your Ladyſhip has with me; --- the little intereſt —

Lady BETTY.

Don't be diſpleas'd with me, my dear Hortenſia, --- I know my intereſt with you is conſiderable. ---I know you love me.

Miſs MARCHMONT.

I wou'd ſacrifice my life for you, Lady Betty: For what had that life been without your generoſity?

Lady BETTY.

If you love me, Hortenſia, never mention any thing of this nature.

Miſs MARCHMONT.

You are too good. —

Lady BETTY.

But to my Lord Winworth. — He has earneſtly requeſted I wou'd become his advocate with you. — He has entirely got the better of his former attachments, and there can be no doubt of his making you an excellent huſband.

Miſs MARCHMONT.

His Lordſhip does me infinite honour; —nevertheleſs —

Lady BETTY. [*eagerly.*]

Neverthelefs, what, my dear?

Miſs MARCHMONT.

I ſay, notwithſtanding I think myſelf highly honour'd by his ſentiments in my favour, — 'tis utterly impoſſible for me to return his affection.

Lady

Lady Betty. [*surprized.*]

Impoſſible for you to return his affection!

Miſs Marchmont. [*aſide.*]

I knew what an intereſt ſhe wou'd take in this affair.

Lady Betty.

And do you really ſay you can't give him a favourable anſwer? — How fortunate! [*aſide.*]

Miſs Marchmont.

I do, my dear Lady Betty;—I can honour, I can reverence him; —but I cannot feel that tenderneſs for his perſon, which I imagine to be neceſſary both for his happineſs and my own.

Lady Betty.

Upon my word, my dear, you are extremely difficult in your choice; and if Lord Winworth is not capable of inſpiring you with tenderneſs, — I don't know who is likely to ſucceed; for, in my opinion, there is not a man in England poſſeſſed of more perſonal accompliſhments.

Miſs Marchmont.

And yet, great as theſe accompliſhments are, my dear Lady Betty, they never excited your tenderneſs. —

Lady Betty.

Why, all this is very true, my dear; — but, though I felt no tenderneſs, — yet I — to be ſure, I — that is — I ſay, nevertheleſs — This is beyond my hopes! [*aſide.*]

Miſs Marchmont. [*aſide.*]

She's diſtreſs'd that I decline the propoſal. — Her friendſhip for us both is generouſly warm;— and ſhe imagines I am equally inſenſible to his merit, and my own intereſt.

Lady BETTY.

Well, my dear, I see your emotion, — and I heartily beg your pardon for saying so much. — I shou'd be inexpressibly concern'd, if I thought you made any sacrifice on this occasion to me. — My Lord, to be sure, possesses a very high place in my esteem, — but —

Miss MARCHMONT.

Dear Lady Betty, what can I do? — I see you are offended with me, — and yet —

Lady BETTY.

I offended with you, my dear! — far from it; I commend your resolution extremely, since my Lord is not a man to your taste. — Offended with you! why shou'd I take the liberty to be offended with you? — A presumption of that nature —

Miss MARCHMONT.

Indeed, Lady Betty, this affair makes me very unhappy.

Lady BETTY.

Indeed, my dear, you talk very strangely: — so far from being sorry that you have refus'd my Lord — I am pleas'd, — infinitely pleas'd, — that is, since he was not agreeable to you. — Be satisfied your acceptance of him wou'd have given me no pleasure in the world; — I assure you it wou'dn't: — on the contrary, as matters are situated, I wou'dn't for the world have you give him the smallest encouragement. [*Exit.*]

Miss MARCHMONT. [*alone.*]

I see she's greatly disappointed at my refusal of an offer so highly to my advantage. — I see, moreover, she's griev'd that his Lordship should meet

meet with a ſecond repulſe, and from a quarter too, where the generoſity of his propoſal might be reaſonably expected to promiſe it ſucceſs. — How ſurpriz'd ſhe ſeem'd, when I told her he cou'dn't make an impreſſion on my heart! and how eagerly ſhe endeavour'd to convince me that ſhe was pleas'd with my conduct; not conſidering that this very eagerneſs was a maniſeſt proof of her diſſatisfaction!—She is more intereſted in this affair than I even thought ſhe wou'd be, — and I ſhould be completely miſerable if ſhe cou'd ſuſpect me of ingratitude. — As ſhe was ſo zealous for the match, I was certainly to blame in declining it. — 'Tis not yet, however, too late. — She has been a thouſand parents to me, — and I will not regard my own wiſhes, when they are any way oppoſite to her inclinations. — Poor Mr. Cecil! — Make me happy after all! — How? — Impoſſible! — for I was born to nothing but misfortune. —

[*Exit.*]

END *of the* THIRD ACT.

ACT

ACT IV.

SCENE, *an Apartment at* Lady BETTY's *House.*

Enter Lady BETTY *and* Mrs. HARLEY.

Lady BETTY.

THUS far, my dear Emmy, there is a gleam of hope. — She determin'd, positively determin'd, againſt my Lord ; — and even ſuſpected ſo little of my partiality for him, that ſhe appear'd under the greateſt anxiety, leſt I ſhou'd be offended with her refuſing him. — And yet, ſhall I own my folly to you ?

Mrs. HARLEY.

Pray do, my dear ; — you'll ſcarcely believe it, — but I have follies of my own ſometimes.

Lady BETTY.

Why you quite ſurprize me !

Mrs. HARLEY.

'Tis very true for all that. — But to your buſineſs.

Lady BETTY.

Why then, greatly as I dreaded her approbation of the propoſal, — I was ſecretly hurt at her inſenſibility to the perſonal attractions of his Lordſhip.

Mrs. HARLEY.

I don't doubt it, my dear. — We think all the world ſhou'd love what we are in love with ourſelves.

Lady

Lady BETTY.

You are right. — And though I was happy to find her reſolution ſo agreeable to my wiſhes, my pride was not a little piqued to find it poſſible for her to refuſe a man upon whom I had ſo ardently plac'd my own affection. — The ſurprize which I felt on this account, threw a warmth into my expreſſions, and made the generous girl apprehenſive that I was offended with her.

Mrs. HARLEY.

Well, this is a ſtrange world we live in. — That a woman without a ſhilling ſhou'd refuſe an Earl with a fine perſon and a great eſtate, is the moſt ſurprizing affair I ever heard of. — Perhaps, Lady Betty, my Lord may take it in his head to go round the family: — If he ſhou'd, my turn is next, and I aſſure you he ſhall meet with a very different reception.

Lady BETTY.

Then you wou'dn't be cruel, Emmy?

Mrs. HARLEY.

Why no; — not very cruel. —— I might give myſelf a few airs at firſt: — I might bluſh a little, and look down: — wonder what he cou'd find in me to attract his attention; — then pulling up my head, with a toſs of diſdain, — deſire him, if ever he ſpoke to me on that ſubject again, ——

Lady BETTY.

Well!

Mrs. HARLEY.

To have a licence in his pocket; --that's all.— I wou'd make ſure work of it at once, and leave it to your elevated minds to deal in delicate abſurdities. — But I have a little anecdote for you, which

which proves, beyond a doubt, that you are as much as ever in poſſeſſion of Lord Winworth's affection.

Lady BETTY.

What is it, my dear Emmy?

Mrs. HARLEY.

Why about an hour ago, my woman, it ſeems, and Arnold, my Lord's man, had a little converſation on this unexpected propoſal to Miſs Marchmont; in which Arnold ſaid, — "Never "tell me of your Miſs Marchmonts, Mrs. Nelſon; "— between ourſelves — but let it go no farther— "Lady Betty is ſtill the woman, and a ſweet crea- "ture ſhe is, that's the truth on't, but a little "fantaſtical, and doesn't know her own mind —

Lady BETTY.

I'll aſſure you! — Why Mr. Arnold is a wit.

Mrs. HARLEY.

Well, but hear him out: — "Mrs. Nelſon, I "know as much of my Lord's mind as any "body; let him marry whom he pleaſes, he'll "never be rightly happy but with her Ladyſhip; "and I'd give a hundred guineas, with all my "ſoul, that it cou'd be a match." — Theſe Nelſon tells me were his very words. — Arnold is an intelligent fellow, and much in the confidence of his maſter.

Lady BETTY.

Indeed, I always thought my Lord happy in ſo excellent a ſervant. — This intelligence is worth a world, my dear Emmy. ——

Enter Miſs MARCHMONT.

Miſs MARCHMONT.

I have been looking for your Ladyſhip.

Lady

Lady BETTY.

Have you any thing particular, my dear Hortensia? — But why that gloom upon your features? — What gives you uneasiness, my sweet girl? Speak, and make me happy by saying it is in my power to oblige you.

Miss MARCHMONT.

'Tis in your power, my dear Lady Betty, to oblige me highly, — by forgiving the ungrateful disregard which I just now shew'd to your recommendation of Lord Winworth; —

Mrs. HARLEY. [*aside.*]

Now will I be hang'd if she doesn't undo every thing by a fresh stroke of delicacy.

Lady BETTY.

My dear!

Miss MARCHMONT.

And by informing his Lordship that I am ready to pay a proper obedience to your commands.

Mrs. HARLEY. [*aside.*]

O the devil take this elevation of sentiment!

Lady BETTY.

A proper obedience to my commands, my dear! I really don't understand you.

Miss MARCHMONT.

I see how generously you are concern'd, for fear I shou'd, upon this occasion, offer violence to my inclination: — But, Lady Betty, I shou'd be infinitely more distress'd by the smallest act of ingratitude to you, than by any other misfortune. — I am therefore ready, in obedience to your wishes, to accept of his Lordship; and if I can't make him a fond wife, I will, at least, make him a dutiful one.

Mrs. HARLEY. [*aside.*]

Now her delicacy is willing to be miserable.

Lady BETTY.

How cou'd you ever imagine, my dear Hortensia, that your rejection of Lord Winworth cou'd possibly give me the smallest offence? — I have a great regard for his Lordship, 'tis true, but I have a great regard for you also; and wou'd by no means wish to see his happiness promoted at your expence: — think of him, therefore, no more, and be assur'd you oblige me in an infinitely higher degree by refusing, than accepting him.

Miss MARCHMONT.

The more I see your Ladyship's tenderness and delicacy, the more I see it necessary to give an affirmative to Lord Winworth's proposal. — Your generosity must not get the better of my gratitude.

Mrs. HARLEY.

Did ever two fools plague one another so heartily with their delicacy and sentiment? — [*aside.*] Dear Lady Betty, why don't you deal candidly with her? ——

Lady BETTY.

Her happiness makes it necessary now, and I will.

Mrs. HARLEY.

Ay, there's some sense in this. ---

Lady BETTY.

Your uncommon generosity, my dear Hortensia, has led you into an error. ——

Miss MARCHMONT.

Not in the least, Lady Betty.

Lady BETTY.

Still, Hortensia, you are running into very great mistakes. — My esteem for Lord Winworth, let me now tell you, ——

Enter

Enter Lord WINWORTH.

Lord WINWORTH.

Ladies, your moſt obedient. — As I enter'd, Lady Betty, I heard you pronounce my name: — May I preſume to aſk, if you were talking to Miſs Marchmont on the buſineſs I took the liberty of communicating to you this morning?

Mrs. HARLEY. [*aſide.*]

Ay, now 'tis all over, I ſee.

Lady BETTY.

Why, to be candid, my Lord, I have mention'd your propoſal. ——

Lord WINWORTH.

Well, my dear Miſs Marchmont, and may I flatter myſelf that Lady Betty's interpoſition will induce you to be propitious to my hopes? — The heart now offer'd to you, Madam, is a grateful one, and will retain an eternal ſenſe of your goodneſs. — Speak, therefore, my dear Miſs Marchmont, and kindly ſay you condeſcend to accept it.

Mrs. HARLEY, [*aſide.*]

So—here will be a comfortable piece of work.— I'll e'en retire, and leave them to the conſequences of their ridiculous delicacy. [*Exit.*]

Miſs MARCHMONT.

I know not what to ſay, my Lord; — you have honour'd me, greatly honour'd me, — but Lady Betty will acquaint you with my determination.—

Lady BETTY.

I acquaint him, my dear—ſurely you are yourſelf the moſt proper to--I ſhall run diſtracted!--[*aſide.*]

Miſs MARCHMONT.

Indeed, Madam, I can't ſpeak to his Lordſhip on this ſubject.

Lady BETTY.

And I aſſure you, Hortenſia, 'tis a ſubject upon which I do not chuſe to enter.

Lord WINWORTH.

If you had a kind anſwer from Miſs Marchmont, Lady Betty, I am ſure you wou'd enter upon it readily: — But I ſee her reply very clearly in your reluctance to acquaint me with it.——

Miſs MARCHMONT.

Why, Madam, will you force me to ——

Lady BETTY.

And why, Hortenſia — What am I going to ſay? —— [*aſide.*]

Lord WINWORTH.

Don't, my dear Ladies, ſuffer me to diſtreſs you any longer:— To your friendſhip, Madam, I am as much indebted [*addreſſing himſelf to Lady* Betty] as if I had been ſucceſsful; — and I ſincerely wiſh Miſs Marchmont that happineſs with a more deſerving man, which I find it impoſſible for her to confer on me. [*going.*]

Lady BETTY. [*aſide.*]

Now I have ſome hope.——

Miſs MARCHMONT.

My Lord, I entreat your ſtay. ——

Lady BETTY.

Don't call his Lordſhip back, my dear; it will have an odd appearance.

Enter

Enter Lord WINWORTH.

Miſs MARCHMONT.

He is come back; — and I muſt tell him what your unwillingneſs to influence my inclinations, makes you decline.

Lord WINWORTH.

Your commands, Madam? ——

Lady BETTY. [*aſide.*]

Now I am undone again!

Miſs MARCHMONT.

I am in ſuch a ſituation, my Lord, that I can ſcarcely proceed. — Lady Betty is cruelly kind to me; — but as I know her wiſhes——

Lady BETTY.

My wiſhes, Miſs Marchmont! — Indeed, my dear, there is ſuch a miſtake ——

Miſs MARCHMONT.

There is no miſtaking your Ladyſhip's goodneſs; you are fearful to direct my reſolution, and I ſhou'd be unkind to diſtreſs your friendſhip any longer.

Lady BETTY.

You do diſtreſs me indeed, Miſs Marchmont. [*half aſide and ſighing.*]

Lord WINWORTH.

I am all expectation, Madam! ——

Miſs MARCHMONT.

I am compell'd by gratitude to both, and from affection to my dear Lady Betty, to break through the common forms impos'd on our ſex, and to declare that I have no will but her Ladyſhip's.

Lady BETTY.

This is ſo provoking! [*aſide.*]

Lord

Lord WINWORTH.

Ten thoufand thanks for this condefcending goodnefs, Madam! — a goodnefs which is additionally dear to me, as the refult of your determination is pronounc'd by your own lips.

Mifs MARCHMONT.

Well, Lady Betty, I hope I have anfwer'd your wifhes now.

Lady BETTY.

You cannot conceive how fenfibly I am touch'd with your behaviour, my dear. [*fighs.*]

Mifs MARCHMONT.

You feel too much for me, Lady Betty.——

Lady BETTY.

Why I do feel fomething, my dear: — this unexpected event has fill'd my heart — and I am a little agitated. — But come, my dear, let us now go to the company.

Mifs MARCHMONT.

How generoufly, Madam, do you intereft yourfelf for my welfare!

Lord WINWORTH.

And for the welfare of all her friends!

Lady BETTY.

Your Lordfhip is too good.——

Lord WINWORTH.

But the bufinefs of her life is to promote the happinefs of others, and fhe is conftantly rewarded in the exercife of her own benignity.

Lady BETTY.

You can't imagine how I am rewarded upon the prefent occafion, I affure your Lordfhip.

[*Exeunt.*]

SCENE

SCENE, *the Paddock behind* Lady BETTY's *Garden.*

Enter Miſs RIVERS *and* SALLY.

SALLY.

Dear Madam, don't terrify yourſelf with ſuch gloomy reflexions.

Miſs RIVERS.

O Sally, you can't conceive my diſtreſs in this critical ſituation! — An elopement, even from a tyrannical father, has ſomething in it which muſt ſhock a delicate mind. — But when a woman flies from the protection of a parent, who merits the utmoſt return of her affection, ſhe muſt be inſenſible indeed, if ſhe does not feel the ſincereſt regret. — If he ſhoudn't forgive me! —

SALLY.

Dear Madam, he muſt forgive you — are'nt you his child? —

Miſs RIVERS.

And therefore I ſhoudn't diſoblige him. — I am half diſtracted, — and I almoſt repent the promiſe I gave Sir Harry, --- when I conſider how much my character may be leſſen'd by this ſtep, and recollect how it is likely to affect my unfortunate father. ---

SALLY.

But I wonder where Sir Harry can be all this time! ---

Miſs RIVERS.

I wiſh he was come. ---

SALLY.

Courage, Madam — I hear him coming.

Miſs RIVERS.

It muſt be he; let's run and meet him.—

Enter

Enter RIVERS. [*Sally ſhrieks and runs off.*]

Miſs RIVERS.

My father!

RIVERS.

Yes, Theodora, — your poor, abandon'd, miſerable father.

Miſs RIVERS.

Oh Sir! —

RIVERS.

Little, Theodora, did I imagine I ſhou'd ever have cauſe to lament the hour of your birth; and leſs did I imagine, when you arriv'd at an age to be perfectly acquainted with your duty, you wou'd throwevery ſentiment of duty off. — In what, my dear, has your unhappy father been culpable, that you cannot bear his ſociety any longer? — What has he done to forfeit either your eſteem or your affection? — From the moment of your birth to this unfortunate hour, he has labour'd to promote your happineſs. — But how has his ſolicitude on that account been rewarded? You now fly from theſe arms, which have cheriſh'd you with ſo much tenderneſs; when gratitude, generoſity and nature, ſhould have twin'd me round your heart. —

Miſs RIVERS.

Dear Sir!

RIVERS.

Look back, infatuated child, upon my whole conduct ſince your approach to maturity: Hav'n't I contracted my own enjoyments on purpoſe to enlarge yours, and watched your very looks to anticipate your inclinations? Have I ever, with the obſtinacy of other fathers, been partial in favour of any man to whom you made the ſlighteſt objection? — Or have I ever ſhewn the

the leaſt deſign of forcing your wiſhes to my own humour or caprice? On the contrary, hasn't the engagement I have enter'd into been carried on ſeemingly with your own approbation? — And hav'n't you always appear'd reconcil'd, at leaſt, to a marriage with Mr. Sidney?

Miſs RIVERS.

I am ſo aſham'd of myſelf!

RIVERS.

How then, Theodora, have I merited a treatment of this nature? You have underſtanding, my dear, though you want filial affection; and my arguments muſt have weight with your reaſon, however my tranquility may be the object of your contempt.—I lov'd you, Theodora, with the warmeſt degree of paternal tenderneſs, and flatter'd myſelf the proofs I every day gave of that tenderneſs, had made my peace of mind a matter of ſome importance to my child — But, alas! a paltry compliment from a coxcomb undoes the whole labour of my life; and the daughter whom I looked upon as the ſupport of my declining years, betrays me in the unſuſpecting hour of ſecurity, and rewards with her perſon the aſſaſſin who ſtabs me to the heart. —

Miſs RIVERS.

Hear me, dear Sir, hear me!—

RIVERS.

I do not come here, Theodora, to ſtop your flight, or put the ſmalleſt impediment in the way of your wiſhes. — Your perſon is your own, and I ſcorn to detain even my daughter by force, where ſhe is not bound to me by inclination. — Since, therefore, neither duty nor diſcretion, a regard for my peace, nor a ſolicitude for your own welfare, are able to detain you, — go to this man, who has taught you to obliterate the ſentiments of nature, and gain'd a ready way to your heart, by expreſſing a contempt for your father. — Go to him boldly, my child, and laugh at the pangs which tear this unhappy boſom. — Be uniformly culpable, nor add the baſeneſs of a deſpicable flight to the unpardonable want of a filial affection. [*Going*]

Miſs RIVERS.

I am the moſt miſerable creature in the world!—

RIVERS. [*Returns.*]

One thing more, Theodora, — and then farewel for ever. — Though you come here to throw off the affection of a child, I will not quit this place before I diſcharge the duty of a parent, even to a romantic extravagance; and provide for your welfare, while you plunge me into the moſt poignant of all diſtreſs. — In the doating hours of paternal blandiſhment, I have often promis'd you a fortune of twenty thouſand pounds, whenever you chang'd your ſituation. — This promiſe was indeed made when I thought you incapable either of ingratitude or diſſimulation, — and when I fancied your perſon wou'd be given, where there was ſome reaſonable proſpect of your happineſs. — But ſtill it was a promiſe, and ſhall be faithfully diſcharg'd. — Here then, in this pocket-book, is a ſecurity for that ſum. [Miſs RIVERS *ſhews an unwillingneſs to receive the pocket-book.*]--Take it--but never ſee me more. — Baniſh my name eternally from your remembrance:—and when a little time ſhall remove me from a world which your conduct has rendered inſupportable, boaſt an additional title, my dear, to your huſband's regard, by having ſhorten'd the life of your miſerable father. — [*Exit.*]

Enter

Enter SALLY.

SALLY.

What, Madam, is he gone?

Miſs RIVERS.

How cou'd I be ſuch a monſter, — ſuch an unnatural monſter, as ever to think of leaving him!— But come, Sally, let us go into the houſe.—

SALLY.

Go into the houſe, Madam! — Why are'nt we to go off with Sir Harry? —

Miſs RIVERS.

This inſenſible creature has been my confidante too! — O I ſhall eternally deteſt myſelf!—

Enter Sir HARRY *and* CECIL.

Sir HARRY.

I beg a thouſand pardons, my dear Miſs Rivers, for detaining you. — An unforeſeen accident prevented me from being punctual; — but the carriage is now ready, and a few hours will whirl us to the ſummit of felicity. — My couſin Cecil is kindly here to aſſiſt us, — and —

Miſs RIVERS.

Sir Harry, I can never forſake my father. —

Sir HARRY.

Madam!

Miſs RIVERS.

By ſome accident he diſcover'd our deſign, and came to this ſpot while I was trembling with expectation of your appearance. —

Sir HARRY.

Well, my dear creature! —

Miſs RIVERS.

Here, in a melancholy but reſolute voice, he expatiated on the infamy of my intended flight, and mention'd my want of affection for him in terms that pierc'd my very ſoul. — Having done this, he took an abrupt leave, and, ſcorning to detain me by force, forſook me to the courſe of my own inclinations.

Sir HARRY.

Well, my angel, and ſince he has left you to follow your own inclinations, you will not, ſurely, heſitate to —

Miſs RIVERS.

Sir Harry, unlooſe my hand; — the univerſe wou'd'nt bribe me now to go off with you. — O, Sir Harry! if you regarded your own peace, you wou'd ceaſe this importunity; — for is it poſſible that a woman can make a valuable wife, who has prov'd an unnatural daughter?

Sir HARRY.

But conſider your own happineſs, my dear Miſs Rivers!—

Miſs RIVERS.

My own happineſs, Sir Harry! — What a wretch muſt the woman be, who can dream of happineſs, while ſhe wounds the boſom of a father!

CECIL.

What a noble girl! — I ſhall love her myſelf for her ſenſe and her goodneſs.

SALLY, *aſide, to* Sir HARRY.

She won't conſent, I know, Sir Harry; — ſo, if the coach is at hand, it will be the beſt way to carry her off directly.

Sir HARRY.

Then, my dear Miſs Rivers, there is no hope —

Miſs

Miſs Rivers.

Sir Harry, I muſt not hear you. — This parting is a kind of death. ——

Sir Harry.

Part, Madam! — By all that's gracious, we muſt not part! — My whole ſoul is unalterably fix'd upon you; — and ſince —— neither tenderneſs for yourſelf, nor affection for me, perſuade you to the only meaſure which can promote our mutual felicity, you muſt forgive the deſpair that forces you from hence, and commits a momentary diſreſpect to avoid a laſting unhappineſs.

Miſs Rivers.

Hear me, Sir Harry;—I conjure you hear me!

Sir Harry.

Let me but remove you from this place, Madam, and I'll hear every thing. — Cecil, aſſiſt me.

Miſs Rivers.

O, Mr. Cecil, I rely upon your honour to ſave and protect me!

Cecil.

And it ſhall, Madam. — For ſhame, kinſman, unhand the Lady!

Sir Harry.

Unhand her, what do you mean, Cecil?

Cecil.

What do I mean, I mean to protect the Lady. — What ſhou'd a man of honour mean?

Miſs Rivers, *breaking from* Sir Harry.

Dear Mr. Cecil, don't let him follow me

[*She runs off.*]

Sally.

SALLY, *following.*

I'll give her warning this moment, that's the ſhort and the long of it. [*Exit.*]

Sir HARRY.

Mr. Cecil, this is no time for trifling — Didn't you come here to aſſiſt me in carrying the Lady off?

CECIL.

With her own inclinations, kinſman; — but as they are now on the other ſide of the queſtion, ſo am I too. — You muſt not follow her, Sir Harry. —

Sir HARRY.

Zounds! but I will.

CECIL.

Zounds! but you ſhan't. — Look'ye, Harry, I came here to aſſiſt the purpoſes of a man of honour, not to abet the violence of a ruffian. — Your friends of the world, your faſhionable friends, may, if they pleaſe, ſupport one another's vices; but I am a friend only to the virtues of a man; and where I ſincerely eſteem him, I always endeavour to make him honeſt in ſpite of his teeth.

Sir HARRY.

An injury like this —

CECIL.

Harry! — Harry! — don't advance: — I am not to be terrified, you know, from the ſupport of what is juſt; — and though you may think it very brave to fight in the defence of a bad action, it will do but little credit either to your underſtanding or your humanity.

Sir HARRY.

Dear Cecil, there's no anſwering that. — Your juſtice and your generoſity over power me. —

You

You have reſtor'd me to myſelf. — It was mean, it was unmanly, it was infamous to think of uſing force. — But I was diſtracted; — nay, I am diſtracted now, and muſt entirely rely upon your aſſiſtance to recover her.

CECIL.

As far as I can act with honeſty, Harry, you may depend upon me; — but let me have no more violence, I beg of you.

Sir HARRY.

Don't mention it, Cecil; — I am heartily aſham'd —

CECIL.

And I am heartily glad of it. —

Sir HARRY.

Pray let us go to my houſe and conſult a little. — What a contemptible figure do I make! —

CECIL.

Why, pretty well, I think; but to be leſs ſo, put up your ſword, Harry. —

Sir HARRY.

She never can forgive me.

CECIL.

If ſhe does, ſhe will ſcarcely deſerve to be forgiven herſelf.

Sir HARRY.

Don't, Cecil; 'tis ungenerous to be ſo hard upon me. — I own my fault, and you ſhould encourage me, for every coxcomb has not ſo much modeſty.

CECIL.

Why, ſo I will, Harry; for modeſty, I ſee, as yet, ſits upon you but very aukwardly. [*Exeunt.*]

END *of the* FOURTH ACT.

ACT

ACT V.

SCENE, *an Apartment at* Lady BETTY's.

Enter RIVERS *and* SIDNEY.

SIDNEY.

I AM deeply ſenſible of Miſs Rivers's very great merit, Sir; — but —

RIVERS.

But what, Sir? —

SIDNEY.

Hear me with temper, I beſeech you, Colonel.

RIVERS.

Hear you with temper! — I don't know whether I ſhall be able to hear you with temper; — but go on, Sir. —

SIDNEY.

Miſs Rivers, independent of her very affluent fortune, Colonel, has beauty and merit which would make her alliance a very great honour to the firſt family in the kingdom. — But, notwithſtanding my admiration of her beauty, and my reverence for her merit, I find it utterly impoſſible to profit either by her goodneſs or your generoſity.

RIVERS.

How is all this, Sir! Do you decline a marriage with my daughter?

SIDNEY.

A marriage with Miſs Rivers, Sir, was once the object of my higheſt ambition; and, had I been honour'd with her hand, I ſhou'd have ſtudied to ſhew my ſenſibility of a bleſſing ſo invaluable; — but at that time, I did not ſup-

poſe

poſe my happineſs to be incompatible with her's. —I am now convinc'd that it is ſo, and it becomes me much better to give up my own hopes, than to offer the ſmalleſt violence to her inclinations.

RIVERS.

Death and hell, Sir! — what do you mean by this behaviour? — Shall I prefer your alliance to any man's in England? — ſhall my daughter even expreſs a readineſs to marry you? — and ſhall you, after this, inſolently tell me you don't chooſe to accept her? —

SIDNEY.

Dear Colonel, you totally miſconceive my motive; — and I am ſure, upon reflexion, you will rather approve than condemn it. — A man of common humanity, Sir, in a treaty of marriage, ſhould conſult the lady's wiſhes as well as his own; and if he can't make her happy, he will ſcorn to make her miſerable.

RIVERS.

Scorn to make her miſerable! — Why the fellow's mad, I believe. — Doesn't the girl abſolutely conſent to have you? — Would you have her drag you to the altar by force? — Would you have her fall at your feet, and beg of you, with tears, to pity one of the fineſt women, with one of the beſt fortunes, in England?

SIDNEY.

Your vehemence, Sir, prevents you from conſidering this matter in a proper light. — Miſs Rivers is ſufficiently unhappy in loſing the man of her heart; but her diſtreſs muſt be greatly aggravated, if, in the moment ſhe is moſt keenly ſenſible of this loſs, ſhe is compell'd to marry another. — Beſides, Colonel, I muſt have my feelings too. — There is ſomething ſhocking in an union with a woman whoſe affections we know to be alienated; and 'tis difficult to ſay which is moſt entitled to contempt, he that ſtoops to accept of a pre-engaged mind, or he that puts up with a proſtituted perſon.

RIVERS.

Mighty well, Sir! — mighty well! But let me tell you, Mr. Sidney, — that under this ſpecious appearance of generoſity, I can eaſily ſee your motive for this refuſal of my daughter; — let me tell you, I can eaſily ſee your motive, Sir; — and let me tell you, that the perſon who is in poſſeſſion of your affections, ſhall no longer find an aſylum in this houſe.

SIDNEY.

Colonel, if I had not been always accuſtom'd to reſpect you, — and if I did not even conſider this inſult as a kind of compliment, I don't know how I ſhou'd put up with it. As to your inſinuation, you muſt be more explicit before I can underſtand you.

RIVERS.

Miſs Marchmont, — Sir. — Do you underſtand me now, Sir? If Miſs Marchmont had not been in the caſe, my daughter had not receiv'd this inſult. — Sir Harry was right; and had not I been ridiculouſly beſotted with your hypocritical plauſibility, I might have ſeen it ſooner; but your couſin ſhall know of your behaviour, and then, Sir, you ſhall anſwer me as a man.

SIDNEY.

Miſs Marchmont, Colonel, is greatly above this illiberal reflexion; as for myſelf, I ſhall be always ready to juſtify an action which I know to be be right, though I ſhou'd be ſorry ever to meet you but in the character of a friend. [*Exit.*]

RIVERS, [*alone.*]

Well! — well! — well! — but it doesn't ſignify, — it doesn't ſignify, — it doesn't ſignify;— I won't put myſelf in a paſſion about it;—I won't put myſelf in a paſſion about it.—I'll tear the fellow piece-meal. — Zounds! I don't know what I'll do. [*Exit.*]

Enter Mrs. HARLEY *and* CECIL.

CECIL.

Why this is better and better.

Mrs. HARLEY.

What a violent paſſion he's in!

CECIL.

This is the very thing I cou'd wiſh — 'twill advance a principal part of our project rarely. — Well isn't Sidney a noble young fellow; and doesn't he richly deſerve the regard which my poor little girl entertains for him?

Mrs. HARLEY.

Why really I think he does.—But how ſecretly my Lady Sentimental carried matters! — O, I always ſaid that your grave, reflecting, moralizing damſels, were a thouſand times more ſuſceptible of tender impreſſions than thoſe lively open-hearted girls who talk away at random, and ſeem ready to run off with every man that happens to fall into their company.

CECIL.

I don't know, widow, but there may be ſome truth in this: you ſee, at leaſt, I have ſuch a good opinion of a madcap, that you are the firſt perſon I have made acquainted with the ſecret.

Mrs. HARLEY.

Well, and havn't I return'd the compliment, by letting you into my deſign about Lady Betty and Lord Winworth?

CECIL.

What a ridiculous buſtle is there here about delicacy and ſtuff!—Your people of refin'd ſentiments are the moſt troubleſome creatures in the world to deal with, and their friends muſt even commit a violence upon their nicety, before they can condeſcend to ſtudy their own happineſs. —But have you done as we concerted?

Mrs. HARLEY.

Yes; I have pretended to Lady Betty that my Lord deſires to ſpeak with her privately on buſineſs of the utmoſt importance; and I have told his Lordſhip that ſhe wants to ſee him, to diſcloſe a ſecret that muſt intirely break off the intended marriage with Miſs Marchmont.

CECIL.

What an aukward figure they muſt make! each imagining that the other has deſir'd the interview,—and expecting every moment to be told ſomething of conſequence.—But you have not given either the leaſt hint of Hortenſia's ſecret inclination for Sidney?

Mrs. HARLEY.

How could you poſſibly ſuppoſe ſuch a thing?

CECIL.

Well, well, to your part of the buſineſs then, while I find out the Colonel, and try what I can do with him for my rattle-pated Sir Harry.

Mrs. HARLEY.

O never doubt my aſſiduity in an affair of this nature! [*Exeunt.*]

Enter

Enter Lady BETTY, *in another Apartment.*

Lady BETTY.

What can he want with me, I wonder?—Speak with me again in private, and upon business of the utmost importance! He has spoken sufficiently to me already upon his business of importance to make me miserable for ever. — But the fault is my own, and I have nobody to blame but myself. — Bless me! here he is.

Enter WINWORTH.

WINWORTH.

Madam! your most devoted: I come in obedience to your commands to ——

Lady BETTY.

My commands, my Lord?

WINWORTH.

Yes, Madam, your message has alarm'd me prodigiously; — and you cannot wonder if I am a little impatient for an explanation.

Lady BETTY.

Impatient for an explanation, my Lord!

WINWORTH.

Yes, Madam, the affair is of the nearest concern to my happiness, and the sooner you honour me with ——

Lady BETTY.

Honour you with what, my Lord?

WINWORTH.

My dear Lady Betty, this reserve is unkind, especially as you know how uneasy I must be 'till I hear from yourself ——

Lady BETTY.

Really, my Lord, I am quite astonish'd! — Uneasy till you hear from myself! — Impatient for an explanation! — I beg your Lordship will tell me what is the meaning of all this?

WINWORTH.

WINWORTH.

Surely, Madam, you cannot ſo ſuddenly change your kind intentions —

Lady BETTY.

My kind intentions, my Lord!

WINWORTH.

I would not, Madam, be too preſuming, but, as I know your Ladyſhip's goodneſs, I flatter myſelf that ——

Lady BETTY.

Your Lordſhip is all a myſtery!—I beg you will ſpeak out; --- for upon my word I don't underſtand theſe half ſentences. ——

WINWORTH.

Why, Madam, Mrs. Harley has told me. —

Lady BETTY, [*with eagerneſs.*]

What has ſhe told you, my Lord?

WINWORTH.

She has told me of the ſecret, Madam, which you have to diſcloſe, that muſt entirely break off my marriage with Miſs Marchmont.

Lady BETTY.

Has ſhe then betray'd my weakneſs? —

WINWORTH.

Madam, I hope you won't think your generous intentions in my favour a weakneſs; for be aſſur'd that the ſtudy of my whole life —

Lady BETTY.

I did not think that Mrs. Harley could be capable of ſuch an action; — but ſince ſhe has told you of the only circumſtance which I ever wiſh'd to be conceal'd, I cannot deny my partiality for your Lordſhip.

WINWORTH.

Madam! —

Lady

Lady BETTY.

This ſecret was truſted with her, and her alone; but though ſhe has ungenerouſly diſcover'd it, her end will ſtill be diſappointed. I acknowledge that I prize your Lordſhip above all the world; — but even to obtain you I will not be guilty of a baſeneſs, nor promote my own happineſs by any act of injuſtice to Miſs Marchmont.

WINWORTH.

I am the moſt unfortunate man in the world! —And does your Ladyſhip really honour me with any degree of a tender partiality?

Lady BETTY.

This queſtion is needleſs, my Lord, after what Mrs. Harley has acquainted you with.

WINWORTH.

Mrs. Harley, Madam, has not acquainted me with particulars of any nature ---

Lady BETTY.

No!

WINWORTH.

No. --- And happy as this diſcovery would have made me at any other time, it now diſtreſſes me beyond expreſſion, ſince the engagements I have juſt enter'd into with Miſs Marchmont, put it wholly out of my power to receive any benefit from the knowledge of your ſentiments. — O Lady Betty! had you been generouſly candid when I ſolicited the bleſſing of your hand, how much had I been indebted to your goodneſs! But now, think what my ſituation is, when, in the moment I am ſenſible of your regard, I muſt give you up for ever.

Enter CECIL *and* Mrs. HARLEY *from oppoſite Places.*

Mrs. HARLEY, [*repeating ludicrouſly.*]

" Who can behold ſuch beauty, and be ſilent!

CECIL

CECIL, [*in the ſame accent.*]

" Deſire firſt taught us words. —

Mrs. HARLEY.

" Man, when created, wander'd up and down,

CECIL.

" Forlorn and ſilent as his vaſſal beaſts;

Mrs. HARLEY.

" But when a heav'n-born maid like you ap-
" pear'd,

CECIL.

" Strange pleaſure fill'd his eyes, and ſeiz'd his
" heart,

Mrs. HARLEY.

" Unloos'd his tongue,

CECIL.

" And his firſt talk was love." [*Both*, ha! ha! ha!]

WINWORTH.

Pray, Mr. Cecil, what is the meaning of this whimſical behaviour?

Lady BETTY.

The nature of this conduct, Mrs. Harley, bears too ſtrong a reſemblance to a late diſingenuity, for me to wonder at.

Mrs. HARLEY.

What diſingenuity, my dear?

Lady BETTY.

Why, pray, Madam, what ſecret had I to diſcloſe to his Lordſhip?

Mrs. HARLEY.

The ſecret which you have diſclos'd, my dear,— [*courtſeying.*]

CECIL.

I beg, my Lord, that we mayn't interrupt your heroics, " when, in the moment you are ſenſible " of "of her regard, — you must give her up for "ever." — A very moving speech, Mrs. Harley! —I am sure it almost makes me cry to repeat it.

WINWORTH.

Mr. Cecil, listening is —

Mrs. HARLEY.

What are we going to have a quarrel? —

CECIL.

O, yes; your lover is a mere nobody without a little bloodshed: two or three duels give a wonderful addition to his character.

Lady BETTY.

Why, what is the meaning of all this?

CECIL.

You shall know in a moment, Madam; — so walk in, good people, — walk in, and see the most surprising pair of true lovers, who have too much sense to be wise, and too much delicacy to be happy.

Mrs. HARLEY.

Walk in, — walk in.

Enter RIVERS, Miss RIVERS, Miss MARCHMONT, Sir HARRY, *and* SIDNEY.

Lady BETTY.

O, Emmy! is this behaving like a friend?

Mrs. HARLEY.

Yes, and like a true friend, as you shall see presently. —

RIVERS.

My Lord, I give you joy, joy heartily. — We have been posted for some time, under the direction of Marshal Cecil and General Harley, in the next room, who have acquainted us with every thing; and I feel the fincereft fatisfaction to think the perplexities of to-day have fo fortunate a conclufion.

WINWORTH.

The perplexities of to-day are not yet concluded, Colonel.

Mifs MARCHMONT.

O Lady Betty, why wou'dn't you truft me with your fecret? I have been the innocent caufe of great uneafinefs to you, and yet my conduct entirely proceeded from the greatnefs of my affection.

Lady BETTY.

I know it, my dear, — I know it well; — but were you to give up Lord Winworth this moment, — be affur'd that I wou'dn't accept of any facrifice made at the expence of your happinefs.

CECIL.

At the Expence of her happinefs! — O, is that all? — Come here, mafter Soberfides [*to* Sidney] and come here, Madam Gravity [*to* Mifs Marchmont] come here, I fay; — I fuppofe, my Lord, I fuppofe, Lady Betty, that you already know from what very manly motives—Sidney, here, has declin'd the marriage with Mifs Rivers?

WINWORTH.

I do; and though I lament the impoffibility of a relation to the Colonel's family, I cannot but admire his behaviour on that occafion.

Lady BETTY.

And I think it extremely generous.

Mrs. HARLEY.

Come, Cecil, ftand by a little; you fhan't have the whole management of this difcovery.

CECIL.

Did you ever fee fuch a woman! Mrs.

Mrs. HARLEY.

Well, my Lord and Lady Betty, ſince we have agreed thus far, you muſt know that Mr. Sidney's behaviour has produc'd more good conſequences than you can imagine. — In the firſt place, it has enabled Colonel Rivers, without a breach of his word, —

CECIL.

To give his daughter to my fooliſh kinſman.

Mrs. HARLEY.

You won't hold your tongue.

CECIL.

And, in the next place, it has enabled Mr. Sidney —

Mrs. HARLEY.

To marry Miſs Marchmont.

CECIL.

Ay, ſhe will have the laſt word. — For it ſeems that between theſe two turtles there has long ſubſiſted —

Mrs. HARLEY.

A very tender affection, —

CECIL.

The devil's in her tongue! — ſhe has the ſpeed of me.

WINWORTH.

What an unexpected felicity?

Lady BETTY.

I am all amazement!

RIVERS.

Well, well, my dear ſiſter,--no wondering about it; — at a more convenient time you ſhall know particulars; for the preſent let me tell you, that now I am cool, and that matters have been properly explain'd to me, I am not only satisfied but charm'd with Mr. Sidney's behaviour, though it has prevented the first wish of my heart; and I hope that his Lordship and you, by consenting to his marriage with Miss Marchmont, will immediately remove every impediment in the way of your own happiness.

WINWORTH.

If my own happiness was not to be promoted by such a step, I shou'd instantly give my consent; --- and therefore, my dear Miss Marchmont, if I have Lady Betty's approbation and your own concurrence, I here bestow this hand upon as deserving a young man as any in the universe. --- This is the only atonement I can make for the uneasiness I have given you; and if your happiness is any way proportion'd to your merit, I need not wish you a greater share of felicity.

SIDNEY.

What shall I say, my Lord?

WINWORTH.

Say nothing, Charles; for if you only knew how exquisite a satisfaction I receive on this occasion, you wou'd rather envy my feelings than think yourself under an obligation. --- And now, my dear Lady Betty, if I might presume ---

Lady BETTY.

That I may not be censur'd any longer, I here declare my hand your Lordship's, whenever you think proper to demand it; for I am now convinc'd the greatest proof which a woman can give of her own worth, is to entertain an affection for a man of honour and understanding.

WINWORTH.

This goodness, Madam, is too great for acknowledgment.

Lady

Lady BETTY.

And now, my dear Theodora, let me congratulate with you: I rejoice that your inclinations are consulted in the most important circumstance of your life; and I am sure Sir Harry will not be wanting in gratitude for the partiality which you have shewn in his favour.

Miss RIVERS.

Dear Madam, you oblige me infinitely.

Sir HARRY.

And as for me, Lady Betty, it is so much my inclination to deserve the partiality with which Miss Rivers has honour'd me, as well as to repay the goodness of her family, that I shall have little merit in my gratitude to either. I have been wild, I have been inconsiderate, but I hope I never was despicable; and I flatter myself I shan't be wanting in acknowledgment only to those, who have laid me under the greatest of all obligations.

RIVERS.

Sir Harry, say no more. — My girl's repentance has been so noble; your Cousin Cecil's behaviour has been so generous; and I believe you, after all, to be a man of such principle, — that, next to Sidney, I don't know who I shou'd prefer to you for a son-in-law. — But you must think a little for the future, and remember, that it is a poor excuse for playing the fool, to be possess'd of a good understanding.

WINWORTH.

Well, there seems but one thing remaining undone: — I just now took the liberty of exercising a father's right over Miss Marchmont, by disposing of her hand; 'tis now necessary for me—

CECIL.

CECIL.

Hold, my Lord ;—I guefs what you are about, but you fhan't monopolize generofity, I affure you. — I have a right to fhew my friendfhip, as well as your Lordfhip; fo, after your kinfman's marriage, whatever you have a mind to do for him fhall be equall'd, on my part, for Mifs Marchmont; guinea for guinea, as far as you will, and let's fee who tires firft in going through with it.

WINWORTH.

A noble challenge, and I accept it.

Lady BETTY.

No, there's no bearing this. ——

Mifs MARCHMONT.

Speak to them, Mr. Sidney, for I cannot. ——

SIDNEY.

I wifh I had words to declare my fenfe of this goodnefs.

RIVERS.

I didn't look upon myfelf as a very pitiful fellow, but I am ftrangely funk in my own opinion, fince I have been a witnefs of this tranfaction.

CECIL.

Why, what the devil is there in all this to wonder at? People of fortune often throw away thoufands at the hazard table to make themfelves miferable, and nobody ever accufes them of generofity.

WINWORTH.

Mr. Cecil is perfectly right; and he is the beft manager of a fortune, who is moft attentive to the wants of the deferving.

Mrs.

Mrs. HARLEY.

Why now all is as it ſhou'd be, — all is as it ſhou'd be!--This is the triumph of good ſenſe over delicacy. — I cou'd cry for downright joy. — I wonder what ails me! --- this is all my doing!

CECIL.

No, — part of it is mine; — and I think it extremely happy for your people of refin'd ſentiments to have friends with a little common underſtanding.

RIVERS.

Siſter, I always thought you a woman of ſenſe.--

Mrs HARLEY.

Yes, ſhe has been a long time intimate vith me, you know.

CECIL.

Well ſaid, ſauce-box!

Sir HARRY.

If this ſtory was to be repreſented on the ſtage, the poet wou'd think it his duty to puniſh me for life, becauſe I was once culpable.

WINWORTH.

That wou'd be very wrong. The ſtage ſhou'd be a ſchool of morality; and the nobleſt of all leſſons is the forgiveneſs of injuries.

RIVERS.

True, my Lord. — But the principal moral to be drawn from the tranſactions of to-day is, that thoſe who generouſly labour for the happineſs of others, will, ſooner or later, arrive at happineſs themſelves.

F I N I S.

EPILOGUE,

Written by DAVID GARRICK, Esq.
Spoken by Mrs. DANCER.

WHEN with the comic muse a bard hath dealing,
The traffic thrives, when there's a mutual feeling;
Our author boasts, that well he chose his plan,
False Modesty! — *Himself*, an Irishman.
As I'm a woman, somewhat prone to satire,
I'll prove it all a bull, *what he calls nature;*
And you, I'm sure, will join before you go,
To maul False Modesty, — *from* Dublin *ho!*
Where are these Lady Lambtons *to be found?*
Not in these riper times, on English ground.
Among the various flowers which sweetly blow,
To charm the eyes, at Almack's *and* Soho,
Pray does that weed, False Delicacy, *grow?*
O, No. ———
Among the fair of fashion; common breeding,
Is there one bosom, where Love lies a bleeding?
In olden *times your grannams unrefin'd,*
Ty'd up the tongue, put padlocks on the mind;
O, *Ladies, thank your stars, there's nothing now confin'd.*
In love you English *Men, — there's no concealing,*
Are most, like Winworth, *simple in your dealing;*
But Britons, *in their natures as their names,*
Are diff'rent as the Shanon, Tweed, *and* Thames.
As the Tweed *flows, the bonny* Scot *proceeds,*
Wunds slaw, and sure, and nae obstruction heeds;
Though oft repuls'd, his purpose still hauds fast,
Stecks like a burr, and wuns the Lass at last.
The Shannon, *rough and vigorous, pours along,*
Like the bold accents of brave Paddy's *tongue:*
Arrah, dear creature — can you scorn me so?
Cast your sweet eyes upon me, top and toe!
Not fancy me? — *Pooh! — that's all game and laughter,*
First marry me, my jew'l — ho! — you'll love me after.
Like his own Thames, *honest* John Trot, *their brother,*
More quick than one, *and much less bold than t'other,*
Gentle not dull, *his loving arms will spread;*
But stopt — in willows hides his bashful head;
John *leaves his home, resolv'd to tell his pain;*
Hesitates — I — love — Fye, Sir — 'tis in vain, —
John *blushes, turns him round, and whistles home again.*
Well! is my painting like? — Or do you doubt it? —
What say you to a trial? — let's about it.
Let Cupid *lead* three Britons *to the field,*
And try which first can make a damsel yield;
What say you to a widow? — *Smile consent,*
And she'll be ready for experiment.

A WORD TO THE WISE

A

WORD TO THE WISE,

A

C O M E D Y,

AS IT WAS PERFORMED

AT THE

THEATRE ROYAL, in DRURY-LANE.

WRITTEN BY HUGH KELLY,
OF THE MIDDLE-TEMPLE,
AUTHOR of FALSE DELICACY.

L O N D O N,
PRINTED FOR THE AUTHOR,
AND SOLD BY
DODSLEY, IN PALL-MALL; J. AND E. DILLY, IN
THE POULTRY; G. KEARSLY, IN LUDGATE-STREET
AND T. CADELL, IN THE STRAND.
MDCCLXX.

A N

ADDRESS to the PUBLIC.

THE comedy here offered to the world, having been banished from the theatre, through the rage of political prejudice, and the author having, through that prejudice, been no less attacked in his reputation than wounded in his fortune, it becomes necessary for him to justify his character as a man, however poor his abilities may be as a writer. — Popular resentment has had it's victim, and the sacrifice being now over, perhaps a few words may be heard in his defence.

For a considerable time, previous to the exhibition of the following scenes, two charges were industriously propagated against the author; and to these charges the unexampled severity exercised on his play may be wholly attributed: The first was, that Mr. Kelly prostituted the Public Ledger, a daily paper then under his direction, to the purposes of administration, in consequence of an annual pension he received; and, instead of conducting it upon principles of impartiality, would admit no letters whatever, unless professedly written in favour of government. — This accusation, though constantly rendered absurd by his readiness to insert every proper letter on each side of every public subject, gained no little credit, but gained it intirely among those who would not be at the trouble of examining into the truth. — At length the calumny grew serious enough to demand some notice, and accordingly, on the 14th of February, 1769, the following reply was published in the Ledger, to a fresh attack by an anonymous correspondent upon the independency of that paper.

" We can assure this gentleman (meaning the correspon-
" dent) that we have never suppressed any thing in favour of
" Mr. Wilkes's cause, which was in the least proper for pub-
" lication: But declare on the contrary, that we always *have*
" been and always *shall* be as ready to insert the productions
" of his friends, as the letters of his enemies. — Many pieces
" on *both* sides have reached us, which we were under a ne-
" cessity of rejecting, because they were too dangerous, or too
" absurd for admittance: yet we can with great truth aver,
" that we strictly keep to our title, and maintain the most dis-
" passionate impartiality, — we profess *ourselves open to all*

 parties,

" *parties*, and cannot consistently with this profession refuse " *any* performance which seems dictated by a spirit of can " dour, or an appearance of rational argument. Our cor- " respondent, therefore, before he calls us *partial*, should " really *prove* us so; and should first of all favour us with his " essays in *defence* of Mr. Wilkes, before he pronounces posi- " tively, that we will *not* indulge them with a *place*.

" In fact, a paper to maintain a *real* impartiality, must be " actuated by the principles of *justice*, not by the fear of *cen-* " *sure* on the one hand, nor the hope of *approbation* on the " other; and the conductors of it must be more solicitous to " *deserve* the applause of their readers, than to *obtain* it. — " Had the managers of the Ledger for instance, rejected any " piece which came *against* the cause of Mr. Wilkes, through " an apprehension of incurring the popular displeasure, they " would have violated the assurance of *impartiality*, which they " have so solemnly given to the public, and the opponents of " that gentleman, would have a reasonable plea to reproach " them with their palpable breach of faith. To accuse them " consequently of *partiality*, argues a *partiality* in their accu- " sers; and it is rather unfair in those, to deny others a li- " berty of speaking upon national affairs, who constantly " lay claim to such a privilege themselves,

" These gentlemen must however remember, that, though " the Ledger is *open* to all parties, it is influenced by *none*: " And that the conductors, to *merit* the good opinion of *all*, " must no more make a sacrifice of their justice at the shrine " of *popularity*, than at the altar of *government*: they can " therefore only repeat, that the advocates for Mr. Wilkes, " will always be as acceptable to them, as any other corres- " pondents, and they *call* upon his friends in this manner, " to favour them with productions in his defence. What " more can be desired at their hands? If the popular writers " decline this candid invitation, the editors of the Ledger " are intirely free from blame. They have bound themselves " in a promise of undeviating impartiality to the *whole* public, " and must by no means act inequitably to those who *do* " oblige them with pieces for insertion, out of an unreason- " able deference for those who do *not*."

This advertisement Mr. Kelly flattered himself would effectually undeceive the public; but here he was unhappily disappointed. Many who had repeatedly heard the charge against him, never once honoured the defence with a perusal; while many more who really read it, considered the very candour of it's declaration as a proof of criminality, and would not allow any weight to the argument of *justice*, when opposed to what they looked upon as the cause of the people. — Mr. Kelly, however, determined, at

all

all events, to do his duty, conducted the Ledger on it's customary plan of *impartiality*, and many of the most popular gentlemen who have arraigned his conduct in the capacity of a public editor, well know that their letters, instead of being rejected, have been frequently inserted at the warning of an hour. — Besides, a review of the Ledger during Mr. Kelly's superintendency, will convince the most incredulous, that the severest animadversions were admitted on the proceedings of administration. — It was not Mr. Kelly's fault if the publications on the contrary side were the most numerous. — The correspondents of a news-paper will make it what they please, and the editor is not to consider in whose favour they write, but whether their writings are proper for insertion. — Whatever Mr. Kelly's own sentiments might be on political affairs, this was the only object of his inquiry: and it will appear, on a retrospection of the pieces printed, while he directed the Ledger, that Mr. Kelly has frequently complimented popular writers on account of their abilities, and civilly requested a continuation of their correspondence. — As to Mr. Kelly's own letters in the Ledger, they appeared but occasionally, from the number of volunteers who eagerly crowded to the general service: Yet he will candidly confess, that when they did appear, they were not always in favour of popularity. This constitutes the second charge against him; and as he is above the despicable littleness of prevaricating, he will enter with confidence, and he hopes with decency, upon his justification.

Whether it has been Mr. Kelly's merit or demerit, to think from principle unpopularly, on the subject of the present unhappy dissensions, he will not pretend to say, but certainly it has been his misfortune; and though several of his discreeter friends repeatedly warned him of the danger his next piece would run on the stage, from an open declaration of his political opinions; still he did not imagine, that his profession as a public writer was to deprive him of his independence as a man —As he never presumed to be offended with the sentiments of others on matters of a national tendency, he claimed a right of expressing his own; and did not suppose his literary character, precluded him from speaking upon a point which was the continual object of literary investigation. — Besides this, he little conceived that the advocates for freedom of thinking, would be the first to manacle the mind; that the professed friends of candour would be the first to condemn without a hearing; and the avowed enemies of oppression be the only persons ready to exercise an unwarrantable severity — He had at least a right to justice, if he had no pretence to favour, and merited surely a trial, though he might afterwards deserve to be condemned.——

The heated hour of prejudice however, is not the hour of sober reflection; at such a season the very virtues of our hearts frequently lead us into mistakes; and we run into excesses which our cooler reason must disapprove, from an actual rectitude of intention. This was the case of numbers who opposed the exhibition of Mr. Kelly's play: they had been told he was a despicable mercenary, hired to write away their liberties, and therefore considered him as a very improper candidate for public approbation — they had been informed, that at the memorable trials of Mr. Gillam, and of the soldier at Guildford, in consequence of the unhappy affair in St. George's fields, he had stood forth an advocate for the effusion of innocent blood; of course they beheld him with detestation; and their motive was really respectable, though their resentment was wholly excited by misinformation or mistake.

It is true indeed Mr. Kelly, as well as an account of the two remarkable trials just mentioned, wrote, during the course of our domestic disunion, many other papers in support of government, and in vindication of parliament; but he never exercised his trifling pen where he did not suppose both to be right, nor delivered a single sentence that was not the result of his amplest conviction. — With regard to the two trials, he represented them as they really *were*, not as they might be *wished* in print, by the *over* zealous advocates of freedom. — And so far was he from being once employed, since his existence, by administration, to exert his poor abilities in their cause, that he here protests, before the public, he never *expected* or *received* the smallest emolument for his little services. — Never was *directly* or *indirectly* connected with a minister in his days, nor has he even at this moment, though suffering so severely on account of his attachment to government, either *solicited* or *received* a shilling compensation for that bread, which he and his family have lost in it's defence.

Here possibly Mr. Kelly may be asked, how, "unplac'd, un- "pension'd, no man's heir or slave," he could be idle enough to risk the favour of a town, that had honoured him with the warmest marks of approbation in his first dramatic attempt, for the mere purpose of serving a government from which he had not received the minutest favour or protection? To this Mr. Kelly replies, that in serving government, where he thought it *ought* to be served, he looked upon himself as rendering very essential benefit to the community. — Knowing it the duty of every good subject to promote, instead of disturbing, the national tranquility, he used his humble endeavours, rather to extinguish than animate the torch of public discord, and strove, as far as so insignificant an individual

dividual could ſtrive, to wreſt it from the hand of every political enthuſiaſt, who madly attempted to ſet his country in flames. With this view he particularly gave an account of the two trials that have expoſed him to ſo much unmerited obloquy. Being well convinced, that, during the rage of party, truth would undergo a torture upon the wheel of prejudice, Mr. Kelly, determined to give a faithful narrative of theſe remarkable deciſions. He accordingly attended; he accordingly gave a real ſtate of both to the world; and though he has been calumniated in the groſs, as a ſhameleſs abettor of murder, no attempt has hitherto been made to point out, in his repreſentation, the ſmalleſt perverſion of a fact. — This was eaſy to be done, had he been employed as the verniſher of guilt; the trials were not carried on in ſecret, but in the full face of day; not ſolely before the retainers of a court, but before the warmeſt ſons of popularity: Mr. Kelly was not culpable if the priſoners were wholly without blame; he only acquitted thoſe in his relation, who were acquitted by the laws of their country, and only explained *how* that innocence was made apparent, which the *too* deciſſive voice of partiality had previouſly condemned.

Mr. Kelly's account of the trials was received with general ſurprize, becauſe the public, by a ſucceſſion of papers in the daily and other prints, had been taught to conſider Mr Gillam and the ſoldier unqueſtionably guilty. — On their acquittal therefore the *intemperate* friends to the popular cauſe, (Mr. Kelly ſays the *intemperate* friends, becauſe he knows many of the moſt rational, as well as the moſt worthy members of the community, from *principle* in oppoſition,) wiſhed to throw a ſtigma on the court, where they were tried, and wiſhed to prejudice the world with an opinion, that both owed their preſervation more to the dexterity of judicial chicane, than to their real innocence. — Mr. Kelly, however, by ſetting the tranſactions in a plain, an honeſt light, prevented the intended inſult to the courts, but drew the whole weight of party reſentment upon himſelf, and the doctrine having been long ſucceſsfully inculcated among the people, that whoever ſpoke, much leſs whoever wrote, againſt popular prejudices, muſt neceſſarily be the hireling of government, Mr. Kelly became gradually ſtigmatized into ſuch a portion of politcal conſequence, that the ſuppreſſion of his comedy was conſidered as a triumph over adminiſtration; ſo that the curtain was no ſooner raiſed on the firſt night than a loud hiſſing prevented the performersfrom beginning the play a conſiderable time; — while on the other hand, the plaudits of Mr. Kelly's numerous friends, to whoſe goodneſs he ſtands eternally indebted, as well as of the unprejudiced, who deſired to give him a fair hearing, and afterwards to expreſs their cenſure or approbation, rendered the confuſion general. At laſt the performance commenced

menced — but went on with inceſſant interruptions, except only in the third act, to the concluſion. The performers totally diſconcerted by the tumult, were unable to exerciſe their abilities, or to remember their parts — whole ſpeeches, eſſentially neceſſary to the conduct of the fable, were left out, and others mutilated for the ſake of brevity. — In ſhort, the ſole conſideration was to get the comedy through the five acts in *any manner*. — This, with much difficulty, was effected, and it was given out for the following Monday. A new conteſt now aroſe: the oppoſers of the play inſiſted, with an uncuſtomary ſeverity, that it ſhould never be exhibited again. — The ſupporters inſiſted that it ſhould, on the Monday, according to the public intimation from Mr. King; but Mr. Kelly, fearing the conſequences of a diſpute that appeared extremely ſerious, propoſed behind the ſcenes, to withdraw his piece at once, for the ſake of reſtoring peace, and the tragedy of Cymbeline was given out in it's room.

This conciliating meaſure, however, was not attended with the deſired effect. The friends of the play, who were greatly the majority, would by no means admit the comedy to be withdrawn; and, after the farce, above two hundred gentlemen calling out for the manager, and threatening immediate demolition, to the houſe, if A WORD to the WISE was not performed, as originally given out, Mr. Lacy, the only manager then in town, ſent Mr. Hopkins, the prompter, to aſſure the company it ſhould, and all terminated peaceably for that evening.

It was no difficult matter to foreſee that the theatre, on the ſucceeding Monday night, would be a ſcene of freſh tumult; and the conſequences appearing more and more alarming to Mr. Kelly, he went to Mr. Garrick, who came to town on the Sunday morning, to conſult with him on the beſt means of preſerving peace, and it was concluded, that Mr. Kelly ſhould wait on his friends, and requeſt that they would give up the point. — Mr. Kelly accordingly did ſo, obſerving, that the intereſts of a ſingle individual were of little conſideration, when weighed againſt the repoſe of a whole public. — He obſerved, as he has repeatedly done in the courſe of the preſent narrative, that prejudices had been ſtrongly propagated againſt him, and that the very ſeverity he had experienced from many of his enemies, though unjuſtifiable in the manner, yet in the motive was really laudable. The moment of party heat, he frequently added, was not the moment to reaſon; and that however he might be injured in his circumſtances, by the ſuppreſſion of his play, he would ſuffer the injury with pleaſure, if he could by any means reſtore the tranquility of the town, which he had ſo unhappily, though ſo innocently, diſturbed. — To this his friends replied, that the cauſe was not his cauſe now, but

the

the public's; that if party disputes were once introduced into the theatre, our most rational amusements must be quickly at an end, that the number of writers at present for the stage was sufficiently small, and that they would not suffer the town to be controuled in it's pleasures from private pique or personal resentment: all they contended for was a fair hearing for the piece; that if it deserved condemnation, they themselves would be the first to give it up; but, till it received an equitable trial, they would not allow a triumph to prejudice professed, and acknowledged partiality.

In this state the affair rested till the Monday evening, when, on Mr. King's appearance, to speak the prologue, the opposition, with increased numbers, hissed, cat-called, and threw oranges: on the other side the demand for the new play was equally violent, the supporters turned several out of the house, whom they considered as general disturbers; however Mr. Garrick went on, in the author's name, with a formal renunciation of every emolument, of every reputation arising from his small endeavours for the public amusement; adding, that he was not only ready, but desirous to concur with their pleasure, though to the total disappointment both of his wishes and interest, and begged the sacrifice he then so chearfully offered might be allowed to terminate the contention. Things nevertheless continued in the same confusion for a considerable time, — during which Mr. Garrick often retired and returned, — but at last advanced with a paper in his hand, from Mr. Kelly, containing a written repetition of the foregoing request, and desiring permission, as the only means of re-establishing harmony, to withdraw his comedy wholly from the theatre.

When Mr. Garrick attempted to read this paper, a demand was made from the gallery, to know whether it was a political production, but though the demand occasioned no little laughter among the opposers of the piece, it only augmented the spirit of the author's friends, by rendering the views of party still more and more visible. — The play of Cymbeline being loudly insisted upon on the one hand, was loudly prohibited on the other; and near three hours having passed in acts of annoyance and hostility, Mr. Kelly was so exceedingly alarmed for the event, that he came himself into the front boxes, and from the front boxes, on the galleries calling out they could not see him, into the pit, and there, turning towards the audience, he expressed his apprehensions for their safety, begged they would be satisfied with what he had done, which was all he had in his power to do for their preservation, and not, by injuring one another, wound him irreparably in his peace.

Though in no degree so successful as he wished, he nevertheless so far prevailed, that a proposition on his

retiring

retiring was suggested for False Delicacy to be given the ensuing night, for his benefit by way of compromise: a gentleman then stood up in the pit, and asked Mr. Garrick, whether consenting to these measures would, or would not, be an impediment to Mr. Kelly's bringing any future productions on the stage — to which that gentleman had no sooner given a negative, than a second person from the gallery cried out, Expulsion means incapacitation. Mr. Kelly, acquainted with these particulars, went to Mr. Garrick and declined the favour intended him — observing, that he by no means meant to wring a benefit from the charity of the public — that if he deserved one benefit he was intitled to three, and that the theatre had already sustained sufficient loss upon his account. — But Mr. Garrick generously told him, that the theatre was much the best able to bear a loss; though, supposing the case otherwise, neither he nor Mr. Kelly, as public men, had a right on that occasion to dispute a determination of the public. Here the matter rested for that night, as there was no play, the money was returned, and the audience retired seemingly well reconciled.

Notwithstanding the compromise of the foregoing evening, and notwithstanding Mr. Kelly desired that the play-bills should contain no intimation that the performance of False Delicacy was intended for his benefit, a report universally prevailed that the opposition were determined not to suffer the exhibition of False Delicacy, which had long been honoured with the approbation of all parties, merely because it was written by the author of a Word to the Wise. Mr. Kelly on this, imagining that the circumstance of his being to receive the profits, of the night, and not any objection which could be raised to an established comedy, must be the sole foundation of this fresh resentment, waited upon his friends and begged they would allow him to relinquish his title to these profits since they were so likely to renew the disturbances of the theatre. His friends however were for a long time inflexible — they pronounced a violation of the compromise, no less injurious to the public, than insulting to them, and added, that they would never have listened to any compromise, if he had not been so importunately solicitous to give up every thing for peace —— but Mr. Kelly representing the prejudice the managers must necessarily sustain, by a contention of the present nature between the public, and pointing out the prejudice also which every individual belonging to the play-house must as necessarily sustain, by an interruption of the customary business — his friends yielded to these arguments, and permitted Mr. Kelly to forego the advantages of the night, to prevent the managers and the performers from ſuffering in a diſpute, where it was equally their intereſt and their duty to conſult the wiſhes of the auditors.

Theſe precautions being taken by Mr. Kelly, he repaired to the theatre on the Tueſday evening with ſome degree of ſatisfaction; but, on the opening of the play the confuſion was as violent as ever, though Mr. Garrick, from Mr. Kelly, aſſured the oppoſition, that the play was not to be performed for the benefit of the author — This aſſurance however was by no means ſufficient; the comedy of Falſe Delicacy was written by Mr. Kelly, and therefore though in poſſeſſion of the ſtage among the number of ſtock plays, was now to be condemned — to effect this purpoſe, an uproar in the theatre was not only judged neceſſary, but the following hand bill was diſtributed at all the doors.

To the PUBLIC.

"YOU cannot be ignorant that one wretch in that infamous banditti, hired by adminiſtration to explain away the rights of an inſulted people, is the author of a *Word to the Wiſe*. As a comic writer, his univerſal want of abilities has rendered him contemptible. As a politician, his principles are deteſtable. For theſe united reaſons, you were pleaſed to forbid the repreſentation of his play on Saturday, and prevent it's performance laſt night.

"The author himſelf begged leave to withdraw it: yet his party are now determined, that you ſhall ſupport the writer, though you reject the play. This night's repreſentation is for his *benefit*. Shall he with impunity aſſume a power repugnant to your own? —— If the priviledge of managers be impoſition, the duty of an Engliſh audience muſt be obedience."

Tueſday, March 6, 1770.

The heat with which proceedings were thus conducted on the part of oppoſition, gave room to imagine, that the audience would, as upon the preceding night, be diſmiſſed without any play. — But Mr. Kelly's friends were now no longer able to ſuppreſs their indignation, and being determined to make no farther conceſſions, they exerted themſelves ſo effectually, that Falſe Delicacy was performed, though with very conſiderable interruption. — Whole ſpeeches, nay, whole ſcenes were obliged to be omitted, and ſuch was the rage of undiſtinguiſhing prejudice, that it even attacked the perſonal ſafety of the female performers — This was not all, when the attempt to ſuppreſs Falſe Delicacy proved abortive, the enemies of the author demanded their money, and appeared unwilling to pay for the mischief they really *did*, because, they had not effected as much as they actually *wished* to *do*.

The conclusion of the farce happily produced a general calm, and though the theatrical horizon seemed pregnant with a storm the succeeding evening, it's serenity still continued, and perhaps, will never be again disturbed by any of Mr. Kelly's productions. There is nothing more necessary to add with regard to the exhibition of *A Word to the Wise*, than that such was the judicious conduct of Mr. Garrick and Mr. King, that what they gained on the one hand, they never lost on the other, – so as the amusement of the public had in the first instance been the only object of their attention, so it was apparent the public tranquility was, in the second, the only object of their care: And whatever inconveniences they themselves might be exposed to, they were incapable of deviating from the rules of politeness, of good sense, and manly condescension.

After a sacrifice of his interest, so ample, so unreserved, for the sake of restoring tranquility in the theatre, it might perhaps be expected that Mr. Kelly's enemies would have thought themselves sufficiently gratified; but prejudice has many appetites to glut, and we seldom listen to the sentiments of justice, where we have publicly committed a violence upon our reason.—It was therefore no way wonderful, though his cause was the common cause of letters, to find many of the periodical prints constantly filled with the grossest scurrilities against him; but, in this they rather gratified his pride, than wounded his sensibility; they only exalted him on the roll of slander, among the most illustrious characters in the kingdom, and made him an object of importance, by making him an object of implacable resentment.

One attack however he cannot help mentioning in this place, though it leads to a repetition of the Guildford Trial, because it came from a quarter wholly unexpected; and from a quarter also too respectable to be overlooked, from the reverend Mr. Horne, at the meeting of the Middlesex freeholders at Mile-End, on Friday the 30th of April. At this meeting Mr. Horne, in summing up the various grievances under which he supposed the nation groaning from the tyranny of administration, took occasion to descant on the soldier's trial for the murder of the unfortunate Mr. Allen, and expressed himself thus —— "It is necessary to give you an account of "Maclean's trial, because the judge forbad it's being taken "down by any one, *except it was government*.—It has never "been published—A very false account of this trial has indeed "been published by Mr. KELLY, who was paid and brought "to Guildford for that purpose, and who had lodgings taken "for him there, and who was familiarly conversant with a gen-"tleman, whose name I shall not mention now, lest it should

seem

" ſeem to proceed from reſentment in me, for an account I " have to ſettle with him next week; however one circumſtance " I ought to tell you; this gentleman was foreman of the " grand jury.——

Without dwelling on Mr. Horne's extraordinary tenderneſs to the gentleman whoſe name he will not mention, while he points him clearly out to every apprehenſion, Mr. Kelly will ſuppoſe that what was aſſerted with regard to him, Mr. Horne himſelf believed to be indiſputably true — Nay, Mr. Kelly is ſeriouſly of this opinion, becauſe many gentlemen of unqueſtionable veracity have aſſured him, that, abſtracted from the intemperance of party, Mr. Horne is in his underſtanding enlarged, and in his diſpoſition liberal. On theſe accounts however, Mr. Kelly differed from the politician, he always reſpected Mr. Horne's private character, and did juſtice to what he conſidered the well meaning, though miſtaken zeal of the ſpirited freeholder, in the moment of his deepeſt concern at hearing a miniſter of peace, preaching diſcord through his country, and expreſſing an impatience of dying the veſtments of his ſacred function, in the blood of his fellow ſubjects.

But though Mr. Kelly readily makes this conceſſion in favour of Mr. Horne's private character, he muſt obſerve, that the conſtitution of this country, for the purity of which Mr. Horne is ſo ſtrenuous an advocate, does not allow the mere *belief* of any man to be *poſitive* evidence, nor compliment his ſimple *conjecture* with the force of a *fact*. — For this reaſon, Mr. Horne ſhould be extremely cautious how he aſſerts any thing to the prejudice of another's reputation; *hearſay* authority is not enough for this purpoſe; he ſhould know of his own *knowledge* what he aſſerts upon his own *word*; and be *certain* in his *proof*, where he is *peremptory* in his *accuſation*. ——If a circumſpection of this nature is neceſſary in every man of honour, it muſt give Mr. Horne much mortification to hear, after he has repreſented Hugh Kelly, to the freeholders of Middleſex, as a venal ſcribler, a ſhameleſs inſtrument of power, an atrocious defender of murder, that the whole charge ſhould be utterly groundleſs—That Kelly's account of Maclean's trial, ſhould be true in every circumſtance, that Kelly never expected or received a ſhilling for writing it, and that in the courſe of his days he has not once changed a ſyllable with Mr Onſlow, notwithſtanding the *converſant familiarity* at Guildſord.

Strange however as all theſe things muſt appear, after Mr. Horne's poſitive affirmation to the contrary, all theſe things are moſt religiouſly veritable; and Mr. Horne is in this public manner called upon to prove an iota of his charge; it is his buſineſs to ſupport his own allegations, not Mr. Kelley's, to

endeavour

endeavour at eſtabliſhing negatives. — Let him therefore ſpiritedly proceed to his proofs. —— He has pronounced Mr. Kelly guilty, let him now ſhew in what his guilt conſiſts. — The moſt tyrannical miniſter can do no more than convict without evidence—in him however deſpotiſm is to be expected. But ſurely the rigid advocate for juſtice will not follow ſo dangerous an example; he will act reaſonably while he contends for reaſon, and conduct himſelf upon principles of legality, while he is generouſly ſtruggling for the preſervation of the laws.

In reality, if there is no more foundation in Mr. Horne's celebrated ſpeech, for the charges brought againſt government, than for the charges urged againſt Mr. Kelly, the catalogue of public grievances is rather ludicrous than melancholy. But without troubling Mr. Horne to ſupport his aſſertions, Mr. Kelly will ſhew theſe very aſſertions ſelf-refuted; he will prove them as inconſiſtent, as they are poſitive, and reſt his defence entirely on the nature of Mr. Horne's accuſation.

Mr. Horne ſets out with ſaying that the judge would not ſuffer the trial to be taken down by any body, except it was for government — Several nevertheleſs took it down, and among the reſt Mr. Chinnery and Mr. Gurney the profeſſed ſhort hand writers—Numbers beſides committed the moſt material paſſages to paper, and ſome to Mr. Kelly's knowledge *not* for Government; but, Mr. Kelly will ſay, that had he been hired by *adminiſtration* for the infamous purpoſe Mr. Horne mentions, it is not likely that the uſe of a pen would have been at all permitted in the court; it is not likely, that the judge would allow a *real* account of a trial to be taken, where a proſtitute writer was particularly employed to *miſrepreſent* it, nor is it likely that the miniſtry, while wiſhing to ſtand well with the world, would furniſh ſuch palpable evidence of it's own diſhonour—If there was any thing illegal in the proceeding of the court —— If an unwarrantable ſtretch of power reſcued the priſoner from juſtice, why has not the tranſaction been held up to univerſal indignation? — Why is it not recorded in the liſt of grievances preſented to the throne?—To make a ſolemn court of judicature the pandar of deſpotic authority would have been a crime of the firſt magnitude; it would have ſhaken the conſtitution to it's centre, and overwhelmed the miniſter with inevitable deſtruction. — But, wicked as ſome gentlemen in oppoſition might ſuppoſe the Government, they could not ſuppoſe it weak enough to overturn the laws thus deſperately at once, for the mere end of ſaving a private foot ſoldier from puniſhment; a pardon was an eaſy expedient, and mercy was not then conſidered criminal—Beſides, were the oſtenſible men in power as ruthleſs as they have been painted, they would have

have given the priſoner up at once, they would have been regardleſs of his fate, nor would they have attempted to ſave him from the gibbet, by methods that muſt have unavoidably hurried themſelves to the block. The queſtion is not whether the unhappy Mr. Allen loſt a ſon, but whether that ſon fell by the hands of Maclean?—Humanity is melted when it thinks of a ſlaughtered child, and a weeping father—But humanity muſt ſtill be juſt—it muſt not wiſh for victims without guilt, nor dry up the tears of ſorrowing relations with a ſacrifice of unoffending blood.

The laſt part of Mr. Horne's aſſertion is to the full as extraordinary as the firſt. Mr. Kelly is made culpable for being *farmiliarly converſant* with the foreman of the grand jury at *Guildford*; though certainly, if there was a neceſſity for any mention of the grand juryman he ought to be mentioned with reſpect; becauſe the grand jury *found* the bill *againſt* Maclean, and conſequently, in that circumſtance, advanced the very wiſhes of popularity—Inſtead therefore of condemning Mr. Kelly for his intimacy with Mr. Onſlow in the preſent caſe, that intimacy ought to be an argument in Mr. Kelly's favour—But the truth is, Mr. Kelly in the whole courſe of his exiſtence, never once ſpoke to Mr. Onſlow, the grand juryman alluded to, knowing who he was, nor he believes at any rate, becauſe he knows Mr. Onſlow's perſon, and is flattered with the poſſeſſion of a tolerable memory——however, if Mr. Horne has evidence to the contrary—let him produce it—if not, let him for the future be more certain of his facts, or leſs peremptory in his aſſertions.

But poſſibly, though Mr. Horne is a ſtrong enemy to examination by interrogatory, he may nevertheleſs chooſe to aſk Mr. Kelly what buſineſs carried him to Guildford, if he did not go as a literary proſtitute in favour of government? To this Mr. Kelly will reply with another queſtion, What buſineſs had Mr. Horne there? Mr. Kelly ſurely has as much right to indulge his curioſity, and to ſupport what he conceives a juſt cauſe, as that gentleman—Mr. Horne cannot be a warmer well wiſher to true freedom, and to national happineſs than Mr. Kelly, though he purſues a very different plan of promoting them—Mr. Kelly's political opinions may be erroneous—but his intention is right—Had he been the venal thing he is repreſented, he might have carried his venality to a certain market—Popular applauſe is always fortune to a public writer of prudence, and the part Mr. Kelly has taken may be an impeachment of his judgment, but argues no depravity of his heart.

Upon the whole, with regard to Mr. Horne, if Mr. Kelly's account of the Guildford trial is falſe, let Mr. Horne point the fallacy out; if Mr. Kelly has been hired to write it, let Mr. Horne mention by whom --- and if it is criminal to be *familiarly converſant* with Mr. Onſlow, let Mr. Horne ſupport a ſingle inſtance of Mr. Kelly's familiarity with that gentleman.—— Mr. Horne ſoon after Mr. Kelly's account of the Guildford trial appeared, promiſed the world *a true ſtate* of that remarkable affair, and if Mr. Kelly ſhamefully miſrepreſented facts, the appearance of Mr. Horne's pamphlet was doubly neceſſary — That pamphlet has never yet appeared; and it cannot be ſuppoſed that a temper ſo ready to fire at light occaſions as Mr. Horne's, would ſuppreſs it, had there been any material cauſe of complaint to lay before the people.

Mr. Kelly has taken up a great deal of room with his trifling concerns, for which he ought to apologize, but as the publication of his play by ſubſcription, proceeded entirely from the generous partiality of his friends, he thought it his duty to let them at leaſt ſee, that though they might be ſupporting a dull writer, they were encouraging an honeſt man—The piece, with all it's imperfections on it's head, is now before the world; and the author hopes, if it ſhould even ſet the reader faſt aſleep, that nothing it contains will rouze his indignation: the moſt careful father he thinks may put it into the hands of his daughter, without any fear of wounding her delicacy, or unhinging her principles—This is it's chief, perhaps it's only merit, and perhaps, had it been heard on the ſtage with patience, it might have been condemned with juſtice —— Mr. Kelly will therefore conſole himſelf with his optimiſt Willoughby, by thinking every thing happens for the beſt, and look upon that very prejudice which has ſuppreſſed his poor performance as ultimately fortunate, ſince it may have been the means of preſerving his little ſhare of reputation.

He cannot however conclude this addreſs without an obſervation or two upon the melancholy ſituation of dramatic writers --- and as it is poſſible that he himſelf may never more venture a production on the ſtage, he hopes what he has further to advance, will merit an additional conſideration from his readers.

The great decline of dramatic genius in this country, has been for many years an object of general concern with the public, and the lovers of the theatre have ardently wiſhed, that ſome happy ſtimulus might be diſcovered to encreaſe the number of writers for the ſtage; yet, though this wiſh has prevailed univerſally, and though the credit, as well as the emolument ariſing from a ſucceſsful play is not a little tempting, ſtill the danger attending the repreſentation of the beſt pieces, is ſo conſiderable, that the few writers bleſſed with eaſy fortunes do not chooſe to run the hazard, and

moſt

most of those who live by the sale of their productions, are content to follow studies less profitable, for a more certain reward of their labours.

Besides this, the difficulty, the toil, the downright drudgery of writing a good play is inconceivable; it is a work which requires long time and a close application; it is a work in which neither the most extensive erudition, nor the most accurate understanding can ensure an author success——In every other species of composition, judgment, genius, and education are almost certain of a triumph—but here knowledge of the world is indispensibly requisite—An acquaintance with the manners, and with the passions is requisite.—Nor are these sufficient without an invention to strike out variety; and a skill to produce effects, by a forcible display of situation—It is not the good sense only of an audience which is addressed—but their feelings; they must be agreeably surprized while they are publicly instructed, and the Muse, like other beauties, must be ravishing to the general eye, before she can be dear to the general heart.

When therefore the difficulty attending a dramatic work is so considerable; when perhaps there is another considerable difficulty to get a play received by the stage, and another still to find a capital company of performers to represent it, instead of wondering that the number of writers is so small, we should in reality wonder how it is so respectable.—But if we look still farther, we shall be surprized that *any* author risks his bark upon the dangerous ocean of the theatre.—It is a melancholy truth, that the people who write most for the stage, are rather remarkable for their ingenuity than their opulence.—On this account a disappointment to them is an essential misfortune. Yet a few private enemies can at all times frustrate their expectations. In vain an unfortunate man of letters may labour for many months with a laudable view of entertaining the town, and improving his own circumstances;—and in vain he may exert his utmost efforts to merit the protection of an audience, if he has unhappily given one individual an offence. The moment his piece is talked of, a party is possibly formed to damn it; and many who would not join this party from malevolence, give it countenance, for the pleasure, as it is called, *of kicking up a riot in the playhouse.*—Thus the littleness of personal pique, and the levity of inconsiderate laughter, have the poet totally at their mercy.—The curtain rises, and the storm begins; nor can the generous interposition of nine tenths among the auditors preserve the play from destruction. There is as much confusion created by the desire of "*go on, go on,*" as by the cry, "*go off, go off.*" Whatever disturbs the representation has a tendency to injure it;

ſo that a performance exhibited during a ſtate of contention muſt deſpair of ſucceſs;—the ſupporters conſtantly interrupted have no opportunity of being entertained, and naturally enough, perhaps attribute the fault to the author; while the oppoſition deciſively pronouncing upon what is predetermined not to hear, kindly brands him with the epithet of an incorrigible, dunce, and, not content with the injury done to his fortune, makes an equal attack upon his literary character.

Such being the ſituation of dramatic genius in this country, let the public themſelves judge, whether an author has any mighty encouragement to write for the ſtage.—Perhaps the poet, treated in the manner now deſcribed, has no dependence but his talents; perhaps upon the ſucceſs of the very piece thus ſuppreſſed he built his chief eſtabliſhment in life, and founded every future proſpect of bringing up a growing family with reputation. — What muſt his feelings then be, to find his hopes all blaſted in a ſingle hour—to find the very labour, poſſibly of years, deſtroyed in an inſtant, by the people for whoſe entertainment he laboured; and to ſee the bread not only wreſted from the hands of his unoffending little ones, but to ſee them even expoſed to the ſtill perſecuting reſentment of prejudice, for the imaginary offences of their father.—What muſt be his feelings—Yet forbear humanity to inquire—the anſwer will harrow up your boſom—Generoſity, turn away from the picture, it muſt deluge you with tears. --- The ſcene of poetical diſtreſs however ſketched to the reader's imagination, thanks to the goodneſs of Providence, is far from being Mr. Kelly's ſituation; but it often has been, and often may be, the ſituation of a much worthier man. --- Mr. Kelly is affluent beyond his merits --- nay, beyond his utmoſt hopes, he poſſeſſes the riches of content in a very extenſive manner, and can ſit down to his humble repaſt with pleaſure, in the honeſt recollection that it is punctually paid for.

The difficulties here pointed out, for dramatic genius to encounter, are difficulties to which every writer for the ſtage is conſtantly expoſed; but the danger becomes infinitely more formidable, if, in times of party feud, he renders himſelf in the leaſt diſagreeable to the popular ſide of the queſtion; the unreflecting virtue of numbers then, as in Mr. Kelly's caſe, will arm againſt him, and think it meritorious to condemn the production, that puniſhment may be inflicted upon the imputed delinquency of the man.—In times like the preſent therefore, what is a dramatic writer to do?—To hold his tongue, replies cold blooded prudence.— And what has the unfortunate man of letters committed, that he alone of all the community is to be denied the privilege of ſpeaking his ſentiments? Say, ye various ſons of ſcience, will you ſubmit

mit to this deſpicable ſlavery of the mind? Are you, above the generality of mankind, diſtinguiſhed for your education and your underſtanding, to be refuſed an opinion, where an opinion is deemed the birth-right of your meaneſt fellow-ſubject? Shall it be your glory to inculcate leſſons of generoſity and independence, and yet be your crime to practiſe theſe leſſons yourſelves? — Shall your writings breathe the nobleſt ſpirit of candour, and your lives be a round of the pooreſt diſſimulation? —— Shall you think your country in danger, and yet be afraid to ſpeak a ſyllable for it's preſervation? — No, you will not tear the finer principles from your breaſts; you will not ſet an example of ſo abject a diſingenuity. — Whatever meets the approbation of your judgment, will be ſupported by the ſanction of your voice, and however you may meet with reproach, you will at leaſt be careful not to deſerve it. — When adminiſtration is indefenſible, you will be too honeſt to combat in it's cauſe; but, at the ſame time you will not heſitate to condemn the errors of popularity. — You will be always animated by a real ſolicitude for the public, and be as careful to guard againſt the extravagance of it's over-zealous friends, as to provide againſt the machinations of it's moſt politic enemies. — Acting thus you may be poor, but you will ever be reſpectable. — Poſterity will do you juſtice, if you are even oppreſſed by your cotemporaries, and you will find ample reſources in the conſciouſneſs of your integrity, to compenſate for the ſevereſt diſappointments in your fortune.

To conclude — If men of talents have an equal right of thinking with the reſt of their fellow-ſubjects, and if they are not precluded by the generally acknowledged ſuperiority of their underſtandings, from declaring their ſentiments upon ſubjects of national importance, the lovers of the drama muſt ſee that nothing can be ſo dangerous to the exiſtence of genius, as the introduction of political diſputes into the theatre. The party which condemns a writer of different principles on one day, may ſee a favourite author, ſacrificed the very next by their enemies in politics; and the violence may continue till there is ſcarcely an individual hardy enough to furniſh our managers with a piece. The ſtate of the ſtage is at preſent ſufficiently deplorable; and it's literature, inſtead of wanton oppoſition, calls loudly for the generous hand of public encouragement. — Give it this encouragement therefore, ye wiſe, and ye worthy — reſcue your writers from the worſt of all tyrannies, and no longer form your minds by the ſentiments of thoſe, who are not allowed to poſſeſs any minds of their own.

THIS

COMEDY

IS INSCRIBED TO

ROBERT LADBROKE, Esq.

AS A PUBLIC TESTIMONY

OF THE

VERY HIGH ESTEEM

IN WHICH

THE AUTHOR HOLDS HIS FRIENDSHIP,

AND A SINCERE MARK

OF THE

VERY JUST RESPECT HE ENTERTAINS

FOR

HIS PRIVATE CHARACTER.

PROLOGUE.

WRITTEN BY MR. KELLY.

SPOKEN BY MR. KING.

WELL, here you are, and comfortably ſqueez'd ——
But do you come *quite* willing to be pleas'd?—
Say, do you wiſh for bravo — fine — encore ——
Or — hiſs — off, off, — no more — no more — no more ——
Tho' for true taſte I know the warmth you feel,
A roaſted poet is a glorious meal ——
And oft I've known a miſerable wit,
Thro' downright laughter faſtn'd on the ſpit,
Baſted, with cat-call ſauce, for very fun,
Not till quite ready —— but till quite undone ——
And yet you ſerv'd the puppy as you ought ——
How dare he think to tell you of a fault ——
What fair one here from prudence *ever* ſtrays,
What lover here *e'er* flatters or betrays?
What huſband here is *ever* found to roam,
What wife is here that does not *doat* on home?
In yon gay circle, not a blooming face
From Club's rude king cou'd point you out the face;
No ſober trader, in that crowed pit,
'Till clear, broad day will o'er his bottle ſit;
Nor while our commerce *fatally* decays,
Erect his villa, or ſet up his chaiſe ——
Nay, you above, in cake-conſuming bow'rs,
Who thro' whole Sundays munge away your hours;

P R O L O G U E.

You are ſo mild, ſo gentle, that ev'n here,
Your ſweet ton'd voices never wound the ear;
Ne'er make the houſe for tune or prologue ring,
Roaſt-beef — roaſt-beef — the prologue, prologue — King —
Why then, thus weigh'd in truth's ſevereſt ſcale,
Shall each pert ſcribbler impudently rail,
With dull morality diſgrace the ſtage,
And talk of vices in ſo *pure* an age;
Your wiſe forefathers, in politer days,
Had ev'n their faults commended in their plays,
To cheat a friend, or violate a wife,
Was then true humour, comedy, and life ——
But now the bard becomes your higheſt boaſt,
Whoſe ill-bred pen traduces you the moſt;
Whoſe ſaucy muſe can hardily aver
That ſtill a *lady* poſſibly can err;
That ſtill a *lord* can trick you at a bet,
And fools and madmen are exiſting yet ——
Be rous'd at laſt — nor, in an age ſo nice,
Let theſe grave dunces teize you with advice ——
What, tho' ſome taylor's oft protracted bill
May hang all trembling on the author's quill,
Regard it not, remove the growing evil —
A well dreſt poet is the very devil ——
Do taverns dun him — What, can ſcribblers treat?
Fine times, indeed, when ſcribblers think to eat ——
Do juſtice then — to-night, ten minutes here
May blaſt the bard's whole labour of a year ——
What do I ſee! — reſentment in your eyes?
'Tis true, the fellow at your mercy lies;
And of all wreaths, the Briton's nobleſt crown,
Is ne'er to ſtrike an enemy when down ——

*

Dramatis Perſonæ.

M E N.

Sir George Hastings,	Mr. King.
Sir John Dormer,	Mr. Reddiſh.
Willoughby,	Mr. Aickin.
Captain Dormer,	Mr. Palmer.
Villars,	Mr. Cautherly.
Footmen,	Mr. Watkins. Mr. Wrighten.

W O M E N.

Mrs. Willoughby,	Mrs. Jefferys.
Miss Willoughby,	Mrs. Baddely.
Miss Dormer,	Miſs Younge.
Miss Montagu,	Mrs. Barry.
Jenny,	Mrs. Smith.
Lucy,	Miſs Platt.

A
WORD to the WISE.

ACT I.

SCENE, *an Apartment in* Sir JOHN DORMER'S *House*.

Enter Sir JOHN DORMER, Miſs DORMER, and Miſs MONTAGU.

Sir JOHN.

WELL but, my dear Caroline, tho' I grant you that Sir George Haſtings has his peculiarities, ſtill you muſt grant me that he has many very amiable qualities.

Miſs DORMER.

I never denied Sir George's merit, Sir, but all his good qualities cannot conceal his unaccountable coxcombry; his attention is conſtantly centered in himſelf, and there is no enduring a man who fancies that every woman muſt at firſt ſight fall violently in love with him.

Sir JOHN.

Do you hear her, Miſs Montagu?

Miſs MONTAGU.

Why, Sir John, there is no accounting for inclination, you know; — however, I cannot look upon Sir George in the very ridiculous light he appears to Miſs Dormer.

Miſs DORMER.

No — why he is a narciſſus that continually makes love to his own ſhadow, and I can't bear the idea of a huſband, in whoſe affection I am likely to be every moment rival'd by the looking-glaſs.

Miſs MONTAGU.

Nay now, my dear, you are rather hard upon him. —Sir George may poſſibly be a little too fond of himſelf ——

Sir JOHN.

But that does'nt prevent him from entertaining very tender ſentiments for Caroline Dormer.

Miſs MONTAGU.

He may be unneceſſarily attentive to the niceties of dreſs ——

Sir JOHN.

But then he is attentive to every law of juſtice and generoſity.

Miſs MONTAGU.

And if his foibles provoke us to an occaſional ſmile, his worth muſt always excite our warmeſt admiration.

Miſs DORMER.

Upon my word, Harriot, a very florid winding up of a period, and very proper for an elevated thought in a ſentimental Comedy;—but I tell you, I ſhould reliſh theſe encomiums on Sir George well enough, if he was not ſo particularly recommended

mended to my attention. — I really can't ſupport the imagination of vowing honour and obedience to the object of my own ridicule, and it wou'd mortify my pride beyond conception, to ſee my huſband the conſtant jeſt of his acquaintance.

Sir JOHN.

My dear Caroline, don't be too difficult in your choice, nor entertain any romantic idea of finding a huſband, all perfection.—The expectation of too much before marriage, frequently imbitters the union after;—and as the beſt men will have their little blemiſhes, we may ſurely number thoſe among the beſt, in whoſe characters we can diſcover nothing more than a few trifling peculiarities.

Miſs DORMER.

I ſee, Sir, you make a point of this affair.

Sir JOHN.

I wou'd not make a point of any thing, my dear, which I thought wou'd be in the leaſt repugnant to your happineſs:—but, really, when I conſider this propoſal in every reſpect, when I conſider the rank, the fortune, and what is above all, the merit of the man, I cannot but wiſh that you wou'd give him a favourable reception; and this the more eſpecially, as I am convinced, if the match ſhould take place, that your fine ſenſe and ſweetneſs of temper, will eaſily mould your huſband to your wiſh, and quickly remove every trace of thoſe foibles, which are at preſent the only reaſon of your objection.

Miſs DORMER.

You are very good, Sir.

Sir JOHN.

This morning, my dear, Sir George purpoſes to declare himſelf in form.—If you can receive his addreſſes, you will make him happy, and oblige me exceedingly; — but if you cannot, deal ingenuouſly, and reject him; the juſtice which I owe to him, as well as the tenderneſs which I have for you, makes this advice doubly requiſite.

Enter a SERVANT.

SERVANT.

Mr. Willoughby, Sir.

Sir JOHN.

I'll wait upon him inſtantly. [*Exit Serv.*] Think therefore ſeriouſly, Caroline, before you determine, for I neither wiſh to cheat my friend into the poſſeſſion of a reluctant heart, nor to ſacrifice my daughter to the object of her averſion. [*Exit.*]

Miſs DORMER.

Well, Harriot, what ſhall I do?—You hear he has actually mention'd him to me in the moſt ſerious terms, and that this very morning he is to make a formal declaration.

Miſs MONTAGU.

And what then, does'nt Sir John deſire you to reject him, if he is really diſagreeable?—Can you poſſibly wiſh for a greater degree of indulgence?

Miſs DORMER.

And yet that very indulgence, my dear Miſs Montagu, is likely to render me extremely miſerable.

Miſs MONTAGU.

Why indeed, *Miſs* Dormer—remember, child, you complimented me firſt with the cold reſpect-ful

ful epithet of Miſs—the men in general ſay that the ſureſt way of making a woman wretched is to indulge her inclinations——But pray, my dear, why is this liberty which Sir John allows you, of promoting your own happineſs, ſo very likely to make you miſerable.

Miſs DORMER.

Ah, Harriot! don't you ſee that while he is ſo generouſly anxious to conſult my wiſhes, I am bound by gratitude, as well as juſtice, to pay the greateſt regard to his expectations.

Miſs MONTAGU.

You are really an excellent girl, my dear. But pray anſwer me one queſtion ſeriouſly.

Miſs DORMER.

What is it?

Miſs MONTAGUE.

Is this diſlike, which you entertain to your father's choice, entirely the reſult of your averſion to Sir George? or is it, be honeſt now, the conſequence of a ſecret partiality for ſomebody elſe?

Miſs DORMER.

A ſecret partiality for ſomebody elſe? Pray, my dear, for whom is it likely I ſhould entertain a partiality?

Miſs MONTAGU.

Caroline, Caroline, this reſerve is ill ſuited both to the nature of our friendſhip and the cuſtomary frankneſs of your temper—yet notwithſtanding the ſecreſy you have hitherto ſo unkindly obſerv'd, I can eaſily ſee that Mr. Villars——What, conſcious, Caroline?

Miſs

Miſs DORMER.

O Harriot, ſpare me—nor be offended that I have endeavour'd to keep a ſecret from you, which I abſolutely ſhudder to whiſper to myſelf—to deal candidly, my dear, I muſt acknowledge that your charge is but too juſt—and notwithſtanding every effort of my pride, and every argument of my prudence, I find this humble yet deſerving Villars poſſeſſes a much higher place in my eſteem than can be conſiſtent with my happineſs.

Miſs MONTAGU.

Why, to do the young fellow juſtice, he is really very agreeable, and has ſomething in his manner that would do credit to a more eligible ſituation—but——

Miſs DORMER.

Ay, Harriot, there's the misfortune—agreeable as he is in every reſpect, he is ſtill a total dependent on my father, and thinks himſelf extremely happy that his talents have obtain'd him even a temporary eſtabliſhment in an opulent family.

Miſs MONTAGU.

Well, my dear, Sir John is generous, and Mr. Villars is very uſeful to him in his literary reſearches; beſides, I am not a little pleas'd at the diſtinction with which he, as well as the Captain, conſtantly treats Mr. Villars.

Miſs DORMER.

I don't know how it is—Mr. Villars has a manner of commanding reſpect from every body; he is humble without ſervility, and ſpirited——

Miſs MONTAGU.

Oh! he is every thing that's amiable, no doubt—and the ſtars have been exceedingly relentleſs in not giving him a large fortune—however, if I have any ſkill in the buſineſs of the heart, Villars is to the full as uneaſy upon your account as you can poſſibly be on his—he is always contriving excuſes for converſing with you, yet when he does, he is in viſible confuſion; and it was only yeſterday evening, when I beg'd he wou'd put a letter for me into the poſt-office, that he ſtammer'd out, in the utmoſt perplexity, "I ſhall "take particular care, Madam, to deliver it to "Miſs Dormer."

Miſs DORMER.

If this be the caſe, Harriot, I muſt indeed behave with particular circumſpection to him; and yet, tho' I ſee the impoſſibility of ever being his, he has given me an inſuperable averſion to the reſt of his ſex.

Miſs MONTAGU.

What then do you intend to do with Sir George?

Miſs DORMER.

To reject him; but ſtill to do it without giving any offence to my father.

Miſs MONTAGU.

And how do you propoſe to manage it?

Miſs DORMER.

By throwing myſelf honeſtly upon Sir George's humanity, by telling him my affection is engaged, and by begging of him to withdraw his addreſſes in ſuch a manner as ſhall appear to be the reſult of his own choice, and not the conſequence of my diſinclination—Sir George, notwithſtanding his egregious vanity is uncommonly good-natur'd—but let us retire to my room, my dear, I am unfit

unfit for company at preſent, and here we are likely to be broken in upon.——O Harriot.

Miſs MONTAGU.

And O, Caroline, what a very fooliſh figure does a woman make, when ſhe is lamentably in love. [*Exeunt.*]

Enter Sir GEORGE HASTINGS *and* Captain DORMER.

DORMER.

Well, my brother-in-law elect,—you are very ſplendidly dreſs'd this morning.

Sir GEORGE.

Why, Jack, I think, I do make a pretty tolerable appearance.

DORMER.

And do you think this appearance calculated to make an impreſſion upon a woman of ſpirit.—Zounds, man, give up your pretenſions, for nothing but a fellow of life is likely to ſucceed with my ſiſter I can promiſe you.

Sir GEORGE.

A fellow of life, Jack;—that is, I ſuppoſe, a fellow of profligacy:—truly you pay your ſiſter a very pretty compliment.

DORMER.

And why pray do you neceſſarily connect the idea of life with the idea of profligacy?

Sir GEORGE.

Becauſe, in the vocabulary of libertines, like you, Jack, the word life always means a round of every thing that is fooliſh or unwarrantable.

DORMER.

DORMER.

Why, what the devil are you turn'd fanatic, George, that you begin to deal ſo much in ſecond-hand morality?

Sir GEORGE.

In ſhort, your fellows of ſpirit never allow a man a ſcruple of common-ſenſe, till he has entirely proſtituted his underſtanding; nor ſuppoſe him to be fit for a commerce with the world, till he abſolutely merits to be hunted out of ſociety.

DORMER.

Well but, George, there is one exceſs of which you yourſelf have been guilty; and I have known the time, when you took a bottle ſo freely, that you were generally made toaſt-maſter of the company.

Sir GEORGE.

Yes, but I ſoon found out that drinking was deteſtable, and toaſting the greateſt of all abſurdities.

DORMER.

Why how wou'd you wiſh to paſs an evening? — Can any thing exceed the pleaſure of ſociety, with a few ſelect friends of good-nature and vivacity?

Sir GEORGE.

O nothing to be ſure is ſo delightful as guzzling down half a dozen bottles, and enjoying the rational diſcourſe—of where does the toaſt ſtand—with you, Sir William—no, with you, Sir George—fill him a bumper, Captain Dormer—fill him to the top.——O, an evening ſpent in this manner muſt be delectable, eſpecially if a couple of fools ſhould happily quarrel in their cups, and cut one another's throat to prove the ſuperiority of their underſtanding.

DORMER.

Ha! ha! ha!—But was this all your objection to the bottle?

Sir GEORGE.

No, for it made my heach ach, and disorder'd my dress beyond bearing.

DORMER.

Disorder'd your dress, ha! ha! ha! what unaccountable coxcombry.

Sir GEORGE.

Why to be sure it's a very ridiculous thing for a man to shew a little regard for decency.

DORMER.

Well, notwithstanding you are a coxcomb systematically, I am sure the character will not be a strong recommendation to my sister.

Sir GEORGE.

Your sister, Jack, is a woman of sense, and must see that she has a much stronger chance of being happy with me, than poor Miss Montagu has of being happy with her brother.—My heart is unadulterated, and is therefore worth any woman's acceptance.

DORMER.

O no doubt it is a very valuable acquisition.

Sir GEORGE.

Whereas, you fellows of life, hawk about your hearts from commoner to commoner, till they become quite contemptible; and then with the additional merit of broken constitutions,—tottering limbs,—pale cheeks, and hollow eyes, you politely offer the refuse of the stews to ladies of fortune, family, and character.

DORMER.

And so your affection is unadulterated;—ha! ha! ha!

Sir GEORGE.

Ay, laugh on and welcome; — but who have we here?

DORMER.

Mr. Willoughby, who will keep you in countenance with maxims of mufty morality.

Sir GEORGE.

What, my good-natur'd optimift, who thinks every thing happens for the beft?

DORMER.

Ay, Candide to perfection, who is continually bleffing his ftars the more they load him with misfortunes;—and pray heaven his bufinefs here this morning has not been to talk with Sir John about my intimacy in his family. [*afide.*]

Enter WILLOUGHBY.

WILLOUGHBY.

Sir George, your moft obedient.—Captain, I am your humble fervant.

Sir GEORGE.

Mr. Willoughby, yours.—How do the ladies, Sir?—the good Mrs. Willoughby, and your amiable daughter.

WILLOUGHBY.

Why my daughter, Sir George, is very well;—and my wife is as ufual, continually embittering every comfort of life, and lamenting the miferies attendant on mortality.

Sir GEORGE.

I wonder fhe does not chufe to follow the fenfible example you fet her, and endeavour rather to leffen, than to aggravate the meafure of unavoidable misfortunes.—She's a young woman, and mifanthropy at her age is rather out of character.

WILLOUGHBY.

Why yes, Sir George, ſhe's twenty good years younger than I am, and yet ſhe is twenty times more impatient under the ſmalleſt diſappointment.

Sir GEORGE.

But, my good friend, you don't think her youth a very unfortunate circumſtance?

WILLOUGHBY.

O, Sir George, my principle is to think every thing for the beſt.

DORMER.

Well ſaid, Mr. Willoughby.

WILLOUGHBY.

It was'nt her youth, however, that ſtruck me, but the ſobriety of her conduct, and her affection for my daughter;—ſhe was beſides a diſtant relation of my firſt wife's—liv'd with us in the ſame houſe; and ſome how I lik'd her, becauſe having no fortune, it gave her but little expectation of a better huſband.

Sir GEORGE.

But why don't you teach her to adopt ſome part of your own fortitude under diſappointment?

DORMER.

Perhaps it is not in her power to exerciſe ſo deſirable a philoſophy.

WILLOUGHBY.

My dear Captain, life has misfortunes enough without our being induſtrious to encreaſe the number of them—when an accident therefore happens, we ſhou'd conſider that, bad as it may be, it might have been ſtill worſe; and inſtead of arrogantly murmuring at the diſpenſations of providence, we ſhou'd thankfully acknowledge the goodneſs that did not plunge us into a deeper degree of affliction.

Sir

Sir GEORGE.

Upon my word I think there is much reaſon in this argument.

WILLOUGHBY.

Ay, and much policy too, Sir George — we ſhou'd always imagine that every thing happens for the beſt—about ten years ago I broke my leg by a fall from a horſe—

DORMER.

And pray did this prove a fortunate accident?

WILLOUGHBY.

Yes; for your father, who generouſly pitied my ſituation, got my place continued to my family; ſo that, if I drop off to-morrow, there's a comfortable proviſion for them—Indeed when the accident happened I cou'dn't foreſee this conſequence — however, I made the beſt of matters—was thankful that I hadn't broke both my legs, and drew a kind of negative good fortune from a ſtroke of real calamity.

Sir GEORGE.

Why what the devil is this fellow Dormer laughing at?

DORMER.

Why how the devil can I help laughing, when the very evils of life are made ſo many indirect inſtruments of happineſs.

WILLOUGHBY.

Oh! let him laugh, Sir George; he can by no means joke me out of my ſentiments—why when my ſon was ſtolen from me in his infancy—I found a conſolation in reflecting that I had not loſt my daughter too;—and tho' I have never ſince been able to hear any account of my poor boy, I am ſatisfied he was taken from me for the beſt, and I bear my lot with reſignation.

DORMER.

DORMER.

How! do you ſet down the loſs of your ſon in the chapter of fortunate accidents?

Sir GEORGE.

Negatively he may, Dormer; for he might have turned out a libertine like yourſelf, and in that caſe his being loſt is indeed a very fortunate circumſtance.

DORMER.

Very ſmart truly—but I ſuppoſe you bear your lot with reſignation too, Sir George,—for you have lately got a good two thouſand a year by the death of this young fellow's godfather, old Webly the humoriſt; and it is your intereſt to pray that he never may be found, as there is a certain clauſe in the will you know, which—

Sir GEORGE.

Which obliges me to inveſt him with this eſtate if ever he is diſcovered—a mighty hardſhip really; and you muſt be a very pretty fellow to ſuppoſe it any way difficult for an honeſt man, to do a common act of juſtice.

WILLOUGHBY.

All for the beſt ſtill, Captain.—Sir George we are certain will do good with his fortune,—whereas had it been poſſeſſed by my boy,—how am I ſure that it wou'd not be applied to very different purpoſes: —yet who knows that it might either; —who knows but—however [*ſtifling his emotion*] I am poſitive every thing happened for the beſt, —and ſo—and ſo a good morning to you. [*Exit.*]

Sir GEORGE.

Poor man, how ſenſibly he feels the loſs of his ſon, notwithſtanding his endeavours to be chearful.—But what am I throwing away my time upon you for, when I have buſineſs of ſo much importance with your ſiſter? Good bye, Jack, and now let us ſee if profligates only are to meet encouragement from the ladies. [*Exit.*]

DORMER.

Ha! ha! ha! was there ever ſuch a compound of ſentiment and vanity.—Caroline muſt keep the fellow in a glaſs caſe, or he'll kill himſelf before the honey-moon is over, with the fatigue of ſeeing company. [*Going.*]

Enter Sir JOHN.

Sir JOHN.

Jack, Jack, come back a little—I want a word or two with you.

DORMER.

I fear'd as much [*aſide.*] What are your commands, Sir?

Sir JOHN.

Why, Jack, I need not tell you how anxious I am to have you ſettled in the world, nor is it neceſſary for me to put you in mind of the engagement I enter'd into with my late worthy friend, Sir Ralph Montagu.

DORMER.

I know your obliging ſollicitude for me extremely well, Sir, and I feel it with the moſt grateful ſenſibility,—but ſure there is yet time enough before I undertake the important charge of a family.

Sir JOHN.

Come, come, you have ſeen enough of the world to become, if you pleaſe, a uſeful member of ſociety;—beſides, Miſs Montagu is now without a father, and ſhou'd be treated with an additional degree of attention.—Nothing therefore can be more improper than to keep a young lady of her merit and

and fortune waiting for the reſult of your determination, when you ought to think it a very great honour that ſhe can be prevail'd upon to receive you as a huſband.

DORMER.

Miſs Montagu, Sir, will, I dare ſay, be no way offended at the delay, if I can judge from the indifference with which ſhe conſtantly behaves to me.

Sir JOHN.

And how can ſhe behave otherwiſe, when you conſtantly treat her with indifference?——To be plain with you however, Jack, I fear you are too wild, too diſſipated, to think ſeriouſly:—you moreover poſſeſs a ſpirit of gallantry, which gives me many an uneaſy moment,—and I am not a little troubled at your continual viſits to Mr. Willoughby's.

DORMER.

To Mr. Willoughby, Sir,—to your own particular friend!

Sir JOHN.

Yes, and the more I eſteem him, the more uneaſy I muſt naturally be at your viſiting there ſo frequently.—Miſs Willoughby has a fine perſon, and a feeling heart; ſhe thinks, beſides, I have obliged her father, and may in the fulneſs of her gratitude, imbibe ſentiments for the ſon of his benefactor. — Take care, therefore, take care; gallantry, tho' a faſhionable crime, is a very deteſtable one; and the wretch who pilfers from us in the hour of his neceſſity, is an innocent character, compared to the plunderer who wantonly robs us of happineſs and reputation.

DORMER.

I hope, Sir, I ſhall never do any thing to bring a reflection upon the honour of my family.

Sir

Sir JOHN.

I hope not, Jack, and therefore I cou'd wish you were not a man of gallantry :—to engage the confidence of the innocent on purpose to betray it, is as mean as it is inhuman.

Enter a SERVANT.

SERVANT.

Every thing is ready in the library, Sir.

Sir JOHN.

Very well—[*Exit Serv.*] Come, Jack, think a little on what I have said ;—in my son let me for once find a friend ; — the honour of my family is now materially trusted in your hands, and tho' my tenderness for you may feel at any prostitution of that honour, be assur'd that my justice will never allow me to pardon it. [*Exit Sir John.*

Enter VILLARS.

DORMER.

Well, Villars, I fancy Willoughby has at last made a complaint to my father, for I am commanded, in the most positive terms to think of an immediate marriage with Miss Montagu.

VILLARS.

And isn't it by much the most sensible course you can follow ? — Miss Montagu is a very fine young lady.

DORMER.

True—but you have never seen Miss Willoughby.

VILLARS.

Besides the great fortune—

DORMER.

Miss Willoughby.

VILLARS.

That courts your acceptance, if I may so express myself—

DORMER.

Miſs Willoughby.

VILLARS.

Oh—I ſee how it is;—and are you then determin'd to marry Miſs Willoughby?

DORMER.

Not ſo faſt—not quite ſo faſt, my dear Villars, I beg of you:—Miſs Willoughby certainly poſſeſſes a greater ſhare of my affection than any other woman in the world; and I don't know, if my father could be brought to approve of ſuch a match, that I ſhould find the leaſt diſinclination to marry her: — but as matters ſtand at preſent there's no likelihood of ſuch a circumſtance, and therefore I wou'dn't chooſe to diſoblige Sir John in ſo material a point, eſpecially as my wiſhes with regard to Miſs Willoughby may poſſibly be indulg'd without ſo conſiderable a ſacrifice.

VILLARS.

I don't underſtand you.

DORMER.

Why Miſs Willoughby knew all along of my engagement with Miſs Montagu, and conſequently had no reaſon to ſuppoſe that my intentions cou'd be very matrimonial; beſides, ſhe let nobody into the ſecret of my addreſſes but her ridiculous ſtep-mother, who is a miſerable compound of avarice and affectation:—indeed, to do the young lady juſtice, it was a conſiderable time before ſhe wou'd hear a ſyllable of a tender nature from me, on account of my connection with Miſs Montagu.

VILLARS.

And how did you manage it at laſt?

DORMER.

Why in the cuſtomary manner: — I talk'd a damn'd deal of nonſenſe with a very tragical tone and a very melancholy countenance — exclaim'd againſt

againſt the tyranny of fathers who wanted to force the inclinations of their children from deſpicable motives of intereſt—and curs'd the poor ſtars for giving her ſo much beauty, and making me ſo ſenſible of it: — then preſſing her tenderly by the hand, I uſually ran out of the room, as if in violent emotion, affecting to gulp down a torrent of tears, and left her own pity to be my advocate the moment ſhe recovered the uſe of her recollection.

VILLARS.

What, and did this anſwer your purpoſe, Sir?

DORMER.

Oh, perfectly; the women are inconceivably fond of the pathetic, and liſten to you with rapture if you talk about death or diſtraction—ſpring but the mine of their pity, you ſoon blow their hearts into a flame — and reap more ſervice from an hour of compleat ſubſtantial miſery than from a whole year of the moſt paſſionate adoration.

VILLARS.

Well, Captain, and may I preſume to aſk what uſe you intend to make of Miſs Willoughby's partiality for you?

DORMER.

Why faith, Villars, that's a very puzzling queſtion upon the whole; — notwithſtanding all my levity, you know I have the deepeſt reverence for my father, and he muſt not be diſoblig'd upon any account, — tho' to deal honeſtly with you, I have no mighty inclination to Miſs Montagu.

VILLARS.

And what muſt become of poor Miſs Willoughby?

DORMER.

Why I ſhou'd'nt like to be a raſcal there neither, —yet what can one do; — where a woman's weak enough to encourage the addreſſes of a man whom ſhe knows to be pre-engaged, ſhe gives him a kind of title to deceive her: — besides, Villars, Miss Willoughby has herself shewn a genius for duplicity in this affair which shou'd make a man of any sense a little considerate.

VILLARS.

How so, pray?

DORMER.

Don't you recollect she has deceiv'd her father thro' the whole transaction? and it is a maxim with me that the woman who can forget the sentiments of nature, has half an inclination to forget the sentiments of virtue.

VILLARS.

Poor Miss Willoughby!

DORMER.

You are mightily concern'd for a woman you never saw in your life; however, be easy — I am as sentimental for a libertine, you know, as any fellow in the kingdom, and it shall be Miss Willoughby's own fault if matters are carried to extremities.—But, Villars, step with me to my agent's, and we'll talk farther on this subject:—few people despise money more than myself, and yet there are few to whom a snug sum would at this moment be more acceptable.

VILLARS.

You promise me then that in this affair of Miss Willoughby's—

DORMER.

Zounds, Villars, I won't brag too much neither, —I am still flesh and blood, — and these make a very dangerous composition in the hour of love and opportunity.

VILLARS.

My dear Captain, this is no jesting matter—the happiness of a deserving young lady is at stake, and a laugh will but poorly repay a violation of your honour, or a breach of your humanity. [*Exeunt.*]

END *of the* FIRST ACT.

ACT II.

SCENE, WILLOUGHBY's *House*.

Enter Mr. *and* Mrs. WILLOUGHBY.

Mrs. WILLOUGHBY.

AND ſo my prudenr, ſage, conſiderate dear, you have actually adviſed Sir John Dormer to reſtrain his ſon's viſits to our houſe?

WILLOUGHBY.

Yes, that was my buſineſs at Sir John's this morning.

Mrs. WILLOUGHBY.

And you imagine this wiſe meaſure will turn out for the beſt I ſuppoſe?

WILLOUGHBY.

I do really ——

Mrs. WILLOUGHBY.

What? You think it for the beſt to let your poor family continue always in obſcurity;—and look upon it as a great unhappineſs, whenever they have the leaſt chance of riſing in the world?

WILLOUGHBY.

And you think I have done a mighty fooliſh thing in preſerving the peace as well as the honour of my poor family, from the greateſt of all misfortunes?

Mrs. WILLOUGHBY.

From the greateſt of all misfortunes! did any body ever hear the like?——Why I tell you Captain Dormer is in love, paſſionately in love with your daughter.

WIL-

WILLOUGHBY.

So much the worse —

Mrs. WILLOUGHBY.

So much the worse! this is the only thing in which you ever forgot your all for the best principle. — So much the worse! so much the better I tell you;—and in all likelihood he might have married her, if your ridiculous fear of being happy, had not put Sir John upon his guard, to prevent so desirable a circumstance.

WILLOUGHBY.

What, madam, wou'd you have me trepan the only son of my benefactor, into a marriage with my daughter, and at a time too when I know him engaged to a lady of Miss Montagu's family and fortune.—O, Mrs. Willoughby, I am ashamed of these arguments; and if there is no way to be rich without being despicable, let us look upon poverty as the most eligible of all situations.

Mrs. WILLOUGHBY.

Don't tell me of Miss Montagu's family, Mr. Willoughby, your daughter is not her inferior in that respect;—besides, a woman of beauty, educated as I have educated Cornelia, even if she has not altogether so much money, has merit enough to deserve the first man in the kingdom. — I am sure if I was a single woman again ———

WILLOUGHBY.

You have been a single woman, madam, and are now married to a fellow old enough for your father.

Mrs. WILLOUGHBY.

I don't deserve to be reproach'd by you, Mr. Willoughby;—you are, at least, a gainer by my pity.

WILLOUGHBY.

I think so, my dear — I think all for the best.

Mrs. WILLOUGHBY.

What all for the beſt; my marrying a man as old as my father?—Have a little gratitude, Mr. Willoughby.

WILLOUGHBY.

Well, well, my dear,—'tis fooliſh for a man and wife to quarrel, becauſe they muſt make it up again.—However, we were here talking of Captain Dormer,—and what is our girl's beauty and education to the purpoſe?

Mrs. WILLOUGHBY.

Very much to the purpoſe.—They ſhew there would have been no impropriety in ſuffering Captain Dormer to marry Cornelia, and they ſhew that you behav'd very abſurdly in ſtriving to prevent the advancement of your own daughter.

WILLOUGHBY.

Madam, madam, young women are apt enough to err of themſelves, but a father has indeed a great deal to anſwer for, who expoſes his daughter to unneceſſary temptations—Captain Dormer has been already too ſucceſsful in ſome families of our acquaintance; and if, while we are contriving to trap him into a marriage with Cornelia, he ſhould find it poſſible to rob her of her honour, we ſhall be very properly puniſhed for the baſeneſs of our deſigns.

Mrs. WILLOUGHBY.

And do you think that poſſible, after the ſhare I have had in her education?—tho' I am but her mother-in-law———

WILLOUGHBY.

My good wife, it is by ſuppoſing our own children wiſer than the children of other people, that ſo many are conſtantly ruined.—If we are deſirous, therefore, of preſerving them unſullied,

we

we ſhould always keep them out of danger;—but our ridiculous partiality, conſtantly paints them in the moſt flattering colours of perfection, and we never ſuppoſe them capable of committing the ſmalleſt miſtake, till they are totally undone.

Mrs. WILLOUGHBY.

Well, it is in vain to talk with you;—but remember I ſay, you will always be the enemy of your own family.

WILLOUGHBY.

I ſhall always endeavour, madam, to act as becomes a father,—but I ſhall alſo ſtrive to act as becomes an honeſt man,—and therefore Captain Dormer ſhall have no more interviews with my daughter.

Mrs. WILLOUGHBY.

No?——

WILLOUGHBY.

No.—My avarice ſhall neither lead me to injure the happineſs of my friend's family, nor ſhall my weakneſs betray the honour of my own.—Every thing will, I dare ſay, turn out for the beſt; tho' if the worſt ſhou'd happen, I ſhall ſtill find a conſolation in having taken every juſtifiable method to prevent it. [*Exit.*]

Enter Miſs WILLOUGHBY.

Miſs WILLOUGHBY.

O, madam, I have heard all:—what will become of me?

Mrs. WILLOUGHBY.

Ah, my poor dear child, was there ever ſo prepoſterous a fool as your father!

Miſs WILLOUGHBY.

Dear madam, ſay ſomething to comfort me.—You have kindly made yourſelf the confidant of my ſentiments for Captain Dormer, and I muſt be be the moſt miſerable creature in the world, if my father is inflexibly determined to drive him from the houſe.

Mrs. WILLOUGHBY.

I can ſay nothing to you, Cornelia, but what muſt add to your regret: — there is no hope of any favourable turn in the affairs of our family: — day after day produces freſh diſappointments; and inſtead of having any agreeable proſpect to cheer us as we go on, the view becomes more and more clouded with misfortunes.—No, there's no enduring life upon theſe terms; — no, there's no poſſibility of enduring it.

Miſs WILLOUGHBY.

O that I had never ſeen Captain Dormer,—or that he had been leſs amiable! —

Mrs. WILLOUGHBY.

Ah, my dear child, I know but too well how to pity your diſtreſs: — I have been in love myſelf; ſtrangely as he now neglects my advice, I was once very deſperately in love with your father: — He was the firſt man that ever ſaid a tender thing to me;—and Mexico, if he was dead tomorrow, would not purchaſe a ſingle glance of regard for another, nor the mines of Peru obtain a ſmile of approbation.

Miſs WILLOUGHBY.

Well, madam, it is happy for me that you have yourſelf been ſuſceptible of the ſofter impreſſions, ſince that ſuſceptibility has induc'd you to aſſiſt me, during my acquaintance with Captain Dormer.

Mrs. WILLOUGHBY.

It is happy for you, Cornelia, and it ſhall be happy for you.—My tenderneſs is more than the tenderneſs of a ſtep-mother,—and there is nothing I admire ſo much as conſtancy in love. — My thoughts, therefore, have not been idle on this affair, and I believe you will allow my underſtanding to be tollerable.

Miſs WILLOUGHBY.

The whole world concurs in an opinion of your good-ſenſe, madam, but few entertain a higher idea of it than Captain Dormer.

Mrs. WILLOUGHBY.

The Captain, my dear, is a man of taſte and diſcernment.

Miſs WILLOUGHBY.

And yet I muſt give him up for ever.

Mrs. WILLOUGHBY.

'Tis your own fault;—why won't you take my advice, and make him yours ſecurely?—there is but one way——

Miſs WILLOUGHBY.

O, madam, you know my abhorrence of an elopement——I have often told you——

Mrs. WILLOUGHBY.

Yes, and I have often told you,—that your father's forgiveneſs may be eaſily obtain'd;—but that Dormer once married to that Harriot Montagu, is loſt for ever.—Do you imagine, child, I wou'd adviſe you to an impropriety?

Miſs WILLOUGHBY.

But how can I betray the dignity of my ſex, in propoſing ſo bold a meaſure to the Captain?

Mrs. WILLOUGHBY.

To be ſure it's very bold in a woman who has given away her heart, to make an honourable of-

fer

fer of her hand to a lover.—However, ſtay child—let poor Dormer be forc'd into this marriage with Miſs Montagu,—let him be torn irrecoverably from you,—and let your obſtinacy, like your father's, continually counteract the happineſs of your family;—were you once Mrs. Dormer, very handſome things might be done for Mr. Willoughby.

Miſs WILLOUGHBY.

O, madam, don't attack me in ſo tender a point!

Mrs. WILLOUGHBY.

Come up ſtairs, child;—ſuſpecting your father's buſineſs to Sir John Dormer's this morning, and dreading the conſequence, I have pack'd up all your things ready for an expedition to Scotland: —you muſt determine, therefore, inſtantly;—and if you determine to have Dormer, you muſt act inſtantly too.

Miſs WILLOUGHBY.

What will become of me!

Mrs. WILLOUGHBY.

I don't know what will become of you, if you don't take my advice;—and I am ſure, on the preſent occaſion, I give you advice that wou'd be very agreeable to half the young ladies within the bills of mortality. [*Exeunt.*]

The SCENE *changes to a Room at* Sir JOHN DORMER'S.

Miſs DORMER *and* Sir GEORGE *diſcovered.*

Sir GEORGE.

Nay, my dear Miſs Dormer, there is no bearing ſo unjuſt an inſenſibility to the power of your own attractions.

Miſs DORMER.

Indeed, Sir George, you over-rate my little merits exceedingly;—and probably the greateſt I can boaſt, is my conſciouſneſs of their being contracted within a very limited circle.

Sir GEORGE.

Well, madam, the very modeſty which induces you to decline every pretenſion to the admiration of the world, is but a freſh proof how greatly you deſerve it.

Miſs DORMER.

You have much politeneſs, Sir George, but politeneſs is your peculiar characteriſtic ———

Sir GEORGE.

At leaſt, madam, I have much ſincerity;—and if Sir John's mediation in my favour, together with as fervent an attachment as ever warm'd the boſom can obtain a look of approbation from Miſs Dormer, ſhe may reſt ſatisfied that the buſineſs of my life, will be an unremitting ſollicitude for the advancement of her happineſs.

Miſs DORMER.

I am infinitely honour'd by this declaration,—and I believe there are not many ladies ———

Sir GEORGE.

Why, madam, if the vanity may be excuſed, I flatter myſelf there are not many ladies who wou'd highly diſapprove my addreſſes. — I have more than once reſiſted ſome flattering overtures, and from very fine women too;—but my heart was reſerv'd for Miſs Dormer, and ſhe will make me the happieſt man exiſting, by kindly condeſcending to accept it.

Miſs DORMER.

I am very ſenſible how juſt a value ſhou'd be plac'd

plac'd upon ſuch an affection as yours, Sir George, and it gives me no little ———

Sir GEORGE. [*aſide.*]

So the Captain imagin'd I ſhou'd not ſucceed with her.

Miſs DORMER.

You will pardon my confuſion, Sir George,—but the declaration I am going to make ———

Sir GEORGE.

Will demand my everlaſting gratitude, madam.

Miſs DORMER.

I ſhall be very happy to find you really of this opinion.

Sir GEORGE.

I muſt be eternally of this opinion; condeſcenſion and benignity, madam, are animating every feature of that beautiful face, and I am ſatisfied you will be prevail'd upon, not utterly to diſregard the heart that ſo paſſionately ſolicits your acceptance.

Miſs DORMER.

Indeed, Sir George, I muſt own you are poſſeſs'd of extraordinary merit.

Sir GEORGE.

This goodneſs is too much, madam.

Miſs DORMER.

Your underſtanding is enlarg'd.

Sir GEORGE.

Dear Miſs Dormer!

Miſs DORMER.

Your perſon is unexceptionable.

Sir GEORGE.

You diſtreſs me, madam, by this exceſſive generoſity.

Miſs DORMER.

Your manners are amiable.

Sir GEORGE.

I want words to thank you, madam.

Miſs DORMER.

And your humanity is unbounded.

Sir GEORGE.

What I am, madam, take me:—I am yours and only yours; nor ſhou'd the united graces, if proſtrate at my feet and ſoliciting for pity, rival you a moment in my affection.—No, Miſs Dormer, your happineſs will ever be the ulimate object of my attention, and I ſhall no longer wiſh to exiſt, than while I am ſtudious to promote it.

Miſs DORMER.

Sir George, I fear you miſunderſtand me,—and yet it is in your power to make me very happy.

Sir GEORGE.

How can I miſunderſtand you, my deareſt creature, if it is in my power to make you happy.

Miſs DORMER.

'Tis in your power indeed, Sir George.

Sir GEORGE.

Bewitching lovelineſs, how you tranſport me; —ſo the Captain thought I ſhou'd'nt ſucceed with her. [*aſide.*]

Miſs DORMER.

But if you wou'd wiſh to ſee me happy,——— you muſt withdraw your addreſſes.

Sir GEORGE.

Miſs Dormer!

Miſs DORMER.

It is impoſſible for me ever to return your affection.

Sir GEORGE.

Miſs Dormer!

Miſs DORMER.

And I ſhall be miſerable beyond belief by a continuance of your ſollicitation.

Sir GEORGE.

Miſs Dormer!

Miſs DORMER.

O, Sir George, to the greatneſs of your humanity let me appeal againſt the prepoſſeſſion of your heart. — You ſee before you a diſtreſſed young creature, whoſe affection is already engaged; — and who, tho' ſhe thinks herſelf highly honoured by your ſentiments, is wholly unable to return them.

Sir GEORGE.

I am extremely ſorry, madam,—to have been —I ſay, madam,—that—really I am ſo exceedingly diſconcerted, that I don't know what to ſay. ——

Miſs DORMER.

O, Sir George, you have no occaſion for apologies, tho' I have unhappily too much;—but I know the nicety of your honour, and I depend upon it with ſecurity.—Let me then entreat an additional act of goodneſs at your hands, which is abſolutely neceſſary, as well for my peace, as for my father's: — this is to contrive ſuch a method of withdrawing your addreſſes, as will not expoſe me to his diſpleaſure.—Let the diſcontinuance of them appear, not to be the reſult of my requeſt, but the conſequence of your own determination; he is a zealous advocate for you, and I ſhou'd incur his ſevereſt reſentment, if he was to be acquainted with the real impediment to the match. — You are diſtreſſed, Sir George, and I am ſinking with confuſion; —I ſhall therefore only add that I truſt you with more than life, and that I conjure you to compaſſionate

passionate my situation. — By this conduct you will engage my eternal esteem, and merit that happiness with a much more deserving woman, which it is impossible for you ever to enjoy with me. [*Exit.*]

Sir GEORGE.

What is all this! — a dream!——No, 'tis no dream, and I feel myself awake but too sensibly. — What then, am I rejected, despis'd, where I suppos'd myself certain of success and approbation.—This is too much;—neither my pride nor my tenderness can support the indignity,—and I shall—what shall I do? Shall I meanly betray the poor girl who has generously thrown herself upon my humanity, and convince the world by such a conduct that she was right in refusing me:——no, damn it—I scorn a littleness of that nature, and I must shew myself worthy of her affection, tho' her unfortunate pre-engagement wou'd not suffer me to obtain it. But how in the name of perplexity shall I manage the matter?—A refusal on my side necessarily incurs the general resentment of the family, and the censure of the world into the bargain; — so that in all probability I shall not only have the honour of risquing my life but my reputation, and this for the happiness of giving the woman I admire to the arms of my rival. ———Really the prospect is a very comfortable one. [*Exit.*]

Enter Miss MONTAGU *and* Miss DORMER.

Miss MONTAGU.

Upon my word, Caroline, you have acted a very heroic part;—but this unaccountable love is able to carry the most timid of the romantic ladies thro' the greatest difficulties.—Now had I been

been in your ſituation, I cou'd no more have aſk'd the man to take my fault upon himſelf, than I cou'd have made downright love to him.

Miſs DORMER.

Ah, Harriot, you little know to what extremities a ſtrong prepoſſeſſion is capable of driving a woman, even where there is the moſt evident impoſſibility of ever obtaining the object of her inclinations.

Miſs MONTAGU.

O, my dear, I ſee very plainly that it is capable of driving a woman to very great extremities.

Miſs DORMER.

Well I am convinc'd that if any thing was to prevent your marriage with my brother, you wou'd, notwithſtanding this ſeeming inſenſibility, look upon the reſt of his ſex with the utmoſt averſion.

Miſs MONTAGU.

I wonder, Caroline, after my repeated declarations of indifference with regard to your brother, that you can imagine I conſider him with the ſmalleſt partiality.—There was indeed a time when I might have been prevailed upon to endure the creature,—but his negligence quickly alarmed my pride, and prevented me from ſquandering a ſingle ſentiment of tenderneſs, upon a man who ſeem'd ſo little inclin'd to deſerve it.

Miſs DORMER.

Well, my dear, I am in hopes that you will have but little reaſon to blame his negligence for the future,—becauſe I know he intends this very day to ſolicit your approbation.

Miſs MONTAGU.

O he does me infinite honour, and I ſuppoſe you imagine he is entitled to one of my beſt curtfies for fo extraordinary an inftance of his condefcenfion;—but, Caroline, I am not altogether fo critically fituated as to be glad of a hufband at any rate —nor have I fuch a meannefs of difpofition as to favour any addreffes which are made to me with a vifible reluctance.

Mifs DORMER.

A vifible reluctance, my dear ——?

Mifs MONTAGU.

Yes, Caroline, a vifible reluctance.——'Tis true indeed there are a good many kind-hearted creatures who can ftoop to flatter a fellow's vanity, even while he treats them with contempt;—but I am made of different materials, my dear, — I love to mortify the prefumption of thofe confident puppies, who afk my hand with as much familiarity as if they afk'd a pinch of fnuff, and feem to fay, "fo child, I want to make you the "upper fervant of my family."

Mifs DORMER.

You are a whimfical creature, Harriot, — but how can you contrive to invalidate the contract between my brother and you, if you are even ferious in your determination?

Mifs MONTAGU.

If I can guefs right, your brother will himfelf find a very expeditious method of breaking it.— However, if he fhou'd not, I am in no great hurry for a tyrant, and my Strephon's impudent brow fhall be pretty well loaded with wrinkles, before he finds me in the humour of faying, "whenever you pleafe, good Sir,—and I am "very much oblig'd to you."

Mifs DORMER.

Well, well, Jack muft folicit for himfelf, and I am fure, notwithftanding this pretended want of of feeling, you are no way destitute of good-nature and sensibility.

Miss MONTAGU.

Good-nature and sensibility, Caroline;——ay, 'tis this good-nature and sensibility that makes the men so intolerably vain, and renders us so frequently contemptible.——If a fellow treats us with ever so much insolence, he has only to burst into a passionate rant, and tell a gross lie with a prodigious agitation; —— in proportion as he whines we become softened; till at last, bursting into tears, we bid the sweet creature rise,—tell him that our fortune is entirely at his service, and beg that he will immediately assume the power of making us compleatly miserable

Miss DORMER.

What a picture!

Miss MONTAGU.

While he, scarcely able to stifle his laughter, retires to divert his dissolute companions with our weakness, and breaking into a yawn of insolent affectation, cries, "poor fool she's doatingly fond of me."—However, Caroline, to convince you at once with regard to my sentiments for your brother ——

Miss DORMER.

Well!

Miss MONTAGU.

Let me tell you now you have determin'd against Sir George, that this very coxcomb as you call him, this Narcissus, who can love nothing but himself, according to your account ——

Miss DORMER.

Astonishment!

Miss MONTAGU.

I the only man I shall ever think of seriously.—

There, wonder,—be amaz'd that I don't ſee with your eyes,—and deſpiſe my want of taſte;—I'm a mad girl, you know, and poſſibly like Sir George for his peculiarities,—but ſtill foibles are leſs culpable than faults, Caroline, and the vanities even of a coxcomb are more eaſily cured than the vices of a libertine.

Enter a FOOTMAN.

FOOTMAN.

Mr. Villars ladies, ſends his compliments, and is ready if you are diſengaged, to play over the new air which you commended laſt night at the Opera.

Miſs DORMER.

O we'll wait upon him inſtantly.

[*Exit Footman.*]

Miſs MONTAGU. [*ludicrouſly.*]

O yes, we'll wait upon him inſtantly!

Miſs DORMER.

How can you be ſo provoking, Harriot?

Miſs MONTAGU.

What, provoking to wait upon your Corydon inſtantly.—Come, my ſweet ſhepherdeſs, let me ſhew it to the parlour. [*Exeunt.*]

The SCENE *changes to* WILLOUGHBY'S.

Enter Mrs. WILLOUGHBY.

Mr. Willoughby is return'd I find, and has got the letter Cornelia left for him.—Well, by this time ſhe's with her huſband that is to be, and will, I ſuppoſe, be ſpeedily on her journey.—The Captain can't recede now, and let his father be pleaſed or diſpleaſed, he is ſtill heir to his title and fortune.—What a difficulty I had to ſhew her the neceſſity,—nay the propriety of this meaſure;—

fond

fond as ſhe is of Dormer, it was hardly poſſible to engage her in it, and ſhe ſeem'd at one time more determin'd to give him up for ever, than betray the dignity of the female character. —Dignity indeed—I think I know what belongs to female dignity, as well as moſt people;—theſe very young girls, however, are ſtrange creatures; — their nicety is not in the leaſt wounded when they tell a man they love him.—But O 'tis a deviation from dignity to own they wiſh him for a huſband.—Here comes Mr. Willoughby; —he mus'nt know my ſhare in this tranſaction 'till he finds himſelf happy in the good conſequences, and owns there is at leaſt one ſenſible head in the family.

Enter WILLOUGHBY. [*ſpeaking to a ſervant behind.*]

WILLOUGHBY.

Let a coach be call'd directly,—ſhe muſt certainly be gone off to this libertine Dormer.

Mrs. WILLOUGABY.

Well, have your elevated notions done you any ſervice, or has all turn'd out for the beſt now?

WILLOUGHBY.

Madam, madam, don't diſtract me, — don't diſtract me,—I am ſufficiently miſerable without theſe unneceſſary reproaches.

Mrs. WILLOUGHBY.

O you are! I am heartily glad of it —

WILLOUGHBY.

Yet ſomething whiſpers at my heart that all will ſtill turn out for the beſt —

Mrs. WILLOUGHBY.

Indeed!

WILLOUGHBY.

Yes,—the diſpenſations of providence are always

ways founded on juſtice;——and none are ever ſufferers in the end, but thoſe who have merited the utmoſt ſeverity from its hands.

Mrs. WILLOUGHBY.

Fine philoſophy truly;——and I ſuppoſe you wou'd have thought it for the beſt if you had loſt me, as well as your daughter?

WILLOUGHBY. [*ironically.*]

I wou'd have tried at leaſt, madam, to be as eaſy as poſſible under ſo great a misfortune.

Mrs. WILLOUGHBY.

You wou'd you barbarous man,——but you are miſerable enough without ſuch a circumſtance, and that's ſome comfort to me.——Your obſtinacy has made your only child deſperate, and you have thought it better to run the hazard of her ruin, than to eſtabliſh her happineſs on a certain foundation.

WILLOUGHBY.

I tell you, madam, any diſtreſs is preferable to the perpetration of a crime; and there was no way of acting upon your principles, without the blackeſt ingratitude to the common benefactor of my family.——I feel for the indiſcretion of this unhappy girl with the ſevereſt poignancy, but I rejoice that my partiality for her led the father into no action that could impeach the probity of the man.

Mrs. WILLOUGHBY.

Mighty fine.

WILLOUGHBY.

This, madam, is a conſolation, a great conſolation in this hour of affection; and let me tell you that in the ſevereſt trials, the truly honeſt feel a ſatisfaction, which is never experienced in the moſt flattering moments of a guilty proſperity.

Mrs.

Mrs. WILLOUGHBY.

Well, well, follow your own courſe, and anſwer for the conſequences.——Had my advice been taken, — but who indeed takes ſenſible advice now-a-days;——you never took my advice in your life, and you ſee what the effect has proved to your unfortunate family.

WILLOUGHBY.

A truce with your wiſdom, madam, I beſeech you; for if it only teaches you to be worthleſs, it wou'd be happy for you to be the greateſt idiot in the kingdom:——but I have no time to waſte in words, every poſſible meaſure muſt be taken for the recovery of this infatuated girl ——

Mrs. WILLOUGHBY.

And ſuppoſe you ſhou'd not be able to recover this infatuated girl as you call her,——what medicine will your philoſophy in that caſe adminiſter for ſo great a misfortune.

WILLOUGHBY.

The beſt of all medicines,——the conſciouſneſs of having never deſerv'd it. [*Exit.*]

Mrs. WILLOUGHBY.

Why you ill-bred brute won't you take me along with you.—I muſt go with him to ſee that every thing is conducted with propriety. [*Exit.*]

The END *of the* SECOND ACT.

ACT III.

SCENE *the Park.*

VILLARS *alone.*

INTO how very hopeleſs a ſituation has my fortune at laſt plung'd me, and how unluckily has the very accident which I conſider'd as the moſt happy circumſtance of my life, turn'd out a ſource of diſappointment and diſtreſs. — Here, while I was rejoicing on being entertained by Sir John Dormer, was it poſſible for me to ſuppoſe that his amiable daughter wou'd have made ſo abſolute a conqueſt of my heart. — But on the other hand, was it poſſible to ſee ſo much ſweetneſs, affability, and merit, without the warmeſt admiration? — Yet to what purpoſe do I continually indulge myſelf in thinking of Miſs Dormer?—My lot in life is as precarious as it is poor, whereas ſhe is entitled to cheriſh the nobleſt expectations.——'Tis true indeed, Captain Dormer has favour'd me with his friendſhip, and I am in hourly hope of an enſigncy by his means—And will an enſigncy——No——I'll lock the ſecret eternally in my boſom, and ſince I cannot raiſe myſelf up to the importance of her proſpects, ſhe ſhall never be reduc'd to the penury of mine.

Enter DORMER.

DORMER.

All alive and merry, my dear Villars, I am now in caſh enough; but here my boy is the commiſſion I have been ſoliciting for you.—'Tis juſt ſign'd,—and you muſt do me the additional favour of accepting this note to buy regimentals.

VIL-

VILLARS.

You overwhelm me with this generoſity—

DORMER.

Nay, no heſitating,—you ſhall give me a draft upon the agent for the money, or do any thing your ridiculous nicety requires, ſo you only condeſcend to oblige me.

VILLARS.

I am at a loſs for words to ——

DORMER.

I am very glad of it, as I don't want to be thank'd for an act of common juſtice; the neceſſities of the worthy have a conſtant claim upon the ſuperfluities of the rich, and we in reality only pay a debt, where the world imagines we confer an obligation.

VILLARS.

This way of thinking is ſo noble, that ——

DORMER.

Poh,—poh,—poh man, let's have none of theſe elaborate acknowledgements, eſpecially at this time—when I have news for you;—ſuch news,—wou'd you believe it, Miſs Willoughby has actually left her father, and is now at my private lodgings in Pall-mall.

VILLARS.

You aſtoniſh me!

DORMER.

Read this letter, and it will inform you of every thing.

VILLARS *reads.*

"My deareſt Dormer, my unrelenting father "has this morning commanded me, never to re- "ceive a viſit from you more ——

DORMER.

There's a touch of the pathetic, Villars. —— My unrelenting father has this morning commanded me, never to receive a viſit from you more. [*ludicrouſly.*]

VILLARS.

" But there's no poſſibility of exiſting without
" my Dormer ——

DORMER.

But there's no poſſibility of exiſting without my Dormer.

VILLARS.

" I have therefore ſent ſome cloathes, and a
" few ornaments, to the houſe in Pall-mall,
" where I have occaſionally met him, and ſhall
" follow them immediately myſelf ——

DORMER.

And ſhall follow them immediately myſelf.—— Ay, there ſhe drops the heroic, and ſenſibly proceeds to buſineſs.

VILLARS.

" If my Dormer's paſſion is as ſincere and as
" honourable as I think it, he will take inſtant
" meaſures for carrying me to Scotland ——

DORMER.

No——Scotland is too far to the north, Villars ——too far to the north——but mind what follows.

VILLARS.

" And put it out of the power of the moſt ma-
" lignant deſtiny ——

DORMER.

There ſhe's in heroics again, Villars.

VILLARS.

" To rob him of his Cornelia Willoughby."

DORMER.

To rob him of his Cornelia Willoughby.——O you muſt ſpeak that with all the emphaſis of tra-

gedy

gedy tendernefs, man:——your voice muft be broken,——your bofom muft be thump'd,——your eyes muft be fix'd.——Zounds it will never do without a deal of the paffionate.

VILLARS.

How can you turn a woman into ridicule, whofe partiality for yourfelf, is the only caufe of her indifcretion?

DORMER.

And how can you fuppofe that her partiality for me, fhou'd render me blind to the impropriety of her conduct?——I can fee when a woman plays the fool with myfelf, as foon as when fhe plays it with other people.

VILLARS.

Well, but what do you intend to do, you fee her elopement is upon an abfolute fuppofition of your intending to marry her?

DORMER.

I don't know that, nor do I fee how I am bound to take more care of a lady's honour, than fhe choofes to take herfelf.——But even admitting the force of your fuppofition, what can I do?——It is not in my power to marry her, fhe knows herfelf it is not in my power, and I fhou'd cut a very ridiculous figure in the eye of the world, if after a fine girl threw herfelf voluntarily into my arms, with a perfect knowledge of my fituation, I was to read her a lecture of morality with a prim, puritanical phyz, and to cry, "you fhan't ftay "with me, Mifs, you muft go home and be du-"tiful to your papa."

VILLARS.

My dear Captain, a fond woman always judges of her lover by herfelf; and Mifs Willoughby imagines, becaufe fhe is ready to run any rifk for your ſake, that you will as readily run any hazard for her's,—ſhe therefore truſts you ——

DORMER.

Zounds, Villars, how prepoſterouſly you argue;——doesn't every woman who truſts entirely to the diſcretion of a lover,—truſt a robber with her purſe, and an enemy with her reputation? A woman of real principle will never put it into a man's power to be perfidious, and I ſhou'd not care to truſt any of theſe eloping damſels with my honour, who are ſuch miſerable guardians of their own.

VILLARS.

You are a very extrrordinary man indeed, to think meanly of a woman, for giving you the greateſt proof which ſhe can poſſibly ſhew of her affection.

DORMER.

I muſt think meanly of any woman who, gives me an improper proof of her affection, tho' I may be inclin'd to take an advantage of it.

VILLARS.

Indeed!

DORMER.

O, Villars, if the women did but know how we doat upon them for keeping us at a ſenſible diſtance, and how we deſpiſe them where they are forwardly fond, their very pride wou'd ſerve them in the room of reaſon, and they would learn to be prudent even from the greatneſs of their vanity.

VILLARS.

So then you think Miſs Willoughby fair game, now ſhe has ——

DORMER.

Undoubtedly;—formerly, indeed, I had ſome ſcruples on her father's account,—but now ſhe has

has gone this length, there is no resisting the temptation.——As I told you before, Villars, she knows I can't marry her, she knows I am already engag'd,——and what the devil do you think she wants with me——hey?

VILLARS.

Why but ——

DORMER.

Why but, —— why but what? Only consider man what a mind a woman must have, who can plunge her whole family in wretchedness for any fellow's sake; honour believe me, Villars, never took root in a bosom which is dead to the feelings of nature; nor are those in the least to be pitied who are willingly destroy'd.

VILLARS.

Well, well, I stay still ——

DORMER.

But well, well,——I hav'nt time to hear what you wou'd say,——for I want you to go to Pall-mall directly to see that Miss Willoughby is properly accommodated.——I know the moment she is miss'd I shall be suspected, so I'll go to my father's and be in the way there, to save appearances as much as possible,

VILLARS.

Why hav'nt you been at Pall-mall yourself to receive her?

DORMER.

Yes, but I had only time to take a few trifling liberties,——and I am now going to make love very much against my inclination to Miss Montagu——My father read me a damn'd severe lecture this morning, and the best way of preventing any suspicion from fastening on me about Miss Willoughby, is to shew every mark of readiness to comply

comply with his inclinations;—but go, my dear boy, about the businefs, and I'll do as much for you, whene'er a pretty woman brings you into difficulties.

VILLARS.

O, I am much oblig'd to you.

DORMER.

The people of the houfe will admit you directly; —-and remember, that a trifling lie or two muft choak neither of us, if any body fhou'd queftion us about the little run-away.

[*Exeunt feverally.*]

SCENE *changes to Sir* JOHN DORMER'S.

Enter Sir GEORGE.

Sir GEORGE.

Why how the plague fhall I act in this affair, —or with what face can I poffibly tell Sir John that I am defirous of declining an alliance with his family, after I have fo repeatedly folicited his influence with Mifs Dormer.——I promifed to wait till he return'd from the Cocoa-tree——I wifh he was come back with all my heart—for my prefent fituation is none of the moft agreeable.——Upon my word it was a mighty modeft requeft of the young lady, at the very moment fhe refus'd me, to defire I wou'd take the whole blame upon myfelf.——Your women of fentiment, however, have a very extraordinary manner of doing things—— O but here comes Sir John, what the devil fhall I fay to him.

Enter Sir JOHN.

Sir George I give you joy,—joy a thoufand times.—I met Caroline as I was coming up ftairs, and by her filence as well as blufhing, I read

read her readineſs to comply with my wiſhes, and find her the excellent girl I always imagin'd her.

Sir GEORGE.

She is a very excellent young lady indeed, and I am very much oblig'd to her.

Sir JOHN.

You can't now, conceive the tranſport of my heart at her chearful concurrence, but I hope you will one day experience, that a dutiful child is the firſt of all human felicities.

Sir GEORGE.

It muſt be a very great happineſs indeed, Sir John.

Sir JOHN.

Well, Sir George, our lawyers ſhall meet this very evening, and every thing ſhall be ſettled to our mutual ſatisfaction.

Sir GEORGE.

Yes, Sir John, I wiſh to ſettle every thing to your ſatisfaction.

Sir JOHN.

There will be no great occaſion for expenſive preparations.

Sir GEORGE.

O none in the world, none in the world.

Sir JOHN.

I don't ſee any neceſſity you have to move out of our preſent houſe in Berkeley-ſquare.

Sir GEORGE.

Nor I either.

Sir JOHN.

You have room enough there.

Sir GEORGE.

Plenty.

Sir JOHN.

Why what's the matter, Sir George, you ſpeak with an air of coldneſs and embarraſſment that ſurprizes me?

Sir

Sir George.

Sir John, I am incapable of a duplicity.

Sir John.

Well.

Sir George.

And notwithſtanding my wiſhes for Miſs Dormer are as ardent as ſhe is deſerving,—a circumſtance has happen'd, which muſt for ever deny me the bleſſing of her hand.

Sir John.

You aſtoniſh me!—but what circumſtance—ſhe is ready—

Sir George.

Yes, yes, ſhe is very ready, Sir John.

Sir John.

Then pray acquaint me with the impediment.

Sir George.

My dear Sir John, a point, a very nice point of honour prevents the poſſibility of my indulging you in this requeſt: you may, however, ſafely aſſure yourſelf that I am now no leſs worthy of your good opinion, than when you favour'd me with the warmeſt recommendation to Miſs Dormer.

Sir John.

Mighty well, Sir George, mighty well,—and ſo you come into my houſe to ſolicit my influence in your favour, over the affections of my daughter, obtain her approbation, and then, without producing one cauſe for a change in your ſentiments, affront us both in the groſſeſt manner, by inſtantly receding from your engagements.

Sir

Sir GEORGE.

You are warm, Sir John.

Sir JOHN.

Have I not abundant cauſe for warmth, when you deny a reaſon for the affront which on this occaſion you have offered to my family. — If you know any thing in my daughter's conduct that renders her unworthy of your alliance, pronounce it freely — and I ſhall myſelf be the firſt to approve your rejection of her. — But, Sir George, if you capriciouſly decline a treaty which you yourſelf took ſo much pains to commence, without aſſigning a ſufficient cauſe for your behaviour; be aſſur'd I will have ample ſatisfaction. — Nor ſhall the altar itſelf protect you from the united vengeance of an injur'd friend and an inſulted father.

Sir GEORGE.

Sir John, I eaſily conceive the purport of this menace: — but whatever meaſures you intend to take, let me tell you, I ſhall one day have your thanks for the conduct which now excites your indignation; and, let me alſo tell you, that the very moment in which your hand is raiſed againſt my life, will be the moment in which I ſhall prove myſelf the trueſt friend to your family.

Sir JOHN.

Away, away, you are all profeſſion and falſhood. — My daughter told me that you were incapable of loving any thing but yourſelf.

Sir GEORGE.

I thank her very heartily, Sir.

Sir JOHN.

And that the wiſhes of your heart were entirely centred in the admiration of your own adorable perſon.

Sir GEORGE.

O, I am infinitely oblig'd to her.

Sir JOHN.

But inſignificant, as ſhe juſtly repreſented you—

Sir GEORGE.

Inſignificant!

Sir JOHN.

That inſignificence ſhall not be your protection.

Sir GEORGE.

My protection! — So, I want to be protected!

Sir JOHN.

Therefore, unleſs you wou'd prove yourſelf as deſtitute of courage as of honour, meet me at the Cocoa-tree in an hour; we can eaſily have a private room, and, if you fail, I ſhall ſet ſuch a ſtigma on the coward, as will render him a ſcorn even to the greateſt profligate in the kingdom.

[*Exit.*

Sir GEORGE.

So — now I am engag'd in a pretty piece of buſineſs — and muſt hazard my life for a woman, who has not only rejected my addreſſes, but mention'd me with contempt; and danger join'd to inſult is my reward, where, in reality, I ought to meet with thanks and approbation, la la la la lalla, *(hums a French air)* — Well, be it as it will, Miſs Dormer's ſecret ſhall be inviolably preſerv'd. — A thruſt through the guts is, to be ſure, diſagreeable enough, but if fellows every day hazard it in defence of the baſeſt actions, there can be no mighty heroiſm in running a little riſque, to ſupport the cauſe of honour and generoſity. [*Exit.*

SCENE,

SCENE, DORMER'S *Lodgings in* Pall-Mall.

Enter Miſs WILLOUGHBY.

Miſs WILLOUGHBY.

Where ſhall I hide my miſerable head, or how ſhall I avoid the ſtroke of impending deſtruction. — The man who ſhou'd have been the guardian, is himſelf the perſon that attacks my honour, and the unlimited confidence which I raſhly repos'd in his affection, is now made uſe of to cover me with diſgrace. — O that my unhappy ſex would learn a little prudence, and be well convinc'd, when they fly from the imaginary oppreſſion of a father, that they are ſeeking protection from the moſt cruel of all enemies, thoſe who mean to ſacrifice their peace, and blaſt their reputation.

Enter LUCY.

LUCY.

Madam, there is a Gentleman from Captain Dormer come to wait upon you.

Miſs WILLOUGHBY.

What can he want with me?

LUCY.

I really can't ſay, Madam. — But, if you pleaſe, I'll ſend him up, and then you can know his buſineſs from himſelf.

Miſs WILLOUGHBY. [*Walking about in diſorder.*]

How am I inſulted and expos'd! But the woman deſerves no reſpect from others, who does not ſhew a proper regard for her own character.

LUCY. [*Aſide.*]

Lord! what a mighty fuſs we make, though I don't ſee we are a bit handſomer than other people. — Well, Madam, what ſhall I ſay to the gentleman?

Miſs WILLOUGHBY

Shew the gentleman up.

LUCY. [*Pertly.*]

Yes, Madam. [*Exit.*

Miſs WILLOUGHBY.

Whoever he is he cannot increaſe my fears, and may poſſibly bring me ſome intelligence to mitigate their ſeverity.

Enter VILLARS.

VILLARS.

Madam, your moſt obedient. — I wait upon you with Captain Dormer's reſpects, to apologize for his unavoidable abſence a few hours, and to hope that every thing here is quite to your ſatisfaction.

Miſs WILLOUGHBY.

As the Captain, Sir, has engag'd your good offices on this occaſion, I ſuppoſe you are acquainted with the hiſtory of my indiſcretion.

VILLARS.

The Captain, Madam, gave me no particular account of matters, but only ſent me as a friend, on whoſe ſecreſy he cou'd rely, to apologize for his abſence, and to enquire how you approved of this ſituation.

Miſs WILLOUGHBY. [*With emotion.*]

Sir, I don't approve of this ſituation at all.

VILLARS.

I ſhou'd be ſorry, Madam, that my preſence diſtreſſed you.

Miſs WILLOUGHBY.

'Tis not your preſence, Sir, which diſtreſſes me, 'tis the conſciouſneſs of my own folly; 'tis the danger to which I have expos'd myſelf. — But, Sir, your appearance is the appearance of humanity; and I think you look with compaſſion on an unhappy young creature, whom the perfidy of a man too tenderly eſteem'd, has devoted to diſtruction; if you do, Sir, ſave me — I conjure you, by all you hold moſt dear, to ſave me from diſhonour.

honour. — I have been indiſcreet, but not criminal, and the purity of my intention has ſome claim to pity, though the raſhneſs of my flight may be wholly without excuſe.

VILLARS.

Be compos'd, Madam — Pray be composed — You affect me exceedingly. — And you ſhall find a protector in me, if you have any juſt cauſe to apprehend the leaſt violence from Captain Dormer.

Miſs WILLOUGHBY.

If I have any cauſe, Sir. — Why, inſtead of proceeding with me to a place where we might be ſecurely united, am I detained in this unaccountable houſe? — Why did he here attempt liberties, that muſt be ſhocking to the mind of ſenſibility? — And why at his departure did he give the people here orders to confine me to theſe apartments.

VILLARS.

You feel too ſtrongly, Madam.

Miſs WILLOUGHBY.

Can I feel too ſtrongly, Sir, where my everlaſting peace of mind is deſtroy'd; and where the man who declared he only exiſted for my ſake, is cruelly induſtrious to plunge me into infamy? — Unknowing in the ways of the world, I cou'd not diſtinguiſh between the language of ſincerity, and the voice of diſſimulation. — By my own integrity I judg'd of his truth, and cou'd not think that any man wou'd be monſter enough to return a tender partiality for himſelf with diſgrace and deſtruction.

VILLARS.

Madam, there is ſomething in your manner — there is ſomething in this generous indignation

that

that diſpoſes me very warmly to ſerve you, and if you really deſire to leave this houſe, you ſhall leave it inſtantly; the people have directions to obey me in every thing, and I do not think myſelf oblig'd to anſwer Mr. Dormer's expectations, where his demands are evidently contrary to the principles of virtue.

Miſs WILLOUGHBY.

Sir you charm me with theſe ſentiments.

VILLARS.

Madam, they are ſentiments which ſhould regulate the conduct of every man; for he who ſuffers a bad action to be committed when he has the power of preventing it, is, in my opinion, as guilty as the actual perpetrator of the crime.

Miſs WILLOUGHBY.

I am eternally indebted to this generoſity, Sir.

VILLARS.

Not in the leaſt, Madam. — For, abſtracted from my general abhorrence of what is indefenſible, I find, I know not how, an irreſiſtable inclination to ſerve you. — But we loſe time. — I'll order a coach directly to the door, and leave you at perfect liberty to follow your own inclinations.

Miſs WILLOUGHBY.

I have a fix'd reliance on your honour, Sir, and only lament that I have nothing but thanks to ſhew my gratitude for this goodneſs.

VILLARS.

My dear Madam, your thanks are more than I deſerve. What I have done, humanity made my duty; and the moſt contemptible of mankind, is he who declines the performance of a good action becauſe he has not an expectation of being rewarded.

END *of the* THIRD ACT.

ACT

ACT IV.

SCENE, *Sir* JOHN DORMER's.

Enter DORMER *followed by* WILLOUGHBY.

WILLOUGHBY.

CAPTAIN Dormer, don't keep me on the rack, but give me up my daughter.

DORMER.

Sir, I have repeatedly told you—

WILLOUGHBY.

Yes, Sir, you have repeatedly told me, that you are wholly unconcern'd in her flight—But this is the only thing in which I cou'd find it any way difficult to believe you.

DORMER.

Mr. Willoughby, this doubt of my veracity is neither kind nor delicate.

WILLOUGHBY.

Don't insult me, Captain Dormer, while you are loading me with calamity, or possibly I may forget that you are the son of my benefactor.—However, Sir, I do not come here to menace, but to supplicate.—I do not come here to provoke the warmth of your temper, but to interest the sensibility of your heart.—You see me a distress'd, unfortunate, miserable old man.—The whole happiness of my life is wrapp'd up in the inconsiderate girl you have stolen from my arms—and if she is not instantly return'd, my portion will be distraction.—Restore her therefore, I beseech you, and restore her while she is innocent.—The

blow

blow is a barbarous one, which is aim'd at the boſom of a friend; and the triumph is deſpicable indeed, which is purchaſed at the expence of humanity.

DORMER. [*Aſide.*]

Why, how contemptible a raſcal is a libertine!

WILLOUGHBY.

For pity's ſake give me back my child; nor deſtroy, in your giddy purſuit of pleaſure, the eternal peace of a man who wou'd readily riſque his life for the advancement of your happineſs. — You have generoſity, Captain Dormer, and you have underſtanding — yet you combat the natural benevolence of your heart, and oppoſe the evident ſenſe of your own conviction: You are cruel, becauſe it is gallant; and you are licentious, becauſe it is faſhionable. — But, Sir, let my diſtreſs, my anguiſh, reſtore you to yourſelf, and teach you, in ſome meaſure, to anticipate the feelings of a father. Early in life an only ſon was taken from me; and the evening of my days is now to be mark'd with the pollution of an only daughter. — O! Mr. Dormer, you men of pleaſure know not how wide a ruin you ſpread in the progreſs of your unwarrantable inclinations. — You do not recollect, that, beſides the unhappy victim ſacrific'd, there is a family to participate in her injuries; a mother, perhaps to die at her deſtruction, and a wretch like me to madden at her diſgrace.

DORMER.

I cannot be the raſcal I intended. [*Aſide.*] Sir, — Mr. Willoughby, be ſatisfied. — Miſs Willoughby is ſafe and well — nor ſhall I ever entertain a wiſh to diſturb your happineſs, or to injure her reputation.

WILLOUGHBY.

Eternal bleſſings on you for this generous declaration. — But, if you ſpeak your real ſentiments, conduct me inſtantly to my child.

DORMER.

With pleaſure, Sir — and I have great reaſon to imagine, that the anxiety ſhe has ſuffer'd in conſequence of this little Indiſcretion, will make her additionally worthy of your affection.

WILLOUGHBY.

Why, I always ſaid, that every thing happens for the beſt; and that many accidents are really bleſſings in diſguiſe, which we lament as abſolute misfortunes.

DORMER.

Your philoſophy will be juſtified in the preſent caſe, I aſſure you.

WILLOUGHBY.

Give me your hand, Captain. — I eſteem you more than ever. — But come; I am impatient to ſee my poor girl. — Her fault was the reſult of her inexperience; and if we were all to be puniſh'd for the errors of indiſcretion, what wou'd become of the beſt of us?

DORMER.

Juſtly conſider'd, Sir.

WILLOUGHBY.

Come along, come along, man: I want to be gone — and my miſerable wife, whom I didn't care to bring in, for fear ſhe ſhou'd be clamorous, waits for me in a coach at the end of the ſtreet.

DORMER.

I attend you, Sir — yet, if half the gay fellows about town were inform'd of the buſineſs I am going upon — I fancy they'd laugh at me pretty heartily.

WILLOUGHBY.

Ah, Captain! a man of ſenſe ſhou'd deſpiſe the ridicule of the profligate, and recollect, that the laughter of a thouſand fools is by no means ſo cutting as the ſeverity of his own deteſtation. [*Exeunt.*

SCENE *changes to another Apartment in Sir* JOHN DORMER'S.

Enter Miſs MONTAGU *and Miſs* WILLOUGHBY.

Miſs WILLOUGHBY.

Thus, my dear Madam, have I given you the whole hiſtory of my infatuation; and I have now only to repeat my ſincere concern for thinking it poſſible that Captain Dormer cou'd be inſenſible of your very great merit, and to intreat the favour of your interpoſition with my father.

Miſs MONTAGU.

My dear girl, there is no occaſion whatſoever for this generous apology.

Miſs WILLOUGHBY.

Indeed, Madam, there is—I was unpardonably vain in attempting to diſpute a heart with you, and I was extremely culpable, in forgetting how much the completion of my own wiſhes might diſturb the peace of a family, to which my father had ſo many obligations.

Miſs MONTAGU.

My dear Miſs Willoughby, we women are all fools when we are in love, and it is but natural that our own happineſs ſhou'd be more immediately the object of our attention than the happineſs of other people—But I want to aſk you a queſtion about this recreant of ours, to which I beg you will give me an ingenuous anſwer.

Miſs

Miſs WILLOUHGBY.

Pray propoſe your queſtion, Madam.

Miſs MONTAGU.

Then, my dear, ſuppoſe matters cou'd be ſo brought about, that Sir John wou'd approve the Captain's attachment to you, cou'd you, tell me candidly, forgive the inſolent uſe which he has juſt made of your generoſity?

Miſs WILLOUGHBY.

Dear Miſs Montagu, why do you aſk me ſuch a queſtion?

Miſs MONTAGU.

Becauſe I am pretty ſure you may ſtill have him, if you think him worth your acceptance.

Miſs WILLOUGHBY.

I really don't underſtand you.

Miſs MONTAGU.

You ſhall underſtand me then—I never will marry Captain Dormer.

Miſs WILLOUGHBY.

Madam!

Miſs MONTAGU.

He's not a man to my taſte.

Miſs WILLOUGHBY.

No!

Miſs MONTAGU.

No—he is worſe to me, to make uſe of an affected ſimile, than prepar'd chicken gloves, or almond paſte.

Miſs WILLOUGHBY.

Indeed!

Miſs MONTAGU.

Yes—he is more offenſive than Naples dew, or Venitian cream, the eſſence of daffodil, or the Imperial milk of roſes.

Miſs WILLOUGHBY.

You can't be ſerious ſurely—not like him!

Miſs MONTAGU.

No, poſitively, I do not like him.

Miſs WILLOUGHBY.

Why, where can there be ſo—

Miſs MONTAGU.

O bravo.
" Is he not more than painting can expreſs,
" Or youthful poets fancy when they love."

Miſs WILLOUGHBY.

You reprove me very juſtly, Madam—and I bluſh to ſpeak of a man with ſoftneſs, whom I ſhou'd always conſider with indignation.

Miſs MONTAGU.

Come, come, my dear, the Captain is a very agreeable young fellow after all—But I know he is as indifferent about me, as I can poſſibly be about him, and I ſhou'd never have a ſyllable of the tender kind from him—if he was not extremely unwilling to diſoblige his father.

Miſs WILLOUGHBY.

Has he yet declar'd himſelf, Madam?

Miſs MONTAGU.

Why, not expreſſly—but I expect him every moment to open with the uſual formality, and if you pleaſe, we can not only render the ſcene a whimſical one, but make him ſmart very ſenſibly for the liberties of this morning.

Miſs WILLOUGHBY.

In what manner pray?

Miſs MONTAGU.

Why the moment he comes, you ſhall retire into this cloſet—and in the midſt of all his profeſſions to me, I ſhall take an opportunity of mentioning

tioning your name with an air of jealous resentment.

Miss WILLOUGHBY.

Well!

Miss MONTAGU.

This I am sure will induce him to make violent protestations, that this heav'nly face of mine alone is the object of his adoration; and, as the men think it no way dishonourable to tell a trifling little fib to a woman, I shall soon have him vowing everlasting fidelity and swearing,

"The envious moon grows pale and sick with grief,
"That I, her maid, am far more fair than she."

Miss WILLOUGHBY.

I conceive the whole design, Madam.

Miss MONTAGU.

Well then, when he is in the meridian of all his nonsense—do you steal softly out of the closet and sit in that chair—I'll take care that he doesn't see you—If he forswears his passion for you, give him a gentle pull by the sleeve—and, looking him stedfastly in the face, leave all the rest to accident.

Miss WILLOUGHBY.

I am afraid I shan't have spirits to go through with it.

Miss MONTAGU.

Courage, child; havn't I given you spirits enough in declaring that I'll never marry him?—I think you said my woman let you in, and that you saw nobody else.

Miss WILLOUGHBY.

Yes.

Miss MONTAGU.

Why then she shall keep your being here a secret from every body, and I warrant we'll pay the Captain off pretty handsomely—but why so melancholy?

Miſs WILLOUGHBY.

Why, my dear Miſs Montagu, I don't know, if in juſtice to you, I ſhou'd think any more of Dormer — he has ſo many accompliſhments —

Miſs MONTAGU.

Well, my dear, to make you entirely eaſy, there is a man in the world who is, in my opinion, much more accompliſh'd ; — but not a word to any body on this matter for your life — I only mention it to you in confidence, and to ſhew the probability of your yet being happy with Dormer.

Enter JENNY.

JENNY.

Madam, the pens and paper are laid in the next room.

Miſs MONTAGU.

Very well — go — and Jenny —

JENNY.

Madam.

Miſs MONTAGU.

Don't give the leaſt hint to any of the family that Miſs Willoughby is here.

JENNY.

By no means, Madam. [*Exit.*

Miſs MONTAGU.

And now we'll prepare a letter to your father — But come, my dear girl, you muſt not be ſo dejected — Your little error is amply attoned for by the generoſity of this conduct ; and there are ſome faults which, like happy ſhades in a fine picture, actually give a forcible effect to the amiable light of our characters. [*Exeunt.*

SCENE

SCENE *changes to the* Pall-mall *apartments.*

Enter WILLOUGHBY, *Mrs.* WILLOUGHBY, DORMER, *and* LUCY.

DORMER.

Come in, my dear Sir — come in — don't be alarm'd Miſs Willoughby — your father is prepared to overlook every —— Why, ſhe isn't here!

LUCY.

Pray, Sir, didn't I tell you ſo?

Mrs. WILLOUGHBY.

What isn't ſhe here?

LUCY.

No, Madam.

WILLOUGHBY.

No!

LUCY.

Lord bleſs you, Sir, didn't I tell you ſo as you came up?

DORMER.

And where is ſhe gone to?

LUCY.

Do you deſire I ſhou'd tell the truth?

WILLOUGHBY.

Ay, ſpeak the truth child, and fear nothing — But let's take a peep into this room.

[*Goes into another room.*

LUCY.

Then the truth is——

Mrs. WILLOUGHBY.

That's a good girl, ſpeak up.

LUCY.

The truth is, I don't know where ſhe's gone.

DORMER.

Death and confuſion, — where can ſhe be gone to?

LUCY.

That I don't know, as I ſaid before — But ſhe went with your friend — the gentleman you ſent here on a meſſage to her. [*Exit.*

Mrs. WILLOUGHBY.

O, ſhe's gone away with a friend of your's, is ſhe — for ſhame Captain Dormer — you a tender lover — you animated with that exquiſite ſoftneſs which ſouls of ſenſibility feel.

DORMER.

Death, Madam, why will you teaze me in this manner—I tell you I have been betray'd.——

Re-enter WILLOUGHBY.

WILLOUGHBY.

No, Sir, it is I who am betray'd. — And ſo a friend of his has carried her off.

[*To Mrs. Willougbby.*

Mrs. WILLOUGHBY.

Yes, and every thing happens for the beſt now — does not it?

DORMER.

Mr. Willoughby, hear me.

WILLOUGHBY.

Captain Dormer, after this re-iterated inſult, this aggravated cruelty — 'tis infamous to talk with you. — However, Sir, old as you think me, and little as you dread my reſentment, you ſhall feel it heavily. — No! injur'd as I am, you ſhall never receive a ſtroke from me. — I am too miſerable myſelf by the loſs of a child, to ſtab my beſt benefactor even in the perſon of a worthleſs ſon. — You are therefore ſafe

afe. — Safe as the fears of cowardice can wiſh. — But, if you have feelings, to thoſe feelings I conſign you. — They will wake a ſcorpion in that boſom to avenge my wrongs. — For know, though bad men may find it poſſible to elude the juſtice of a whole univerſe, they are yet utterly without means of flying from their own recollection.

DORMER.

Mr. Willoughby, let me only explain the matter——

WILLOUGHBY.

Sir, I'll talk to no monſters.

DORMER.

Dear Mrs. Willoughby, your huſband is ſo impetuous —

Mrs. WILLOUGHBY.

Don't ſpeak to me, Sir — don't ſpeak to me. — A perfidious lover ſhall never gain an audience from Mr. Willoughby. — But, my dear, — what do you intend doing?

WILLOUGHBY.

Pray, Madam, don't teaze me.

Mrs. WILLOUGHBY.

Why, you ill-natur'd — but I won't forget the bounds of propriety — eſpecially as you are not madman enough to fight — It wou'd be little for the better if you were killed.

WILLOUGHBY.

Death, Madam, any thing wou'd be for the better, that ſet me free from your intollerable impertinence. [*Exit.*

Mrs. WILLOUCHBY.

Did the world ever hear ſuch a vulgar fellow — But theſe huſbands have no more breeding! — And here he has gone without giving me his hand. — In a little time I ſuppoſe the fair ſex will be entirely neglected. — [*Going, returns.*] But, Sir, a word in your ear. — You are a base man. — I would not violate propriety for the world — but you are a base man. Sir John shall know every thing instantly. — 'Twas I that urg'd my poor girl to repose that implicit confidence in your honour — and since my advice has lost — my assiduity will do any thing to recover her. [*Exit.*

DORMER.

Why, how just is it that profligacy shou'd be constantly attended with punishment, and how reasonable is it, that those who make no scruple of wounding the happiness of others, shou'd be conspicuously miserable themselves. — How shall I look my father in the face, when this matter comes to be known; or how shall I see this unhappy old man, whom I have so infamously wrong'd. — What a poor, what a paltry, what a merciless passion, is this passion of gallantry; yet it reflects no scandal whatever upon it's followers, though it begins in the most despicable falshood, and terminates in the most irreparable destruction. — A man of gallantry, is the only wretch who can despise the sense of shame, and stifle the feelings of gratitude without reproach; take him into your house, he attempts the sanctity of your bed; — load him with obligations, and he betrays the purity of your daughter. — The sensible world however allows him to be a man of honour all the time, and he stabs you with impunity to the heart for presuming to complain of your wrongs. — Why did not I see the blackness of this character a little earlier. — But — no — My cursed pride would resist the arguments of my conviction. — And for a pitiful triumph over an unsuspecting innocent, I must basely divest myself both of reason and humanity. Where can this girl be fled to? — Villars I am sure is incapable of betraying me, and as she came here with her own con-

sent

ſent ſhe was prepared for the conſequences of courſe.

Enter VILLARS.

My dear Villars you are come moſt luckily, here Miſs Willoughby is gone off, and the people of the houſe have the impudence to ſay, by your means.

VILLARS.

Well, and they ſay very juſtly.

DORMER.

How's this?

VILLARS.

I ſuffer'd her to eſcape — I aſſiſted in her eſcape — and am now ready to anſwer for the conſequences.

DORMER.

Indeed!

VILLARS.

But firſt, Sir, let me return you the commiſſion, and the note with which you were this morning ſo kind as to preſent me. — I do not mean to keep your favours while I counteract your views, and I ſcorn to profit by the generoſity of any man, unleſs upon terms that merit my approbation.

DORMER.

Death and the devil, Sir, how dare you uſe me in this manner: how dare you betray my confidence ſo ſcandalouſly, draw, and give me inſtant ſatisfaction.

VILLARS.

I came here on purpoſe to give you ſatisfaction — but before I draw ſuffer me to aſk a queſtion or two in my turn. — And now, Sir, how dare you ſuppoſe, that I was to be made the inſtrument of your licentiouſneſs; how dare you ſuppoſe that I

 wou'd

wou'd be the pander to your vices, and join with you in a barbarous contrivance of deſtroying a young creature, whoſe inexperience was her only crime?

DORMER.

Here's a fellow!

VILLARS.

But I ſuppoſe you inſulted me on account of my ſituation, and imagin'd, becauſe I was poor that I was conſequently worthleſs; however, Sir, be now undeceiv'd, and, in the midſt of your affluence, and my poverty, know, that I am your ſuperior, for the beſt of all reaſons, becauſe I diſdain to commit a deſpicable action.

DORMER.

I am aſtoniſh'd at the very impudence of his rectitude, and can't ſay a ſyllable to him.

VILLARS.

When I came here, inſtead of a willing victim to your wiſhes, I found Miſs Willougby in the utmoſt affliction, conſcious of her indiſcretion in flying from her father, and ſhuddering with apprehenſion of violence from you. — She ſoon inform'd me of her fears, and lamented, in the moſt pathetic terms, how greatly ſhe had been deceiv'd in the object of her affection. — She imagin'd an honourable union with you, wou'd have been the conſequence of her flight; and little ſuppoſed that the man ſhe lov'd wou'd make uſe of her partiality for himſelf to cover her with diſgrace. — Thus diſappointed, thus betray'd, ſhe aſk'd for my protection, ſhe receiv'd it — and now, Sir, *(drawing)* take your revenge.

DORMER.

Yes, Sir, I will take my revenge, but it ſhall be thus: *(throwing down his ſword and ſhaking Villars*

Villars by the hand) Thus, my dear Villars, let me thank you for the ſuperiority of your principles; I am myſelf juſt awakened to a ſenſe of true honour, and cannot, now I know the real motive of your conduct, reſent, as an injury, what I muſt look upon with the higheſt admiration.

VILLARS.

How agreeably you ſurprize me, Sir.

DORMER.

Dear Villars, take theſe trifles again, or I ſhall not think you forgive me. *(Villars accepts the commiſſion, &c.)* But, my poor girl — and ſo ſhe has principle after all — what a raſcal have I been! — Do tell me where ſhe's gone.

VILLARS.

Indeed I cannot. — I only ſaw her into a coach; but I ſuppoſe ſhe is returned to her father's.

DORMER.

No — ſhe is not — her father is but juſt gone — he came to me, as I ſuſpected, on the very firſt knowledge of her flight; and ſhew'd ſo deep a diſtreſs, that I cou'dn't perſevere in my deſign of ſeeming wholly ignorant of her elopement.

VILLARS.

Well!

DORMER.

I therefore brought him here to give her back; and the poor man was actually in extaſies — but when he found ſhe was gone, he loſt all patince; and, naturally enough, imagining that ſhe was carry'd off by my contrivance, treated me with a freedom, which nothing but the conviction of my guilt could enable me to endure, even from the father of Miſs Willoughby.

VILLARS.

Upon my word, this affair has drawn you into a very diſagreeable ſituation.

DORMER.

DORMER.

Into a diſagreeable ſituation! — into a damn'd one — and I ſhall hate the word Gallantry as long as I live. — My friend's daughter too! — ſhame — ſhame — ſhame — Zounds! Villars, a man ought to be good even from policy, if he is not ſo from inclination. — Damn it; you don't know half the perplexities of my ſituation.

VILLARS.

No!

DORMER.

No. — Diſtracted as I am, I muſt aſſume a calm unruffled face immediately, before Miſs Montagu.

VILLARS.

What, are you going to Miſs Montagu directly?

DORMER.

Yes, inſtantly. — I have myſelf requeſted a tete a tete, to make a formal declaration — and truly I am in a pretty frame of mind to make love to a woman of her vivacity.

VILLARS.

Why, indeed, your hands are pretty full of buſineſs.

DORMER.

Yes, yes, I have buſineſs enough; and my father will know every thing preſently. — But I muſt be a man of gallantry, and be damn'd to me! — Villars, you now ſee, that the greateſt of all idiots is he who makes himſelf deſpicable to deſtroy his own happineſs. [*Exeunt.*

SCENE *changes to a Room at the* Cocoa-tree.

Sir GEORGE (*alone.*)

Well, here I am; and a pleaſant affair I have to go through! — I wiſh it was well over: —

For

For, though there may be a great deal of bravery in venturing one's life, I can't ſay that there is a great deal of ſatisfaction.

Enter a WAITER.

WAITER.

Sir John Dormer, Sir.

Sir GEORGE.

Shew Sir John up. — Now for it.

The WAITER *returns, introducing* Sir JOHN, *and exits.*

Sir GEORGE.

Sir John, your moſt obedient.

Sir JOHN.

Well, Sir George; I ſee you are a man of courage at leaſt; and ſo far I find you worth my reſentment.

Sir GEORGE.

No reproaches now, my dear Sir John: For the greateſt enemies make a point of being perfectly well bred, when they are going to cut one another's throats.

Sir JOHN.

Then, Sir George, that I may anſwer your ideas of politeneſs, let me beg of you to draw inſtantly.

Sir GEORGE.

There is no refuſing a requeſt which is made with ſo much civility; and now, Sir, I am all obedience to your commands.

Sir JOHN.

And now to puniſh the infamous inſult which has been offer'd to my family.

Miſs DORMER *ruſhes from a door at the head of the ſtage; and, falling upon her knees, exclaims,*

Then puniſh it here, Sir: For I alone am culpable.

Sir

Sir JOHN.

How's this!

Miſs DORMER.

O Sir, hear me with pity: For the dread of your reſentment is inſupportable.

Sir GEORGE.

A lady upon her knees! Pray, Madam, ſuffer me raiſe you up.

Miſs DORMER.

No, Sir George: This attitude beſt becomes a creature like me, who has not only expos'd her benefactor to danger, but even rais'd a ſword againſt the life of her father.

Sir JOHN.

Riſe, Caroline.—But tell me, in the name of wonder, what am I to underſtand by this?

Miſs DORMER.

My indiſcretion, Sir—my diſobedience:—For, though you have ever treated me with the moſt unbounded indulgence, I have nevertheleſs ungratefully diſappointed your views, and plac'd my affection upon an object that can never be intitled to your approbation.

Sir GEORGE.

So my throat ſeems to be pretty ſafe this time.

Sir JOHN.

Go on.

Miſs DORMER.

Actuated by my regard for this object, though utterly deſpairing to obtain him, I truſted Sir George with the ſecret, in the fulneſs of my heart; and begg'd he would not only withdraw his addreſſes, but withdraw them in ſuch a manner, as might ſave me even from the ſuſpicion of any unwillingneſs to pay an implicit obedience to your commands.

Sir

Sir JOHN.

This is very extraordinary.

Sir GEORGE.

Yes, but it's very true for all that.

Miſs DORMER.

Sir George ſaw my diſtreſs, and kindly complied with my requeſt; and hadn't I accidentally overheard the altercation which produc'd this meeting, the beſt of fathers or the nobleſt of men (*pointing to Sir* George) had perhaps fallen a ſacrifice to the unhappy prepoſſeſſion of an inconſiderate daughter.

Sir GEORGE.

I never knew ſo ſenſible a woman in my life.

Miſs DORMER.

Diſtracted at the extremity to which matters were carried, I knew not how to act—The moment I was capable of reſolving, I reſolv'd to fly here and wait for your arrival—not coming to any determination till you, Sir, and Sir George had quitted the houſe—here I hinted to the people my apprehenſion of a miſunderſtanding between you, and deſir'd to be plac'd in the next room to that which he told me was reſerv'd for your uſe—the reſt is already known—and I am now to intreat Sir George's forgiveneſs, for the danger to which his unexampled greatneſs of mind had ſo nearly expos'd him—and to implore your pardon, Sir, for daring to entertain even a hopeleſs prepoſſeſſion, when I knew it muſt combat with the favourite object of your inclinations.

Sir GEORGE.

Come, Sir John—what the devil are you dreaming of—you and I are friends now—and therefore we need not ſtand altogether upon ceremonies.

Sir JOHN.

I am confidering, Sir George, whether I ought moft to be pleas'd, or offended with my daughter.

Sir GEORGE.

Zounds, man, be pleas'd with her, for it will be moft to your own fatisfaction.

Sir JOHN.

Then, Caroline, let me tell you that I am charm'd with your franknefs upon this occafion — though I am forry it was not fhewn a little earlier — had you ingenuoufly told me the fituation of your heart when I talk'd to you this morning, you wou'd have fav'd yourfelf much anxiety, and prevented me from behaving in a manner to Sir George that I muft be eternally afham'd of.

Mifs DORMER.

Indeed, Sir, if you knew my motive—

Sir GEORGE.

Come, come, my dear Mifs Dormer — don't let us pain ourfelves with the recollection of paft anxieties — when we may indulge ourfelves with the profpect of future happinefs — I have no notion of the wifdom that makes us miferable — and therefore, Sir John muft and fhall, if he expects me to overlook his cavalier conduct of to-day, do me the favour to confult your inclinations.

Mifs DORMER.

You are too good, Sir George — but—

Sir JOHN.

Speak up my dear, and tell us candidly who you have diftinguifh'd with your approbation — I am not one of the fathers who wifh to maintain a defpotic authority, nor will I make my daughter wretched, to convince the world that I am mafter in my family.

Sir

Sir GEORGE.

O fye, Sir John, there are a great many good fathers who never refuſe any thing but happineſs to their children.

Miſs DORMER.

I am ſo overwhelm'd with this goodneſs—it is at preſent too much for me. As we go home in the coach I ſhall endeavour to let you know every thing—Eſpecially as the object of my choice is—

Sir JOHN.

Is he a man of merit, my dear—is he a good man—he that is worthy in himſelf, is above the deſpicable neceſſity of ſtealing a reputation from the virtue of his progenitors; the riches of the heart are the nobleſt of all poſſeſſions.

[*Exeunt* Sir John, *and* Miſs Dormer.

Sir GEORGE.

I am entirely of Sir John's opinion—the riches of the heart are the nobleſt of all poſſeſſions, and I don't think that, on the preſent occaſion, I have proved myſelf the pooreſt fellow in the kingdom—notwithſtanding my recent inſignificance.

[*Exit.*

End of the Fourth ACT.

ACT V.

SCENE *Sir* JOHN DORMER'*s* *House*.

Enter Miſs MONTAGU, *and Miſs* WILLOUGHBY.

Miſs MONTAGU.

Why, what can keep this hopeful Corydon of ours.

Miſs WILLOUGHBY,

Poſſibly ſome other attachment.

Miſs MONTAGU.

Jealouſy, Miſs Willoughby—rank jealouſy, my dear girl—O that we ſhou'd be ſuch fools as to beſtow a ſingle thought upon theſe wretched fellows, who are not ſenſible of the obligation.

Enter JENNY.

Madam, Madam, Captain Dormer is coming up. [*Exit.*

Miſs MONTAGU.

To your ambuſh, my dear—and be ſure you watch a proper opportunity of annoying the enemy.

Miſs WILLOUGHBY (*retiring into a cloſet.*)

O you ſhan't have any occaſion to queſtion my generalſhip.

Enter DORMER.

DORMER.

Miſs Montagu, your moſt obedient

Miſs MONTAGU.

Captain Dormer, your moſt devoted humble ſervant.

DORMER.

I am come my dear Miſs Montagu.—

Miſs

Miſs MONTAGU.

I ſee you are, my dear Captain Dormer.

DORMER.

The amiable vivacity of your temper, Madam, has always been an object of my admiration—but I come now to ſolicit you in regard to a ſubject—

Miſs MONTAGU.

Upon which it is criminal I ſuppoſe to exerciſe my amiable vivacity.

DORMER.

I need not inform you, Madam, of the engagement which, ſo happily for me, ſubſiſts between our families—nor need I remind you—

Miſs MONTAGU.

Why then do you give yourſelf this trouble, Sir, if the information is ſo very unneceſſary?

DORMER.

That I may tell you, Madam, I am inexpreſſibly fortunate in the honour of this interview, and that I may aſſure the moſt charming of her ſex the whole felicity of my life materially depends upon her approbation.

Miſs MONTAGU.

Upon my word, a very pretty ſpeech, Captain, and very tolerably expreſs'd—but do you know now, that I look upon the whole buſineſs of making love to be mighty fooliſh, and have no notion of a woman's ſenſe, who is to be flatter'd out of her liberty, by a flimſy compliment to her perſon.

DORMER.

This livelineſs is charming—but you muſt not however rally me out of my purpoſe—ſuffer me therefore, my dear Miſs Montagu, to implore—

Miſs

Miſs MONTAGU.

Now poſitively I muſt ſtop you, for there is no bearing the inſolence of this humility.

DORMER.

What inſolence—my dear Miſs Montague—Is it inſolence thus to fall at your feet—Is it inſolence—

Miſs MONTAGU.

For heaven's ſake Dormer don't make a fool of yourſelf—for I tell you the humbleſt ſupplications with which you men can poſſibly teaze the women, are an unaccountable mixture of pride and abſurdity.

DORMER.

There is ſomething ſo very new in this opinion, Madam, that I ſhould be glad you'd let me know how it is to be ſupported.

Miſs MONTAGU.

O 'tis very eaſily ſupported, if you only ſuffer me to put the general purport of all love addreſſes, from the time of the firſt pair, down to the preſent hour, into ſomething like plain Engliſh.

DORMER.

Pray do.

Miſs MONTAGU.

Why then ſuppoſe, that a tender lover, like you, ſhou'd offer up his adoration at the altar of ſome terreſtrial divinity like myſelf, let me aſk you if this wou'd not be the meaning of his pretty harangue, however he might ſtudy to diſguiſe his deſign with the plauſible language of adulation.

DORMER.

Now for it.

Miſs MONTAGU.

Don't interrupt me—Madam, your beauty is ſo exquiſite, and your merit is ſo tranſcendent, that Emperors themſelves might juſtly tremble to ap-

proach

proach you, and languifh in the deepeft defpair of being allied to fo much perfection.

DORMER.

Well faid.

Mifs MONTAGU.

Yet, though all hearts are yours, and though you were born to triumph over an admiring world, I defire you will inftantly appoint me the mafter of your fate—my happinefs depends upon your being a flave, and I muft be eternally wretched, without the power of making you miferable — you muft therefore promife to know no will but my humour, and no pleafure but my inclination— Your prefent ftate of freedom you muft exchange for the moft mortifying dependence, and throw your whole fortune at my feet, for the honour of managing the domeftic concerns of my family. If you—

DORMER.

What the devil is there more of it?

Mifs MONTAGU.

If you behave well, that is if you put up with every caprice of my temper, and every irregularity of my conduct; if you meanly kifs the hand that ftrikes at your repofe, and treat me with reverence when I offer you the groffeft indignities, you fhall have an occafional new gown, and fometimes the ufe of your own chariot— Nay, if you are very good indeed, I may carry my kindnefs ftill farther, and ufe you with nearly as much civility as any of my fervants.

DORMER.

What hav'nt you done yet?

Mifs MONTAGU.

O I cou'd go on for an hour—But what do you think of this fpecimen — Isn't it a true tranflation of all the love fpeeches that have been made fince the

the commencement of the world, and aren't you men a ſet of very modeſt creatures, to ſuppoſe that an addreſs of this elegant nature is calculated to make an inſtant conqueſt of our affections?

DORMER.

This ſpirit is bewitching, and increaſes my admiration, though it treats me with ſeverity.

Miſs MONTAGU.

Well, notwithſtanding the frightful idea which I entertain of matrimony, I am nevertheleſs half afraid I ſhall be at laſt cheated out of my freedom as well as the reſt of my ſex — but then I muſt be perfectly convinc'd of my admirer's ſincerity.

DORMER.

A decent hint that, though I wiſh it had been ſpar'd. — [*Aſide.*] And can you, my dear Miſs Montagu, poſſibly doubt the ſincerity of my profeſſions, and cruelly turn away thoſe irreſiſtible eyes when I vow an everlaſting fidelity? — What, ſtill ſilent, my angel — not a word — not one word to reſcue me from deſtraction — but be it ſo — If Miſs Montagu decrees my fate, I ſubmit without murmuring, for death itſelf is infinitely preferrable to the idea of offending her. [*Going.*] I think I am pretty ſafe now. [*Aſide.*]

Miſs MONTAGU

Now, who wou'd believe that this fellow cou'd lye with ſo very grave a countenance. [*Aſide.*] Why you are in a violent hurry Captain Dormer.

DORMER.

O, zounds, ſhe calls me back does ſhe? [*Aſide.*] What, my dear Miſs Montagu, do you relent, do you feel the leaſt compaſſion for the diſtreſſes of a heart that adores you?

Miſs MONTAGU.

Sit down, Captain. — Sit down here — I am a ſtrange, fooliſh creature — and cannot diſguiſe

my

my ſentiments. — But if I thought myſelf the only object. —

DORMER.

By all my hopes —

Miſs MONTAGU.

Well, don't ſwear — I muſt believe you. — And yet I am ſtrangely apprehenſive that in the extenſive circle of your acquaintance you muſt have form'd ſome attachments. — The world has been talking — and 'tis no ſecret that Miſs Willoughby has accompliſhments.

Miſs WILLOUGHBY *enters unobſerved by* DORMER, *and ſits down.*

DORMER.

Yes, Madam — Miſs Willoughby has accompliſhments, but they are very trifling.

Miſs MONTAGU.

Then you never entertained any tenderneſs for her, I ſuppoſe.

DORMER.

For Miſs Willoughby, Madam — O my dear Miſs Montagu, you don't think me altogether deſtitute of underſtanding!

Miſs MONTAGU.

Why, you juſt now own'd that ſhe had accompliſhments.

DORMER.

Yes, I ſaid that ſhe had trifling ones.

Miſs MONTAGU.

And no more?

DORMER.

The baby's face is regular enough — and might ſerve very well for the window of a toy-ſhop.

Miſs MONTAGU.

Then I find there is nothing to be apprehended on her account.

DORMER.

On her account, my angel, you ſhan't leſſen the merit of your own attractions ſo much as to admit the poſſibility of ſuppoſing it.

Miſs WILLOUGHBY, (*Giving him a pull by the ſleeve.*)

I am very much oblig'd to you, Sir.

Miſs MONTAGU. (*Ludicrouſly.*)

Not a word, not one word to reſcue me from diſtraction ——

Miſs WILLOUGHBY.

The baby's face is regular enough, and might ſerve very well for the window of a toy-ſhop —

Miſs MONTAGU.

But be it ſo — If Miſs Montagu decrees my fate, I ſubmit without murmuring. —

Miſs WILLOUGHBY.

O don't think the Gentleman altogether deſtitute of underſtanding ——

Miſs MONTAGU.

For death itſelf is infinitely more preferrable to the idea of offending her —— There Miſs Willoughby is a man of honour for you —

Miſs WILLOUGHBY.

And are theſe the men who value themſelves ſo much upon their veracity?

Miſs MONTAGUE.

O my dear, they have veracity to a very prudent degree, for they never tell a falſhood to any body who is capable of calling them to an account — But come, Miſs Willoughby, let us leave

leave the Gentleman to himſelf — he has a very pretty ſubject for a reverie, and it wou'd be cruel to diſturb him in his agreeable reflections — Sir, your moſt obedient —— Give it him home, my dear girl — have no mercy on him — [*Aſide to Miſs* WILLOUGHBY.]

Miſs WILLOUGHBY.

Sir, your moſt reſpectful —

Miſs MONTAGU.

That's right — Sir, your moſt oblig'd —

Miſs WILLOUGHBY.

Your moſt faithful —

Miſs MONTAGU.

Bravo! — And moſt devoted humble ſervant. [*Exeunt laughing.*

DORMER. [*After a long pauſe of confuſion.*]

So; I have had a hopeful time on't — my evil genius has been along arrear in my debt, and now pays me off with a witneſs. — What a ſneaking, what a pitiful puppy do I appear — thus detected, and thus laughed at — But I deſerve it all — I woudn't ſee the infamy of practiſing deceit upon a woman — I muſt even think myſelf call'd upon to betray, becauſe the object was a woman; and laugh at the anguiſh I gave a worthy heart, becauſe it was lodg'd in a female breaſt —— Notwithſtanding all my mortification, however, I am overjoyed at finding Miſs Willoughby ſafe — I may now perhaps prevent the matter from reaching my father's ears — not that I fear he will diſcard — but what is infinitely worſe, if he knows it, will eternally deſpiſe me —— How merry the girls were with me — Sir, your moſt reſpectful — Sir, your moſt oblig'd — Sir, your moſt faithful —

Enter Sir JOHN.

Sir JOHN.

Sir, your moſt devoted humble ſervant —

DORMER. [*Aſide.*]

O! now I am completely done for —

Sir JOHN.

Well, Sir, what can be urg'd for you now? — Is this the reformation I was to expect — and is this the regard which you entertain for the credit of your family?

DORMER.

If you'll give me leave to clear this matter up, Sir —

Sir JOHN.

'Tis already clear'd up — Mr. Willoughby — Miſs Montagu have clear'd it up — And now ſuppoſe Mr. Willoughby, liſtening only to the dictates of his rage, and not to the pleadings of his friendſhip for me, had demanded reparation for his wrongs, how, after robbing him of his daughter, cou'd you come prepar'd againſt his life — And how, after deſtroying a young lady's reputation, cou'd you attempt to embrue your hands in the blood of her father? —— But, Sir, you are a man of ſpirit, you are a man of honour, and that ſpirit, and that honour are to be ſufficient pleas for every violence offer'd to juſtice, and ev'ry outrage commited upon humanity—You have a title to be guilty, becauſe you have the character of being brave, and you may perpetrate the blackeſt crime with impunity, becauſe you have the diabolical reſolution to defend it.

DORMER.

There is ſo much propriety in this reproach, Sir — that I feel myſelf unable to anſwer it —

Sir

Sir John.

That ſword I gave you, Sir, to be exerted in the cauſe of honour, not to be drawn in the ſupport of infamy — I gave it to be us'd in the defence of your country, not to be exercis'd in the violation of her laws — but why do I talk of honour to him who looks with admiration upon ſhame, and thinks himſelf accompliſh'd in proportion as he becomes profligate — why do I reaſon with a man who glories in the proſtitution of his underſtanding, and imagines he exalts his character as he deſtroys the peace of ſociety ? — Perhaps, in his ideas of bravery he may be oblig'd even to raiſe his arm againſt my boſom, and perhaps he may puniſh a reproachful mention of his vices, though it comes from the lips of his father.

Dormer.

Sir, I have been culpable — extremely culpable — but my preſent intention is to remove Mr. Willoughby's diſtreſs — not to defend the injury I offered him — and I can with truth affirm, that the principal part of my miſconduct in this affair, originally proceeded from the great veneration which I entertained for that very father, who now thinks me ſo profligate and unnatural.

Sir John.

Mighty well!

Dormer.

I lov'd Miſs Willoughby, Sir, tenderly lov'd her, before you enter'd into any engagement about Miſs Montagu — But fearful of diſobliging you, I kept the circumſtance of my paſſion a ſecret, as I did not ſuppoſe you wou'd countenance a union, where there was ſo material a diſparity of ſituations.

Sir JOHN.

And, pray, Sir, how dare you ſuppoſe that I ſhou'd be more offended at the performance of a good action — than at the commiſſion of a diſhonourable one?—How dare you imagine I ſhou'd be diſpleas'd at your marriage with Miſs Willoughby, and that I ſhou'd not be infinitely more diſpleas'd at this ſcandalous ſeduction? — But it was your regard for me which led you to betray the confidence of your friend, as well as to attempt the innocence of his daughter — Yes, Sir, your regard for me is extremely evident — You knew how much my happineſs depended upon your reputable riſe in the world, and how warmly I expected you wou'd be a credit to your country, as well as an ornament to your family — Your natural advantages were great, and your education has been liberal — Yet, inſtead of the flattering proſpects with which my imagination was once delighted, I have now nothing before me but a gloomy ſcene of diſappointment and regret — Inſtead of hearing my ſon's name with joy, and exulting in the growing dignity of his character, I am hourly mortified with ſome freſh accounts of his licentiouſneſs, and hourly trembling, leſt the hand of well-grounded reſentment, or the ſword of public juſtice, ſhould cut him off in the perpetration of his crimes — Inſtead of finding him the ſupport of my age, he inceſſantly ſaps the foundation of my life, and inſtead of kindly nouriſhing the lamp of my exiſtence with his virtues, he ſinks me down into the grave, an equal victim of ſorrow and diſgrace.

DORMER. [*Falling at his father's feet.*]

No more, Sir, I beſeech you no more — nor ſuppoſe me ſuch a monſter — My life hitherto has been a ſcene of folly and diſſipation, and I reflect, with the deepeſt concern, upon the anxiety which the beſt of fathers has ſuffer'd on my account — but if he can be prevail'd upon to forgive the paſt, the future, I will boldly ſay, ſhall merit his approbation — for I am now ſatisfied that nothing can be conſiſtent with the principles of honour, which is any way repugnant to the laws of morality.

Sir JOHN.

Riſe, and be my ſon again — there is a candour, there is a generoſity in this acknowledgment which engages my confidence, and I ſtill flatter myſelf with a belief, that you will anſwer my warmeſt expectations.

DORMER.

You are too good, Sir —— But the freedom with which I ſhall communicate the moſt unfavourable circumſtances of this affair, as well as my readineſs to fulfill all your commands, ſhall in ſome meaſure prove the certainty of my reformation.

Sir JOHN.

Why, Jack, this is ſpeaking like my ſon — And to let you ſee that your inclination is the only object of my wiſhes, Miſs Willoughby's hand now waits to crown your return to virtue.

DORMER.

Miſs Willoughby's, Sir!

Sir JOHN.

Yes, — Miſs Montagu, juſt as I entered, acquainted me with the whimſical diſtreſs of your courtſhip ſcene, in terms equally conſiſtent with her uſual good-nature and vivacity, and on account, of your attachment to Miſs Willoughby, as well

as

as her own fix'd diſinclination to be your's, requeſted I wou'd not think any longer of the treaty between our families — Finding her determin'd in the ſolicitation, I wou'd by no means force her wiſhes — and am now rejoic'd at ſo lucky an opportunity of rewarding, as you yourſelf cou'd deſire, the merit of your preſent character.

DORMER.

There is no doing juſtice to the generoſity of your ſentiments, Sir —

Sir JOHN.

Poh, poh, man, the parent that makes his children happieſt always gives them the beſt fortunes —— We'll, now join the company chearfully — But remember for the future, my dear boy, what every ſon ſhou'd conſtantly have in view, that more than your own happineſs and your own honour are truſted to your care, and that you cannot experience a misfortune, nor ſuffer a diſgrace, without ſenſibly wounding the boſom of your father. [*Exeunt.*

SCENE *another Room at Sir* JOHN DORMER'S.

Enter Sir GEORGE.

So then, it ſeems, I am not quite deteſtible after all. — It ſeems there are ſome women, though I have been rejected, who can ſtill think me amiable — and declare, if ever they change their ſituation, I muſt poſitively be the man. — Villars had the ſecret from Miſs Dormer — and Miſs Dormer had the acknowledgement of Miſs Montagu's regard for me, from Miſs Montague herſelf — her refuſal of Dormer moreover

over corroborates the intelligence, even if there was any thing very improbable in my having engag'd a lady's affection. — Upon my ſoul I don't ſee but Harriot is to the full as handſome as Caroline; and then her underſtanding — Yes, I think 'tis pretty evident that ſhe has the advantage in underſtanding — Ay, but can I ſo readily forget Caroline — Can I ſo quickly remove my addreſſes, and offer up that heart at the ſhrine of the one which has been ſo recently rejected at the altar of the other — Why, to be ſure, there will be nothing extremely gallant in ſuch an affair — But, at the ſame time, there will be nothing extremely prepoſterous — It doesn't follow, becauſe I have been repuls'd by one woman, that I ſhould forſwear the whole ſex; and, in a fit of amorous lunacy, like the knight errants of old, nobly dedicate my life to deſpair, becauſe I unfortunately loſt the original object of my affections — Beſides, at the preſent period, changing hands is all the faſhion; and while it is ſo meritorious in men of quality to part with their wives, it cannot ſurely be very criminal to part with our miſtreſſes — here, by all that's opportune, ſhe comes — what a bewitching girl — O! 'twou'd be barbarous to let her pine — I'll give her encouragement at once, and put an end to her anxiety.

Enter Miſs MONTAGU.

Miſs MONTAGU.

O! there's no bearing their loves, and their joys — their tears, and their congratulations — Sir John has join'd the hands of another couple — and Caroline has now Miſs Willoughby to keep her in countenance — But pray, Sir George, wasn't poor Villars overjoy'd when you told him of Sir John's design of receiving him as a son-in-law.

Sir GEORGE.

He was, both with gratitude and astonishment — however, I carried him immediately to Sir John; here Miss Dormer was sent for, and, without the least hint of her private sentiments, Sir John, who had properly sounded the young fellow's inclinations, introduc'd him as a man whom he found worthy to be his son-in-law, and her husband.

Miss MONTAGU.

I pity'd her situation most heartily.

Sir GEORGE.

I pity the situation of every lady in love, Madam

Miss MONTAGU.

I am sure Miss Dormer thinks herself much indebted to your generosity.

Sir GEORGE.

Perhaps, Madam, I may yet have obligations to the prepossession of Miss Dormer.

Miss MONTAGU.

Prepossessions are strong things, Sir George.

Sir GEORGE.

And, in a lady's bosom, Madam, very troublesome.

Miss MONTAGU.

Not where the object is attainable ——

Sir GEORGE.

True, Madam — and he must be a barbarian who, conscious of a lady's tenderness, possesses the ability without the inclination to return it — I think that hint will give her some consolation. [*Aside.*]

Miss

Miſs MONTAGU.

The men, I believe, Sir George, have but few opportunities of exerciſing ſuch a barbarity — Indications of tenderneſs ſeldom firſt proceed from the ladies.

Sir GEORGE.

I don't know that, Madam — but was I happy enough to be the object of a lady's eſteem — I wonld ſacrafice much to remove her anxiety — This will make her ſpeak or the devil's in't. [*Aſide.*]

Miſs MONTAGU.

Kind creature! and ſo you'd condeſcend to take pity on her.

Sir GEORGE.

I would do every thing to make her happy, Madam — why, what the plague muſt ſhe be in love, and is the courtſhip to come entirely from my ſide? [*Aſide.*]

Miſs MONTAGU.

Well! you are a whimſical creature, and ſo I leave you —

Sir GEORGE.

Stay, Miſs Montagu —

Miſs MONTAGU.

For what?

Sir GEORGE.

I will be generous and ſpare her bluſhes [*Aſide.*] I have ſomething very ſerious to ſay to you.

Miſs MONTAGU.

Serious indeed if one may judge by your gravity.

Sir GEORGE.

Miſs Montagu, I am inexpreſſibly concerned — I ſay inexpreſſibly concern'd to ſee you of late ſo melancholy.

Miſs MONTAGU.

To ſee me of late ſo melancholy!—Why, Sir George, I never had better ſpirits.

Sir GEORGE.

No!

Miſs MONTAGU.

No — really —

Sir GEORGE.

I cou'd not imagine it.

Miſs MONTAGU.

And why ſo, pray?

Sir GEORGE.

Why ſo, Madam? Nay, I have no particular reaſon — but Miſs Montagu, I ſhould be ſorry to ſee you labour under the ſmalleſt uneaſineſs — I have the higheſt opinion of your merit, Madam — and —

Miſs MONTAGU.

Surely Caroline has not—[*Aſide.*] I ſhall be always proud of poſſeſſing a place in the good opinion of Sir George Haſtings.

Sir GEORGE.

You do poſſeſs the principal place in my good opinion, Madam — and ——

The back ſcene thrown open diſcovers Sir JOHN, *Captain and Miſs* DORMER, VILLARS, *Mr. Mrs. and Miſs* WILLOUGHBY.

Sir GEORGE.

Zounds, this interruption is abominable.

DORMER.

Ay, this is right; now the rooms are thrown together, we ſhall have ſpace enough for a country dance in the evening — Villars we now are brothers.

VILLARS.

VILLARS.

To my unſpeakable tranſport.

Sir JOHN, *to* Willoughby, *who ſeems in private converſation with him.*

Nay, no acknowledgment, my dear Mr. Willoughby — I am acting no more than an intereſted part, and conſulting my own wiſhes in the wiſhes of my children.

WILLOUGHBY, *to his wife.*

Doesn't every thing happen for the beſt now?— And isn't this excellent young man, to whom I probably owe my child, another proof, that if we are deſirous of happineſs we muſt labour to deſerve it.

Mrs. WILLOUGHBY. [*Aſide.*]

My Scotch ſcheme has help'd the buſineſs greatly for all that.

Sir JOHN.

We'll have a public wedding — the friends of all our families ſhall be invited — and Mr. Villars, let not any humility in the ſituation of your's, prevent you from calling the worthy to be witneſſes of the juſtice which fortune renders to your merit.

VILLARS.

Sir, your goodneſs is unbounded — but juſtice obliges me to tell you, that the man thus honour'd with your eſteem, is even more humble than you think him; that he has no family, no relations — and, out of this company, no friends.

WILLOUGHBY.

How's this?

Sir JOHN.

Pray wasn't Mr. Villars, the clergyman in my neighbourhood, your uncle?

VILLARS.

VILLARS.

He was the beſt of men; and more than a father to me in every thing but the actual relation.

WILLOUGHBY, [*Impatiently.*]

Stand out of the way—

Mrs. WILLOUGHBY.

My dear, I deſire you won't forget the rules of propriety.

WILLOUGHBY.

You ſaid, Sir, you were ignorant of your family.

VILLARS.

I did, Sir.

WILLOUGHBY.

Some unhappy father, like me, now bleeds for the loſs of a ſon — Pray go on—

Mrs. WILLOUGHBY.

My dear—

VILLARS.

At an early ſtage of infancy, ſome wandering miſcreants ſtole me from my friends, and carried me into a diſtant part of the country, where a woman, who call'd herſelf my mother, being committed to priſon for a theft, fell ill of a fever, that put a period to her life—with her dying breath ſhe related this circumſtance, and wou'd have told more, but the laſt agonies taking away her utterance, prevented the poſſibility of any farther declaration.

Sir JOHN.

How unfortunate!

Miſs DORMER.

How extremely unfortunate!

VILLARS.

It wou'd have been ſtill more unfortunate, hadn't the good Mr. Villars, who kept a little academy in the place, attended the poor wretch with medicines, and look'd with an eye of compaſſion on my helpleſs ſituation — Mr. Villars was the univerſal friend of mankind, the rich never mentioned him without reverence, and the poor never beheld him without joy — But his income was too narrow for the extent of his benevolence, and he was involved in continual diſtreſſes from the uncommon excellence of his heart.

Sir GEORGE.

Zounds, no perſon doubts his being a good man.

VILLARS.

Mr. Villars, without heſitating, ordered me to be taken care of, and as ſoon as I was capable of inſtruction, receiv'd me into his houſe, where I was educated in common with the reſt of his pupils — and at laſt grew ſufficiently qualified to be his aſſiſtant; but his neceſſities encreaſing with the exerciſe of his virtues, notwithſtanding my utmoſt aſſiduity, he was oblig'd to ſell his academy, and I had at laſt the mortification of cloſing his eyes in the very priſon, from which I was originally reſcu'd by the greatneſs of his humanity.

Miſs DORMER.

And was it juſt at this time that Sir John bought the ſeat in your neighbourhood?

VILLARS.

It was, Madam — and it was at this time alſo, that hearing Sir John had an occaſion for an aſſiſtant in ſome literary employments, I procur'd the recommendation to him which has given me the

the honour of being known in this family — The only trace of what I ever was, is this picture; which was by some means in my possession when I was stolen, as the woman who stole me declar'd in the course of her imperfect narration; fearing to dispose of it, she kept it to the hour of her death, and then delivered it up as a possible means of finding out my family —

Sir JOHN.

Let me see this picture.

WILLOUGHBY.

No, let me see it for the love of heaven — O Sir John — Sir John — this was Lady Dormer's picture — she made a present of it to my first wife, and here on the setting are the initials of her name.

Sir JOHN.

I remember it perfectly — I myself ordered the letters to be engrav'd.

VILLARS.

I can scarce speak.

WILLOUGHBY.

While I have power to ask — tell me, Sir, what is your age.

VILLARS.

Twenty-two.

WILLOUGHBY

Receive my thanks, receive my thanks, kind heav'n! — O my boy, my boy! Providence still orders all things for the best, and I am in reality your father.

VILLARS.

O, Sir! bless your son, and assure him he has a father.

Miss WILLOUGHBY, *embracing him.*

My brother my deliverer too! — this is happiness indeed —

Mrs.

Mrs. WILLOUGHBY.

Let me embrace you too — Your ſiſter will tell you what a mother-in-law I am, and how much ſhe is indebted to my leſſons of propriety. Well! I begin myſelf to think every thing happens for the beſt, after the unexpected good fortune of this morning.

DORMER.

Not to Sir George, I am ſure — for he loſes a good eſtate by this unexpected diſcovery. [*Here Miſs* MONTAGU, *Miſs* DORMER, *Sir* JOHN, *and* DORMER *ſeem congratulating* VILLARS — *ſo does Sir* GEORGE.]

Sir GEORGE.

What, you begin to crow again, do you? — But, let me tell you, I think every accident happens for the beſt, which enables me to do an act of juſtice, and advance the welfare of the deſerving.

Miſs MONTAGU.

Generouſly conſider'd indeed, Sir George — few people, I believe, would give up a fortune ſo eaſily.

Sir GEORGE.

Why, my friend Jack there, if he loſt both an eſtate and a miſtreſs in a couple of hours, wou'd hardly ſet ſo good a face upon matters, notwithſtanding he is much my ſuperior in ſerenity of countenance.

Sir JOHN.

And perhaps, Sir George, even you, may be a conſiderable gainer in the end, if we can but contrive to make an actnal comedy of to-day's adventures, by your marriage with a certain lady in this company. [*Looking at Miſs* MONTAGU.]

Sir George.

And poſſibly that might be yet effected, through your interpoſition, Sir John, with Miſs Montagu.

Miſs Montagu.

What? is your denouement to be produc'd at my expence; upon my word, I ſhould be much oblig'd to Sir John's interpoſition for ſuch a purpoſe!

Sir George.

I ſhou'd at leaſt, Madam — and though I come rather with an ill grace after ſo recent a rejection—

Dormer.

Your affection is not unadulterated now George.

Sir George.

Why, no — But I hav'nt yet told Miſs Montagu — that death itſelf is infinitely preferable to the idea of offending her — [*ludicrouſly*] though I wou'd readily riſk my life to purchaſe her favourable opinion. [*Turning to her.*]

Miſs Montagu.

Well, don't talk to me on this ſubject now, Sir George — You have to be ſure merited much — and you are in every reſpect ſo greatly the oppoſite of my confident ſwain there, who thought I muſt fly into his arms the moment he condeſcended to receive me — that — however, I won't hear a ſyllable from you now — if you can make a tollerable bow to me do, but don't let me hear a ſyllable of nonſenſe, I beg of you.

Sir George.

This goodneſs —

Dormer.

Didn't the lady ſay ſhe wou'dn't hear a ſyllable of nonſenſe —

Sir

3

Sir George.

And ſo you begin to talk to her, do you?

Mrs. Willoughby.

Mighty fine! is it nonſenſe to make a grateful acknowledgment for the kindneſs of a lady — What will the men come to at laſt? —

Sir George.

So he thinks, Madam—Though Villars [*Aſide to Villars*] 'tis a little hard, becauſe Miſs Montagu chooſes to conſult her own happineſs, that I am to acknowledge the receipt of an obligation.

Sir John.

My dear Sir George, Miſs Montagu has too much diſcernment not to ſee the value of ſo deſerving a lover — Addreſs her therefore certain of ſucceſs, and look ſecurely for happineſs according to Mr. Willoughby's principle, becauſe you richly merit it.

Willoughby.

Right, Sir John — Providence looks down delighted on the actions of the worthy, and, however it may command adverſity to frown on the beginning of their days, they will acknowledge with me, that all it's diſpenſations are full of benignity in the end.

THE END.

EPILOGUE.

SPOKEN BY MRS. BARRY.

MODISH divines, at court and in the city,
Are in their pulpits hum'rous, gay, and witty——
They've now chang'd hands, the ſtage and pulpit teaching,
Sermons are plays, and plays are merely preaching——
A Word to the Wiſe, a pretty pert adviſer !——
As if 'twere poſſible to make you wiſer :
Yet as each here, may think the Poet labours
Not to teach him, but to inſtruct his neighbours ;
As the bright regents of that ſplendid row
Sneer on the pit, for beings much below ;
And theſe in turn, as things in order move,
Toſs up the ſneer to thoſe who mount above :
The gods look down, and let *their* pity fall
On front, ſide, green, ſtage-boxes, pit, and all.
Let me, before your carriages appear,
Breathe one ſhort word, ye wiſe ones, in your ear.
You, ſtop your chairs, *(to the ſide-boxes)* your hacks, *(to the pit)*
won't run away ;
And ladies, *(to the gallery)* put not on your pattins pray :
And firſt, ye ſoft, ye ſweet romantic maids,
Who die for purling ſtreams, and ſylvan ſhades,
And think for better and for worſe, to take
The beſt of huſbands, in a darling rake ;
Who brings a ſhatter'd fortune to the fair,
With mind and body wanting vaſt repair ;

Shall

E P I L O G U E.

Shall I for once your tender thoughts reveal?
'Tis fine to hear him ſwear, to ſee him kneel;
His tongue with worn-out extacies will run,
'Till he has triumph'd, 'till the wife's undone;
And then that tender ſtrain, ſo love-creating,
Turns to, "Death, Madam, hold your curſed prating,—
"You quite diſtract me — prithee farther ſtand——
"I won't be teaz'd — Zounds, take away your hand —"
This is a ſad change, ladies, but 'tis common,
Man will be man, and woman will be woman;
For Villars is a phœnix, where's his brother?
'Twill take a hundred years to find another.
Yet you, ye Sires, whom time ſhould render wiſe,
You act as if each moment it could riſe;
Forgetting all, what you yourſelves have been,
You truſt your girls with Dormers at fifteen;
Throw your poor lambkins in the tyger's way,
Then ſtare to find a rake — a beaſt of prey.
Learn prudence here — and, O! you precious blades,
Whether cockaded, or without cockades;
Whether haranguing for the public good,
You ſhake St. Stephens — or the Robinhood——
Who ring our charms for ever in our ears,
Yet inly triumph at a virgin's tears;
Be now convinc'd — the libertine diſclaim,
And live to honour, if not dead to ſhame.
What is the plaudit of a fool when mellow,
Roaring in raptures, *a damn'd honeſt fellow*?
Will that repay you for the boſom ſtings?
Damn'd honeſt fellows, oft are worthleſs things——
But I'll ſtop here, I will not ſermonize——
A fooliſh woman can't inſtruct the wiſe.

CLEMENTINA

CLEMENTINA,

A

TRAGEDY.

A NEW EDITION.

[Price One Shilling and Six-pence.]

CLEMENTINA,

A

TRAGEDY,

As it is Perform'd with universal Applause at the

Theatre-Royal in COVENT-GARDEN.

A NEW EDITION.

LONDON:
Printed for EDWARD and CHARLES DILLY,
in the Poultry,
And T. CADELL, in the Strand.
MDCCLXXI.

TO

GEORGE COLMAN, Esq;

DEAR SIR,

WHEN I inscribe this Tragedy to you, I mean to pay myself a very high compliment; the utmost I could possibly say of you, would by no means extend your Reputation; but it will do me much honour to declare, that so celebrated a writer has distinguished CLEMENTINA with the most essential attention; and that so valuable a man has given me leave to sign myself, what I truly am,

DEAR SIR,

His most faithful

and most obliged

humble servant,

The AUTHOR.

ADVERTISEMENT.

THE Author of this Tragedy has printed several lines for the Closet, which, in the Representation, were omitted for the sake of brevity. —The chief business of this advertisement, however, is to acknowledge his obligations to the inimitable performance of Mrs. YATES, and to thank Mr. BENSLEY, Mr. SAVIGNY, and Mr. WROUGHTON, for their great good-nature, in undertaking their respective characters at the short notice of a week, when Mr. ROSS unexpectedly returned the part of *Anselmo* *, which had been in his possession above a fortnight, and left it no more than barely possible for the utmost diligence of these Gentlemen, to exhibit a piece, which the public have since been kindly pleased to honour with the most generous approbation.

* This circumstance obliged Mr. BENSLEY, who was cast for *Palermo*, to undertake Mr. SAVIGNY's part, which was originally *Granville*—Mr. SAVIGNY taking *Anselmo*, and Mr. WROUGHTON, *Palermo*.

PROLOGUE,

By GEORGE COLMAN, Esq;

Spoken by Mr. BENSLEY.

IN these, our moral and religious days,
Men dread the crying sin of writing Plays;
While some, whose wicked wit incurs the blame,
Howe'er they love the trespass, fly the shame.
If, a new holy war with Vice to wage,
Some preacher quits the pulpit for the stage,
The Rev'rend Bard, with much remorse and fear,
Attempts to give his Evening-Lecture here.
The work engender'd, to the world must rise;
But yet the father may elude our eyes.
The parish on this trick of youth might frown,
And thus, unown'd, 'tis thrown upon the Town.
At our Director's door he lays the sin,
Who sees the Babe, relents, and takes it in;
To swathe and dress it first unstrings his purse,
Then kindly puts it out to You—to nurse.
Should some young Counsel, thro' his luckless star,
By writing Plays turn truant to the Bar,
Call'd up by you to this High Court of Wit,
With non inventus *we return the writ.*
No latitat *can force him to appear,*
Whose failure and success cause equal fear.
Whatever fees his clients here bestow,
He loses double in the Courts below.
Grave solemn Doctors, whose prescribing pen
Has in the trade of Death kill'd many men,

With

With vent'rous quill here tremblingly engage
To ſlay Kings, Queens, and Heroes, on the ſtage.
The Great, if great men write, of ſhame afraid
Come forth incog.—*and Beaux, in maſquerade.*
Some Demireps in wit, of doubtful fame,
Tho' known to all the town, withhold their name.
Thus each by turns ungratefully refuſe
To own the favours of their Lady-Muſe;
Woo'd by the Court, the College, Bar and Church,
Court, Bar, Church, College, leave her in the lurch.
'Tis your's to-night the work alone to ſcan;
Arraign the bard, regardleſs of the man!
If Dulneſs waves her poppies o'er his play,
To Critic fury let it fall a prey;
But if his art the tears of Pity draws,
Aſk not his name—but crown him with applauſe!

Dramatis Personæ.

ANSELMO - - - Mr. SAVIGNY.
GRANVILLE - - Mr. BENSLEY.
PALERMO - - - Mr. WROUGHTON.
ADORNO - - - - Mr. GARDNER.

CLEMENTINA - - Mrs. YATES.
ELIZARA - - - - Miſs PEARCE.

CITIZENS, GUARDS, *&c.*

SCENE, VENICE.

TIME—The Time of Repreſentation.

CLEMENTINA,

A

TRAGEDY.

ACT I.

An Apartment in ANSELMO'*s Palace.*

Enter CLEMENTINA *and* ELIZARA.

CLEMENTINA.

DISTRACTION! here ſo ſoon?

ELIZARA.

This very hour—
Your good, your noble, yet miſguided father,
This moment chill'd me with the hated tale;
Then ſeizing eagerly my trembling hand,
" Tell Clementina, tell your ſtubborn friend,"
Cry'd he, in accents poſitive and ſtern,
" That brave Palermo, juſt return'd from chains,
" Chains greatly purchas'd in his country's cauſe,
" Muſt now receive ſuch welcome, ſuch affection,
" As ſuits her virtue, and Anſelmo's daughter.—
" Tell her, my word's irrevocably giv'n,
" And bid her guard the honour of her father."

CLEMENTINA.

Why let the ſtorm exert its utmoſt rage,
And burſt in thunder on my wretched head!
Let this ſevere, this unrelenting father,
Caſt me a houſeleſs wand'rer on the world,
Yet ſhall my ſoul with unabating firmneſs
Deny her ſanction to Palermo's claim.
O Elizara, you who know the cauſe,
The endleſs cauſe of Clementina's tears,
Who ſaw the awful, tho' the ſecret rite
That gave this hand, now widow'd, to Rinaldo;
Is there, in all the various rounds of woe,
A curſe ſo great, a pang ſo exquiſite,
As this poor breaſt is ſingled out to feel?

ELIZARA.

Indulge not thus a painful recollection!

CLEMENTINA.

Oh memory! ev'n madneſs cannot loſe it!
Mangled with wounds, amidſt unnumber'd foes,
My hapleſs huſband for his country fell!
Yet, the ſad ſtory of our loves conceal'd,
I was allow'd no privilege of tears,
But doom'd to hide the anguiſh of my heart.—
And now, in all the fulneſs of deſpair,
To have another forc'd upon me! horror!
It is not to be borne!—But I'm reſolv'd,
And will devote the remnant of my life
To loſt Rinaldo's memory, or die
Some little hour before my griefs would end me.

ELIZARA.

Alas, I feel the ſorrows of your boſom,
With all the ardent ſympathy of friendſhip;
And know how ſouls ſo delicate as yours,
Muſt ſpurn th' idea of a ſecond lord.
Yet blame no more the ſternneſs of Anſelmo;

The

The antient hate too long, too idly cherifh'd,
Between your angry father and Rinaldo's,
Firft urg'd the meafure of a private union.
A ftranger therefore to your grief, Anfelmo
Claims but the right which cuftom, and which nature,
Have long giv'n parents o'er their children's hearts.

CLEMENTINA.

What claim, what right, misjudging Elizara,
Can tyrant cuftom plead, or nature urge
To force the free election of the foul?
Say, fhould affection light the nuptial torch,
Or fhould the rafh decifion of a father
Doom his fad race to wretchednefs for ever?
No, Elizara; cuftom has no force,
Nature no right, to fanctify oppreffion;
And parents vainly tell us of indulgence,
When they give all but happinefs to children.

ELIZARA.

True—yet a cruel crifis in your fate,
Has much to offer for the good Anfelmo.
He fondly thinks his daughter difengag'd;
Believes too, fondly, that Palermo's merit
Muft touch the gentle bofom of my friend:
If then determin'd to reject his choice,
At once throw off conftraint—at once be open,
And feal his lips for ever on the fubject,
By a frank mention of your fatal ftory.

CLEMENTINA.

What! and expofe my dear Rinaldo's kindred
To all the fury of enrag'd Anfelmo,
The now acknowledg'd ruler of the ftate;
Who, tho' renown'd for wifdom and for juftice,
Yet in the points, the cruel points of honour,
Is rigid, ftern, and fatally fevere?
No, Elizara; tho' thefe fading eyes

No more muſt hope to gaze upon Rinaldo,
Tho' the ſoul-ſwelling language of my woes,
Falls unregarded on the ſilent tomb,
And boaſts no pow'r to call my ſlaughter'd hero
From the dark, dreary manſions of the dead;
Still let me guard whatever he held dear,
Nor pluck down added ruin on his houſe!

ELIZARA.

Anſelmo's juſtice will o'ercome his hatred—
Were he inclin'd to make his will his law,
Or wiſh'd for means to gratify reſentment,
He has the pow'r already; but his mind,
Superior ever to the thought of wrong,
Can feel no paſſion to diſgrace his virtue.

CLEMENTINA.

The beſt may err, nor will I tempt his rage;
The mighty meaſure of my woe is full—
Why then, when fate's unmerciful decree
Has curs'd me up to ſuch a height of ill,
Why ſhould I ſhudder at the gathering ſtorm,
Or ſeek for ſhelter in another's ſorrow?
I now have no aſylum but the grave:
Tho' did peace court me from the bow'rs of bliſs,
My ſoul would ſcorn to hear the charmer's voice,
If ſhe requir'd me to perform a deed,
That either ſhock'd my juſtice, or my honour.

ELIZARA.

Then ſummon all your firmneſs, Clementina!
For here Anſelmo comes, and brings Palermo;
O that your terrors for Rinaldo's kindred,
May ſtill ſubſide, and hear the voice of reaſon!
Your ſoul is ill adapted to diſguiſe;
And without cauſe to diſappoint his views,
Muſt be as fatal as to tell him all.

CLEMENTINA.

They're here—let us retire—Palermo's presence
Is now a thousand deaths—and tho' prepar'd
With fortitude to act—still, Elizara,
While I can shun the conflict, let me spare,
Spare ev'n the feelings of a cruel father! [*Exeunt.*

Enter ANSELMO *and* PALERMO.

ANSELMO.

Gone so abruptly!—gone at our approach!—
And yet, my son, the crimson hue of virtue
Will always deepen at a lover's sight,
Who comes to ask his certain day of transport,
And knows the hour of apprehension o'er.

PALERMO.

'Tis just, my lord—But still however lovely,
The soft emotion of these gentle terrors,
Spreads in the blooming daughters of perfection,
Still Clementina might have kindly giv'n
A long lost lover welcome from his bonds;
And nobly told him that his ruin'd fortunes
Were ev'n deem'd merit with Anselmo's daughter.

ANSELMO.

Think not, Palermo, of your ruin'd fortunes;
My Clementina, with her father's eyes,
Regardless looks on dignity and wealth;
And holds the mind pre-eminent in both,
That boasts a bright pre-eminence in virtue.

PALERMO.

When sharp adversity has stung the mind,
It makes us doubly conscious of neglect:
And sure a soul less sensible than mine
Had room to start at Clementina's coldness.
Judge then by all that headlong fire of youth

 Which

Which once ſwell'd up your own impaſſion'd breaſt,
If I could let indifference paſs unnotic'd?
He never lov'd that bore a ſlight with temper,
Nor ever merited a worthy heart,
Who meanly ſtoop'd, contented with a cold one.

ANSELMO.

No more, my ſon!—This day rewards your ſuff'rings,
For Clementina ſhall to-day be yours;
And while love courts you with his ripeſt roſes,
The golden ſun of honourable greatneſs
Shines out to crown you with his warmeſt beams—
Our native land—but what exceeds all price,
Our native liberty ſhall ſoon be ours;
And ſoon Palermo nobly ſhall revenge
On haughty Ferdinand, that ſcourge of earth,
The wrongs ill-fated Venice has ſuſtain'd,
The wrongs which heedleſs of a ſoldier's glory
Th' imperial plund'rer on my ſon himſelf
So poorly, meanly, infamouſly heap'd,
When in a baſe exaction for his ranſom,
He ſeiz'd his all, nor left th' indignant warrior
A home to reſt in from the weight of chains—
Our French ally, the nobly-minded Lewis,
This hour diſpatches an embaſſador,
To give our country renovated being,
And burſt aſunder ev'ry yoke of Spain.

PALERMO.

The glorious news o'erpays an age of bonds!
O for a curſe, a quick diſpatching curſe,
To blaſt the ruthleſs tyrant on his throne,
And mark him out thro' all ſucceeding ages,
A dread example to deſpotic kings!
But ſay, and bleſs me with ſome certain hope;
On what foundation does the royal Lewis,
Bid us thus boldly, confidently look
For inſtant vengeance, and for inſtant freedom?

ANSEL-

ANSELMO.

That I am yet to learn.—But noble ſtill
I ever found him in our various treaties;
And therefore cannot, will not, doubt him now.
Sunk by his late diſtreſſes, Ferdinand
Now mourns his dreams of univerſal empire,
And ſhrinks in ſecret at the arms of France.

PALERMO.

Eternal praiſes to the God of battles!
Yes, ſcepter'd ſavage, we may reach you yet,
And boldly tell you in the face of nations,
That royal robbers from unerring juſtice
Demand a double meaſure of perdition!—
The needy ruffian, in his hour of hunger,
Has ſome excuſe for prowling on his neighbour;
But when the arm, the mighty arm of kings,
That ſhou'd protect all mankind from oppreſſion,
Is ſtretch'd to ſeize on what it ought to guard,
Then heaven's own brand in aggravated fire,
Shou'd ſtrike th' illuſtrious villain to his hell;
And war in mercy for a groaning world.

ANSELMO.

Oh, nobly ſaid!—Our cauſe is juſt, and heaven
Fights on our ſide: for late, the Spaniſh troops
In two great fields were wholly overthrown,
And fill'd the plains with myriads of their dead.
Our navies too, tho' ſome Venetian cities
Lye humbled ſtill beneath the tyrant's yoke,
Fill Spain with conſtant and with juſt alarms;
For ſuch a blaze of unexampled glory
Has crown'd the fleets entruſted to my care,
That tho' depriv'd of more than half our realm,
We ſtill remain a formidable foe,
And rule triumphant o'er the boundleſs wave.

PALERMO.

How the bright profpect burfts upon my view,
And lifts me up in fancy to the ftars!
O did the fair, the matchlefs Clementina,
View me with eyes lefs rigidly fevere,
This one bleft hour had madden'd me with rapture.

ANSELMO.

Again, Palermo?—But I ceafe to chide,
And go, my fon, to end your doubts for ever.—
If I know aught of Clementina's heart,
'Twill beat in honeft unifon to mine,
And give an added welcome to your claim,
Becaufe you've now, an added need of fortune.

PALERMO.

Too generous Anfelmo!

ANSELMO.

Nay, no thanks!
The man who bears not to a friend diftrefs'd
A double will to ratify engagements,
Stands felf-convicted at the bar within,
The bafe affaffin of his native honour. [*Exit.*

PALERMO *alone.*

Why did I wound his venerable bofom,
With any doubt of Clementina's truth?
And yet difquiet hangs about my heart;
A fecret voice inceffantly fuggefts,
That Clementina was not born for me:
But let me not anticipate misfortune!
When fate has ftruck, 'tis time enough to feel;
And he is beft prepar'd againft the blow,
Whofe confcious virtue never has deferv'd it. [*Exit.*

Scene

Scene changes to CLEMENTINA'*s Apartment.*

CLEMENTINA *alone.*

Now, Clementina,—now the trial comes—
Call up th' inherent greatneſs of your ſoul,
And ſhew Anſelmo, ſhew this rigid ſire,
That his own firmneſs animates his daughter!
What, does he think that force can move my temper?
No; ſacred ſpirit of my dear Rinaldo,
If kindly hov'ring round your wretched wife,
You ſtill obſerve her in this world of woe,
Look, and applaud her in an hour of terror!
Look, and behold, how faithful to her vows,
She braves a ſure deſtruction for your ſake;
Braves all the ſtings of poverty and ſcorn,
Her father's fury, and her houſe's hate,
To live the ceaſeleſs mourner of your fall!

Enter ANSELMO.

ANSELMO.

Well, Clementina,—Have I yet a daughter?

CLEMENTINA.

Say rather, Sir—if I have yet a father?

ANSELMO.

Yes, Clementina, an unhappy father,
Who now implores compaſſion from his child
I ſee, I ſee with infinite regret,
Your ſcorn, your fix'd averſion to Palermo;
And tho' I came, determin'd to exact
A ſtrict, a rigid inſtance of your duty,
My aching ſoul, quite melted at your tears,
Rejects the ſterner ſentiment of force,
And bends the weeping ſuppliant to a daughter.

CLEMENTINA.

O could the ſecret volume of my heart,
Be laid this moment openly to view,

My father there, would read my pride to pleaſe him.
Let him aſk all from Clementina's duty,
Which wretched Clementina can perform ;
Let him do this, and he's at once obey'd.
But when he aſks her to direct her wiſhes,
To turn the mighty current of the mind,
And join the ſtreams, the ever-warring ſtreams
Of boundleſs love and limitleſs averſion ;
There he exceeds her utmoſt ſtretch of pow'r,
And only gives occaſion for her tears.

ANSELMO.

Look round on all th' accompliſh'd ſons of Venice,
And ſay who ſhines ſuperior to Palermo ?
Take then his hand, and bleſs your doating father !—
Let us not now in poverty deſert him,
Nor aid the arrow of a galling need,
With the keen dart of diſappointed love !
No, Clementina, let us nobly claim
A great alliance with his ruin'd fortunes,
And give a bright example to our country,
That worth is all things, with the truly worthy !

CLEMENTINA.

Palermo's merits, and Palermo's wants,
Alike receive my praiſes, and my pity ;
But, venerable Sir, if e'er my peace,
My ſoul's dear peace, was tender to your thoughts,
Spare me, O ſpare me, on this cruel ſubject !
Let the brave youth, ſo honour'd with your friendſhip,
Partake your wealth, but do not kill your daughter.
Do not, to give him a precarious good,
Doom me to certain wretchedneſs for ever !
I have an equal claim upon your heart,
And call as much for favour as Palermo.

ANSELMO.

A little time, ſweet ſoother of my age,
Will charm that gentle boſom into reſt,

And

And ev'n return Palermo love for love.
Then, Clementina! O my ſoul's whole comfort,
Refuſe a kneeling father if you can. [*Kneels.*
Here at your feet, the author of your being,
Who never ſtoop'd to aught before but heaven,
Begs for compaſſion—Muſt he beg in vain?

CLEMENTINA.

O mercy, mercy! Will you kill your daughter?
Riſe Sir, O riſe, and ſave me from diſtraction!

ANSELMO *riſing.*

My word, my child, has never yet been broken.—
Do not in age expoſe me to diſhonour!—
Save your poor father at the verge of life,
O nobly ſave him from the guilt of falſhood!
In this reverſal of Palermo's fortunes,
The ſland'rous tongue of all my houſe's foes,
Will mark me out to univerſal ſhame;
And tell the world his poverty alone,
Has loſt the daughter of the baſe Anſelmo.

CLEMENTINA.

No more—I yield—and am a wretch for ever.

ANSELMO.

O ſay not ſo, my ſoul's ſupreme delight!
Applauding heav'n ſhall bleſs your filial virtue,
And give your heart that joy you give your father.
My tranſport grows too mighty to be borne—
O let me haſten to the brave Palermo,
And raiſe him from deſpondency to rapture! [*Exit.*

CLEMENTINA *alone.*

Rinaldo's widow, wedded to Palermo!
Where ſhall I now find refuge from reflection,
Or how root up the agonizing thought,
That brings this horrid marriage to my view?
I was prepar'd for all a father's fury,

But was not arm'd againſt a father's tears.
How could I ſee him weeping at my feet,
Toſt in a whirlwind of contending paſſions,
And yet retain the purpoſe of my ſoul?
Ev'n if the ſainted ſpirit of my huſband,
From the bright manſions of eternal day,
Beheld the anguiſh of his ſtruggling heart,
It muſt have kindly prompted me to pity.—
O this Palermo!—This deteſted union!—
Married to him?—The widow of Rinaldo?—
Give me, ye bleſſed miniſters of peace,
Some inſtant portion of that ſoothing ſtream,
Which pours a deep oblivion on the mind,
And drowns the ſenſe of memory for ever!

ACT

ACT II.

An Apartment in ANSELMO's *Palace.*

Enter GRANVILLE *and* ELIZARA.

ELIZARA.

AND is it poſſible? Do I once more
Behold Rinaldo?—

GRANVILLE.

Yes, my Elizara;
Yet, lovely maid, take heed alone to know me
For what I ſeem—Th' ambaſſador of France.
As ſuch alone Anſelmo has receiv'd me,
And ſuch my king confirms me.—But declare,
How fares my Clementina?—How does ſhe
Support the oft proclaim'd, the general tale,
That now ſix moons has rank'd me with the dead?

ELIZARA.

She bears it like a wife that truly lov'd—
But by what miracle again reſtor'd
Acquaint me!—for concurring multitudes
Beheld your fall in battle, and reported,
That in a pile of greatly-ſlaughter'd heroes,
A Gallic ſquadron bore you from the field.

GRANVILLE.

I fell indeed amidſt the gen'ral carnage,
And lay ſome hours among the honour'd dead;
For whom the vanquiſh'd, France's gen'rous ſons
Made one bold effort to obtain a grave:
Here a brave youth of that exalted nation,

Close by whose side with emulative fire
I fought for Venice on that hapless day;
Beheld the man he deign'd to call his friend,
And by a kind of miracle restor'd me.—
Then to the king in terms of warmest weight,
Proclaim'd my fancied merits.—Royal Lewis
Received the story with a gracious ear,
And pour'd profuse, his favours on Rinaldo.

ELIZARA.

Why then, O why, distinguish'd thus, thus honour'd,
Did not Rinaldo sooth his sorrowing friends,
And ease the torments of a wife's despair?

GRANVILLE.

O Elizara! how my soul has felt
For all the anguish she was doom'd to suffer,
That heaven, which knows the greatness of my love,
Alone can witness.—But the conquering arms
Of widely wasting Ferdinand, cut off
Our commerce with the world—and had not fate,
In two late fields propitious smil'd upon us,
Rinaldo yet, distracted and forlorn,
Had drag'd a chain of miserable being;
Nor known, as now he shall, th' extatic bliss
Of speaking peace to weeping Clementina.

ELIZARA.

But whence this transformation?—Why conceal'd
Beneath the garb of France, does brave Rinaldo
So closely seek to hide himself in Granville?

GRANVILLE.

For ends of moment.—If the charge I bear
Meets, as I hope, and as I think it ought,
A warm reception from Anselmo—Then
I come determin'd to avow my marriage;
And gracious Lewis will, I trust, remove
The fatal feuds that shake our angry houses.

ELIZARA.

But ſhou'd Anſelmo diſapprove your charge,
What meaſure then remains to be purſu'd,
And what becomes of wretched Clementina?

GRANVILLE.

There my diſguiſe is ſuited to aſſiſt me;
Shou'd he refuſe to join the views of France,
My orders are that inſtant to return,
And my deſign, to bear off Clementina.

ELIZARA.

You talk, Rinaldo, with an air of triumph;
Think you the firſt of our Venetian daughters,
Can in a moment thus be borne away;
Borne from her palace compaſs'd round with guards,
Surrounding virgins, and a watchful father?

GRANVILLE.

My name conceal'd and all my train inſtructed,
My king's credentials bearing but the title,
Which he himſelf has giv'n me, and which yet
Has reach'd no ear of Venice but your own,
Can there exiſt a doubt of my ſucceſs?
Unknown—unnotic'd—unſuſpected quite,
A truſty friend ſhall lead her to the beach,
If Clementina, like myſelf, diſguis'd
Will venture aught to bleſs her faithful huſband.

ELIZARA.

Rinaldo ſhou'd purſue a diff'rent courſe,
A courſe more ſuited to his worth and honour.
Now independent, now ſo rais'd in France,
What can you dread from Venice or its leader?
Your fortunes now are equal to your birth.
Shou'd then your embaſſy diſpleaſe Anſelmo,
Act like yourſelf!—throw off this dark diſguiſe,
And nobly claim your wife.—You know his juſtice,
And know beſides he cannot hate you farther.

GRAN-

GRANVILLE.

Fain, gentle maid, wou'd I purſue this counſel,
And in the face of day aſſert my right;
But if the purport of my public buſineſs,
Which heaven avert! ſhou'd raiſe Anſelmo's anger,
My life, once known, muſt expiate my crime.
I come, I hope, to bleſs the ſtate of Venice;
But I come alſo, with a foreign ruler—
This, you know well, is death by law declar'd;
Nor cou'd th' ambaſſador of France, preſerve
Th' offending ſubject from the ſtroke of juſtice.

ELIZARA.

May heaven indulgent ſmile upon your hopes!
But oh! I dread, I dread a diſappointment.
And ſee, impatience frowning on his brow,
Hither Anſelmo comes.—Let me fly hence,
And bleſs my friend, with tidings of her lord!

[*Exit.*

Enter ANSELMO, *with Papers.*

ANSELMO.

Well, Sir, the views of Lewis are at length
Reveal'd; and here, I ſee, he ſpeaks them plainly.

GRANVILLE.

Why, ſage Anſelmo, this offended brow?
I truſt my maſter's offers have deſerv'd
Your higheſt approbation; for they breathe
Nought but attachment, and regard for Venice.

ANSELMO.

Is this the baſis of his love for Venice?
Has he ſtood forth a champion for our freedom,
Merely himſelf to tread us into ſlaves?
And ſav'd us from the arm of haughty Spain,
To make us bear his own oppreſſive yoke?
Go tell your king, and tell him from Anſelmo,

That France and Venice can be friends no more;
Tell him, to us, all tyrants are the ſame;
Or if in bonds the never-conquer'd ſoul
Can feel a pang more keen than ſlav'ry's ſelf,
'Tis when the chains, that cruſh us into duſt,
Are forg'd by hands from which we hop'd for freedom.

GRANVILLE.

And what idea does my buſineſs raiſe,
Of ſlaves or tyrants, ſervitude or chains?
'Tis true, the gracious Lewis has propos'd
To take the ſtate of Venice to his care,
If ſage Anſelmo, her illuſtrious leader,
Approves the ſcheme of well-concerted empire—
He ſees with deep, with nobly-minded ſorrow,
How, ſtill expos'd to ev'ry pow'rful neighbour,
You fall a victim to alternate ſpoilers;
Hence, with paternal tenderneſs, he wiſhes
T' enroll your ſons among the ſons of France,
And make the ſubjects of his diff'rent realms,
One equal, common, and united people.
If this be ſlav'ry ——

ANSELMO.

'Tis the worſt of ſlav'ry,
Tamely to bend our necks beneath the yoke,
And ſuffer fraud, to talk us out of freedom.—
If we muſt yield before ſuperior force,
Let us at leaſt deſerve the name of men;
Let us fall nobly, if we are to fall,
And give the world in characters of blood,
Eternal cauſes to lament our fate,
But never one occaſion to deſpiſe us!

GRANVILLE.

Far from my boſom be the abject thought!
To ſtoop the ſervile miniſter of greatneſs,
Or crouch the advocate for lawleſs pow'r:
The heir myſelf of heav'n-deſcended freedom,
I wiſh the ſame bright heritage to all.

And inly ſcorn a brotherhood with ſlaves.
Yet ſure, ſome form your government muſt know;
The reins of ſtate muſt ſomewhere be devolv'd
And he who holds them, name him as you pleaſe,
Muſt be your prince, and you muſt be his ſubjects.
Why then, if Lewis ſolemnly ſhall ſwear,
To hold your rights inviolably ſacred;
Still to maintain the ſpirit of your laws,
And never know another line of action;
Why ſhould you turn indignantly away,
And ſlight the offer of a mighty monarch,
Who knows that form of government is beſt,
Which beſt ſecures the welfare of the people?

ANSELMO.

Becauſe your monarch, in this very offer,
Seeks to ſubvert our glorious conſtitution;
Seeks to erect hereditary rule,
Where virtue only, gives ſuperior rank;
And where the genius of deſcended Rome,
Has levell'd all diſtinctions but in goodneſs.
What is his promiſe to maintain us free?
Sir, we'll maintain that freedom for ourſelves;
And to maintain it, we reject your maſter.
The pow'r, ſo ſafe in his benignant hand,
Is ſafer ſtill, retain'd within our own;
We know the worth of liberty too well,
Ever to caſt the bleſſing baſely from us,
Or ſtill more baſely to ſurvive our honour.

GRANVILLE.

You need not caſt the mighty bleſſing from you.—
The king my maſter, wiſhes for no more,
Than ſuch mere title to the realms of Venice,
As to his ſubjects and the world may warrant,
A warm exertion of continual care
For this his dear ally.—And mark, my lord;
[*ſhewing a paper.*

The

The moment Venice owns him for her ſovereign,
This inſtrument confirms the viceroy's office,
With all the active rule, to great Anſelmo
And his heirs for ever.—

ANSELMO.

Am I awake?
Or can I truſt my reaſon?—Patience—Patience!
Are all the bright atchievements of my life
Unable now to ſave me from diſgrace?
Thus to the winds I give the vile propoſal:
[*tearing the paper.*
Thus tear the record of imputed ſhame;
Nor let ſucceeding ages be inform'd
That mortal man has dar'd to doubt my honour!

GRANVILLE.

No more, my lord! my king I ſee has err'd,
In off'ring peace and happineſs to Venice.
Yet let me mourn for you, her wretched race!
Her ſlaughter'd ſons, and violated virgins;
For you, her ſhrieking matrons; and for you,
O ye unconſcious, unoffending babes,—
Driv'n from your humble yet your chearful homes,
To timeleſs graves, or everlaſting exile!
Anſelmo dooms you to this dreadful fate,
And ſpurns the friendſhip offer'd to preſerve you.

ANSELMO.

Eternal curſes on the baleful friendſhip,
That ſeeks to cheat us of our native juſtice!
And did your mean, your poorly-thinking prince
Suppoſe Anſelmo would betray his country,
Hang up his name to everlaſting ſcorn,
And ſell the brighteſt birthright of a people,
To gain a robber's portion of the plunder!
What cou'd repay me for internal peace,
Or give diſtinction where I ſold my honour?
The wildeſt prodigal the world can know,
Is he who madly caſts away his virtue;

And tho' he gains a ſceptre in return,
He's ſtill a wretched loſer by the change—

GRANVILLE.

Enough, my lord; we end our conf'rence here.—
Venice, 'tis true, admires the good Anſelmo,
And truſts her preſent ſafety to his wiſdom;—
Yet if his fellow-citizens ſhall hear,
How light their happineſs is held, when weigh'd
In glory's grand, tho' too romantic ſcale,
Well may they mourn this honourable madneſs,
This dread, tho' bright, delirium of the mind,
Which ſeeks for ſafety in aſſur'd deſtruction,
And blindly murders nations to preſerve them.

ANSELMO.

Whene'er they ſhew ſuch turpitude of ſoul,
Make them again an offer of your chains!—
But now, the purport of your buſineſs o'er,
And public character thrown wholly off,
In the plain province of a private man,
Let me ſalute the noble lord of Granville;
And beg, while Venice boaſts of ſuch a gueſt,
He'll not diſdain the dwelling of Anſelmo!

GRANVILLE.

My lord, with equal gratitude and pleaſure,
I meet your kindneſs for my little ſtay;
My ſcarce furl'd ſails muſt quickly court the wind,
And bear me back to my expecting maſter.

ANSELMO.

Th' aſſembled ſenate now requires my preſence—
My lord, farewell!—I treat you as a friend.—
I never dealt in ceremony yet; and you'll excuſe
Th' unpoliſh'd manners of Venetian ſailors.

GRANVILLE.

The gen'rous frankneſs of your temper here,
Beſpeaks a native honeſty and wiſdom,

4 That

That makes me doubly anxious for the ſtate,
And doubly mourn your harſh reply to Lewis.

ANSELMO.

Mourn not for us, my lord!—a free-born people
Can have but two bright objects of ambition;
A life of honour, or a death of glory:
And when for virtuous liberty they fall,
They ſhare at leaſt the ſecond greateſt bleſſing,
Which heav'n e'er pour'd in mercy on mankind. [*Exit.*

GRANVILLE *alone.*

How I admire his fortitude of ſoul,
And love his pride, tho' adverſe to my wiſhes!
Once my own boſom vehemently flam'd
With all the phrenzy of his noble zeal,
And look'd on death more eligible far,
Than ev'n a government of certain bliſs,
Beneath the reign of any foreign ruler.—
But I now wake from all this glitt'ring dream
Of fancied virtue and ideal honour—
My Clementina!—

Enter CLEMENTINA.

CLEMENTINA.

My long-loſt Rinaldo!
'Tis he—'tis he, and Elizara err'd not!
The grave has giv'n him back.—All-ſeeing heaven,
In kind compaſſion to a wife's deſpair,
By ſome benignant miracle has rais'd him;
And theſe tranſported arms again enfold
The beſt belov'd, the moſt deplor'd of huſbands.

GRANVILLE.

My life's great bliſs! here let me grow for ever.

CLEMENTINA.

It is too much—I ſhall run wild with rapture—
How are you ſav'd, and wherefore thus diſguis'd?

Yet

Yet do not anſwer—partly Elizara
Has told me of your views—and 'tis enough
I ſee you ſafe—That providence be prais'd!
Whoſe mercy ſent you at an hour of dread,
To ſnatch me from deſtruction!—

GRANVILLE.

O my love!
I cannot tell you half of what I feel;
Words are too poor.—Yet ſay, my chiefeſt good,
Say, do you love with ſuch tranſcendent truth,
That if the kindneſs of indulging fate,
Shou'd point out ways of flying with Rinaldo,
To ſome ſecure, ſome hoſpitable coaſt,
Alike propitious to our peace and fortune;
Wou'd Clementina, wou'd a wife prefer
The fond, the ardent boſom of a huſband,
To the ſtern manſion of a ruthleſs father?

CLEMENTINA.

Wou'd ſhe prefer?—O quickly let him lead her
Thro' dreary waſtes, and never-trodden wilds,
Where heat, cold, famine, in their dread extremes,
At each new footſtep ſtrike an added horror;
Thro' the noon-blaze of fierce autumnal ſuns,
O'er burning deſarts inſtantly conduct her;
Or where the ſtiff'ning nations of the night,
In more than winter freeze beneath the pole;
Thro' theſe bear off your faithful Clementina;
And tho' a filial anguiſh drowns her eye,
At what her poor, her rev'rend father feels,
O never queſtion if ſhe loves Rinaldo!

GRANVILLE.

Thus let me preſs you to my grateful boſom,
Thus ſpeak the raptures of my ſwelling heart!

CLEMENTINA.

O I have much to tell you of my ſorrows.—
But what are ſorrows now?—The gracious being,
Who from a precipice of guilt and woe,
In this dread criſis, ſnatch'd me by your hand,
O'erpays me tenfold for my paſt afflictions,
And all my tears were miniſters of joy.

[*Exeunt.*

ACT

ACT III.

ANSELMO's *Palace.*

Enter ANSELMO *with a Paper, and* ADORNO.

ANSELMO.

FROM Ferdinand himſelf.—

ADORNO.

From Ferdinand!

ANSELMO.

From him, Adorno.—But obſerve his words!—
" Touch'd with the various miſeries of Venice,
" The firſt of Europe's kings ſalutes the ſenate;
" And offers peace, nay friendſhip to their realms,
" Peace uncondition'd, and eternal friendſhip."

ADORNO.

What! has the royal ruffian been inform'd
That France has ſued us to become her ſubject;
And does he, fearful of our baſe aſſent,
Fearful his rival ſhou'd obtain our homage,
Give up his own deſpotic claim upon us,
And rather chooſe to ſet us wholly free,
Than ſee his foe acknowledg'd for our maſter?

ANSELMO.

Too plain.—Perdition on his recreant head!
His motive may be ſeen.—Too plain, his fears
Wou'd now uſurp the guiſe of high-ſoul'd virtue:
But tho' we know the ſource of this propoſal,
Tho' we are certain that his late defeats,
Join'd to his dread of our receiving Lewis,

Have

Have dragg'd the trembling tyrant from his throne,
To daſtard ſupplication—ſtill his offers
Demand our prompt acceptance—he conſents
To yield up all our towns—our captive ſons—
To ceaſe for ever his deteſted claim,
And treat us henceforth, as a ſep'rate nation,
A dear ally, but independent people.

ADORNO.

But ſay, my lord, what miniſter he ſends,
To ſign theſe terms of unexpected peace?
Fraud and the royal hypocrite are one;
Nor can we truſt ſecurely to his word,
When once his int'reſt urges him to break it.

ANSELMO.

That very int'reſt is our hoſtage now—
And here too, conſcious of our glad concurrence,
He ſpeeds his Alva to confirm the treaty;
Who comes beneath ſafe-conduct from Colonna,
(Supplying now my abſence in the fleet)
And will arrive at Venice ere the eve.

ADORNO.

So ſoon?

ANSELMO.

So ſays the letter.—But, my friend,
Haſte hence!—Convene the ſenators— the people!—
Within an hour I'll meet them at Saint Mark's;
There, when our peace is happily reſtor'd,
They ſhall receive their government again,
And find a ſubject in their preſent ruler.

[*Exit* Adorno.

Enter PALERMO.

Joy to my ſon!—to Venice boundleſs joy!—
O my Palermo! I have news that aſks
An angel's tongue.—

PALERMO.

And I have news, that howl'd
In deepeſt hell, wou'd make the demons tremble.—
Clementina——

ANSELMO.

Ha! what of her, Palermo?

PALERMO.

Is falſe, perfidious——

ANSELMO.

How?

PALERMO.

Doats upon another!

ANSELMO.

Beware, Palermo, this capricious temper!
Doubt ſeldom lodges in a noble mind;
And he ſcarce merits to be treated juſtly,
Whoſe jealous ſoul, on light foundation, queſtions
Th' unſullied luſtre of another's virtue—
Retract then quick this haſty accuſation,
And kindly ſay my hapleſs child is dead,
But dare not once to tell me ſhe is worthleſs!

PALERMO.

On light foundation did I doubt, my lord,
This ſharp reproach had been indeed deſerv'd;
But if inceſſant coldneſs, if contempt,
If open inſult for proteſting love,
And ev'n a noon-day fondneſs for a ſtranger,
Are honeſt grounds of rational ſuſpicion,
Then have I cauſe for rage and indignation—

ANSELMO.

By heav'n, 'tis falſe! nor ſhall my child be wrong'd
By any coinage of a dotard's madneſs;

Her

Her soul, superior to the sland'rous charge,
Has prov'd its worth to more than Roman greatness;
And if she meant not to accept your vows,
Her sense—her pride—her virtue had repuls'd them
—Fond of a stranger—Tell me, Sir—what stranger,
What mighty object has alarm'd your fears,
And kindled hell's most fiercely blazing fire,
The fire of groundless jealousy within you?

PALERMO.

Why will Anselmo treat me with contempt,
And wound the wounded with the darts of scorn?
Think you I rave, or that my restless brain,
Ingenious, seeks out sources of misfortune?
But what if hid within yon secret arbour
You shou'd yourself detect them—what if there
You knew them long conceal'd? What if you saw
Her alabaster arm, as I have seen it,
O damning sight! thrown round the happy villain,
Wou'd you not then with me conclude her lost,
And think this ample evidence to prove
The plain perdition of her monstrous falshood?

ANSELMO.

And were you, Sir, a father, like Anselmo,
Like me, a doating father—had your child
Thro' life maintain'd an unsuspected honour,
And rose in virtue as she rose in beauty;
Wou'd you believe, at reason's full meridian,
A maid thus pure, thus eminently spotless,
Cou'd plunge at once in infamy eternal,
And set fame, fortune, happiness at nought,
Thro' instant passion for a total stranger?

PALERMO.

My Lord, I come not with an idiot's tale,
Or wish Anselmo in an angry mood
Shou'd, as an infant, chide a thoughtless daughter:

No; I disdain the thought—I come to guard
No less his honour than my own—to shew
Our mutual danger—and advise, that Granville
May be this moment order'd to his France—
As yet, tho' highly erring, Clementina
Cannot be compleatly guilty—Send, then,
Her new-found fav'rite instantly from Venice—
She still is undestroy'd; and Granville,
Tho' thrice my sword avengingly was drawn,
Safe from this arm, enjoys the law of nations.

ANSELMO.

Rash—desp'rate youth, forbear to urge my temper—
Or, by yon heav'n, the friendship which I hold you,
No more o'erlooks this treatment of my child—
She false—She shameless—Kneel, blasphemer, kneel,
Fall at her feet, and own you've lost your reason;
For nought but madness can excuse the wound,
Which virtue feels in injur'd Clementina.

PALERMO.

They're in the arbour yet—convince yourself—
And see how far I wound the cause of virtue,
In this report of faithless Clementina.

ANSELMO.

I will this instant—But remember, Sir,
Unless your charge proceeds from some mistake
Of probable appearance—unless it springs
From some plain source of obvious misconception,
The purpos'd union never shall take place——
I prize my child's repose too dearly, Sir,
To trust it with a madman—Nor will she
Be e'er prevail'd on to receive a lover,
Who dares to think her capable of baseness. [*Exit.*

PALERMO *alone.*

To think her base—O that I cou'd not think it—
What tho' her person spotless and unsullied,

May

May vie with Zembla's now-descending snows,
What tho' her error is ideal yet,
And actual guilt has stamp'd no sable on her;
Is not her mind, that all-in-all of virtue,
Polluted, stain'd, nay prostitute before me?
Do I not take, O torture! to my arms,
A mental wanton, in the rage, the madness
Of flaming will, and burning expectation?
Will not this fiend, damnation on him, Granville,
Will he not dart like light'ning to her memory,
And fire her fancy ev'n——O hold my brain—
Let me avoid the mere imagination—
It stabs—it tears—On love's luxurious pillow
It blasts the freshest roses, and leaves scorpions,
Eternal scorpions only, in their room. [*Exit.*

Scene changes to the Arbour in the Garden.

CLEMENTINA *and* GRANVILLE *discovered.*

CLEMENTINA.

No more, my love!—'tis time we reach the palace—
But remember, if aught adverse shou'd arise,
Which heav'n forbid, to intercept our flight,
On no account reveal yourself; reflect,
Our law is death to all Venetian subjects,
Who dare propose a government of strangers!

GRANVILLE.

Fear not, my Clementina:—with strict prudence,
A prudence render'd doubly nice by love,
The whole shall be conducted.—

CLEMENTINA.

For my sake
Let it—Reveal'd, your public character
Wou'd now destroy, and not protect you; jealous,
To fury jealous for their antient customs,
The multitude, with all my father's rage,

Wou'd

Wou'd burn—and O, thus wonderfully ſav'd,
Again my love, I cannot, muſt not loſe you.
[*Embracing him.*

Enter ANSELMO.

ANSELMO.

Death to my ſight!

CLEMENTINA.

Ha! I behold my father!

ANSELMO.

Yes, bluſhleſs girl, you do behold your father.—
And you, O baſe, inhoſpitable lord!
You too, behold the much-abus'd Anſelmo.—
But hence to France, the native nurſe of wiles:
This moment hence to France, or know the next
Is big with fate, and teeming with deſtruction!

GRANVILLE.

What is my crime, and wherefore ſhou'd I go?
Is it a crime to doat upon your daughter?
If that, my Lord, is deadly in your ſight,
I am indeed a criminal moſt guilty:
But ſure my rank, my fortune, and my fame,
Are no way leſs, than your approv'd Palermo's.

CLEMENTINA *kneeling.*

O Sir, O Father, O rever'd Anſelmo!
By ev'ry name of tenderneſs and duty;
By the dear mem'ry of that ſainted matron,
Who gave me birth, and from her well-earn'd heav'n
Beholds me proſtrate at your feet for pity;
Break off the curſt engagement with Palermo.—

ANSELMO.

Kneel not to me, ungrateful, kindleſs girl!
I have been proſtrate at your feet in vain.
Aſk not my pity, yet deny your own;

Nor think a father's fond forgiving heart,
While deeply bleeding, monster! at your shame,
Can quite forget this base capricious falshood,
Forget the vow scarce cold upon your lip,
To wrong'd Palermo, your affianc'd Lord,
And give its sanction to this guilty change—
A wanton's passion for a slave of France.

CLEMENTINA.

A wanton's passion!

GRANVILLE.

Wanton!—hear, Anselmo—

CLEMENTINA.

No, let me speak; and let me here assert
The equal rights of justice and of nature;
A wanton's passion—I'm your daughter, Sir,
But am not therefore to be deem'd a slave;
I bear you all the rev'rence, the regard,
That can inform a filial bosom—yet
My heart is free, and must consult its feelings;—
I cannot teach these feelings what you wish,
I cannot rush, deep perjur'd, to the altar;
Nor in the presence of attesting heav'n,
Profess to honour, what I now despise,
And swear to love the object of my horror.

ANSELMO.

Shameless deceiver, peace!—You, Sir, to France!
Th' impatient winds are swell'd to fill your sails;
Hence then, ard fly the fury of Anselmo!

GRANVILLE.

Flight was not made for soldiers, nor befits
Th' ambassador of kings—I claim protection
From the known law of nations—Mark, my lord!—
And think in time, I represent a monarch,
Who will not bear the shadow of an insult.

ANSEL-

ANSELMO.

Dare you aſſert the ſacred law of nations,
To ſcreen deceit, or ſanctify diſhonour?
I ſpurn all cuſtoms oppoſite to truth,
And own no rule, but what is own'd by virtue.—
A guard there ſtrait!

CLEMENTINA.

Yet force him not away.
Behold theſe tears, my father—O look back
On all the paſt tranſactions of my life!
Have I not ever walk'd with innocence,
And held one courſe of unſuſpected honour?
Strong as appearances may ſpeak againſt me,
Think, kindly think, there may be yet a cauſe—
What wou'd I ſay—Diſtraction! Murder Granville?
And muſt Anſelmo's boſom bleed?—O mis'ry!
Where ſhall I turn?—Indeed—indeed, my father,
I am not criminal—and O believe
At once I cannot be intirely worthleſs!

ANSELMO.

O impudence of guilt!—when my own eyes,
With ſhame have witneſs'd your licentious fondneſs!
Nought but that proof cou'd ever have convinc'd me;
For O I lov'd you with ſuch wild exceſs,
And held your purity in ſuch opinion,
That had an angel told me of this change,
This rapid, dire tranſition into vice,
I ſtill had wanted occular conviction.
What ho! a guard!—And can this be my child?
O nature, nature! this my Clementina?
And can ſhe thus deſert me after all?
In the cold ev'ning of my age deſert me,
For this once-ſeen, this hoſt-betraying ruffian?
Who, gracious heav'n! O who wou'd be a father!

Enter a Guard.

Arreſt that lord!—and bear him to his ſhip.

GRANVILLE.

Stand off, ye ſlaves! by heav'n, he dies that ſtirs.

CLEMENTINA.

Oh mercy!

ANSELMO.

Strike, if madly he reſiſt you!

CLEMENTINA.

Strike here then! pay obedience to your chief,
And kill his child, his wretched child, before him.
Diſpatch us both, or let us both depart;
We go together, or together fall.

GRANVILLE.

And muſt I live to ſee you raviſh'd from me?
To think perhaps another—that Palermo—
O ſnatch me, ſnatch me from the horrid thought!
It breaks, it rends me on a thouſand wheels,
And any death is extaſy to this.—

CLEMENTINA.

And do you judge ſo poorly of my love?
O know me better, and be quite at reſt!
This arm, if it muſt come to that, ſhall free me.—
Yet, while our hope ſupplies one glimmering ray,
Let us not urge our fate, before 'tis needful;
Conceal your name and quality with care;
And recollect 'tis time enough to die,
When ev'ry means of living is deny'd us?

ANSELMO.

What ſhallow air of myſtery is this?
Trifle not, guards,—but execute your orders!

GRANVILLE.

Off, barbarians, off!

CLEMENTINA.

You ſhall not part us.—

ANSELMO.

Hew them aſunder!

GRANVILLE.

O my Clementina! [*Borne off.*

CLEMENTINA.

It is too much. [*Faints.*

ANSELMO.

She faints.—

Enter ELIZARA.

Aſſiſt her, quick!
Yet why aſſiſt her? O my breaking heart!
Shou'd it not now in mercy be my wiſh,
To cloſe her eyes for ever on her ſhame,
And end her being and her crime together?

ELIZARA.

Patience! ſhe's innocent; and ſee, my Lord,
See, ſhe revives!

ANSELMO.

O gentle Elizara,
Cou'd the bright luſtre of her mind revive,
I might again behold her as I have done;
But that is ſet in one eternal night,
And now my dream of happineſs gives way
To ſure diſgrace, and aggravated anguiſh.
Ye fathers, tear the feelings from your hearts!
Ye mothers, drag your infants from the breaſt,
Daſh them remorſeleſs on their kindred flint,
And kill the embryo ſavageneſs within them.
They'll elſe blaſt all the comforts of your life,
And, viper-like, with death return your fondneſs—
O nature, nature, can this be my child!
Loſt Clementina; wretched, curſt Anſelmo! [*Exit.*

ELIZARA.

ELIZARA.

How does my Clementina?—Look, O look,
And ſee your trueſt friend!—

CLEMENTINA.

Where have I been?
And why am I reſtor'd?—'Tis Elizara.—
Say, O ſay kind maid—where is my huſband?
Where is he hurried by his brutal guard?

ELIZARA.

Are you a ſtranger to your father's order?

CLEMENTINA.

No—no—I rave—I know it but too well—
O this relentleſs, this unfeeling father!
Yet why do I exclaim?—His cauſe for rage
Is juſt—He only acts as virtue dictates;
And his poor heart is torn for my offence.—
'Tis fate alone that marks me out for woe,
And I ſhall never ſee Rinaldo more.

ELIZARA.

Perſiſt not thus in unavailing grief;
But praiſe the goodneſs that preſerves your huſband.
Ev'n now the head-ſtrong multitude, enrag'd
At Granville's embaſſy to change the ſtate,
Throng round the palace, and in thouſands threat
A quick and public meaſure of revenge.
Had he but ſtay'd another hour, a moment,
Perhaps Anſelmo's, ev'n your father's pow'r,
Had been too weak, tho' exercis'd, to ſave him.

CLEMENTINA.

What does this do, but aggravate my ſorrows?
But ſhew how curs'd, how doubly curs'd my fate,
My cruel fate, has mercileſsly made me?

Conceal'd, my husband falls a dreadful victim
To popular resentment.—If acknowledg'd,
His country's justice leads him to the scaffold—
And flying, gracious, and immortal pow'rs!
Anselmo, burning at my seeming crime,
Presses that fell Palermo to his bed.—
Why this is woe, 'tis thick substantial woe,
And shall behold a breast unshrinking here—
Burst from your cells ye demons of despair!
Ye furies clad in tenfold snakes arise!
Yawn quick ye graves with all your timeless dead!
Ye cannot now strike terror to my soul;
Rinaldo's lost, and I can fear no farther!

ELIZARA.

Why this distrust in heav'n's unending mercy?
Has it not now pour'd blessings on your head,
And work'd an actual miracle to save you,
From the wide horror of a double marriage?
What is there now but to refuse Palermo,
To slight the man you meant this morn to slight,
And end a suit you can receive no longer?
Hope therefore still, and think the gracious hand,
Which led your lord at such a crisis here,
Will crown your truth with happiness at last.

CLEMENTINA.

Go talk of hope to wretches at the stake,
To shrieking mothers o'er their infants dead—
Go bid the murd'rer, while his hands yet reek
With unoffending blood, hope to regain
His former peace of mind, or ever know
A tranquil thought, a tranquil slumber more!—
O, I cou'd curse this base deceiver, hope,
Till echo thunder'd execration back,
And rent the air with imprecating phrenzy.— [*A shout.*
What means that shout? Ha! my fears inform me.
Perhaps ev'n now the savage multitude

Have ſeiz'd my huſband; and perhaps they now
Glut their fell vengeance on his quiv'ring limbs.
Shout.] Again—it muſt be ſo—Barbarians, ſtay—
For me, for me he falls—'Twas Clementina—
'Twas I who led him to your fatal ſhores—
Wreak then your vengeance on his wretched wife,
But ſpare, O ſpare Rinaldo! [*Runs out wildly, Elizara following.*

ACT

ACT IV.

Scene ANSELMO's *Palace.*

Enter ANSELMO *and* PALERMO.

ANSELMO.

WELL, my Palermo—this unlook'd-for rival
Ploughs back his way to tyranny and France.
I ſaw his canvaſs whitening on the breeze,
As well to know him certainly departed,
As to reſtrain the fury of the people,
Who, fir'd with honeſt, tho' miſguided zeal,
Forgot his ſanctity of public character,
And rav'd for vengeance on a foe to freedom.

PALERMO.

The people's voice, howe'er it ſometimes errs,
Means always nobly, and is rais'd by virtue;
Their very faults, illuſtrious from their motives,
Demand reſpect, nay, aſk for admiration,
And ſoar, at leaſt, half ſanctify'd to juſtice—
There—hear their voice—'tis now ſwell'd up with rapture.
Alva, the welcome miniſter of peace,
Excites their joy, and ev'ry order hails
The white-wing'd moment, that preſerves the ſtate,
And crowns the gen'rous labours of Anſelmo.

ANSELMO.

He comes, e'en earlier than my utmoſt hope,
And proves how much his ſovereign was alarm'd

At

At the now lucky embaſſy from Lewis—
Come, my Palermo, let us haſten hence!
And ſhew due honour to the noble Alva!

PALERMO.

Fain would I greet him; but alas, my gloom
Would chill the pleaſure which it meant to grace.

ANSELMO.

Remain then here—I wou'd not have it ſaid
That aught cou'd wound a citizen of Venice
Who liv'd to ſee his liberty reſtor'd.
I am the father of that wretched girl,
Who clouds your brow with grief and diſappointment;
I am, and feel her conduct like a father:
But when I think upon the countleſs millions,
Whom this unlook'd-for providence of heav'n
Deſigns to bleſs, I caſt away my griefs,
And in my country, ſtrive to loſe my daughter.

PALERMO.

Your ſpirit fires me—I adopt its juſtice,
And will attempt, if poſſible, myſelf
To loſe all memory of this ſweet deceiver.

ANSELMO.

Do—and be dearer to my heart than ever—
Your worth firſt made you mine; the ſame, that worth,
Shall keep you—Clementina now is ſunk
Below your thought; to wed her would be baſeneſs.
Deſpiſe her, therefore, as you prize my friendſhip,
And know I'd ſcorn to give a ſhameleſs woman,
Tho' ten times mine, to any man of honour. [*Exit.*

PALERMO.

He's right—he's right—I were a ſlave indeed,
A ſoul-leſs ſlave, to proſtitute a thought,
A ſingle thought, on ſuch a woman longer—
Were ſhe as fair as luxury has painted

The

The nymphs of Paradiſe to Eaſtern minds,
I ought to ſpurn her now—Her heart is loſt—
'Tis all debas'd by this licentious paſſion,
And he who weds the object of his ſcorn,
May boaſt of love, but never talk of honour— [*Exit.*

Scene changes to St. Mark's.

Enter ADORNO, *Senators*, *Citizens*, *Guards*, &c.

ADORNO.

Now is the time, my friends, to preſs him cloſe,
And make him wholly ſov'reign of the ſtate;
Which his great talents and unequal virtue
Have thus ſo happily, ſo nobly ſav'd—
The nations round us, owe their chiefeſt ſtrength
To regal government—How were we torn
With jarring int'reſts till the rule ſupreme,
To one great arm was truſted—to Anſelmo!
France—Ferdinand—and ev'ry pow'rful neighbour,
May ſtill divide us with their ſep'rate factions:
But if we chooſe a monarch of our own,
His and the public welfare muſt be one.—

Firſt CITIZEN.

Is he acquainted with our views, Adorno?
Have you inform'd him of our grateful purpoſe?

ADORNO.

No—For I fear'd his ſtern diſapprobation,
And only hope the people's gen'ral voice
Will now induce him to accept a throne.

Second CITIZEN.

See where he comes.—

Enter

Enter ANSELMO, *preceded by a Proceſſion of Prieſts Biſhops, Senators,* &c.

ANSELMO.

Well, my brave countrymen!
I once more ſee you free; the ſolemn league
Is happily concluded; and to heaven
Our deepeſt thanks we gratefully muſt pour,
For life, for peace, for liberty immortal!
Here now my labour and commiſſion end.
This ſacred ſword, the badge of ſov'reign pow'r,
Which in the ſtorms and perils of the ſtate,
Your gen'ral voice entruſted to my care,
And bade me carry as your common leader,
'Till death or freedom finiſh'd my command,
This ſacred pledge becomes your own again—
Here to your uſe I ſolemnly reſign it,
And ſink with tranſport, to a private ſtation;
More proud the ſubject of a free-born ſtate,
Than if I rul'd a univerſe of ſlaves—

ADORNO.

My lord Anſelmo, your applauding country
Gives back the ſword to that experienc'd hand,
Which crowns her ſons with liberty and peace:
Thro' me ſhe offers you a crown, a throne,
And hails her monarch, in her great preſerver.
Start not!—with me the gen'ral voice cries out,
Long live our king—long live the good Anſelmo.
[*A flouriſh.*

ANSELMO.

Shall I with thanks, or deep-ſtruck indignation,
With grateful heart, or juſtly kindled ire,
Receive this flatt'ring inſtance of your favour?
Warm to the voice of virtuous approbation,
I feel a joy beyond the pow'r of words,
To find my actions honour'd with your praiſe:
But in the riſing raptures of the man,

The honeſt citizen muſt do his duty;
He muſt refuſe, reſentingly refuſe,
Th' unthinking bounty, which to pay his ſervice,
Wou'd plunge his country in immediate bondage.

ADORNO.

This ſelf-denying dignity of ſoul,
Serves but to ſhew the wiſdom of our choice,
And proves how ſafe a confidence repos'd,
Will lodge in hands ſo worthy as Anſelmo's.

ANSELMO.

Long, my brave friends, againſt the Spaniſh tyrant,
Have the exalted citizens of Venice
Fought the great cauſe of juſtice and mankind:
And will you now, triumphant over force,
From downright gratitude embrace a chain?
What has your glorious fortitude effected,
If in the full fraught tranſport of your ſouls,
You lift the man you fondly call deliverer,
To ſov'reign rule, and crown him for your maſter?
In ſuch a caſe your bleſſing is your bane,
And Spain, a foe leſs deadly than Anſelmo.

ADORNO.

Does not the uſe which you have made of pow'r,
Proclaim how much, how amply we ſhou'd truſt you?
Have you employ'd it, but for public good,
Or wiſh'd to keep it, when that good was anſwer'd?
Hear then your grateful countrymen, and know
Adorno ſpeaks the wiſhes of the people,
The people's wiſhes joyfully conven'd,
Who with one voice now offer you a kingdom.

ANSELMO.

I ſcorn the kingdom that can court a tyrant,
And while I live my country ſhall be free.
If then my voice deſerves the leaſt attention,
Let me exhort, nay, ſhame you from your purpoſe.

I fought

I fought to ſave you from deſpotic pow'r,
Not, giddy men, to be myſelf your lord:
You may forget your duty to the ſtate,
But I'll remember mine, and keep all equal,
Tho' I myſelf am ſingled out for maſter.

Firſt CITIZEN.

We'll urge the point no more.

ADORNO.

I ne'er had urg'd it,
But for the public welfare, from belief,
That all rewards were properly his due,
Whoſe arm and wiſdom had preſerv'd our freedom.

ANSELMO.

Rewards, Adorno! talk not of rewards—
The man is half a traitor to the ſtate,
Who only ſerves it from a ſordid motive—
Yet, if too warm, too rude in my refuſal,
I give offence to any ſon of Venice,
Here I abjure th' intention of offending,
And beg my kind, my too indulgent friends,
May now diſperſe, and ſeek their ſeveral homes—
Who moſt loves freedom, will keep order moſt;
And know, the beſt way each can ſerve his country,
Is to hold tumult in a deep abhorrence,
And labour cloſely in his private ſtation.

ADORNO.

Long live Anſelmo—long live great Anſelmo.
[*Exit.* Adorno, Citizens, *&c.*

ANSELMO *alone.*

Lo there—the phrenzy of a nation's virtue!
Who cou'd abuſe their elevated weakneſs?
Curſe on the deſpicable ſlave that cou'd!—
Curſe on the ſlave, however he poſſeſſes
A nation's confidence, whoſe grov'ling intereſt,

Or abject pride, can tempt him to betray it!
The more his weight, his merit with a country,
The more he's bound, by ev'ry tye of honour,
To guard the laws; and he's a double villain,
When once he vilely turns that very power,
Which he derives from popular esteem,
To sap the bulwarks of the public freedom.

Enter an Officer.

What means this haste?

OFFICER.

To tell my lord Anselmo,
That Granville's vessel, which so late you forc'd
To sea, has unexpectedly borne back,
And seems to steer directly for the point
Which bounds the palace-garden from the surge—

ANSELMO.

Where is my daughter?—Where is Clementina?
I've scarcely left a soldier at the palace,
Sole tho' it stands, and sep'rate from the city—
Hence quick, and seize on Granville, if he lands.
Take ample force—My soul forebodes his purpose—
[*Exit Officer.*
Yet shou'd he dare—by heaven's high host he dies—
No character can sanctify such outrage—
The laws—the laws shall vindicate themselves,
And teach the ministers of neighb'ring kings,
To look for safety, only in their justice. [*Exit.*

Scene changes to an Apartment in ANSELMO's *Palace.*

Enter PALERMO, *followed by* CLEMENTINA.

CLEMENTINA.

Nay, for your own sake, give me up, Palermo;
Give me again my former peace of mind,

Give

Give me again, my father's dear regards,
Of which your fatal paſſion has depriv'd me:
O prideleſs lord, tho' dead to my repoſe,
At leaſt reflect and tremble for your own.
What joy, what comfort ever can you hope
From one, not only ſickening at your ſight,
But hear, and fly me—doating on another—
To madneſs doating—

PALERMO.

O, I know it well—
Your once-ſeen Granville, light capricious beauty!
And ſeen too, while your plighted vow to me
Was yet all warm, and flying up to heaven!
For him you trampled on your ſacred promiſe;
For this light Frenchman, in a ſingle moment,
Broke ev'ry roſy nicety of ſex,
And at a word, a glance—nay, without either—
Loſt a whole life of innocence and honour.—

CLEMENTINA.

Licentious railer—therefore give me up!
Nought but contention, wretchedneſs, and ſhame,
Can wait a union circumſtanc'd like ours.
Thro' life our fiend-like fury to each other,
Muſt make our home the dwelling of deſpair;
And after death, our ſtill oppoſing ſpirits,
If after death our enmity can live,
With thoſe in ſtory of the Thæban brothers,
Will ſhun all commerce, and as hating here,
Diffuſe their hate throughout the whole hereafter.—

PALERMO.

Swell not the picture with a needleſs horror,
Nor once imagine that my ſoul requires
Such ſtriking pleas to ſhun an obvious baſeneſs—
Think you I mean, perſiſting in my claim—
To ſeize a hand that juſtice bids me ſcorn;
No: I deſpiſe the meanneſs, and intend

Not

Not to aſſert my title, but reſign it ;
I am a lover,—yet I'm ſtill a man ;
Acquainted therefore with the blotted mind,
I turn affrighted from the faultleſs perſon,
And wed diſtraction ſooner than diſhonour.

CLEMENTINA.

Bleſt may you be for this exalted ſcorn,
This noble warmth of manly indignation,
Dearer to me than all the melting ſtrains
Which ſong e'er fancied for proteſting love—
My ſoul is now ſecurely at her eaſe,
And glows with grateful rev'rence for Palermo.

PALERMO.

Deem not unjuſtly, Madam, of my feelings ;
You may betray, but never ſhall deſpiſe me—
I come no whimp'rer of a tragic ſtory,
To ſhield beneath an angry father's ſanction,
And act the legal ruffian on averſion.
Falſe, therefore, Clementina, you are free—
Take back your vows—take your engagements back—
And tho' I own this heart muſt bleed profuſely,
For ſtill, O ſtill your image triumphs here :
Yet know, I'd ſooner tear it from my boſom,
Than once be rivall'd in the woman's thought,
Who made my wife, ſhould think alone for me.

Enter GRANVILLE.

GRANVILLE.

Where, where is Clementina?

CLEMENTINA.

Granville again!
Yet here again in danger.

GRANVILLE.

My love! away—
Fly hence—Eſcape is certain now.

PALERMO.

PALERMO *pushing him away.*

Vile Franc,
Stand off, 'tis death, 'tis death again to touch her—

GRANVILLE.

Forbear, rash man, to tempt my greedy vengeance.
Wild with my wrongs, its appetites are raging—
There is not now a coward guard to call;
My friends make pris'ners of your paltry force,
And e'er a band superior can arrive,
That lady will be safe on board—Dare not,
Therefore, to withstand us—her heart is mine—
So shall her hand be, tho' yours grasp'd the thunder.

PALERMO.

Heaven's own red bolt will not be then more deadly—
For know, injurious lord, tho' I despise
The hand and heart, that can descend so low;
Yet while I wield this sword, my noble friend
Shall not be basely plunder'd of his daughter:
Draw, Granville, boldly then, and prove which arm
Can best protect its master.

CLEMENTINA.

Hold, O hold
Your dread destructive swords—For my sake, Granville,
Plunge not thus in blood—And O Palermo!
If the bright flame of honour fires your soul,
As sure it does, from sentiments so noble,
Restrain your rage—The man whose life you seek—

GRANVILLE.

No more, my Clementina—Why entreat
Where we command with absolute dominion?
Without there, friends——

Enter a Party of Guards.

My spirited companions,
Secure that headstrong lord—I join you on the instant.

 Treat

Treat him, however, with a juſt reſpect!
I know him noble, though he is my foe,
And ev'n admire him for his very hatred—

PALERMO.

Coward, is this your boaſted reſolution,
Is this the way you dare me to the fight,
And raiſe your merit with your peerleſs miſtreſs?

GRANVILLE.

And thinks Palermo that I fear his ſword,
Or uſe this method to elude his fury?
No—once eſcap'd from this oppreſſive ſtate,
Demand your reparation, and receive it——
The fate of many hangs upon me now,
And honour bids me rather bear you hence,
Than take your life in vengeance for your virtue.
Lead him away.

PALERMO.

O infamous aſſaſſin.
Now more than ever worthy of her heart—
But let your murd'rers bind me down ſecurely:
For if I once can ruſh upon your throat,
Theſe hands, unarm'd, ſhall do a noble vengeance,
And tear you piece-meal, inſtantly before her.

GRANVILLE.

Lead him away— [*Palermo is carried off.*

CLEMENTINA.

O ſay, my dear Rinaldo,
Say while ſurprize and joy have left me words,
By what bleſt accident again I ſee you?
Heaven ſure exhauſts its mercy on our heads,
And all its wonders are reſerv'd for love!

GRANVILLE.

The time will ſcarce admit ſufficient anſwer—
In brief know, therefore, that when torn from hence,
I heard

I heard Anſelmo's order to the troops,
To line the ſpacious quarters of St. Mark's;
Some angel then inſpir'd me with the thought
Of ſteering back, and forcing to my love,
Left now unguarded in a palace, diſtant
From inſtant aid, and dreaming not of danger;
Th' event, how happy! juſtified the action.
My brave attendants caught my honeſt flame,
And, heaven-aſſiſted, eaſily acquir'd
A bloodleſs conqueſt o'er your people.
[*A Shout without, and a claſhing of ſwords.*

CLEMENTINA.

Ha!
What means that ſhout, this ſudden claſh of arms?

GRANVILLE.

Stand firm, my friends; I fly to your ſupport. [*Exit.*

ANSELMO *without.*

Seize him, ſeize Granville.

CLEMENTINA.

O almighty heav'n!
We're loſt again—again undone—

ANSELMO *without.*

Palermo,
Send off his bravoes to the common dungeon.

CLEMENTINA.

Some mountain fall on my devoted head,
And ſhield me from the fury of Anſelmo!—
My dear Rinaldo! How ſhall I preſerve him!
O that the daughters of indulgent ſires
Cou'd know my ſorrows, know my anguiſh now!
They'd fly from diſobedience, and wou'd ſhudder
In downright prudence, to admit a thought
That madly tended to deceive a Father.

Enter ANSELMO, GRANVILLE, *Guards*, &c.

ANSELMO.

And now conduct the hero to his priſon.
His monarch maſter, tho' in priſon here,
Shou'd not unpuniſh'd violate our laws,
Nor offer ſuch an outrage to Anſelmo.

GRANVILLE.

Why all this pomp of needleſs preparation?
I know my crime, and dare your inſtant ſentence.
Bring forth your knives, your engines, or your fires—
Next to ſucceeding in a noble cauſe,
The gen'rous mind eſteems to ſuffer nobleſt.
Bring forth your racks then, witneſs to my triumph,
And be yourſelf, obdurate Lord, the judge,
Which is moſt brave, the torturer or tortur'd.

CLEMENTINA.

Stop not with him—Prepare your racks for me—
I am moſt guilty, and to heav'n I ſwear,
Whate'er his fate is, that is Clementina's.
Yet, my dear Granville, if we are to fall,
We'll vindicate our fame; and tho' offending,
Aſſert at leaſt the honour of our loves.
Let us inform this venerable chief,
It is a ſon he hurries to the block,
And that my fancy'd ſpoiler is my huſband.

ANSELMO.

Your huſband, traitreſs!—infamous evaſion,
To varniſh o'er your unexampled baſeneſs,
And ſnatch, if poſſible, this foreign caitiff,
This foul offender, from the ſtroke of juſtice.

GRANVILLE.

Take heed, reveal not all, my Clementina.
Fate's worſt is done, and dying undiſcover'd,

Guards

Guards thoſe I prize much dearer than my life.
Remember this; and O remember too,
Known, or unknown, that equal death awaits me.

CLEMENTINA.

My father, hear me—Yes, he is my huſband.
However ſtrange, myſterious, or unlikely—
I muſt no more—But time, a little time,
Will prove it all—Then, gracious Sir, diſtreſs
No longer an unhappy pair, whoſe hands
High heaven has join'd—Allow the wretched wife
To gain her wedded lord; and judge, O judge,
If aught but this, the firſt of human duties,
Cou'd tear her thus from Venice and her father.

ANSELMO.

Your huſband—married—when—by whom, and where?
Away, degen'rate, infamous deceiver,
Away, and from the world hide quick
That guilty head—Your minion dies this hour—
The next, a cloyſter ſhuts you in for ever.
Take him from hence—

CLEMENTINA.

And take me with him.

GRANVILLE.

Unman me not with this exceſſive ſoftneſs,
My life's ſole joy; but let me meet my fate
As may become a ſoldier—Where's my dungeon?
Perhaps Anſelmo, when a little calmer,
May think my blood ſufficient expiation,
And let my guiltleſs followers eſcape,
Whoſe only crime is duty to their leader.
Gracious heav'n compoſe her— [*Borne off.*

CLEMENTINA *to the Guard preventing her.*

Off—let me go—
Is this a time to drag me from my huſband?

Will not his blood ſuffice your utmoſt rage,
But muſt he, in the bitter hour of death,
Loſe the poor comforts of a wife's attendance?
Where is the mighty freedom of your ſtate,
Where your ſtrict love of liberty and juſtice?
Why, ſay, O why, ye too benignant pow'rs!
Did you from ruin ſnatch this barbarous realm,
Where ev'n our virtues are conſider'd crimes,
And ſoft compaſſion's conſtituted treaſon—
Revoke, revoke your merciful decrees;
From your dread ſtores of everlaſting wrath
Hurl inſtant fury down, and blaſt thoſe laws
Which talk of freedom, yet enſlave the mind,
And boaſt of wiſdom, while they chain our reaſon!

ANSELMO.

Blaſpheming monſter—ſtop that impious tongue,
Nor thus provoke me longer, to commit
Some dreadful deed of honourable phrenzy:
Already driv'n beyond a father's patience,
I ſcarce can ſpare the very life I gave.
Hence from my ſight then, execrable wretch—
To urge me farther, is to ruſh on death,
And add new horrors to the fate of Granville.

CLEMENTINA.

Do ſtrike at once—behold my ready boſom—
Yet ſpare, Anſelmo, my unhappy huſband:
He is not what he ſeems—O Sir—he is—
My brain—my brain—When, when ſhall I have reſt?
My father, be conſiſtently ſevere,
Wreak not this cruel murder on my peace,
And think that nature ſanctifies my perſon.

ANSELMO.

He is not what he ſeems—Declare who is he?
How loſs of truth attends the loſs of honour!
Abandon'd girl, your arts are all in vain,

Are

Are all unable to prevent his fate.
At my requeſt, th' aſſembling ſenate now
Prepare to hear his crime, and will pronounce
His doom directly—Nay, this wretched tale
Shall ev'n give vengeance wings—accelerate
His fall; and, like the dreadful whirlwind, ſweep
Him to deſtruction. [*Exit.*

CLEMENTINA.

Stay, Anſelmo, ſtay—
He is—but that is alſo certain death,
And I myſelf prepare the horrid axe
If I reveal him—Which way ſhall I act?
The lab'ring globe convulſing to its baſe,
Is downy ſoftneſs to my mad'ning boſom:
I'm all diſtraction—Reaſon drops her rein,
And the next ſtep is dreadful deſperation. [*Exit.*

ACT

ACT V.

Scene a Priſon.

Enter GRANVILLE *in Chains.*

GRANVILLE.

WHERE ſhall I turn—they have me now ſecure—
Was I however ſingled out alone,
To bear the utmoſt malice of the ſtars,
I cou'd, unſhrinking, look upon theſe chains;
But when I think what Clementina ſuffers,
When in the eye of agonizing fancy,
I paint my wife all weltring in her blood,
Or what more deeply damns me in reflection,
Suppoſe her drag'd to hot Palermo's bed;
My heart faints inſtantly with apprehenſion,
And almoſt dies at bare imagination;
Yet, gracious fountain of unbounded mercy!
Let one bleſt drop from your exhauſtleſs ſource,
In pity fall, and ſave my Clementina;
Save her, O ſave her in the hour of peril,
And teach the world that——

CLEMENTINA *within.*

Hear me, O Anſelmo!
I conjure you hear me—

GRANVILLE.

She's now in danger—
The ſlaves now tear their victim to the altar.
She is my wife—Barbarians, hear you that!
Theſe chains—theſe chains—damnation on theſe chains—

The

The priſon blazes—Hell yawns quick before me—
Where does this lead? No matter where—Deſpair
Is prudence now— [*Exit.*

Scene changes to an Apartment in ANSELMO's *Palace.*

Enter ANSELMO *and* PALERMO.

ANSELMO.

And yet, my good Palermo,
My ſecret ſoul inclines to hear her too.
O did you mark her undiſſembled anguiſh?

PALERMO.

I did—I did—and felt it moſt ſeverely—
Her burning eye expanding into blood,
Stood deſperately fix'd, while on each cheek,
Each pallid cheek, a ſingle tear hung quiv'ring,
Like early dew-drops on the ſick'ning lily,
And ſpoke a mind juſt verging into madneſs.

ANSELMO.

I'll ſee her once again—for when I weigh
All the nice ſtrictneſs of her former conduct;
When I reflect, that to this curſed day,
She look'd, as if her perſon, wholly mind,
In Dian's breaſt cou'd raiſe a ſigh of envy,
I cannot think her utterly abandon'd:
Abandon'd too, in ſuch a little ſpace!
Deſpiſe me not, Palermo—for the father
Still ruſhes ſtrongly on my aching heart,
And fondly ſeeks for argument to ſave her.

PALERMO.

Check not the tender ſentiments of nature,
But ſee her—make her, if poſſible, diſcloſe
Who Granville truly is, ſince ſhe affirms
He is not what he ſeems, and is her huſband—
That he's a Frenchman, and of noble rank,
Appears too plainly from his high commiſſion—

But ſtill ſome ſecret ſtrongly heaves her ſoul;
And hid beneath this myſtery of woe,
Who knows how far that ſecret may not merit
Compaſſion, or excuſe—

ANSELMO.

I'll try at leaſt—
I'll act as fits the fondneſs of a father;
Forgive, as far as honour can forgive,
And if her guilt exceeds a father's mercy,
I'll beg of heaven the firmneſs of a man— [*Exit.*

PALERMO.

Unhappy, gen'rous, excellent old man!
I cou'd not quench his little ray of hope,
And tell him all I thought of Clementina.
She is indeed diſtreſt—But pride alone,
A diſappointed pride, and lawleſs love,
Now harrow up her ſoul—Had ſhe an honeſt,
Rational excuſe—a tale that cou'd behold
The light—ere now ſhe had diſcover'd it—
This ſeeming myſtery, is wholly art.
To ſave this new-made huſband—Monſtrous—monſtrous!
Shame riſes upon ſhame, and each freſh guilt
Out-damns the former with its deep'ning blackneſs—

Enter GRANVILLE, *burſting from the back Scene.*

GRANVILLE.

I've forc'd a way—Infernal villain, turn!
Chain'd as I am, you ſhall not fly me now.

PALERMO.

Why this exceeds my utmoſt expectation—
This is revenge that pays an age of torture.
Yes, fraudful lord, this meeting gives me tranſport;
And long ere now my vengeance had you felt,
But that the perjur'd partner of your crimes

Appear'd

Appear'd moſt guilty, and to juſtice ſeem'd
Leſs the ſeduc'd, than infamous ſeducer—

GRANVILLE.

Talk not of juſtice, O conſummate coward!
Talk not of juſtice, little-minded ſpoiler!
When, dead alike to ſentiment and ſhame,
You ſeek by force—by force, inhuman ruffian!
To drag a helpleſs woman to your bed;
And tho' deſpis'd—deteſted—execrated—
Attempt, aſſiſted by her ſavage father,
To make her yours, thro' actual rape and murder.

PALERMO.

Ere I reply to this injurious charge,
Let me, tho' fate hangs o'er your guilty head,
On equal terms, allow you room to anſwer.
Here I unlooſe your chains—Now hence with me,
And fight the cauſe of this abandon'd woman.
Palermo dares you forth to ſingle combat:
Palermo too, ſhall arm his vanquiſh'd foe,
Nor ev'n, while Venice dooms him to the axe,
Once name his crimes, to ſhun the claims of honour—

GRANVILLE.

Hence—With the promis'd ſword alone I'll anſwer;
For tho' my ſoul thro' all her enmity,
Feels a kind ſomething for this gallant anger,
In blood alone ſhe'll ſpeak her obligation. [*Exeunt*.

Scene changes to a Chamber.

Enter CLEMENTINA.

CLEMENTINA.

He'll ſee me—endleſs bleſſings on his head—
Yes—Elizara's counſel was moſt juſt:
There is no other way to ſave my huſband—
If I perſiſt in hiding who he is,
He dies beyond a doubt—whereas revealing
The fatal ſecret, tho' replete with horror,

May wake the father in Anſelmo's boſom;
And when he finds his daughter ſtill unſullied,
The ſudden torrent of ſurprize and joy,
May lead him yet to pity and forgiveneſs—

Enter ANSELMO.

ANSELMO.

I come at laſt, unhappy girl, to hear
If there's indeed, in this myſterious conduct,
Aught that can have pretenſions to excuſe?
I come ev'n hoping ardently for motives
To juſtify an offer of my pardon;
For O! I wiſh, I wiſh to find you guiltleſs—
Speak then at once, I earneſtly conjure you:
Give me but room to exerciſe my fondneſs,
And come again ſecurely to my heart—

CLEMENTINA.

O Sir! reſtrain, reſtrain this wond'rous goodneſs!
It pierces like a dagger thro' my heart,
And ſhews me doubly, what a wretch I was
To wrong ſo good, ſo excellent a father.
Had I at firſt reveal'd my wretched ſtory—
Had I but ſaid who Granville truly is,
I ſee, 'twere poſſible to hope for pity.

ANSELMO.

Deſerve that pity, and receive it now—
Prove that you are not loſt—prove that this Granville
Is not the vile ſeducer of an inſtant,
Shew me but this—and leave a partial father,
If you can wipe away the charge of ſhame,
To overlook the crime of diſobedience.

CLEMENTINA.

How cou'd I be a monſter ſo deprav'd,
As once to forfeit tenderneſs like this!

 O Sir—

O Sir—if you can graciously forgive
One fault—one fatal fault—wretch as I am,
We may be happy yet; and long, long days
Of future joy o'erpay these hours of sorrow—
Know then that Granville———

ANSELMO.

Well.

CLEMENTINA.

Is not of France.

ANSELMO.

Proceed.

CLEMENTINA.

He is a citizen of Venice—

ANSELMO.

What citizen?

CLEMENTINA.

Rinaldo—

ANSELMO.

Ha! confusion!
Son of my foe—nay more, a foe to freedom!

CLEMENTINA.

He's not your foe, Sir, nor a foe to freedom.
I need not mention how he fought for Venice;
You saw him fall, and saw his country weep:
A train of wonderful events has since
High-rais'd him in the court of France, and duty
To an indulgent, to a royal master,
Join'd with his wishes to behold your daughter,
Has led him to this dang'rous embassy:
O save him then, my father—I know well
His life is forfeit to the laws—But sure,

As your unequall'd virtue has preſerv'd
The ſtate, the ſtate will readily preſerve
Your hapleſs ſon.

ANSELMO.

'Tis hard, 'tis hard at once
To conquer our reſentments—Hard to take
Thoſe to our hearts, whom we have hated deadly:
But 'tis ſuch bliſs to find you ſtill unſpotted,
That what before had fir'd my ſoul to madneſs,
Brings rapture now, and cancels diſobedience.

CLEMENTINA.

How ſhall I ſpeak the feelings of my heart!
How, ſacred Sir, repay this wond'rous goodneſs!

ANSELMO.

I have a daughter ſtill—Rinaldo never
Was loſt to worth, tho' I abhorr'd his father;
Nor ſhall his country, for this firſt tranſgreſſion,
Forget the merit of his former ſervice.
Now you're my child again—your huſband lives;
Thus, thus I bury your offence for ever, [*Embracing her.*
And fly to bring Rinaldo to your arms. [*Exit.*

CLEMENTINA.

O teach me, heaven! O teach me to expreſs
The ſtrong ſenſations of my ſwelling boſom!
Do not oppreſs me with this weight of mercy,
And yet deſtroy my feeble pow'r to thank you:
But my Rinaldo, my deliver'd lord,
Shall ſpeak our mutual praiſe—Joy, boundleſs joy
And gratitude abſorb my little ſenſe
Beyond the reach of recollection—and
Tranſport grows too exquiſite for words.

Enter

Enter GRANVILLE, *leaning on his Sword, pale and bloody: entering he falls against the side of the Scene, where he continues some time.*

CLEMENTINA.

My husband—horror—welt'ring in his blood!
O who has rais'd his arm against your life?

GRANVILLE.

Behold I come ev'n in the pangs—support me,
Clementina—of death to save my love,
To prove my right—and guard her from dishonour.

CLEMENTINA.

Ye heavenly ministers—O say if this,
If this is all my happiness at last!

GRANVILLE.

My Clementina—But it will not be—
The hand of fate is on me—and Palermo
Triumphs after all—O had I giv'n him
Blow for blow—I cou'd enjoy these pangs—But
Thus, thus to fall——

[*Falling down,* Clementina *kneeling over him.*

CLEMENTINA.

Well now what farther business
Have I with life?—

GRANVILLE.

My dearest Clementina!

CLEMENTINA.

What says my love?

GRANVILLE.

They have not yet undone you?

CLEMEN-

CLEMENTINA.

Am I not yet alive—let that convince you—
Anſelmo too is reconcil'd—And O!
I look'd for years, for long, long years of joy:
But what is reconciliation now?
Or what is joy?—From dreams of heav'n I wake,
To added woe, to aggravated torture—
And muſt we part, Rinaldo?

GRANVILLE.

O for ever!
Life ebbs apace, and all is darkneſs round me,
Save Clementina—Save my gallant friends—
They're yours—my father too—farewel! One look,
One laſt dear look—farewel—farewel for ever. [*Dies.*

CLEMENTINA.

Here too my ſun eternally ſhall ſet—
Rinaldo—friend—companion—lover—huſband—
Hard as our doom is, it is kind in this,
And joins us now, to ſever us no more!

Enter ANSELMO.

ANSELMO.

Palermo has acquainted me with all—
And is he gone ſo ſoon?—O hapleſs girl!
But yet Palermo's not to blame—Rinaldo
Provok'd his fate—He urg'd him to the combat,
And the ſurvivor, conſcious who has fall'n,
Deplores moſt deeply the diſaſt'rous blow.

CLEMENTINA.

Hence with his more than crocodile complaining,
Hence, to th' inferior monſter of the Nile,
Let him teach tears of yet unfancy'd falſhood—
There lies my huſband ſlaughter'd by his hand,
Heav'n's

Heav'n's worſt of woes—Heav'n's worſt of woes upon him!
And thinks he now with ſounds of lamentation,
To charm down griefs of magnitude like mine?
No, here I ſhake off wretchedneſs and life;
Here I attend my dear Rinaldo's ſpirit,
And leave the world to beings like Palermo.
[*Stabs herſelf.*

ANSELMO.

O Clementina—O my child—my child!
Had you no pity for a weeping father?
Was I not curs'd enough, enough a wretch,
Without this blow to rend my breaſt aſunder?

CLEMENTINA.

I ſcarce know what I act—my reaſon totters;
Yet while an interval of ſenſe remains,
O ſee me, Sir, with leſs endearing goodneſs—
Wretched no leſs as daughter than as wife:
In life's decline I mark you out to woe,
And here I murder my unhappy huſband:
'Tis time the grave ſhou'd hide ſo foul a monſter!
My brain, my brain, my brain—Who's that—Palermo—
[*Raving.*
Again—There, ſavage—there, that blow is ample vengeance—
Look down—look down, Rinaldo—ſee your wife!
There lies the murd'rer ſlain by Clementina!
Prepare to meet my ſpirit in the ſkies!
Prepare to meet me in eternal morning!
Elyſium ſpreads upon my raptur'd view,
And I die bleſt, ſince dying I revenge you— [*Sinks.*

ANSELMO.

O when I caſt a retroſpective glance
On all the graces of her infant years;
When I reflect how, rip'ning into beauty,

My

My eager eyes wou'd ſtrain in tranſport on her,
Her faults, her follies vaniſh from my view,
And nought remains but tenderneſs to torture.

CLEMENTINA.

Where am I?—O I ſhall remember ſoon—
That is Anſelmo—that my rev'rend father:
O Sir, forgive me—beg down mercy on me!
And in the grave unite me to Rinaldo. [*Dies.*

ANSELMO.

She's gone—ſhe's gone; my lily there lies blaſted,
No more to know returning ſpring—no more
To bloſſom in the pride of beauty.—Where,
Where ſhall I fly to loſe my recollection?
The world is now deteſtable to thought,
Since all that once delighted me is loſt.
O wretched child—O miſerable father!
But let me not blaſpheme: good heav'n—good heav'n!
I yield ſubmiſſive to the dreadful ſtroke,
And only aſk that this unhappy ſtory,
To future times, may forcibly point out
The dire effects of filial diſobedience. [*Exit.*

THE END.

EPI-

EPILOGUE,

By GEORGE COLMAN, Esq;

Spoken by Mrs. YATES.

FROM Otway's *and immortal* Shakespeare's *page*
Venice *is grown familiar to our stage.*
Here the Rialto *often has display'd*
At once a bridge, a street, and mart of trade;
Here, treason threat'ning to lay Venice *flat,*
Grave candle-snuffers oft in Senate sat.
To-night in Venice *we have plac'd our scene,*
Where I have been—liv'd—died—as you have seen.
Yet, that my travels I may not disgrace,
Let me—since now reviv'd—describe the place!
Nor wou'd the Tour of Europe *prove our shame,*
Cou'd every Macaroni *do the same.*
The City's self—a wonder, all agree—
Appears to spring, like Venus, *from the sea.*
Founded on piles, it rises from the strand,
Like Trifle plac'd upon a silver stand:
While many a lesser isle the prospect crowns,
Looking like sugar-plums, or floating towns.
Horses and mules ne'er pace the narrow street,
Where crouded walkers elbow all they meet:
No carts and coaches o'er the pavement clatter;
Ladies, Priests, Lawyers, Nobles,—go by water:
Light boats and gondolas transport them all,
Like one eternal party to Vauxhall.
Now hey for merriment!—hence grief and fear!
The jolly Carnival leads in the year;

Calls the young Loves and Pleaſures to its aid ;
A three-months jubilee and maſquerade!
With gaiety the throng'd piazza glows,
Mountebanks, jugglers, boxers, puppet-ſhows:
Maſk'd and diſguis'd the ladies meet their ſparks,
While Venus *hails the mummers of* St. Mark's.
There holy friars turn gallants, and there too
Nuns yield to all the frailties—" Fleſh is heir to."
There dear Ridottos conſtantly delight,
And ſweet Harmonic Meetings ev'ry night!
Once in each year the Doge *aſcends his barge,*
Fine as a London *Mayor's, and thrice as large;*
Throws a huge ring of gold into the ſea,
And cries—" Thus We, thy Sov'reign, marry thee.
" Oh may'ſt thou ne'er, like many a mortal ſpouſe,
" Prove full of ſtorms, and faithleſs to thy vows!"
One word of politics—and then I've done—
The ſtate of Venice *Nobles rule alone.*
Thrice happy Britain, *where with equal hand*
Three well-pois'd ſtates unite to rule the land!
Thus in the theatre, as well as ſtate,
Three ranks muſt join to make us bleſs'd and great.
King, Lords, and Commons, o'er the nation ſit;
Pit, Box, and Gallery, rule the realms of wit.

THE SCHOOL FOR WIVES

P. J. De Loutherbourg invent. et sculp.

Act 4th Scene 4th in the School for Wives.

THE

School for Wives.

A

COMEDY.

AS IT IS PERFORMED AT THE

THEATRE-ROYAL

IN

DRURY-LANE.

Embelliſhed with an Etching, by Mr. LOUTHERBOURG.

A NEW EDITION.

LONDON,
Printed for T. BECKET, the Corner of the Adelphi, in the Strand.
MDCCLXXV.

[PRICE ONE SHILLING AND SIX-PENCE.]

THE SCHOOL FOR WIVES,

BEING A COMEDY IN WHICH THE LADIES
ARE PARTICULARLY INTERESTED,
IT SHOULD BE ADDRESSED TO THE FIRST
ORNAMENT OF THE SEX;
AND IS THEREFORE INSCRIBED WITH
THE HIGHEST ADMIRATION AND
THE MOST PROFOUND
REVERENCE,

TO HER MAJESTY;

NOT BECAUSE SHE IS THE GREATEST
OF QUEENS,
BUT BECAUSE, IN THE MILDER AND
MORE ENDEARING RELATIONS
OF LIFE,
SHE IS THE BRIGHTEST PATTERN
OF ALL
THE FEMALE VIRTUES.

January 1, 1774.

P R E F A C E.

THE Author of the following performance cannot commit it to the preſs, without acknowledging the deepeſt ſenſe of gratitude, for the uncommon marks of approbation with which he has been honoured by the Public.

Tho' he has choſen a title uſed by MOLIERE, he has neither borrowed a ſingle circumſtance from that great poet, nor, to the beſt of his recollection, from any other writer.—His chief ſtudy has been to ſteer between the extremes of ſentimental gloom, and the exceſſes of unintereſting levity; he has ſome laugh, yet he hopes he has alſo ſome leſſon; and, as faſhionable as it has been lately for the wits, even

even with his friend Mr. Garrick at their head, to ridicule the Comic Mufe, when a little grave, he muft think that fhe degenerates into farce, where the grand bufinefs of inftruction is neglected, and confider it as a herefy in criticifm, to fay that one of the moft arduous tafks within the reach of literature, fhould, when executed, be wholly without utility.

The author having been prefumptuous enough to affert, that he has not purloin'd a fingle fprig of bays from the brow of any other writer, he may perhaps, be afked if there are not feveral plays in the Englifh language, which, before his, produced Generals, Lawyers, Irifhmen, Duels, Mafquerades, and Miftakes? He anfwers, yes; and confeffes moreover, that all the Comedies before his, were compofed not only of men and women, but that, before his, the great bufinefs of comedy confifted in making difficulties for the purpofe of removing them; in diftreffing poor young lovers; and in rendering a happy marriage the object of every cataftrophe.

Yet tho' the Author of the School for Wives pleads guilty to all thefe charges, ftill, in extenuation of his offence, he begs leave to obferve, that having only men and women to introduce upon the ftage, he was obliged to compofe his Dramatis Perfonæ

Perſonæ of mere fleſh and blood; if, however, he has thrown this fleſh and this blood into *new* ſituations; if he has given a *new* fable, and placed his characters in a point of light hitherto unexhibited—he flatters himſelf that he may call his play, a *new* play; and tho' it did not exiſt before the creation of the world, like the famous Welch pedigree, that he may have ſome ſmall pretenſions to originality.

Two things, beſides the general moral inculcated through his piece, the author has attempted; the firſt, to reſcue the law, as a profeſſion, from ridicule or obliquy; and the ſecond, to remove the imputation of a barbarous ferocity, which dramatic writers, even meaning to compliment the Iriſh nation, have connected with their idea of that gallant people.—The law, like every other profeſſion, may have members who occaſionally diſgrace it; but, to the glory of the Britiſh name, it is well known that, in the worſt of times, it has produced numbers whoſe virtues reflected honour upon human nature; many of the nobleſt privileges the conſtitution has to boaſt of were derived from the integrity, or the wiſdom of lawyers: Yet the ſtage has hitherto caſt an indiſcriminate ſtigma upon the whole body, and laboured to make that profeſſion either odious or contemptible in the theatre, which, if the laws are indeed dear to good Engliſh-

Englishmen, can never be too much respected in this kingdom. There is scarcely a play in which a lawyer is introduced, that is not a libel upon the long robe; and so ignorant have many dramatic writers been, that they have made no distinction whatever, between the characters of the first barristers in Westminster-Hall, and the meanest solicitors at the Old Bailey.

With respect to the gentlemen of Ireland, where even an absolute attempt is manifested to place them in a favourable point of view, they are drawn with a brutal promptitude to quarrel, which is a disgrace to the well known humanity of their country.—The gentlemen of Ireland have doubtless a quick sense of honour, and, like the gentlemen of England, as well as like the gentlemen of every other high-spirited nation, are perhaps unhappily too ready to draw the sword, where they conceive themselves injured—But to make them proud of a barbarous propensity to duelling, to make them actually delight in the effusion of blood, is to fasten a very unjust reproach upon their general character, and to render them universally obnoxious to society. The author of the School for Wives, therefore, has given a different picture of Irish manners, tho' in humble life, and flatters himself that those who are really acquainted with the original, will acknowledge it to be at least a tolerable resemblance.

It would be ungrateful in the higheſt degree to cloſe this preface, without acknowledging the very great obligations which the Author has to Mr. Garrick. Every attention, which, either as a manager, or as a man, he could give to the intereſt of the following play, he has beſtowed with the moſt generous alacrity; but, univerſally admired as he is at preſent, his intrinſic value will not be known, till his loſs is deplored; and the public have great reaſon to wiſh, that this may be a very diſtant event in the annals of the theatre. The Epilogue ſufficiently marks the maſterly hand from which it originated; ſo does the comic commencement of the Prologue, and the elegant writer of the graver part, is a character of diſtinguiſhed eminence in the literary republic.

It has been remarked with great juſtice, that few new pieces were ever better performed than *The School for Wives*. Mr. King, that highly deſerving favourite of the town, was every thing the Author could poſſibly wiſh in General Savage. Mr. Rediſh acquired a very conſiderable ſhare of merited reputation in Belville. Mr. Moody is unequalled in his Iriſhman. Mr. Palmer, from his manner of ſupporting Leeſon, was entitled to a much better part: And Mr. Weſton in Torrington was admirable. Miſs Younge, in Mrs. Belville, extorted applauſe from the coldeſt auditor. Her tenderneſs—her force—her pathos, were the true effuſions of genius, and proved that ſhe has no ſuperior where the feelings are to be intereſted. With reſpect to Mrs. Abington, enough can never be ſaid. The elegance, the vivacity, the critical nicety with which ſhe went through Miſs Walſingham, is only to be gueſſed at by thoſe who are familiar with the performance of that exquiſite actreſs. Her Epilogue was delivered with an animation not to be conceived, and manifeſted the ſtrict propriety, with which ſhe is called the firſt prieſteſs of the Comic Muſe in this country.

Jan. 1, 1774.

PRO-

P R O L O G U E.

Spoken by Mr. KING.

NO coward he, who in this critick age,
Dares set his foot upon the dang'rous stage;
These boards, like Ice, your footing will betray,
Who can tread sure upon a slipp'ry way?
Yet some thro' five acts slide with wond'rous skill,
Skim swift along, turn, stop, or wind at will!
Some tumble, and get up; some rise no more;
While cruel criticks watch them on the shore,
And at each stumble make a hellish roar!
A wise Philospher hath truly noted,
(His name I have forgot, tho' often quoted,)
That fine-spun spirits from the slightest cause,
Draw to themselves affliction, or applause:
So fares it with our Bard.—Last week he meets
Some hawkers, roaring up and down the streets,
Lives, characters, behaviour, parentage,
Of some who lately left the mortal *stage!*
His ears so caught the sound, and work'd his mind,
He thought his own name floated in the wind;
As thus—" Here is a faithful, true relation,
" Of the birth, parentage, and education,
" Last dying speech, confession, character,
" Of the unhappy malefacterer,
" And comick poet, Thomas Addle Brain!
" Who suffer'd Monday *last at Drury-Lane;*
" All for the price of half-penny a-piece;"
Still in his ears these horrid sounds encrease!
Try'd and condemn'd, half executed too,
There stands the culprit; 'till repriev'd by you.

[going.

Enter Miſs YOUNGE.

Miſs YOUNGE.

Pray give me leave—I've *ſomething now to ſay.*

Mr. KING.

Is't at the School for Wives, *you're taught this way?*
The School for Huſbands *teaches to obey.*

[Exit.

Miſs YOUNGE

It is a ſhame, good Sirs, that brother King,
To joke and laughter ſhould turn every thing.
Our frighted poet would have no denial,
But begs me to ſay ſomething on his trial:
The School for Wives, *as it to us belongs,*
Should for our uſe be guarded with our tongues.
Ladies, prepare, arm well your brows and eyes,
From thoſe your thunder, theſe your light'ning flies.
Should ſtorms be riſing in the Pit—look down,
And ſtill the waves thus, fair ones, with a frown:
Or ſhould the Galleries for war declare;
Look up—your eyes will carry twice as far.

* *Our Bard, to noble triumphs points your way,*
Bids you in moral principles be gay;
Something he'd alter in your education,
Something which hurting you, *would hurt a* nation.
Ingenuous natures wiſh you to reclaim?
By ſmiling virtue you'll inſure your aim:
That *gilds with bliſs the matrimonial hours,*
And blends her laurels with the ſweeteſt flowers.

Ye married fair! deign to attend our ſchool,
And without uſurpation *learn to rule:*
Soon will he ceaſe mean objects to purſue,
In conſcience wretched till he lives to you;
Your charms will reformation's pain beguile,
And vice *receive a ſtab from ev'ry* ſmile.

* The concluſion of the Prologue from this line is by another hand.

EPILOGUE.

Spoken by Mrs. ABINGTON.

CAN *it be thought, ye wives! this ſcribbling fool,*
Will draw you here, by calling you to School?
Does not he know, poor ſoul! to be directed
Is what you hate, and more to be corrected!
Long have theſe walls to public fame been known,
An ancient College *to inſtruct the town!*
We've Schools *for* Rakes, *for* Fathers, Lovers, Wives,
For naughty girls and boys, to mend their lives:
Where ſome to yawn, ſome round about to look,
Some to be ſeen, few come to mind their book:
Some with high wit and humour hither run,
To ſweat the maſters—and they call it fun.
Some modiſh ſparks, true ſtoicks, and high bred,
Come, but ne'er know what's done, or ſung, or ſaid;
Should the whole herd of criticks round them roar,
And with one voice cry out, encore! encore!
Or louder yet, off, off! no more! no more!
Should Pit, Box, Gall'ry with convulſions ſhake,
Still are they half aſleep, nor t'other half awake:
O, ladies fair! are theſe fit men to wed?
Such huſbands, half, *had better be* quite *dead.*
But, to return,—vain men, throughout the nation,
Boaſt, they alone, have College *education:*
Are not we *qualify'd to take degrees?*
We've caps, *and* gowns, *nay* bands *too, if you pleaſe,*
Cornellys', *and* Almack'*s, our* Univerſities!
Young female ſtudents riſe, if girls of parts,
From under graduates,—miſtreſſes of arts!
The baſhful ſpinſters, turn important ſpouſes,
Strive to be maſters, *and the* heads of houſes;
Will any of you here, bleſt with a wife,
Diſpute the fact,—you dare not for your life.

Pray

Pray tell me truly, criticks, and be free,
Do you this night prefer the Wife *to* me?
Shall Mrs. Belville *give the Play a name?*
What are her merits? a cold, ſmiling dame,
While I, a ſalamander, liv'd in flame!
Preſs'd by three *lovers!—'twas indeed provoking!*
Ladies, upon my word, it was no joking.
Can you from mortal woman more require,
Than ſave her fingers, and yet play with fire?
The riſks I run, the partial bard upbraids;
Wives won't be taught,—be it the School for Maids.

Dramatis Perſonæ.

M E N.

General Savage,	Mr. King.
Belville,	Mr. Reddish.
Torrington,	Mr. Weston.
Leeson,	Mr. Palmer.
Captain Savage,	Mr. Brereton.
Connolly,	Mr. Moody.
Spruce,	Mr. Baddeley.
Ghastly,	Mr. W. Palmer.
Leech,	Mr. Bransby.
Crow,	Mr. Wright.
Wolf,	Mr. Ackman.

W O M E N.

Miſs Walsingham,	Mrs. Abington.
Mrs. Belville,	Miſs Younge.
Lady Rachel Mildew	Mrs. Hopkins.
Mrs. Tempest,	Mrs. Greville.
Miſs Leeson,	Miſs Jarratt.
Maid,	Mrs. Millidge.

THE

THE

School for Wives.

ACT I.

SCENE, *an Apartment at* BELVILLE'S.

Enter Captain SAVAGE, *and Miſs* WALSINGHAM.

Capt. HA! ha! ha! Well, Miſs Walſingham, this fury is going; what a noble peal ſhe has rung in Belville's ears!

Miſs. Wal. Did ſhe ſee you, Captain Savage?

Capt. No, I took care of that: for tho' ſhe is'n't married to my father, ſhe has ten times the influence of a wife, and might injure me not a little with him, if I didn't ſupport her ſide of the queſtion.

Miſs. Wal. It was a pleaſant conceit of Mr. Belville, to inſinuate the poor woman was diſordered in her ſenſes!—

Capt. And did you obſerve how the termagant's violence of temper, ſupported the probability of the charge?

Miſs Wal. Yes, ſhe became almoſt frantic in reality, when ſhe found herſelf treated like a madwoman.

Capt. Belville's affected ſurprize too, was admirable!

Miſs Wal. Yes, the hypocritical compoſure of his countenance, and his counterfeit pity for the poor woman, were intolerable!

Capt. While that amiable creature, his wife, implicitly believed every ſyllable he ſaid—

Miſs. Wal. And felt nothing but pity for the accuſer, inſtead of paying the leaſt regard to the accuſation. But pray, is it really under a pretence of getting the girl upon the ſtage, that Belville has taken away Mrs. Tempeſt's niece from the people ſhe boarded with?

Capt. It is: Belville, ever on the look-out for freſh objects, met her in thoſe primitive regions of purity, the Green-Boxes; where, diſcovering that ſhe was paſſionately deſirous of becoming an actreſs, he improved his acquaintance with her, in the fictitious character of an Iriſh manager, and ſhe eloped laſt night, to be, as ſhe imagines, the heroine of a Dublin theatre.

Miſs Wal. So, then, as he has kept his real name artfully conceal'd, Mrs Tempeſt can at moſt but ſuſpect him of Miſs Leeſon's ſeduction.

Capt. Of no more; and this, only, from the deſcription of the people who ſaw him in company with her at the play; but, I wiſh the affair may not have a ſerious concluſion; for ſhe has a brother, a very ſpirited young fellow, who is a counſel in the Temple, and who will certainly call Belville to an account, the moment he hears of it.

Miſs Wal. And what will become of the poor creature after he has deſerted her?

Capt. You know that Belville is generous to profuſion, and has a thouſand good qualities to counterbalance this ſingle fault of gallantry, which contaminates his character.

Miſs

Miſs Wal. You men! you men!—You are ſuch wretches that there's no having a moment's ſatisfaction with you! and what's ſtill more provoking, there's no having a moment's ſatisfaction without you!

Capt. Nay, don't think us all alike.

Miſs Wal. I'll endeavour to deceive myſelf; for it is but a poor argument of your ſincerity, to be the confidant of another's falſehood.

Capt. Nay, no more of this, my love; no people live happier than Belville and his wife; nor is there a man in England, notwithſtanding all his levity, who conſiders his wife with a warmer degree of affection: if you have a friendſhip therefore, for her, let her continue in an error, ſo neceſſary to her repoſe, and give no hint, whatever, of his gallantries to any body.

Miſs Wal. If I had no pleaſure in obliging you, I have too much regard for Mrs. Belville, not to follow your advice; but you need not enjoin me ſo ſtrongly on the ſubject, when you know I can keep a ſecret.

Capt. You are all goodneſs; and the prudence with which you have conceal'd our private engagements, has eternally oblig'd me; had you truſted the ſecret even to Mrs. Belville, it wou'dn't have been ſafe; ſhe would have told her huſband, and he is ſuch a rattleſkul, that, notwithſtanding all his regard for me, he wou'd have mention'd it in ſome moment of levity, and ſent it in a courſe of circulation to my father.

Miſs Wal. The peculiarity of your father's temper, joined to my want of fortune, made it neceſſary for me to keep our engagements inviolably ſecret; there is no merit, therefore, either in my prudence, or in my labouring aſſiduouſly to cultivate the good opinion of the General, ſince both were ſo neceſſary to my own happineſs; don't deſpiſe me for this acknowledgment now.

Capt. Bewitching ſoftneſs!—But your goodneſs, I flatter myſelf, will be ſpeedily rewarded; you are now ſuch a favourite with him, that he is eternally talking of you; and I really fancy he means to propoſe you to me himſelf: for, laſt night, in a few minutes after he had declared you would make the beſt wife in the world, he ſeriouſly aſk'd me if I had any averſion to matrimony?

Miſs Wal. Why, that was a very great conceſſion indeed, as he ſeldom ſtoops to conſult any body's inclinations.

Capt. So it was, I aſſure you; for, in the army, being uſed to nothing but command and obedience, he removes the diſcipline of the parade into his family, and no more expects his orders ſhou'd be diſputed, in matters of a domeſtic nature, than if they were delivered at the head of his regiment.

Miſs Wal. And yet Mrs. Tempeſt, who you ſay is as much a ſtorm in her nature as her name, is diſputing them eternally.

Enter Mr. and Mrs. BELVILLE.

Bel. Well, Miſs Walſingham, hav'n't we had a pretty morning's viſitor?

Miſs Wal. Really, I think ſo; and I have been aſking Capt. Savage, how long the lady has been diſordered in her ſenſes?

Bel. Why will they let the poor woman abroad, without ſome body to take care of her?

Capt. O, ſhe has her lucid intervals.

Miſs Wal. I declare I ſhall be as angry with you as I am with Belville. (*Aſide to the Captain.*)

Mrs. Bel. You can't think how ſenſibly ſhe ſpoke at firſt.

Bel. I ſhould have had no conception of her mad-

 neſs

neſs, if ſhe hadn't brought ſo prepoſterous a charge againſt me.

Enter a SERVANT.

Serv. Lady Rachel Mildew, Madam, ſends her compliments, and if you are not particularly engaged, will do herſelf the pleaſure of waiting upon you.

Mrs. Bel. Our compliments, and we ſhall be glad to ſee her ladyſhip. [*Ex. Servant.*

Bel. I wonder if Lady Rachel knows that Torrington came to town laſt night from Bath!

Mrs. Bel. I hope he has found benefit by the waters, for he is one of the beſt creatures exiſting; he's a downright parſon Adams, in good-nature and ſimplicity.

Miſs Wal. Lady Rachel will be quite happy at his return, and it would be a laughable affair, if a match could be brought about between the old maid and the old bachelor.

Capt. Mr. Torrington is too much taken up at Weſtminſter Hall, to think of paying his devoirs to the ladies, and too plain a ſpeaker, I fancy, to be agreeable to Lady Rachel.

Bel. You miſtake the matter widely; ſhe is deeply ſmitten with him; but honeſt Torrington is utterly unconſcious of his conqueſt, and modeſtly thinks that he has not a ſingle attraction for any woman in the univerſe.

Mrs. Bell. Yet my poor aunt ſpeaks ſufficiently plain, in all conſcience, to give him a different opinion of himſelf.

Miſs Wal. Yes, and puts her charms into ſuch repair, whenever ſhe expects to meet him, that her cheeks look for all the world like a raſberry ice upon a ground of cuſtard.

Capt. I thought *Apollo* was the only god of Lady Rachel's

Rachel's idolatry, and that in her paſſion for poetry ſhe had taken leave of all the leſs elevated affections.

Bel. O, you miſtake again; the poets are eternally in love, and can by no means be calculated to deſcribe the imaginary paſſions, without being very ſuſceptible of the real ones.

Enter Servant.

Ser. The man, Madam, from Taviſtock-ſtreet, has brought home the dreſſes for the maſquerade, and deſires to know if there are any commands for him.

Mrs. Bel. O, bid him ſtay till we ſee the dreſſes. [*Ex. Servant.*

Miſs Wal. They are only Dominos.

Bel. I am glad of that; for characters are as difficult to be ſupported at the maſquerade, as they are in real life. The laſt time I was at the Pantheon, a Veſtal Virgin invited me to ſup with her, and ſwore that her pocket had been pick'd by a Juſtice of Peace.

Miſs Wal. Nay, that was not ſo bad, as the Hamlet's Ghoſt that box'd with Henry the Eighth, and afterwards danc'd a hornpipe to the tune of Nancy Dawſon. Ha! ha! ha! — We follow you, Mrs. Belville.

Scene changes to LEESON's *Chambers in the Temple.*

Enter LEESON.

Leeſ. Where is this Clerk of mine? Connolly?

Con. (behind) Here, Sir!

Leeſ. Have you copied the marriage-ſettlement, as I corrected it?

Con. (*enters with Piſtols*) Ay, honey, an hour ago.

Leeſ. What, you have been trying thoſe piſtols?

Con.

Con. By my ſoul I have been firing them this half hour, without once being able to make them go off.

Leeſ. They are plaguy dirty.

Con. In troth, ſo they are; I ſtrove to brighten them up a little, but ſome misfortune attends every thing I do, for the more I clane them, the dirtier they are, honey.

Leeſ. You have had ſome of your uſual daily viſitors for money, I ſuppoſe.

Con. You may ſay that! and three or four of them are now hanging about the door, that I wiſh handſomely hang'd any were elſe for bodering us.

Leeſ. No joking, Connolly! my preſent ſituation is a very diſagreeable one.

Con. Faith, and ſo it is; but who makes it diſagreeable? your aunt Tempeſt would let you have as much money as you pleaſe, but you won't condeſcend to be acquainted with her, though people in this country can be very intimate friends, without ſeeing one another's faces for ſeven years.

Leeſ. Do you think me baſe enough to receive a favour from a woman, who has diſgraced her family and ſtoops to be a kept miſtreſs? you ſee, my ſiſter is already ruin'd by a connection with her.

Con. Ah, Sir, a good guinea isn't the worſe for coming through a bad hand; if it was, what would become of us lawyers? and by my ſoul, many a high head in London would, at this minute be very low, if they hadn't receiv'd favours even from much worſe people then kept miſtreſſes.

Leeſ. Others, Connolly, may proſtitute their honour, as they pleaſe; mine is my chief poſſeſſion, and I muſt take particular care of it.

Con. Honour, to be ſure, is a very fine thing, Sir; but I don't ſee how it is to be taken care of, without a little money; your honour to my knowledge, hasn't been in your own poſſeſſion theſe two

years,

years, and the devil a crum can you honeftly fwear by, till you get it out of the hands of your creditors.

Leef. I have given you a licence to talk, Connolly, becaufe I know you faithful; but I hav'n't given you a liberty to fport with my misfortunes.

Con. You know I'd die to ferve you, Sir; but of what ufe is your giving me leave to fpake, if you oblige me to hould my tongue? 'tis out of pure love and affection that I put you in mind of your misfortunes.

Leef. Well, Connolly, a few days will, in all probability, enable me to redeem my honour, and to reward your fidelity; the lovely Emily you know, has half-confented to embrace the firft opportunity of flying with me to Scotland, and the paltry trifles I owe, will not be mifs'd in her fortune.

Con. But, dear Sir, confider you are going to fight a duel this very evening, and if you fhou'd be kilt, I fancy you will find it a little difficult to run away afterwards with the lovely Emily.

Leef. If I fall, there will be an end to my misfortunes.

Con. But furely it will not be quite genteel, to go out of the world without paying your debts.

Leef. But how fhall I ftay in the world, Connolly, without punifhing Belville for ruining my fifter?

Con. O, the devil fly away with this honour; an ounce of common fenfe, is worth a whole fhip load of it, if we muft prefer a bullet or a halter, to a fine young lady and a great fortune.

Leef. We'll talk no more on the fubject at prefent. Take this letter to Mr. Belville; deliver it into his own hand, be fure; and bring me an anfwer: make hafte, for I fhall not ftir out till you come back.

Con. By my foul, I wifh you may be able to ftir out then—O, but that's true!

Leef. What's the matter?

Con. Why, Sir, the gentleman I laft liv'd clerk with,

with, died lately, and left me a legacy of twenty guineas—

Leeſ What! is Mr. Stanley dead?

Con. Faith, his friends have behav'd very unkindly if he is not, for they have buried him theſe ſix weeks.

Leeſ. And what then?

Con. Why, Sir, I received my little legacy this morning, and if you'd be ſo good as to keep it for me, I'd be much oblig'd to you.

Leeſ. Connolly, I underſtand you, but I am already ſhamefully in your debt: you've had no money from me this age—

Con. O Sir, that does not ſignify; if you are not kilt in this damn'd duel, you'll be able enough to pay me: if you are, I ſhan't want it.

Leeſ. Why ſo, my poor fellow?

Con. Becauſe, tho' I am but your clerk, and tho' I think fighting the moſt fooliſh thing upon earth, I'm as much a gintleman as yourſelf, and have as much right to commit a murder in the way of duelling.

Leeſ. And what then? You have no quarrel with Mr. Belville?

Con. I ſhall have a damn'd quarrel with him tho' if you are kilt: your death ſhall be reveng'd, depend upon it, ſo let that content you.

Leeſ. My dear Conolly, I hope I ſhan't want ſuch a proof your affection.——How he diſtreſſes me!

Con. You will want a ſecond, I ſuppoſe, in this affair: I ſtood ſecond to my own brother in the Fifteen Acres, and tho' that has made me deteſt the very thought of duelling ever ſince; yet if you want a friend, I'll attend you to the field of death with a great deal of ſatisfaction.

Leeſ. I thank you, Connolly, but I think it extremely wrong in any man who has a quarrel, to expoſe his friend to difficulties; we ſhou'dn't ſeek for redreſs, if we are not equal to the taſk of fighting our own battles; and I chooſe you particularly to carry my letter, becauſe you may be ſuppoſed ignorant of the contents, and thought to be acting only in the ordinary courſe of your buſineſs.

Con. Say no more about it honey; I will be back with you preſently. (*Going, returns.*) I put the twenty guineas in your pocket, before you were up, Sir; and I don't believe you'd look for ſuch a thing there, if I wasn't to tell you of it. [*Exit.*

Leeſ. This faithful, noble hearted creature!—— but let me fly from thought; the buſineſs I have to execute will not bear the teſt of reflection. [*Exit.*

Re-enter CONNOLLY.

Con. As this is a challenge, I ſhou'dn't go without a ſword; come down, little tickle-pitcher. (*Takes a ſword.*) Some people may think me very conceited now; but as the dirtieſt black-legs in town can wear one without being ſtared at, I don't think it can ſuffer any diſgrace by the ſide of an honeſt man. [*Exit.*

SCENE *changes to an Apartment at* BELVILLE's.

Enter Mrs. BELVILLE.

Mrs. Bel. How ſtrangely this affair of Mrs. Tempeſt hangs upon my ſpirits, tho' I have every reaſon, from the tenderneſs, the politeneſs, and the generoſity of Mr. Belville, as well as from the woman's behaviour, to believe the whole charge the reſult of a diſturb'd imagination.—Yet ſuppoſe it ſhould be actually true:—heigho! —well, ſuppoſe it ſhou'd;—I wou'd endeavour—I think I wou'd endeavour to keep my temper:—a frowning face never recovered a heart that was not to be fixed with a ſmiling one:—but women, in general, forget this grand article of the matrimonial

trimonial creed entirely; the dignity of inſulted virtue obliges them to play the fool, whenever their Corydons play the libertine; and poh! they muſt pull down the houſe about the traitor's ears, tho' they are themſelves to be cruſh'd in pieces by the ruins.

Enter a Servant.

Ser. Lady Rachael Mildew, madam. [*Exit Ser.*

Enter Lady RACHAEL MILDEW.

Lady Rach. My dear, how have you done ſince the little eternity of my laſt ſeeing you. Mr. Torrington is come to town, I hear.

Mrs. Bel. He is, and muſt be greatly flattered to find that your Ladyſhip has made him the hero of your new comedy.

Lady Rach. Yes, I have drawn him as he is, an honeſt practitioner of the law; which is, I fancy, no very common character—

Mrs. Bel. And it muſt be a vaſt acquiſition to the Theatre.

Lady Rach. Yet the managers of both houſes have refuſed my play; have refuſed it peremptorily! tho' I offered to make them a preſent of it.

Mrs. Bel. That's very ſurpriſing, when you offer'd to make them a preſent of it.

Lady Rach. They alledge that the audiences are tired of crying at comedies; and inſiſt that my Deſpairing Shepherdeſs is abſolutely too diſmal for repreſentation.

Mrs. Bel. What, tho' you have introduced a lawyer in a new light!

Lady Rach. Yes, and have a boarding-ſchool romp, that flaps her mother's face, and throws a baſon of ſcalding water at her governeſs.

Mrs. Bel. Why ſurely theſe are capital jokes!

Lady Rach. But the managers can't find them out.—However, I am determined to bring it out somewhere; and I have discover'd such a treasure for my boarding-school romp, as exceeds the most sanguine expectation of criticism.

Mrs. Bel. How fortunate!

Lady Rach. Going to Mrs. Le Blond, my millener's, this morning, to see some contraband silks, (for you know there's a foreign minister just arriv'd) I heard a loud voice rehearsing Juliet, from the dining-room; and upon enquiry found that it was a country girl just elop'd from her friends in town, to go upon the stage with an Irish manager.

Mrs. Bel. Ten to one, the strange woman's niece, who has been here this morning. (*Aside.*

Lady Rach. Mrs. Le Blond has some doubts about the manager, it seems, though she hasn't seen him yet, because the apartments are very expensive, and were taken by a fine gentleman out of livery.

Mrs. Bel. What am I to think of this?—Pray, Lady Rachel, as you have convers'd with this young actress, I suppose you could procure me a sight of her?

Lady Rach. This moment if you will, I am very intimate with her already; but pray keep the matter a secret from your husband, for he is so witty, you know, upon my passion for the drama, that I shall be teized to death by him.

Mrs. Bel. O, you may be very sure that your secret is safe, for I have a most particular reason to keep it from Mr. Belville; but he is coming this way with Captain Savage, let us at present avoid him. [*Exeunt.*

Enter BELVILLE *and Captain* SAVAGE.

Capt. You are a very strange man, Belville; you are for ever tremblingly solicitous about the happiness

pineſs of your wife, yet for ever endangering it by your paſſion for variety.

Bel. Why, there is certainly a contradiction between my principles and my practice; but if ever you marry, you'll be able to reconcile it perfectly. Poſſeſſion, Savage! O, poſſeſſion, is a miſerable whetter of the appetite in love! and I own myſelf ſo ſad a fellow, that though I wou'dn't exchange Mrs. Belville's mind for any woman's upon earth, there is ſcarcely a woman's perſon upon earth, which is not to me a ſtronger object of attraction.

Capt. Then perhaps in a little time you'll be weary of Miſs Leeſon.

Bel. To be ſure I ſhall; though to own the truth, I have not yet carried my point concluſively with the little monkey.

Capt. Why how the plague has ſhe eſcap'd a moment in your hands?

Bel. By a mere accident.—She came to the lodgings, which my man Spruce prepar'd for her, rather unexpectedly laſt night, ſo that I happened to be engaged particularly in another quarter—you underſtand me—and the damn'd aunt found me ſo much employment all the morning, that I could only ſend a meſſage by Spruce, promiſing to call upon her the firſt moment I had to ſpare in the courſe of the day.

Capt. And ſo you are previouſly ſatisfied that you ſhall be tired of her?

Bel. Tir'd of her?--Why I am at this moment in purſuit of freſh game, againſt the hour of ſatiety:—game that you know to be exquiſite: and I fancy I ſhall bring it down, though it is cloſely guarded by a deal of that pride, which paſſes for virtue with the generality of your mighty good people.

Capt. Indeed! and may a body know this wonder?

Bel. You are to be trusted with any thing, for you are the closest fellow I ever knew, and the rack itself would hardly make you discover one of your own secrets to any body—what do you think of Miss Walsingham?

Capt. Miss Walsingham!—Death and the devil! (*Aside.*

Bel. Miss Walsingham.

Capt. Why surely she has not received your addresses with any degree of approbation?

Bel. With every degree of approbation I cou'd expect.

Capt. She has?

Bel. Ay: why this news surprises you?

Capt. It does indeed!

Bel. Ha, ha, ha! I can't help laughing to think what a happy dog Miss Walsingham's husband is likely to be!

Capt. A very happy dog, truly!

Bel. She's a delicious girl, is'n' she, Savage?—but she'll require a little more trouble;—for a fine woman, like a fortified town, to speak in your father's language, demands a regular siege; and we must even allow her the honours of war, to magnify the greatness of our own victory.

Capt. Well, it amazes me how you gay fellows ever have the presumption to attack a woman of principle; Miss Walsingham has no apparent levity of any kind about her.

Bel. No; but she continued in my house, after I had whispered my passion in her ear, and gave me a second opportunity of addressing her improperly; what greater encouragement cou'd I desire?

Enter SPRUCE.

Well, Spruce, what are your commands?

Spruce, My Lady is just gone out with Lady Rachel, Sir.

Bel.

Bel. I underſtand you.

Spruce. I believe you do. *(Aſide.)* [*Exit.*

Capt. What is the Engliſh of theſe ſignificant looks between Spruce and you?

Bel. Only that Miſs Walſingham is left alone, and that I have now an opportunity of entertaining her; you muſt excuſe me, Savage; you muſt upon my ſoul; but not a word of this affair to any body; becauſe when I ſhake her off my hands, there may be fools enough to think of her upon terms of honourable matrimony. [*Exit.*

Capt. So, here's a diſcovery! a precious diſcovery! and while I have been racking my imagination, and ſacrificing my intereſt, to promote the happineſs of this woman, ſhe has been liſtening to the addreſſes of another; to the addreſſes of a married man! the huſband of her friend, and the intimate friend of her intended huſband!—By Belville's own account, however, ſhe has not yet proceeded to any criminal lengths—But why did ſhe keep the affair a ſecret from me? or why did ſhe continue in his houſe after a repeated declaration of his unwarrantable attachment?—What's to be done?—If I open my engagement with her to Belville, I am ſure he will inſtantly deſiſt;—but then her honour is left in a ſtate extremely queſtionable—It ſhall be ſtill concealed—While it remains unknown, Belville will himſelf tell me every thing;—and doubt, upon an occaſion of this nature, is infinitely more inſupportable than the downright falſehood of the woman whom we love.

[*Exit.*

The END *of the* FIRST ACT.

A C T II.

SCENE, *an Apartment in General* SAVAGE's *House.*

Enter General SAVAGE *and* TORRINGTON.

Gen. ZOUNDS! Torrington, give me quarter, when I ſurrender up my ſword: I own that for theſe twenty years, I have been ſuffering all the inconveniencies of marriage, without taſting any one of its comforts, and rejoicing in an imaginary freedom, while I was really grovelling in chains.

Tor. In the dirtieſt chains upon earth;—yet you wou'dn't be convinc'd, but laugh'd at all your married acquaintance as ſlaves, when not one of them put up with half ſo much from the worſt wife, as you were oblig'd to crouch under, from a kept miſtreſs.

Gen. 'Tis too true. But, you know, ſhe ſacrificed much for me;—you know that ſhe was the widow of a colonel, and refus'd two very advantageous matches on my account.—

Tor. If ſhe was the widow of a judge, and had refuſed a high chancellor, ſhe was ſtill a devil incarnate, and you were in courſe a madman to live with her.

Gen. You don't remember her care of me when I have been ſick.—

Tor. I recollect, however, her uſage of you in health, and you may eaſily find a tenderer nurſe, when you are bound over by the gout or the rheumatiſm.

Gen.

Gen. Well, well, I agree with you that ſhe is a devil incarnate; but I am this day determin'd to part with her for ever.

Tor. Not you indeed.

Gen. What, don't I know my own mind?

Tor. Not you indeed, when ſhe is in the queſtion: with every body elſe, your reſolution is as unalterable as a determination in the houſe of peers; but Mrs. Tempeſt is your fate, and ſhe reverſes your decrees with as little difficulty as a fraudulent debtor now-a-days procures his certificate under a commiſſion of bankruptcy.

Gen. Well, if, like the Roman Fabius, I conquer by delay, in the end, there will be no great reaſon to find fault with my generalſhip. The propoſal of parting now comes from herſelf.

Tor. O, you daren't make it for the life of you.

Gen. You muſt know that this morning we had a ſmart cannonnading on Belville's account, and ſhe threatens, as I told you before, to quit my houſe if I don't challenge him for taking away her niece.

Tor. That fellow is the very devil among the women, and yet there isn't a man in England fonder of his wife.

Gen. Poh, if the young minx hadn't ſurrender'd to him, ſhe would have capitulated to ſomebody elſe, and I ſhall at this time be doubly obliged to him, if he is any ways inſtrumental in getting the aunt off my hands.

Tor. Why at this time?

Gen. Becauſe, to ſhew you how fixed my reſolution is to be a keeper no longer, I mean to marry immediately.

Tor. And can't you avoid being preſs'd to death, like a felon who refuſes to plead, without incurring a ſentence of perpetual impriſonment?

Gen. I fancy you would yourſelf have no objection

jection to a perpetual imprisonment in the arms of Miss Walsingham.

Tor. But have you any reason to think that upon examination in a case of love, she would give a favourable reply to your interrogatories?

Gen. The greatest—do you think I'd hazard such an engagement without being perfectly sure of my ground? Notwithstanding my present connection won't suffer me to see a modest woman at my own house—She always treats me with particular attention whenever I visit at Belville's, or meet her any where else—If fifty young fellows are present, she directs all her assiduities to the old soldier, and my son has a thousand times told me that she professes the highest opinion of my understanding.

Tor. And truly you give a notable proof of your understanding, in thinking of a woman almost young enough to be your grand-daughter.

Gen. Nothing like an experienc'd chief to command in any garrison.

Tor. Recollect the state of your present citadel.

Gen. Well, if I am blown up by my own mine, I shall be the only sufferer—There's another thing I want to talk of, I am going to marry my son to Miss Moreland.

Tor. Miss Moreland!—

Gen. Belville's sister.

Tor. O, ay, I remember that Moreland had got a good estate to assume the name of Belville.

Gen. I haven't yet mentioned the matter to my son, but I settled the affair with the girl's mother yesterday, and she only waits to communicate it to Belville, who is her oracle, you know.

Tor. And are you sure the captain will like her?

Gen. I am not so unreasonable as to insist upon his liking her, I shall only insist upon his marrying her.

Tor. What, whether he likes her or not?

Gen.

Gen. When I iſſue my orders, I expect them to be obey'd; and don't look for an examination into their propriety.

Tor. What a delightful thing it muſt be to live under a military government, where a man is not to be troubled with the exerciſe of his underſtanding.

Gen. Miſs Moreland has thirty thouſand pounds—That's a large ſum of ammunition money.

Tor. Ay, but a marriage merely on the ſcore of fortune, is only gilding the death-warrant ſent down for the execution of a priſoner. However as I know your obſtinate attachment to what you once reſolve, I ſhan't pretend to argue with you; where are the papers which you want me to conſider?

Gen. They are in my library—File off with me to the next room, and they ſhall be laid before you—But firſt I'll order the chariot, for the moment I have your opinion, I purpoſe to ſit down regularly before Miſs Wallingham—who waits there?

Enter a Servant.

Gen. Is Mrs. Tempeſt at home?

Serv. Yes, Sir, juſt come in, and juſt going out again.

Gen. Very well; order the chariot to be got ready.

Serv. Sir, one of the pannels was broke laſt night at the Opera-houſe.

Gen. Sir, I didn't call to have the pleaſure of your converſation, but to have obedience paid to my orders.

Tor. Go order the chariot, you blockhead.

Serv. With the broken pannel, Sir?

Gen. Yes, you raſcal, if both pannels were broke, and the back ſhattered to pieces.

Serv. The coachman thinks that one of the wheels is damag'd, Sir.

Gen. Don't attempt to reaſon, you dog, but execute your orders.——Bring the chariot without the wheels—if you can't bring it with them.

Tor. Ay bring it, if you reduce it to a ſledge, and let your maſter look like a malefactor for high treaſon, on his journey to Tyburn.

Enter Mrs. TEMPEST.

Mrs. Temp. General Savage, is the houſe to be for ever a ſcene of noiſe with your domineering?—The chariot ſhan't be brought—it won't be fit for uſe 'till it is repaired—and John ſhall drive it this very minute to the coach-maker's.

Gen. Nay, my dear, if it isn't fit for uſe that's another thing.

Tor. Here's the experienced chief that's fit to command in any garriſon. *(Aſide).*

Gen. Go, order me the coach then. *(To the Serv.)*

Mrs. Temp. You can't have the coach.

Gen. And why ſo, my love?

Mrs. Temp. Becauſe I want it for myſelf.—Robert, get a hack for your maſter—tho' indeed I don't ſee what buſineſs he has out of the houſe.

[*Exeunt Mrs. Tempeſt and Robert.*

Tor. When you iſſue your orders, you expect them to be obey'd, and don't look for an examination into their propriety

Gen. The fury!—this has ſteel'd me againſt her for ever, and nothing on earth can now prevent me from drumming her out immediately.

Mrs. Temp. (*behind*) An unreaſonable old fool—But I'll make him know who governs this houſe!

Gen. Zounds! here ſhe comes again; ſhe has been lying in ambuſcade, I ſuppoſe, and has over-heard us.

Tor. What if ſhe has? you are ſteel'd againſt her for ever.

Gen. No, ſhe's not coming—ſhe's going down ſtairs;

ſtairs;—and now, dear Torrington, you muſt be as ſilent as a ſentinel on an out-poſt about this affair. If that virago was to hear a ſyllable of it, ſhe might perhaps attack Miſs Walſingham in her very camp, and defeat my whole plan of operations.

Tor. I thought you were determin'd to drum her out immediately. [*Exeunt.*

The SCENE *changes to* Belville's.

Enter Miſs Walsingham, *followed by* Belville.

Miſs Wal. I beg, Sir, that you will inſult me no longer with ſolicitations of this nature—Give me proofs of your ſincerity indeed! What proofs of ſincerity can your ſituation admit of, if I could be even weak enough to think of you with partiality at all?

Bel. If our affections, Madam, were under the government of our reaſon, circumſtanced as I am, this unhappy boſom wouldn't be torn by paſſion for Miſs Walſingham.—Had I been bleſs'd with your acquaintance, before I ſaw Mrs. Belville, my hand as well as my heart, wou'd have been humbly offer'd to your acceptance—fate, however, has ordered it otherwiſe, and it is cruel to reproach me with that ſituation as a crime, which ought to be pitied as my greateſt misfortune.

Miſs Wal. He's actually forcing tears into his eyes.—However, I'll mortify him ſeverely. (*Aſide.*

Bel. But ſuch proofs of ſincerity as my ſituation can admit of, you ſhall yourſelf command, as my only buſineſs in exiſtence is to adore you.

Miſs Wal. His only buſineſs in exiſtence to adore me! (*Aſide.*

Bel. Proſtrate at your feet, my deareſt Miſs Walſingham (*kneeling*), behold a heart eternally devoted to your ſervice.—You have too much good ſenſe, Madam, to be the ſlave of cuſtom, and too much humanity not to pity the wretchedneſs you have cauſed.

caufed.—Only, therefore, fay that you commiferate my fufferings—I'll afk no more—and furely that may be faid, without any injury to your purity, to fnatch even an enemy from diftraction—where's my handkerchief? *(Afide.*

Mifs Wal. Now to anfwer in his own way, and to make him ridiculous to himfelf—*(afide.)* If I thought, if I could think *(affecting to weep)* that thefe proteftations were real.

Bel. How can you, Madam, be fo unjuft to your own merit? how can you be fo cruelly doubtful of my folemn affeverations?—Here I again kneel, and fwear eternal love!

Mifs Wal. I don't know what to fay—but there is one proof—*(affecting to weep.)*

Bel. Name it, my angel, this moment, and make me the happieft of mankind!

Mifs Wal. Swear to be mine for ever.

Bel. I have fworn it a thoufand times, my charmer; and I will fwear it to the laft moment of my life.

Mifs Wal. Why then—but don't look at me I befeech you—I don't know how to fpeak it—

Bel. The delicious emotion—do not check the generous tide of tendernefs that fills me with fuch extafy.

Mifs Wal. You'll defpife me for this weaknefs.

Bel. This weaknefs—this generofity, which will demand my everlafting gratitude.

Mifs Wal. I am a fool—but there is a kind of fatality in this affair—and I do confent to go off with you.

Bel. Eternal bleffings on your condefcenfion.

Mifs Wal. You are irrefiftible, and I am ready to fly with you to any part of the world.

Bel. Fly to any part of the world indeed—you fhall fly by yourfelf then! *(afide.)* You are the moft moſt lovely, the moſt tender creature in the world, and thus again let me thank you: O, Miſs Walſingham, I cannot expreſs how happy you've made me!—But where's the neceſſity of our leaving England?

Miſs Wal. I thought he wou'dn't like to go abroad—(*aſide.*) That I may poſſeſs the pleaſure of your company unrival'd.

Bel. I muſt cure her of this taſte for travelling— (*Aſide.*

Miſs Wal. You don't anſwer, Mr. Belville?

Bel. Why I was turning the conſequence of your propoſal in my thoughts, as going off—going off—you know——

Miſs Wal. Why going off, you know, is going off—And what objections can you have to going off?

Bel. Why going off, will ſubject you at a certainty, to the ſlander of the world; whereas by ſtaying at home, we may not only have numberleſs opportunities of meeting, but at the ſame time prevent ſuſpicion itſelf from ever breathing on your reputation.

Miſs. Wal. I didn't dream of your ſtarting any difficulties, Sir.—Juſt now I was dearer to you than all the world.

Bel. And ſo you are, by heav'n!

Miſs Wal. Why won't you ſacrifice the world then at once to obtain me?

Bel. Surely, my deareſt life, you muſt know the neceſſity, which every man of honour is under, of keeping up his character?

Miſs Wal. So, here's this fellow ſwearing to ten thouſand lies, and yet talking very gravely about his honour and his character. (*Aſide.*) Why, to be ſure in theſe days, Mr. Belville, the inſtances of conjugal infidelity are ſo very ſcarce, and men of faſhion are ſo remarkable for a tender attachment to their wives, that I don't wonder at your circumſpection—But do you think I can ftoop to accept you by halves, or admit of any partnerfhip in your heart?

Bel. O you muft do more than that, if you have any thing to fay to me. (*Afide.*) Surely, Madam, when you know my whole foul unalterably your own, you will permit me to preferve thofe appearances with the world, which are indifpenfibly requifite—Mrs. Belville is a moft excellent woman, however it may be my fortune to be devoted to another—Her happinefs, befides, conftitutes a principal part of my felicity, and if I was publicly to forfake her, I fhould be hunted as a monfter from fociety.

Mifs Wal. Then, I fuppofe it is by way of promoting Mrs. Belville's repofe, Sir, that you make love to other women; and by way of fhewing the nicety of your honour, that you attempt the purity of fuch as your own roof, peculiarly, intitles to protection. For the honour intended to me—thus low to the ground, I thank you, Mr. Belville.

Bel. Laugh'd at, by all the ftings of mortification!

Mifs Wal. Good bye.—Don't let this accident mortify your vanity too much;—but take care, the next time you vow everlafting love, that the object is neither tender enough to fob—fob—at your diftrefs; nor provoking enough to make a propofal of leaving England.—How greatly a little common fenfe can lower thefe fellows of extraordinary impudence? [*Exit.*

Bel. (*alone.*) So then, I am fairly taken in, and fhe has been only diverting herfelf with me all this time:—however, lady fair, I may chance to have the laugh in a little time on my fide; for if you can fport in this manner about the flame, I think it muft in the run lay hold of your wings:—what fhall I do in this affair?—fhe fees the matter in its true light, and there's no good to be expected from thumping of bofoms, or fqueezing white handkerchiefs;—no thefe won't won't do with women of ſenſe, and, in a ſhort time, they'll be ridiculous to the very babies of a boarding ſchool.

Enter Captain SAVAGE.

Capt. Well, Belville, what news? You have had a freſh opportunity with Miſs Walſingham.

Bel. Why, faith, Savage, I've had a moſt extraordinary ſcene with her, and yet have but little reaſon to brag of my good fortune, tho' ſhe offered in expreſs terms to run away with me.

Capt. Prithee explain yourſelf, man; ſhe cou'dn't ſurely be ſo ſhameleſs!

Bel. O, her offering to run away with me, was by no means the worſt part of the affair.

Capt. No, then it muſt be damn'd bad indeed! but prithee, hurry to an explanation.

Bel. Why then, the worſt part of the affair is, that ſhe was laughing at me the whole time; and made this propoſal of an elopement, with no other view, than to ſhew me in ſtrong colours to myſelf, as a very dirty fellow to the beſt wife in England.

Capt. I am eaſy. (*Aſide.*

Enter SPRUCE.

Spruce. Sir, there is an Iriſh gentleman below with a letter for you, who will deliver it to nobody but yourſelf.

Bel. Shew him up then.

Spruce. Yes, Sir.

Capt. It may be on buſineſs, Belville; I'll take my leave of you.

Bel. O, by no means; I can have no buſineſs which I deſire to keep from you, tho' you are the arrant'ſt miſer of your confidence upon earth, and wou'd rather truſt your life in any body's hands, than even a paltry amour with the apprentice of a milliner.

Enter CONNOLLY.

Con. Gintlemin, your moſt obedient; pray which of you is Mr. Belville?

Bel. My name is Belville, at your ſervice, Sir.

Con. I have a little bit of a letter for you, Sir.

Bel. (*Reads.*)

SIR,

The people where Miſs Leeſon lately lodg'd aſſerting poſitively that you have taken her away in a fictitious character, the brother of that unhappy girl thinks himſelf oblig'd to demand ſatisfaction for the injury you have done his family; tho' a ſtranger to your perſon, he is ſufficiently acquainted with your reputation for ſpirit, and ſhall, therefore, make no doubt of ſeeing you with a caſe of piſtols, near the Ring in Hyde Park, at eight o'clock this evening, to anſwer the claims of

To Craggs Belville, Eſq. George Leeſon.

Capt. Eight o'clock in the evening! 'tis a ſtrange time!

Con. Why ſo, honey? A fine evening is as good a time for a bad action as a fine morning; and if a man of ſenſe can be ſuch a fool to fight a duel, he ſhou'd never ſleep upon the matter, for the more he thinks of it, the more he muſt feel himſelf aſham'd of his reſolution.

Bel. A pretty letter!

Con. O yes, an invitation to a brace of bullets is a very pretty thing.

Bel. For a challenge, however, 'tis very civilly written!

Con. Faith, if it was written to me, I ſhou'dn't be very fond of ſuch civility; I wonder he doesn't ſign himſelf, your moſt obedient ſervant.

Capt. I told you Leeſon's character, and what wou'd become of this damn'd buſineſs; but your affairs—are they ſettled, Belville?

Bel. O they are always ſettled—for as this is a country where people occaſionally die, I take conſtant care to be prepared for contingencies.

Con. Occaſionally die!—I'll be very much oblig'd to you, Sir, if you tell me the country where people do not die? for I'll immediately go and end my days there.

Bel. Ha! ha! ha!

Con. Faith, you may laugh gintlemin, but tho' I am a fooliſh Iriſhman, and come about a fooliſh piece of buſineſs, I'd prefer a ſnug birth in this world, bad as it is, to the fineſt coffin in all Chriſtendom.

Bel. I am ſurpris'd, Sir, that thinking in this manner, you would be the bearer of a challenge.

Con. And well you may, Sir.—But we muſt often take a pleaſure in ſerving our friends, by doing things that are very diſagreeable to us.

Capt. Then you think Mr. Leeſon much to blame, perhaps, for hazarding his life where he can by no means repair the honour of his ſiſter.

Con. Indeed and I do—But I ſhall think this gintlemin, begging his pardon, much more to blame for meeting him.

Bel. And why ſo, Sir—You wou'dn't have me diſappoint your friend?

Con. Faith, and that I wou'd—He, poor lad, may have ſome reaſon at preſent to be tir'd of the world, but you have a fine eſtate, a fine wife, a fine parcel of children—In ſhort, honey, you have every thing to make you fond of living, and the devil burn me, was I in your caſe, if I'd ſtake my own happineſs againſt the miſery of any man.

Bel. I am very much obliged to your advice, Sir, tho' on the preſent occaſion I cannot adopt it; be ſo good as to preſent my compliments to your friend, and tell him I ſhall certainly do myſelf the honour of attending his appointment.

Con. Why then upon my ſoul I am very ſorry for it.

Capt. 'Tis not very cuſtomary, Sir, with gentlemen of Ireland to oppoſe an affair of honour.

Con. They are like the gintlemin of England, Sir, they are brave to a fault; yet I hope to ſee the day that it will be infamous to draw the ſwords of either, againſt any body but the enemies of their country. [*Exit.*

Bel. I am quite charmed with this honeſt Hibernian, and would almoſt fight a duel for the pleaſure of his acquaintance.

Capt. Come, ſtep with me a little, and let us conſider, whether there may not be ſome method of accommodating this curſed buſineſs.

Bel. Poh! don't be uneaſy upon my account; my character, with regard to affairs of this nature, is unhappily too well eſtabliſhed, and you may be ſure that I ſhan't fight with Leeſon.

Capt. No—you have injured him greatly?

Bel. The very reaſon of all others why I ſhould not cut his throat. [*Exeunt.*

Enter SPRUCE,

Spruce. What, the devil, this maſter of mine has got a duel upon his hands! Zounds! I am ſorry for that; he is a prince of a fellow! and a good ſubject muſt always love his prince, though he may now and then be a little out of humour with his actions.

Enter General SAVAGE.

Gen. Your hall-door ſtanding open, Spruce, and none of your ſentinels being on guard, I have ſurpriſed your camp thus far without reſiſtance: Where is your maſter?

Spruce.

Spruce. Juſt gone out with Captain Savage, Sir.

Gen. Is your lady at home?

Spruce. No, Sir, but Miſs Walſingham is at home; ſhall I inform her of your viſit?

Gen. There is no occaſion to inform her of it, for here ſhe is, Spruce. [*Exit Spruce.*

Enter Miſs WALSINGHAM.

Miſs Wal. General Savage, your moſt humble ſervant.

Gen. My dear Miſs Walſingham, it is rather cruel that you ſhould be left at home by yourſelf, and yet I am greatly rejoic'd to find you at preſent without company.

Miſs Wal. I can't but think myſelf in the beſt company, when I have the honour of your converſation, General.

Gen. You flatter me too much, Madam; yet I am come to talk to you on a ſerious affair, Miſs Walſingham; an affair of importance to me and to yourſelf: Have you leiſure to favour me with a ſhort audience, if I beat a parley?

Miſs Wal. Any thing of importance to you, Sir, is always ſufficient to command my leiſure.—'Tis as the Captain ſuſpected. (*Aſide.*

Gen. You tremble, my lovely girl, but don't be alarmed; for though my buſineſs is of an important nature, I hope it won't be of a diſagreeable one.

Miſs Wal. And yet I am greatly agitated. (*Aſide.*

Gen. Soldiers, Miſs Walſingham, are ſaid to be generally favour'd by the kind partiality of the ladies.

Miſs Wal. The ladies are not without gratitude, Sir, to thoſe who devote their lives peculiarly to the ſervice of their country.

Gen. Generouſly ſaid, Madam: Then give me leave, without any maſked battery, to aſk, if the heart

of

of an honeſt ſoldier is a prize at all worth your acceptance.

Miſs Wal. Upon my word, Sir, there's no maſked battery in this queſtion.

Gen. I am as fond of a coup de main, Madam, in love as in war, and hate the tedious method of ſapping a town, when there is a poſſibility of entering ſword in hand.

Miſs Wal. Why, really, Sir, a woman may as well know her own mind, when ſhe is ſummoned by the trumpet of a lover, as when ſhe undergoes all the tireſome formality of a ſiege. You ſee I have caught your own mode of converſing, General.

Gen. And a very great compliment I conſider it, Madam: But now that you have candidly confeſs'd an acquaintance with your own mind, anſwer me with that frankneſs for which every body admires you ſo much. Have you any objection to change the name of Walſingham?

Miſs Wal. Why then frankly, General Savage, I ſay no.

Gen. Ten thouſand thanks to you for this kind declaration.

Miſs Wal. I hope you won't think it a forward one.

Gen. I'd ſooner ſee my ſon run away in the day of battle;—I'd ſooner think Lord Ruſſel was bribed by Lewis the XIVth, and ſooner villify the memory of Algernon Sidney.

Miſs Wal. How unjuſt it was ever to ſuppoſe the General a tyrannical father! (*Aſide.*

Gen. You have told me condeſcendingly, Miſs Walſingham, that you have no objection to change your name, I have but one queſtion more to aſk.

Miſs Wal. Pray propoſe it.

Gen. Would the name of Savage be diſagreeable to you?—Speak frankly again, my dear girl!

Miſs Wal. Why then again I frankly ſay, no.

Gen.

Gen. You make me too happy; and though I ſhall readily own, that a propoſal of this nature would come with more propriety from my ſon——

Miſs. Wal. I am much better pleaſed that you make the propoſal yourſelf, Sir.

Gen. You are too good to me.—Torrington thought that I ſhould meet with a repulſe. (*Aſide.*

Miſs. Wal. Have you communicated this buſineſs to the Captain, Sir?

Gen. No, my dear Madam, I did not think that at all neceſſary. I have always been attentive to the Captain's happineſs, and I propoſe that he ſhall be married in a few days.

Miſs Wal. What, whether I will or no?

Gen. O, you can have no objection.

Miſs Wal. I muſt be conſulted, however, about the day, General: but nothing in my power ſhall be wanting to make him happy.

Gen. Obliging lovelineſs!

Miſs Wal. You may imagine, that if I was not previouſly impreſt in favour of your propoſal, it wou'd not have met my concurrence ſo readily.

Gen. Then you own that I had a previous friend in the garriſon.

Miſs Wal. I don't bluſh to acknowledge it when I conſider the accompliſhments of the object, Sir.

Gen. O this is too much, Madam; the principal merit of the object is his paſſion for Miſs Walſingham.

Miſs Wal. Don't ſay that, General, I beg of you, for I don't think there are many women in the kingdom, who could behold him with indifference.

Gen. Ah, you flattering, flattering angel! — and yet, by the memory of Marlborough, my lovely girl, it was the idea of a prepoſſeſſion on your part, which encouraged me to hope for a favourable reception.

Miſs

Miss Wal. Then I must have been very indiscreet, for I labour'd to conceal that prepossession as much as possible.

Gen. You cou'dn't conceal it from me! you cou'dn't conceal it from me!—The female heart is a field which I am thoroughly acquainted with, and which has more than once been a witness to my victories, Madam.

Miss Wal. I don't at all doubt your success with the ladies, General; but as we now understand one another so perfectly, you will give me leave to retire.

Gen. One word, my dear creature, and no more; I shall wait upon you some time to-day, with Mr. Torrington, about the necessary settlements.

Miss Wal. You must do as you please, General, you are invincible in every thing.

Gen. And if you please, we'll keep every thing a profound secret, 'till the articles are all settled, and the definitive treaty ready for execution.

Miss Wal. You may be sure, that delicacy will not suffer me to be communicative on the subject, Sir.

Gen. Then you leave every thing to my management.

Miss Wal. I can't trust a more noble negociator. [*Exit.*

Gen. The day's my own. (*sings.*) *Britons, strike home! strike home! Revenge, &c.* [Exit singing.

END *of the* SECOND ACT.

A C T III.

SCENE, *Miſs* LEESON's *Lodgings*.

Enter Lady RACHEL MILDEW, *Mrs.* BELVILLE, *and Miſs* LEESON.

Lady Rach. WELL, Mrs. Belville, I am extremely glad you agree with me, in opinion of this young lady's qualifications for the ſtage. Don't you think ſhe'd play Miſs Headſtrong admirably in my comedy?

Mrs. Bel. Yes, indeed, I think ſhe poſſeſſes a natural fund of ſpirit, very much adapted to the character.—'Tis impoſſible, ſurely, that this hoyden can have a moment's attraction for Mr. Belville? (*Aſide.*

Miſs Leeſ. You are very obliging, ladies; but I have no turn for comedy; my forte is tragedy entirely.

Alphonſo!—O Alphonſo! to thee I call, &c.

Lady Rach. But, my dear, is there none of our comedies to your taſte?

Miſs Leeſ. O, yes; ſome of the ſentimental ones are very pretty, there's ſuch little difference between them and tragedies.

Lady Rach. And pray, my dear, how long have you been engaged to Mr. Frankly?

Miſs Leeſ. I only came away laſt night, and hav'n't ſeen Mr. Frankly ſince, tho' I expect him every moment.

Mrs. Bel. Laſt night! juſt as Mrs. Tempeſt mentioned. (*Aſide.*

Lady Rach. You had the concurrence of your friends?

Miſs Leeſ. Not I, Madam; Mr. Frankly ſaid, I had too much genius to mind my friends, and as I ſhould want nothing from them, there was no occaſion to conſult them in the affair.

Lady Rach. Then Oſbaldiſton is not your real name, perhaps?

Miſs Leeſ. O no, nor do I tell my real name: I choſe Oſbaldiſton, becauſe it was a long one, and wou'd make a ſtriking appearance in the bills.

Mrs. Bel. I wiſh we cou'd ſee Mr. Frankly.

Miſs Leeſ. Perhaps you may, Madam, for he deſigns to give me a leſſon every day, 'till we are ready to ſet off for Ireland.

Lady Rach. Suppoſe then, my dear, you wou'd oblige us with a ſcene in Juliet, by way of ſhewing your proficiency to Mrs. Belville.

Miſs Leeſ. Will you ſtand up for Romeo?

Lady Rach. With all my heart, and I'll give you ſome inſtructions.

Miſs Leeſ. I beg pardon Ma'am; I'll learn to act under nobody but Mr. Frankly. This room is without a carpet; if you will ſtep into the next, ladies, I'll endeavour to oblige you,

Shall I not be environ'd, diſtraught——

This way Ladies.

Lady Rach. Pray, Madam, ſhew us the way.

[*Exeunt Miſs* Leeſ. *and Lady* Rach.

Mrs. Bel. I'll prolong this mummery as much as poſſible, in hopes the manager may come. Lye ſtill, poor fluttering heart! it cannot be the lord of all your wiſhes! it cannot ſurely be your ador'd Belville! [*Exit.*

Re-enter

Re-enter Miſs Leeſon.

Miſs Leeſ. Hav'n't I left my Romeo and Juliet here? O yes, there it is.

Enter Belville.

Bel. ———*O, were thoſe Eyes in heav'n,*
They'd thro' the ſtarry region ſhine ſo bright,
That birds would ſing, and think it was the morn!

Miſs Leeſ. Ah, my dear Mr. Frankly! I'm ſo glad you are come! I was dying to ſee you.

Bel. Kiſs me, my dear;—why did'nt you ſend me word of your intention to come away laſt night?

Miſs Leeſ. I hadn't time: but as I knew where the lodgings were, I thought I ſhould be able to find you by a note to the coffee-houſe I always directed to.

Bel. Kiſs me again, my little ſparkler!

Miſs Leeſ. Nay, I won't be kiſs'd in this manner; for tho' I am going on the ſtage, I intend to have ſome regard for my character. But, ha! ha! ha! I am glad you are come now: I have company above ſtairs.

Bel. Company! that's unlucky at this time, for I wanted to make you intirely eaſy about your character. (*Aſide.*) And pray, my dear, who is your company? You know we muſt be very cautious, for fear of your relations.

Miſs Leeſ. O, they are only ladies.—But one of them is the moſt beautiful Creature in the world!

Bel. The devil ſhe is!

Miſs Leeſ. *An earth-treading ſtar, and makes dim heaven's light.*

Bel. Zounds! I'll take a peep at the ſtar, who knows but I may have an opportunity of making another actreſs. (*Aſide.*

Miſs Leeſ. Come, charmer! charmer!

Bel. ————*Wer't thou as far,*
As that vaſt ſhore, waſh'd by the fartheſt ſea,
I wou'd adventure for ſuch merchandiſe.

Now let's ſee what fortune has ſent us above ſtairs. [*Exeunt.*

SCENE *changes to a Dining Room at Miſs* LEESON'*s.*

Mrs. Belville, *and Lady* Rachel *diſcover'd.*

Mrs. Bel. This is a moſt ignorant young creature, Lady Rachel.

Lady Rach. Why I think ſhe is—did you obſerve how ſhe ſlighted my offer of inſtructing her?

Enter Miſs Leeſon.

Miſs Leeſ. Ladies!—ladies!—here he is! here is Mr. Frankly!

Enter Belville *bowing very low, and not ſeeing the Ladies.*

Bel. Ladies, your moſt obedient.

Mrs. Bel. Let me, if poſſible, recollect myſelf—Sir, your moſt obedient humble ſervant.

Bel. Zounds! let me out of the houſe.

Lady Rach. What do I ſee?

Miſs Leeſ. You ſeem, ladies, to know this gentleman?

Mrs. Bel. (*Taking hold of him.*) You ſhan't go, renegade—You laugh'd at my credulity this morning, and I muſt now laugh at your embarraſſment.

Bel. What a kind thing it would be in any body to blow out my ſtupid brains?

Lady Rach. I'll mark this down for an incident in my comedy.

Miſs Leeſ. What do you hang your head for, Mr. Frankly?

Bel.

Bel. Be ſo good as to aſk that lady, my dear.— The Devil has been long in my debt, and now he pays me home with a witneſs.

Mrs. Bel. What a cruel thing it is to let Mrs. Tempeſt out, my love, without ſomebody to take care of her!

Miſs Leeſ. What, do you know Mrs. Tempeſt, Madam?

Mrs. Bel. Yes, my dear;——and I am pretty well acquainted with this gentleman.

Miſs Leeſ. What isn't this gentleman the manager of a play-houſe in Ireland?

Bel. The curtain is almoſt dropt, my dear; the farce is nearly over, and you'll be ſpeedily acquainted with the cataſtrophe.

Enter Mrs. TEMPEST.

Mrs. Tem. Yes, Sir, the curtain is almoſt dropt: I have had ſpies to watch your haunts, and the cataſtrophe ends in your detection—Come, you abandon'd ſlut——

Miſs Leeſ. And have I elop'd after all, without being brought upon the ſtage?

Mrs. Temp. I don't know that you would be brought upon the ſtage; but I am ſure you were near being brought upon the town. I hope, Madam, for the future, you'll ſet me down a mad-woman.

(*To Mrs.* Bel.

Mrs. Bel. Mr. Belville, you'll make my apologies to this lady, and acknowledge that I think her perfectly in her ſenſes.

Bel. I wiſh that I had entirely loſt mine.

Lady Rach. (*Writing*) *I wiſh that I had entirely loſt mine.* A very natural wiſh in ſuch a ſituation.

Mrs. Temp. Come, you audacious minx, come away. You ſhall be ſent into Yorkſhire this very evening; and ſee what your poor mother will ſay to you, huſſey.

Miſs Leeſ. I will go on the ſtage, if I die for't; and 'tis ſome comfort there's a play-houſe at York.

[*Exit Mrs.* Tempeſt, *and Miſs* Leeſon.

Bel. Nancy, I am ſo aſham'd, ſo humbled, and ſo penitent, that if you knew what paſſes here, I am ſure you wou'd forgive me.

Mrs. Bel. My love, tho' I cannot ſay I rejoice in your infidelity, yet, believe me, I pity your diſtreſs: let us therefore think no more of this.

Lady Rach. (*Writing*) *And think no more of this.* ——This conduct is new in a wife, and very dramatic.

Bel. Where, my angel, have you acquired ſo many requiſites to charm with?

Mrs. Bel. In your ſociety, my dear; and believe me —that a wife may be as true a friend as any bottle-companion upon earth, tho' ſhe can neither get merry with you over night, nor blow out your brains about ſome fooliſh quarrel in the morning.

Bel. If wives knew the omnipotence of virtue, where ſhe wears a ſmile upon her face, they'd all follow your bewitching example, and make a faithleſs huſband quite an incredible character.

Lady Rach. *Quite an incredible character!*—Let me ſet down that. (*writing.*)

S C E N E *changes to General* SAVAGE's.

Enter General and Captain.

Gen. Yes, Horace, I have been juſt viſiting at Belville's.

Capt. You found nobody at home, but Miſs Walſingham?

Gen. No, but I'd a long converſation with her, and upon a very intereſting ſubject.

Capt. 'Tis as I gueſs'd. (*Aſide.*

Gen.

Gen: She is a moſt amiable creature, Horace.

Capt. So ſhe is, Sir, and will make any man happy that marries her.

Gen. I am glad you think ſo.

Capt. He's glad I think ſo!—'tis plain,—but I muſt leave every thing to himſelf, and ſeem wholly paſſive in the affair. (*Aſide.*

Gen. A married life after all, Horace, I am now convinced is the moſt happy, as well as the moſt reputable.

Capt. It is indeed, Sir.

Gen. Then, perhaps, you wou'd have no objection to be married, if I offered you as agreeable a young woman as Miſs Walſingham.

Capt. 'Twou'd be my firſt pride on every occaſion, Sir, to pay an implicit obedience to your commands.

Gen. That's ſenſibly ſaid, Horace, and obligingly ſaid; prepare yourſelf therefore for an introduction to the lady in the morning.

Capt. Is the lady prepared to receive me, Sir?

Gen. O yes; and you can't think how highly delighted Miſs Walſingham appeared, when I acquainted her with my reſolution on the ſubject.

Capt. She's all goodneſs!

Gen. The more I know her, the more I am charm'd with her. I muſt not be explicit with him yet, for fear my ſecret ſhould get wind, and reach the ears of the enemy. (*Aſide.*) I propoſe, Horace, that you ſhould be married immediately.

Capt. The ſooner the better, Sir, I have no will but your's.

Gen. (*Shaking hands with him.*) By the memory of Marlbro', you are a moſt excellent boy!—But what do you think? Miſs Walſingham inſiſts upon naming the day.

Capt.

Capt. And welcome, Sir; I am ſure ſhe won't make it a diſtant one.

Gen. O, ſhe ſaid, that nothing in her power ſhou'd be wanting to make you happy.

Capt. I am ſure of that, Sir.

Gen. (*A loud knocking.*) Zounds, Horace! here's the diſgrace and puniſhment of my life: let's avoid her as we would a fever in the camp.

Capt. Come to the library, and I'll tell you how whimſically ſhe was treated this morning at Belville's.

Gen. Death and the devil! make haſte. O, I muſt laugh at marriage and be curſt to me! But I am providing, Horace, againſt your falling into my error.

Capt. I am eternally indebted to you, Sir.

[*Exeunt.*

SCENE BELVILLE's *Houſe.*

Enter Mrs. Belville, *and Lady* Rachel.

Lady Rach. Nay, Mrs. Belville, I have no patience, you act quite unnaturally.

Mrs. Bell. What! becauſe I am unwilling to be miſerable?

Lady Rach. This new inſtance of Mr. Belville's infidelity——This attempt to ſeduce Miſs Walſingham, which your woman overheard, is unparponable!

Mrs. Bell. I don't ſay but that I am ſtrongly wounded by his irregularities. Yet if Mr. Belville is unhappily a rover, I wou'd much rather that he ſhould have twenty miſtreſſes than one.

Lady Rach. You aſtoniſh me!

Mrs. Bel. Why, don't you know, my dear Madam, that while he is divided amidſt a variety of objects, 'tis impoſſible for him to have a ſerious attachment!

Lady Rach. Lord, Mrs. Belville! how can you ſpeak with ſo much compoſure! a virtuous woman ſhould be always outrageous upon ſuch an occaſion as this.

Mrs. Bel. What, and weary the innocent ſun and moon from the firmament, like a deſpairing princeſs in a tragedy — No — no—Lady Rachel, 'tis bad enough to be indifferent to the man I love, without ſtudying to excite his averſion.

Lady Rach. How glad I am that Miſs Walſingham made him ſo heartily aſham'd of himſelf: Lord, theſe young men are ſo full of levity: Give me a huſband of Mr. Torrington's age, ſay I.

Mrs. Bel. And give me a huſband of Mr. Belville's, ſay I, with all his follies: However, Lady Rachel, I am pretty well ſatisfied that my conduct at Miſs Leeſon's will have a proper effect upon Mr. Belville's generoſity, and put an entire end to his gallantries for the future.

Lady Rach. Don't deceive yourſelf, my dear.— The gods in the ſhilling gallery would ſooner give up Roaſt Beef, or go without an epilogue on the firſt night of a new piece.

Mrs. Bel. Why ſhould you think ſo of ſuch a man as Mr. Belville?

Lady Rach. Becauſe Mr. Belville is a man: However, if you dare run the riſque—we will try the ſincerity of his reformation.

Mrs. Bel. If I dare run the riſque! I would ſtake my ſoul upon his honour.

Lady Rach. Then your poor ſoul would be in a very terrible ſituation.

Mrs. Bel. By what teſt can we prove his ſincerity?

Lady Rach. By a very ſimple one. You know I write ſo like Miſs Walſingham, that our hands are ſcarcely known aſunder.

Mrs. Bel. Well——

Lady Rach. Why then let me write to him as from her.

Mrs. Bel. If I did not think it would look like a doubt of his honour—

Lady Rach. Poh! dare you proceed upon my plan?—

Mrs. Bel. Moſt confidently: Come to my dreſſing-room, where you'll find every thing ready for writing, and then you may explain your ſcheme more particularly.

Lady Rach. I'll attend you, but I am really ſorry, my dear, for the love of propriety, to ſee you ſo calm under the perfidy of your huſband; you ſhould be quite wretched—indeed you ſhould. [*Ex.*

SCENE, *the Temple.*

Enter LEESON.

The hell-hounds are after me, and if I am arreſted at this time, my honour will not only be blown upon by Brudenell, but I ſhall perhaps loſe Emily into the bargain. [*Exit.*

Enter LEECH, CROW, *and* WOLF, *dreſs'd in fur habits.*

Leech. Yonder, my lads, he darts through the Cloiſters; who the devil cou'd think that he wou'd ſmoke us in this diſguiſe? Crow, do you take the Fleet-Street ſide of the Temple, as faſt as you can, to prevent his doubling us that way—and, Wolf, do you run round the Garden court, that he mayn't eſcape us by the Thames—I'll follow the ſtrait line myſelf, and the devil's in the dice if he is not ſnap'd by one of us. [*Exeunt.*

SCENE

SCENE *changes to another part of the Temple.*

Enter LEESON *on one ſide*, CONNOLLY *on the other.*

Leeſ. Fly, open the chambers this moment—the bailiffs are after me.

Con. Faith and that I will—but it will be of no uſe to fly a ſtep neither, if I havn't the key.

Leeſ. Zounds! didn't you lock the door?

Con. Yes, but I believe I left the key on the inſide —however your own key will do the buſineſs as well.

Leeſ. True, and I forgot it in my confuſion, do you ſtay here, and throw every impediment in the way of theſe raſcals.

Con. Faith and that I will.

Enter CROW *and* WOLF.

Crow. Pray, Sir, did you ſee a gentleman run this way, dreſt in green and gold.

Con. In troth I did.

Wolf. And which way did he run?

Con. That I can tell you too.

Wolf. We ſhall be much oblig'd to you.

Con. Indeed and you will not, Mr. Catchpole, for the devil an information ſhall you get from Connolly; I ſee plainly enough what you are, you black-guards, tho' there's no gueſſing at you in theſe fur-coats.

Crow. Keep your information to yourſelf and be damn'd; here the cull comes, a priſoner in the cuſtody of maſter Leech.

Enter LEESON *and* LEECH.

Leeſ. Well, but treat me like a gentleman—Don't expoſe me unneceſſarily.

Leech. Expoſe you, maſter, we never expoſe any body, 'till gentlemen that expoſe themſelves, venever they compels their creditors to arreſt them.

Con. And where's your ruthority for arreſting the gentleman; let us ſee it this minute, for may be you havn't it about you.

Leech. O here's our authority, ve knew as we had to do vid a lawyer, and ſo we came properly prepar'd, my maſter.

Leeſ. What ſhall I do?

Con. Why harkee, Sir—Don't you think that you and I cou'd beat theſe three theeves, to their hearts content? I have nothing but my carcaſe to venter for you, honey, but that you are as welcome to as the flowers in May.

Leeſ. O, by no means, Connolly, we muſt not fly in the face of the laws.

Con. That's the reaſon that you are going to fight a duel.

Leeſ. Harkee, officer—I have ſome very material buſineſs to execute in the courſe of this evening: here are five guineas for a little indulgence, and I aſſure you, upon the honour of a gentleman, that if I have life, I'll attend your own appointment to morrow morning.

Leech I can't do it, maſter—Five guineas to be ſure is a genteel thing—but I have ten for the taking of you, do you ſee—and ſo if you pleaſe to ſtep to my houſe in Southampton Buildings, you may ſend for ſome friend to bail you, or ſettle the affair as well as you can with the plaintiff.

Con. I'll go bail for him this minute, if you don't want ſome body to be bail for myſelf.

Leeſ. Let me reflect a moment.

Crow to Con. Can you ſwear yourſelf worth one hundred and ſeventy pounds when your debts are paid?

Con. In troth I cannot, nor one hundred and ſeventy

ty pence—unleſs I have a mind to perjure myſelf.—But one man's body is as good as another's, and ſince he has no bail to give you but his fleſh, the fatteſt of us two is the beſt ſecurity.

Wolf. No, if we can't get better bail than you, we ſhall lock up his body in priſon according to law.

Con. Faith, and a very wiſe law it muſt be, which cuts off every method of getting money, by way of making us pay our debts.

Leech. Well, maſter Leeſon, what do you determine upon?

Leeſ. A moment's patience—Yonder I ſee Mr. Torrington—a thought occurs—yet it carries the appearance of fraud——however as it will be really innocent, nay laughable in the end, and as my ruin or ſalvation depends upon my preſent deciſion, it muſt be hazarded.

Crow. Come, maſter, fix upon ſomething, and don't keep us waiting for you.

Con. By my ſoul, honey, he don't want you to wait for him; he'll be very much obliged to you if you go away, and leave him to follow his own buſineſs.

Leeſ. Well, gentlemen—here comes Mr. Torrington: you know him, I ſuppoſe, and will be ſatisfied with his ſecurity.

Leech. O we'll take his bail for ten thouſand pounds, my maſter—Every body knows him to be a man of fortune.

Leeſ. Give me leave to ſpeak to him then, and I ſhall not be ungrateful for the civility.

Leech. Well we will—But harkee, lads, look to the paſſes, that no tricks may be play'd upon travellers.

Enter TORRINGTON.

Leeſ. Mr. Torrington, your moſt obedient.

Tor. Your humble ſervant.

Leeſ. I have many apologies to make, Mr. Torrington,

ton, for preſuming to ſtop a gentleman to whom I have not the honour of being known; yet when I explain the nature of my buſineſs, Sir, I ſhall by no means deſpair of an excuſe.

Tor. To the buſineſs, I beg, Sir.

Leeſ. You muſt know, Sir, that the three gentlemen behind me, are three traders from Dantzick, men of conſiderable property, who, in the preſent diſtracted ſtate of Poland, wiſh to ſettle with their families in this country.

Tor. Dantzick traders.—Ay, I ſee, they are foreigners by their dreſs.

Leech. Ay, now he is opening the affair.

Leeſ. They want therefore to be naturalized—and have been recommended to me for legal advice.

Tor. You are at the bar, Sir.

Leeſ. I have eat my way to profeſſional honour ſome time, Sir.

Tor. Ay, the cooks of the four ſocieties take care that the ſtudents ſhall perform every thing which depends upon teeth, young gentleman.—The eating exerciſes are the only ones never diſpens'd with.

Leeſ. I am, however, a very young barriſter, Mr. Torrington; and as the affair is of great importance to them, I am deſirous that ſome gentleman of eminence in the law ſhou'd reviſe my poor opinion, before they make it a ground of any ſerious determination.

Tor. You are too modeſt, young gentleman, to entertain any doubts upon this occaſion, as nothing is clearer than the laws with reſpect to the naturalization of foreigners.

Con. Faith the old gentleman ſmiles very good naturedly.

Leech. I fancy he'll ſtand it, Crow, and advance the crop for the younker.

Leeſ. To be ſure the laws are very clear to gentlemen

men of your ſuperior abilities.—But I have candidly acknowledged the weakneſs of my own judgment to my clients, and adviſ'd them ſo warmly to ſolicit your opinion, that they will not be ſatisfy'd unleſs you kindly conſent to oblige them.

Tor. O, if nothing but my opinion will ſatisfy them, let them follow me to my chambers, and I'll ſatisfy them directly.

Leeſ. You are extremely kind, Sir, and they ſhall attend you.—Gentlemen, will you be ſo good as to follow Mr. Torrington to his chambers, and he'll ſatisfy you intirely.

Wolf. Mind that!

Con. Muſha! the bleſſing of St. Patrick upon that ould head of yours.

Tor. What, they ſpeak Engliſh, do they?

Leeſ. Very tolerably, Sir!—Bred up general traders, they have a knowledge of ſeveral languages; and it would be highly for the good of the kingdom, if we cou'd get more of them to ſettle among us.

Tor. Right, young gentleman! the number of the people forms the true riches of a ſtate; however, now-a-days, London itſelf is not only gone out of town, but England itſelf, by an unaccountable fatality, ſeems inclin'd to take up her reſidence in America.

Leeſ. True, Sir! and to cultivate the barbarous borders of the Ohio, we are hourly deſerting the beautiful banks of the Thames.

Tor. *(Shaking him by the hand.)* You muſt come and ſee me at chambers, young gentleman! we muſt be better known to one another.

Con. Do you mind that, you thieves?—

Leeſ. 'Twill be equally my pride, and my happineſs to merit that honour, Sir.

Tor. Let your friends follow me, Sir!—and pray do you call upon me ſoon; you ſhall ſee a little plan which

which I have drawn up to keep this poor country, if poffible, from undergoing a general fentence of tranf-portation.—Be pleafed to come along with me, gentlemen—I'll fatisfy you. [*Exit.*

Leech. Well, mafter! I wifh you joy.—You can't fay but we behav'd to you like gemmen!——

[*Exeunt Bailiffs.*

Leef. And if you were all three in the cart, I don't know which of you I wou'd wifh to have refpited from execution; I have play'd Mr. Torrington a little trick, Connolly, but the moment I come back I fhall recover my reputation, if I even put myfelf voluntarily into the hands of thefe worthy gentlemen.—— [*Exit.*

Con. Mufha! long life to you old Shillaley; I don't wonder at your being afraid of a prifon, for 'tis to be fure a bleffed place to live in!—And not let my thick fkull confider if there's any way of preventing this infernal duel.——Suppofe I have him bound over to the peace!—No, that will never do: it would be a fhameful thing for a gentleman to keep the peace! befides, I muft appear in the bufinefs, and people may then think from my connection with him, that he has'n't honour enough to throw away his life!—Suppofe I go another way to work, and fend an anonymous letter about the affair to Mrs. Belville; they fay, tho' fhe is a woman of quality, that no creature upon earth can be fonder of her hufband!—Surely the good genius of Ireland put this fcheme in my head.—I'll about it this minute, and if there's but one of them kept from the field, I don't think that the other can be much hurt, when there will be nobody to fight with him. [*Exit.*

SCENE *changes to Capt.* SAVAGE's *Lodgings.*

Enter Captain SAVAGE *and* BELVILLE.

Capt. Why, faith, Belville, your detection, and fo fpeedily too, after all the pretended fanctity of the

 morning,

morning, muſt have thrown you into a moſt humiliating ſituation.

Bel. Into the moſt diſtreſſing you can imagine: had my wife rav'd at my falſehood, in the cuſtomary manner, I could have brazen'd it out pretty tolerably; but the angel-like ſweetneſs, with which ſhe bore the mortifying diſcovery, planted daggers in my boſom, and made me at that time wiſh her the verieſt vixen in the whole creation.

Capt. Yet, the ſuffering forbearance of a wife, is a quality for which ſhe is ſeldom allow'd her merit; we think it her duty to put up with our falſehood, and imagine ourſelves exceedingly generous in the main, if we practiſe no other method of breaking her heart.

Bel. Monſtrous! monſtrous! from this moment I bid an everlaſting adieu to my vices: the generoſity of my dear girl—

Enter a Servant to BELVILLE.

Ser. Here's a letter, Sir, which Mr. Spruce has brought you.

Bel. Give me leave, Savage—Zounds! what an induſtrious devil the father of darkneſs is, when the moment a man determines upon a good action, he ſends ſuch a thing as this, to ſtagger his reſolution.

Capt. What have you got there?

Bel. You ſhall know preſently. Will you let Spruce come in.

Capt. Where have you acquired all this ceremony?

Bel. Bid Spruce come in.

Ser. Yes, Sir.

Capt. Is that another challenge?

Bel. 'Tis upon my ſoul, but it came from a beautiful enemy, and dares me to give a meeting to Miſs Walſingham.

Capt. How!

Enter SPRUCE.

Bel. Pray, Spruce, who gave you this letter?

Spruce. Miſs Walſingham's woman, Sir: ſhe ſaid it was about very particular buſineſs, and therefore I wou'dn't truſt it by any of the footmen.

Capt. O, damn your diligence. (*Aſide.*

Bel. You may go home, Spruce.

Spruce. (*Looking ſignificantly at his maſter.*) Is there no anſwer neceſſary, Sir?

Bel. I ſhall call at home myſelf, and give the neceſſary anſwer.

Spruce. (*Aſide.*) What can be the matter with him all on a ſudden, that he is ſo cold upon the ſcent of wickedneſs? [*Exit.*

Capt. And what anſwer do you propoſe making to it, Belville?

Bel. Read the letter, and then tell me what I ſhou'd do—You know Miſs Walſingham's hand.

Capt. O perfectly!—This is not—yes, it is her hand!—I have too many curſt occaſions to know it. (*Aſide.*

Bel. What are you muttering about?—Read the letter.

Capt. *If you are not entirely diſcouraged, by our laſt converſation, from renewing the ſubject which* then *gave offence*——

Bel. *Which* then *gave offence.*—You ſee, Savage, that it is not offenſive any longer.

Capt. S'death! you put me out.—*You may at the maſquerade, this evening*—

Bel. You remember how earneſt ſhe was for the maſquerade party.

Capt. Yes, yes, I remember it well:—and I remember, alſo, how hurt ſhe was this morning, about the affair of Miſs Leeſon. (*Aſide.*)—*have an opportunity of entertaining me*——O the ſtrumpet! (*Aſide.*

Bel.

Bel. But mind the cunning with which ſhe ſigns the note, for fear it ſhou'd by any accident fall into improper hands.

Capt. Ay, and you put it into very proper hands. (*Aſide.*) *I ſhall be in the blue domino* —The ſignature is— YOU KNOW WHO.

Bel. Yes, *you know who.*

Capt. May be, however, ſhe has only written this to try you.

Bel. To try me, for what purpoſe? But if you read a certain poſtſcript there, I fancy you'll be of a different opinion.

Capt. If Mr. Belville has any houſe of character to retire to, it wou'd be moſt agreeable, as there cou'd be no fear of interruption.

Bel. What do you ſay now?—Can you recommend me to any houſe of character, where we ſhall be free from interruption.

Capt. O, curſe her houſe of character! (*Aſide.*) But ſurely, Belville, after your late determin'd reſolution to reform——

Bel. Zounds! I forgot that.

Capt. After the unexampled ſweetneſs of your wife's behaviour——

Bel. Don't go on, Savage: there is ſomething here *(putting his hand upon his boſom)* which feels already not a little aukwardly.

Capt. And can you ſtill perſiſt?

Bel. I am afraid to anſwer your queſtion.

Capt. Where the plague are you flying?

Bel. From the juſtice of your cenſure, Horace; my own is ſufficiently ſevere; yet I ſee that I ſhall be a raſcal again, in ſpite of my teeth; and good advice is only thrown away upon ſo incorrigible a libertine. [*Exit.*

Capt. (*alone.*) So then, this diamond of mine proves a counterfeit after all, and I am really the veriest wretch existing at the moment in which I conceived myself the peculiar favourite of fortune. O the cursed, cursed sex! I'll see her once more to upbraid her with her falsehood, then acquaint my father with her perfidy, to justify my breaking off the marriage, and tear her from my thoughts for ever.

Enter a Servant.

Ser. Sir! Sir! Sir!—

Capt. Sir, Sir, Sir.—What the devil's the matter with the booby!

Ser. Miss Walsingham, Sir!

Capt. Ah! what of her?

Ser. Was this moment overturn'd at Mr. Belville's door; and John tells me carried in a fit into the house.

Capt. Ha! let me fly to her assistance. [*Exit.*

Ser. Ha, let me fly to her assistance—O, are you thereabouts. [*Exit.*

SCENE *changes to Mr.* BELVILLE'*s*.

Enter Mrs. BELVILLE, *Miss* WALSINGHAM *and Lady* RACHEL MILDEW.

Mrs. Bel. But are you indeed recover'd, my dear?

Miss Wal. Perfectly, my dear—I wasn't in the least hurt, tho' greatly terrified, when the two fools of coachmen contended for the honour of being first, and drove the carriages together with a violence incredible.

Lady Rach. I sincerely rejoice at your escape; and now Mrs. Belville, as you promised to choose a dress for me if I went in your party to the masquerade this evening, can you spare a quarter of an hour to Tavistock-Street?

Mrs.

Mrs. Bel. I am loath to leave Miſs Walſingham alone, Lady Rachel, ſo ſoon after her fright.

Miſs Wal. Nay, I inſiſt that you don't ſtay at home upon my account; and Lady Rachel's company to the maſquerade is a pleaſure I have ſuch an intereſt in, that I beg you won't delay a moment to oblige her.

Mrs. Bel. Well, then I attend your ladyſhip.

Lady Rach. You are very good; and ſo is Miſs Walſingham. [*Exit.*

Miſs Wal. I wonder Captain Savage ſtays away ſo long! where can he be all this time?—I die with impatience to tell him of my happy interview with the General.

Enter a Servant.

Ser. Captain Savage, Madam.

Miſs Wal. Shew him in. [*Exit Ser.*] How he muſt rejoice to find his conjectures ſo fortunately realized.

Enter Captain SAVAGE.

Capt. So, madam, you have juſt eſcap'd a ſad accident.

Miſs Wal. And by that agreeable tone and countenance, one would almoſt imagine you were very ſorry for my eſcape.

Capt. People, madam, who doubt the kindneſs of others, are generally conſcious of ſome defect in themſelves.

Miſs Wal. Don't madam me, with this accent of indifference. What has put you out of humour?

Capt. Nothing.

Miſs. Wal. Are you indiſpoſed?

Capt. The Crocodile! the Crocodile! (*Aſide.*

Miſs Wal. Do you go to the maſquerade to night?

Capt.

Capt. No, but you do.

Miss Wal. Why not? Come, don't be ill-natur'd, I'm not your wife yet.

Capt. Nor ever will be, I promise you.

Miss Wal. What is the meaning of this very whimsical behaviour?

Capt. The settled composure of her impudence is intolerable. (*Aside.*) Madam, Madam, how have I deserv'd this usage?

Miss Wal. Nay, Sir, Sir, how have I deserv'd it, if you go to that?

Capt. The letter, madam!—the letter!

Miss Wal. What letter?

Capt. Your letter, inviting a gallant from the masquerade to a house of character, madam! — What, you appear surpriz'd?

Miss Wal. Well I may, at so shameless an aspersion.

Capt. Madam, madam, I have seen your letter! Your new lover cou'dn't keep your secret a moment. But I have nothing to do with you,—and only come to declare my reasons for renouncing you everlastingly!

Enter Servant.

Serv. General Savage, madam.

Miss Wal. Shew him up. [*Exit Serv.*] I am glad he is come, Sir; inform him of your resolution to break off the match, and let there be an end of every thing between us.

Enter General Savage.

Gen. The news of your accident reach'd me but this moment, madam——or I should have posted much sooner to reconnoitre your situation. My aid de camp, however, has not been inattentive I see, and I dare say his diligence will not be the least lessen'd, when he knows his obligations to you.

Capt. O, Sir, I am perfectly sensible of my obligations; and the conſciouſneſs of them, was one motive of my coming here.

Gen. Then you have made your acknowledgments to Miſs Walſingham, I hope.

Miſs Wal. He has indeed, General, ſaid a great deal more than was neceſſary.

Gen. That opinion proceeds from the liberality of your temper; for 'tis impoſſible he can ever ſay enough of your goodneſs.

Capt. So it is; if you knew but all, Sir.

Gen. Why who can know more of the matter than myſelf?

Miſs Wal. This gentleman, it ſeems, has ſomething, General Savage, very neceſſary for your information.

Gen. How's this?

Capt. Nay, Sir, I only ſay, that for ſome particular reaſons, which I ſhall communicate to you at a more proper time, I muſt beg leave to decline the lady whoſe hand you kindly intended for me this morning.

Gen. O you muſt!—Why then I hope you decline at the ſame time, all pretenſion to every ſhilling of my fortune? It is not in my power to make you fight, you poltroon, but I can puniſh you for cowardice.

Miſs Wal. Nay, but General, let me interpoſe here. If he can maintain any charge againſt the lady's reputation, 'twould be very hard that he ſhould be diſinherited for a neceſſary attention to his honour.

Capt. And if I don't make the charge good, I ſubmit to be diſinherited without murmuring.

Gen. 'Tis falſe as hell! the lady is infinitely too good for you, in every reſpect; and I undervalued her worth, when I thought of her for your wife.

Miſs Wal. I am ſure the lady is much oblig'd to your favourable opinion, Sir.

Gen.

Gen. Not in the leaſt, madam; I only do her common juſtice.

Capt. I cannot bear that you ſhould be diſpleas'd a moment, Sir; ſuffer me therefore to render the converſation leſs equivocal, and a few words will explain every thing.

Gen. Sirrah, I'll hear no explanation; ar'n't my orders that you ſhou'd marry?

Miſs Wal. For my ſake hear him, General Savage.

Capt. Madam, I diſdain every favour that is to be procur'd by your interpoſition. [*Exit.*

Miſs Wal. This matter muſt not be ſuffer'd to proceed farther tho', provokingly, cruelly as the Captain has behav'd. (*Aſide.*

Gen. What's that you ſay, my bewitching girl?

Miſs Wal. I ſay that you muſt make it up with the Captain, and the beſt way will be to hear his charge patiently.

Gen. I am ſhocked at the brutality of the dog; he has no more principle than a ſuttler, and no more ſteadineſs than a young recruit upon drill. But you ſhall have ample ſatisfaction:—this very day I'll cut him off from a poſſibility of ſucceeding to a ſhilling of my fortune. He ſhall be as miſerable as——

Miſs Wal. Dear General, do you think that this wou'd give me any ſatisfaction?

Gen. How he became acquainted with my deſign I know not, but I ſee plainly, that his mutiny proceeds from his averſion to my marrying again.

Miſs Wal. To your marrying again, Sir! why ſhou'd he object to that?

Gen. Why, for fear I ſhould have other children, to be ſure.

Miſs Wal. Indeed, Sir, it was not from that motive; and, if I can overlook his folly, you may be prevail'd upon to forgive it.

Gen. After what you have ſeen, juſtice ſhou'd make you

you a little more attentive to your own intereſt, my lovely girl.

Miſs Wal. What, at the expence of his?

Gen. In the approaching change of your ſituation, there may be a family of your own.

Miſs Wal. Suppoſe there ſhou'd, Sir; won't there be a family of his too?

Gen. I care not what becomes of his family.

Miſs Wal. But, pray let me think a little about it, General.

Gen. 'Tis hard, indeed, when I was ſo deſirous of promoting his happineſs, that he ſhou'd throw any thing in the way of mine.

Miſs Wal. Recollect, Sir, his offence was wholly confin'd to me.

Gen. Well, my love, and isn't it throwing an obſtacle in the way of my happineſs, when he abuſes you ſo groſly for your readineſs to marry me?

Miſs Wal. Sir!—

Gen. I ſee, with all your good nature, that this is a queſtion you cannot rally againſt.

Miſs Wal. It is indeed, Sir.—What will become of me? [*Aſide.*

Gen. You ſeem ſuddenly diſorder'd, my love?

Miſs Wal. Why really, Sir, this affair affects me ſtrongly.

Gen. Well, it is poſſible, that for your ſake, I may not puniſh him with as much ſeverity as I intended: in about an hour I ſhall beg leave to beat up your quarters again, with Mr. Torrington; for 'tis neceſſary I ſhould ſhew you ſome proof of my gratitude, ſince you have been ſo kindly pleaſed to honour me with a proof of your affection.

Miſs Wal. (*Aſide.*) So, now indeed, we're in a hopeful ſituation. [*Exeunt.*

SCENE *changes to* TORRINGTON'S *Chambers in the Temple.*

Enter TORRINGTON, LEECH, CROW, *and* WOLF.

Tor. Walk in, gentlemen—A good pretty young man that, we parted with juſt now—Pray, gentlemen, be ſeated—

Leech. He is indeed a very pretty young man.

Crow. And knows how to do a genteel thing—

Wolf. As handſome as any body.

Tor. There is a rectitude beſides in his polemical principles.

Leech. In what, Sir?—

Tor. His polemical principles.

Crow. What are they, Sir?

Tor. I beg pardon, gentlemen, you are not ſufficiently intimate with the Engliſh language, to carry on a converſation in it.

Wolf. Yes, we are, Sir.

Tor. Becauſe, if it is more agreeable to you, we'll talk in Latin.

Leech. We don't underſtand Latin, Sir.

Tor. I thought you generally convers'd in that language abroad.

Crow. No, nor at home neither, Sir: there is a language we ſometimes talk in, call'd Slang.

Tor. A ſpecies of the ancient Sclavonic, I ſuppoſe.

Leech. No, it's a little rum tongue, that we underſtand among von another—

Tor. I never heard of it before—But to buſineſs, gentlemen—the conſtitution of your country is at preſent very deplorable, I hear.

Wolf. Why indeed, Sir, there never was a greater cry againſt people in our way.

Tor. But you have laws, I ſuppoſe, for the regulation of your trade.

Leech. To be ſure we have, Sir: nevertheleſs ve find it very difficult to carry it on.

Crow.

Crow. Ve are harrafs'd with fo many oppreffions—

Tor. What, by the Pruffian troops?—

Crow. The Pruffian troops, Sir—Lord blefs you, no: by the courts of law; if ve make never fo fmall miftake in our duties.

Tor. Then your duties are very high, or very numerous—

Leech. I am afraid we don't underftand one another, Sir—

Tor. I am afraid fo too—Pray, where are your papers, gentlemen?—

Leech. Here's all the papers we have, Sir—You'll find every thing right—

Tor. I dare fay I fhall. *(Reads.) Middlefex to wit*—Why this is a warrant from the Sheriff's office to arreft fome body.

Crow. To be fure it is, Sir—

Tor. And what do you give it to me for?

Wolf. To fhew that we have done nothing contrary to law, Sir.

Tor. Who fuppofes that you have?

Leech. Only becaufe you afk'd for our papers, Sir.

Tor. Why what has this to do with them?

Crow. Why that's the warrant for arrefting the young gentleman.

Tor. What young gentleman?

Wolf. Lord blefs your heart, Sir; that ftopp'd you in the ftreet, and that you bail'd for the hundred and feventy pounds.

Tor. I bail'd for an hundred and feventy pounds!

Leech. Sure, Sir, you told me to follow you to chambers, and you wou'd fatisfy us.

Tor. Pray hear me, Sir—aren't you a trader of Dantzick?

Leech. I a trader! I am no trader, nor did I ever before hear of any fuch place.

Tor. Perhaps this gentleman is—

Crow. Lord help your head, I was born in Clare-

 market,

market, and never was farther out of town in my life than Brentford, to attend the Sheriff at the Middlesex election.

Tor. And it may be that you don't want to be naturaliz'd? [*To Wolf.*

Wolf. For what, my Master? I am a Liveryman of London already, and have a vote besides for the four counties.

Tor. Well, gentlemen, having been so good as to tell me what you are not, add a little to the obligation, and tell me what you are?

Leech. Why, Sir, the warrant we have shew'd you, tells that ve are sheriff's officers.

Tor. Sheriff's officers are you—O-ho—Sheriff's officers—then I suppose you must be three very honest gentlemen.

Crow. Sir!---we are as honest—

Tor. As sheriff's officers usually are.—Yet cou'd you think of nobody, but a man of the law, for the object of your conspiracy?

Leech. Sir, we don't understand what you mean?

Tor. But I understand what you mean, and therefore I'll deal with you properly.

Wolf. I hope, Sir, you'll pay us the money, for we can't go 'till the affair is certainly settled in some manner.

Tor. O, you can't—why then I will pay you.—But it shall be in a coin you won't like, depend upon it. —Here, Mr. Molesworth—

Enter MOLESWORTH.

Tor. Make out mittimusses for the commitment of these three fellows, they are disguis'd to defraud people; but I am in the commission for Middlesex, and I'll have you all brought to justice.—I will teach you to go masquerading about the streets.—So take them along, Mr. Molesworth.

Leech.

Leech. Ve don't fear your mittimus.

Crow. We'll put in bail directly, and try it with you, tho' you are a great lawyer.

Wolf. He'll make a flat of himself in this Nantzick affair.

Tor. Mighty well—And, if I find the young barrister, he may, perhaps, take a trip to the barbarous borders of the Ohio, from the beautiful banks of the Thames.

END *of the* THIRD ACT.

ACT IV.

SCENE, *an Apartment at* BELVILLE'S.

Enter Mrs. BELVILLE, *and Captain* SAVAGE.

Mrs. Bel. DON'T argue with me, Captain Savage; but consider that I am a wife, and pity my distraction.

Capt. Dear madam, there is no occasion to be so much alarm'd; Mr. Belville has very properly determin'd not to fight; he told me so himself, and should have been effectually prevented, if I hadn't known his resolution.

Mrs. Bel. There is no knowing to what extremities he may be provok'd, if he meets Mr. Leeson; I have sent for you, therefore, to beg that you will save him from the possibility, either of exposing himself to any danger, or of doing an injury to his adversary.

Capt.

Capt. What wou'd you have me do, Madam?

Mrs. Bel. Fly to Hyde-park, and prevent, if yet poſſible, his meeting with Mr. Leeſon: do it, I conjure you, if you'd ſave me from deſperation.

Capt. Though you have no reaſon whatever to be apprehenſive for his ſafety, Madam, yet, ſince you are ſo very much affected, I'll immediately execute your commands. [*Exit.*

Mrs. Bel. Merciful heaven! where is the generoſity, where is the ſenſe, where is the ſhame of men, to find a pleaſure in purſuits, which they cannot remember without the deepeſt horror; which they cannot follow without the meaneſt fraud? and which they cannot effect, without conſequences the moſt dreadful? The ſingle word Pleaſure, in a maſculine ſenſe, comprehends every thing that is cruel; every thing that is baſe; and every thing that is deſperate: Yet men, in other reſpects the nobleſt of their ſpecies, make it the principal buſineſs of their lives, and do not heſitate to break in upon the peace of the happieſt families, though their own muſt be neceſſarily expos'd to deſtruction.—O Belville! Belville!—my life! my love!---The greateſt crime which a libertine can ever experience, is too deſpicable to be envied; 'tis at beſt nothing but a victory over his own humanity; and if he is a huſband, he muſt be dead indeed, if he is not doubly tortured upon the wheel of recollection.

Enter Miſs WALSINGHAM *and Lady* RACHEL MILDEW.

Miſs Wal. My dear Mrs. Belville, I am extremely unhappy to ſee you ſo diſtreſs'd.

Lady Rach. Now I am extremely glad to ſee her ſo, for if ſhe wasn't greatly diſtreſs'd it wou'd be monſtrouſly unnatural.

Mrs. Bel. O, Matilda!---my huſband! my huſband! my children! my children!

Miſs Wal. Don't weep, my dear! don't weep! pray be comforted, all may end happily. Lady Rachel, beg of her not to cry ſo.

Lady

Lady Rach. Why, you are crying yourſelf, Miſs Walſingham; and tho' I think it out of character to encourage her tears, I can't help keeping you company.

Mrs. Bel. O, why is not ſome effectual method contriv'd, to prevent this horrible practice of duelling?

Lady Rach. I'll expoſe it on the ſtage, ſince the law now-a-days kindly leaves the whole cognizance of it to the theatre.

Miſs Wal. And yet if the laws againſt it were as well enforced as the laws againſt deſtroying the game, perhaps it would be equally for the benefit of the kingdom.

Mrs. Bel. No law will ever be effectual till the cuſtom is render'd infamous.—Wives muſt ſhriek! —mothers muſt agonize!—orphans muſt multiply! unleſs ſome bleſſed hand ſtrips the faſcinating glare from honourable murder, and bravely expoſes the idol who is worſhip'd thus in blood. While it is diſreputable to obey the laws, we cannot look for reformation:—But if the duelliſt is once baniſhed from the preſence of his ſovereign;—if he is for life excluded the confidence of his country;---if a mark of indelible diſgrace is ſtamp'd upon him, the ſword of public juſtice will be the ſole chaſtiſer of wrongs; trifles will not be puniſh'd with death, and offences really meriting ſuch a puniſhment will be reſerv'd for the only proper avenger, the common executioner.

Lady Rach. I cou'dn't have expreſs'd myſelf better on the ſubject, my dear: but till ſuch a hand as you talk of is found, the beſt will fall into the error of the times.

Miſs Wal. Yes, and butcher each other like madmen, for fear their courage ſhould be ſuſpected by fools.

Mrs. Bel. No news yet from Captain Savage?

Lady Rach. He can't have reach'd Hyde-park yet, my dear.

Miſs Wal. Let us lead you to your chamber, my dear; you'll be better there.

Mrs.

Mrs. Bel. Matilda, I muſt be wretched any where; but I'll attend you.

Lady Rach. Thank heav'n I have no huſband to plunge into ſuch a ſituation!

Miſs Wal. And, if I thought I cou'd keep my reſolution, I'd determine this moment on living ſingle all the days of my life. Pray don't ſpare my arm, my dear. [*Exeunt.*

SCENE, *Hyde Park.*

Enter BELVILLE.

Bel. I fancy I am rather before the time of appointment; engagements of this kind are the only ones, in which, now-a-days, people pretend to any punctuality:——a man is allow'd half an hour's law to dinner, but a thruſt through the body muſt be given within a ſecond of the clock.

Enter LEESON.

Leeſ. Your ſervant, Sir.—Your name I ſuppoſe is Belville?

Bel. Your ſuppoſition is very right, Sir; and I fancy I am not much in the wrong, when I ſuppoſe your name to be Leeſon.

Leeſ. It is, Sir; I am ſorry I ſhou'd keep you here a moment.

Bel. I am very ſorry, Sir, you ſhou'd bring me here at all.

Leeſ. I regret the occaſion, be aſſured, Sir; but 'tis not now a time for talking, we muſt proceed to action.

Bel. And yet talking is all the action I ſhall proceed to, depend upon it.

Leeſ. What do you mean, Sir? Where are your piſtols?

Bel. Where I intend they ſhall remain till my next journey into the country, very quietly over the chimney in my dreſſing-room.

Leeſ. You treat this matter with too much levity, Mr. Belville; take your choice of mine, Sir.

Bel.

Bel. I'd rather take them both, if you pleaſe, for then no miſchief ſhall be done with either of them.

Leeſ. Sir, this trifling is adding inſult to injury; and ſhall be reſented accordingly. Didn't you come here to give me ſatisfaction?

Bel. Yes, every ſatisfaction in my power.

Leeſ. Take one of theſe piſtols then.

Bel. Come, Mr. Leeſon, your bravery will not at all be leſſen'd by the exerciſe of a little underſtanding: If nothing leſs than my life can atone for the injury I have unconſciouſly done you, fire at me inſtantly, but don't be offended becauſe I decline to do you an additional wrong.

Leeſ. S'death, Sir, do you think I come here with an intention to murder?

Bel. You come to arm the guilty againſt the innocent, Sir; and that, in my opinion, is the moſt attrocious intention of murder.

Leeſ. How's this?——

Bel. Look'e, Mr. Leeſon, there's your piſtol— (*Throws it on the ground.*) I have already acted very wrongly with reſpect to your ſiſter; but, Sir, I have ſome character (though perhaps little enough) to maintain, and I will not do a ſtill worſe action, in raiſing my hand againſt your life.

Leeſ. This hypocritical cant of cowardice, Sir, is too palpable to diſarm my reſentment; though I held you to be a man of profligate principles, I nevertheleſs conſider'd you as a man of courage; but, if you heſitate a moment longer, by heav'n I'll chaſtiſe you on the ſpot. (*Draws.*)

Bel. I muſt defend my life; though, if it did not look like timidity, I would inform you—(*They fight, Leeſon is diſarm'd.*)—Mr. Leeſon, there is your ſword again.

Leeſ. Strike it through my boſom, Sir;—I don't deſire to out-live this inſtant.

Bel. I hope, my dear Sir, that you will long live

happy

happy—as your ſiſter, tho' to my ſhame I can claim no merit on that account, is recover'd unpolluted, by her family; but let me beg that you will now ſee the folly of deciſions by the ſword, when ſucceſs is not fortunately chain'd to the ſide of juſtice: before I leave you, receive my ſincereſt apologies for the injuries I have done you; and, be aſſured, no occurrence will ever give me greater pleaſure, than an opportunity of ſerving you, if, after what is paſt, you ſhall at any time condeſcend to uſe me as a friend. [*Ex.*

Leeſ. Very well—very well—very well.

Enter CONOLLY.

Leeſ. What, you have been within hearing I ſuppoſe?

Con. You may ſay that.

Leeſ. And isn't this very fine?

Con. Why I can't ſay much as to the finery of it, Sir, but it is very fooliſh.

Leeſ. And ſo this is my ſatisfaction after all!

Con. Yes, and pretty ſatisfaction it is. When Mr. Belville did you but one injury, he was the greateſt villain in the world; but now that he has done you two, in drawing his ſword upon you, I ſuppoſe he is a very worthy gentleman.

Leeſ. To be foil'd, baffled, diſappointed in my revenge!—What tho' my ſiſter is by accident unſtain'd, his intentions are as criminal as if her ruin was actually perpetrated; there is no poſſibility of enduring this reflection!—I wiſh not for the blood of my enemy, but I would at leaſt have the credit of giving him life.

Con. Arrah, my dear, if you had any regard for the life of your enemy, you ſhou'dn't put him in the way of death.

Leeſ. No more of theſe reflections, my dear Conolly; my own feelings are painful enough. Will you be ſo good as to take theſe damn'd piſtols, and come with me to the coach?

Con. Troth and that I will; but don't make your-ſelf

ſelf uneaſy; conſider that you have done every thing which honour required at your hands.

Leeſ. I hope ſo.

Con. Why you know ſo: you have broke the laws of heaven and earth, as nobly as the firſt Lord in the land, and you have convinc'd the world, that where any body has done your family one injury, you have courage enough to do it another yourſelf, by hazarding your life.

Leeſ. Thoſe, Connolly, who would live reputably in any country, muſt regulate their conduct in many caſes by its very prejudices.—Cuſtom, with reſpect to duelling, is a tyrant, whoſe deſpotiſm no body ventures to attack, tho' every body deteſts its cruelty.

Con. I didn't imagine that a tyrant of any kind would be tolerated in England. But where do you think of going now? For chambers, you know, will be moſt delightfully dangerous, till you have come to an explanation with Mr. Torrington.

Leeſ. I ſhall go to Mrs. Crayons.

Con. What the gentlewoman that paints all manner of colours in red chalk?

Leeſ. Yes, where I firſt became acquainted with Emily.

Con. And where the ſweet creature has met you two or three times, under pretence of ſitting for her picture.

Leeſ. Mrs. Crayons will, I dare ſay, oblige me in this exigency with an apartment for a few days. I ſhall write, from her houſe, a full explanation of my conduct to Mr. Torrington, and let him know where I am; for the honeſt old man muſt not be the ſmalleſt ſufferer, tho' a thouſand priſons were to ſtare me in the face —But come, Connolly, we have no time to loſe.—Yet if you had any prudence you would abandon me in my preſent ſituation.

Con. Ah, Sir, is this your opinion of my friendſhip? Do you think that any thing can ever give me half ſo much pleaſure in ſerving you, as ſeeing you ſurrounded by misfortunes?

[*Exeunt.*

SCENE *changes to an Apartment at* BELVILLE's.
Enter General SAVAGE, TORRINGTON, *and* SPRUCE.

Spruce. Miſs Walſingham will wait on you immediately, gentlemen.

Gen. Very well.

Spruce. (*aſide.*) What can old Holifernes want ſo continually with Miſs Walſingham? [*Exit.*

Gen. When I bring this ſweet mild creature home, I ſhall be able to break her ſpirit to my own wiſhes—I'll inure her to proper diſcipline from the firſt moment, and make her tremble at the very thought of mutiny.

Tor. Ah, General, you are wonderfully brave, when you know the meekneſs of your adverſary.

Gen. Envy, Torrington——ſtark, ſtaring envy: few fellows, on the borders of fifty, have ſo much reaſon as myſelf, to boaſt of a blooming young woman's partiality.

Tor. On the borders of fifty, man!—beyond the confines of threeſcore.

Gen. The more reaſon I have to boaſt of my victory then; but don't grumble at my triumph: you ſhall have a kiſs of the bride, let that content you, Torrington.

Enter Miſs WALSINGHAM.

Miſs Wal. Gentlemen, your moſt obedient; General, I intended writing to you about a trifling miſtake; but poor Mrs. Belville has been ſo very ill, that I cou'dn't find an opportunity.

Gen. I am very ſorry for Mrs. Belville's illneſs, but I am happy, Madam, to be perſonally in the way of receiving your commands, and I wait upon you with Mr. Torrington, to talk about a marriage ſettlement.

Miſs Wal. Heavens! how ſhall I undeceive him! (*Aſide.*

Tor. 'Tis rather an aukward buſineſs, Miſs Walſingham, to trouble you upon; but as the General wiſhes that the affair may be as private as poſſible, he thought it better to ſpeak to yourſelf, than to treat with any other perſon.

Gen.

Gen. Yes, my lovely girl; and to convince you that I intended to carry on an honourable war, not to pillage like a free-booter, Mr. Torrington will be a truſtee.

Miſs Wal. I am infinitely oblig'd to your intention, but there's no neceſſity to talk about my ſettlement—for——

Gen. Pardon me, Madam,—pardon me, there is—beſides, I have determin'd that there ſhall be one, and what I once determine is abſolute.—A tolerable hint for her own behaviour, when I have married her, Torrington. (*Aſide to Tor.*

Miſs Wal. I muſt not ſhock him before Mr. Torrington (*aſide.*) General Savage, will you give me leave to ſpeak a few words in private to you?

Gen. There is no occaſion for ſounding a retreat, Madam; Mr. Torrington is acquainted with the whole buſineſs, and I am determin'd, for your ſake, that nothing ſhall be done without him.

Tor. I can have no objection to your hearing the lady *ex parte*, General.

Miſs Wal. What I have to ſay, Sir, is of a very particular nature.

Tor. (*riſing*) I'll leave the room then.

Gen. (*oppoſing him*) You ſhan't leave the room, Torrington. Miſs Walſingham ſhall have a ſpecimen of my command, even before marriage, and you ſhall ſee, that every woman is not to bully me out of my determination. [*Aſide to Tor.*

Miſs Wal. Well, General, you muſt have your own way.

Gen. (*to Tor.*) Don't you ſee that 'tis only fighting the battle ſtoutly at firſt, with one of theſe gentle creatures?

Tor. (*ſignificantly*) Ah, General!

Gen. I own, Madam, your ſituation is a diſtreſſing one; let us ſit down—let us ſit down——

Miſs Wal. It is unſpeakably diſtreſſing indeed, Sir.

Tor. Diſtreſſing however as it may be, we muſt proceed to iſſue, Madam; the General propoſes your jointure to be 1000*l.* a year.

Miſs Wal. General Savage!

Gen. You think this is too little, perhaps?

Miſs Wal. I can't think of any jointure, Sir.

Tor. Why to be ſure, a jointure is at beſt but a melancholy poſſeſſion, for it muſt be purchaſed by the loſs of the huſband you love.

Miſs Wal. Pray don't name it, Mr. Torrington.

Gen. (*kiſſing her hand*) A thouſand thanks to you, my lovely girl.

Miſs Wal. For heaven's ſake let go my hand.

Gen. I ſhall be mad 'till it gives me legal poſſeſſion of the town.

Miſs Wal. Gentlemen—General—Mr. Torrington I—beg you'll hear me.

Gen. By all means, my adorable creature; I can never have too many proofs of your diſintereſted affection.

Miſs Wal. There is a capital miſtake in this whole affair—I am ſinking under a load of diſtreſs.

Gen. Your confuſion makes you look charmingly, though.

Miſs Wal. There is no occaſion to talk of jointures or marriages to me; I am not going to be married.

Tor. What's this?

Miſs Wal. Nor have I an idea in nature, however, enviable I think the honour, of being your wife, Sir.

Gen. Madam!

Tor. Why here's a demur!

Miſs Wal. I am afraid, Sir, that in our converſation this morning, my confuſion, ariſing from the particularity of the ſubject, has led you into a material miſconception.

Gen. I am thunder-ſtruck, Madam! I cou'dn't miſtake my ground.

Tor. As clear a *nol. proſ.* as ever was iſſued by an attorney-general.

Gen.

Gen. Surely you can't forget, that at the firſt word you hung out a flag of truce, told me even that I had a previous friend in the fort, and didn't ſo much as hint a ſingle article of capitulation?

Tor. Now for the rejoinder to this replication.

Miſs Wal. All this is unqueſtionably true, General, and perhaps a good deal more; but in reality my confuſion before you on this ſubject to-day was ſuch, that I ſcarcely knew what I ſaid; I was dying with diſtreſs, and at this moment am very little better;—permit me to retire, General Savage, and only ſuffer me to add, that tho' I think myſelf highly flatter'd by your addreſſes, it is impoſſible for me ever to receive them. Lord! Lord! I am glad 'tis over in any manner. [*Ex.*

Tor. Why, we are a little out of this matter, General; the judge has decided againſt us, when we imagin'd ourſelves ſure of the cauſe.

Gen. The gates ſhut in my teeth, juſt as I expected the keys from the governor!

Tor. I am diſappointed myſelf, man; I ſhan't have a kiſs of the bride.

Gen. At my time of life too!

Tor. I ſaid from the firſt you were too old for her.

Gen. Zounds, to fancy myſelf ſure of her, and to triumph upon a certainty of victory!

Tor. Ay, and to kiſs her hand in a rapturous return for her tenderneſs to you:—let me adviſe you never to kiſs before folks, as long as you live again.

Gen. Don't diſtract me, Torrington! a joke, where a friend has the misfortune to loſe the battle, is a downright inhumanity.

Tor. You told me that your ſon had accus'd her of ſomething that you would not hear; ſuppoſe we call at his lodgings, he perhaps, as an *amicus curiæ*, may be able to give us a little information.

Gen. Thank you for the thought;—But keep your finger more than ever upon your lips, dear Torrington. You know how I dread the danger of ridicule, and it wou'd wou'd be too much, not only to be thraſh'd out of the field, but to be laugh'd at into the bargain.

Tor. I thought when you made a preſentment of your ſweet perſon to Miſs Walſingham, that the bill wou'd be return'd ignoramus. [*Exeunt.*

SCENE, BELVILLE'*s*.

Mrs. BELVILLE *and Lady* RACHEL MILDEW, *diſcovered on a Sopha.*

Lady Rach. You heard what Captain Savage ſaid?

Mrs. Bel. I would flatter myſelf, but my heart will not ſuffer it; the Park might be too full for the horrid purpoſe, and perhaps they are gone to decide the quarrel in ſome other place.

Lady Rach. The Captain enquir'd of numbers in the Park without hearing a ſyllable of them, and is therefore poſitive that they are parted without doing any miſchief.

Mrs. Bel. I am, neverthelefs, torn by a thouſand apprehenſions; and my fancy, with a gloomy kind of fondneſs, faſtens on the moſt deadly. This very morning, I exultingly numbered myſelf in the catalogue of the happieſt wives.—Perhaps I am a wife no longer;—perhaps, my little innocents, your unhappy father is at this moment breathing his laſt ſigh, and wiſhing, O, how vainly! that he had not preferr'd a guilty pleaſure to his own life, to my eternal peace of mind, and your felicity!

Enter SPRUCE.

Spruce. Madam! madam! my maſter! my maſter!

Mrs. Bel. Is he ſafe!

Enter BELVILLE.

Bel. My love!

Mrs. Bel. O, Mr. Belville! (*Faints.*

Bel. Aſſiſtance, quick!

Lady Rach. There ſhe revives.

Bel. The angel-ſoftneſs! how this rends my heart!

Mrs. Bel. O, Mr. Belville, if you cou'd conceive the

the agonies I have endur'd, you would avoid the poſſibility of another quarrel as long as you liv'd, out of common humanity.

Bel. My deareſt creature, ſpare theſe tender reproaches; you know not how ſufficiently I am puniſh'd to ſee you thus miſerable.

Lady Rach. That's pleaſant indeed, when you have yourſelf deliberately loaded her with affliction.

Bel. Pray, pray Lady Rachel, have a little mercy: Your poor humble ſervant has been a very naughty boy,—but if you only forgive him this ſingle time, he will never more deſerve the rod of correction.

Mrs. Bell. Since you are return'd ſafe, I am happy. Excuſe theſe fooliſh tears, they guſh in ſpite of me.

Bel. How contemptible do they render me, my love!

Lady Rach. Come, my dear, you muſt turn your mind from this gloomy ſubject.——Suppoſe we ſtep up ſtairs, and communicate our pleaſure to Miſs Walſingham?

Mrs. Bel. With all my heart. Adieu, recreant!

[*Exeunt Mrs.* Bel. *and Lady* Rach.

Bel. I don't deſerve ſuch a woman, I don't deſerve her.---Yet, I believe I am the firſt huſband that ever found fault with a wife for having too much goodneſs.

Enter Spruce.

What's the matter?

Spruce. Your ſiſter——

Bel. What of my Siſter?

Spruce. Sir, is elop'd.

Bel. My ſiſter!

Spruce. There is a letter left, Sir, in which ſhe ſays, that her motive was a diſlike to match with Captain Savage, as ſhe has plac'd her affections unalterably on another gentleman.

Bel. Death and damnation!

Spruce. Mrs. Moreland, your mother, is in the greateſt diſtreſs, Sir, and begs you will immediately go with the ſervant that brought the meſſage; for he, observing the young lady's maid carrying some bundles out, a little suspiciously, thought there must be some scheme going on, and dogg'd a hackney coach, in which Miss Moreland went off, to the very house where it set her down.

Bel. Bring me to the servant, instantly;---but don't let a syllable of this matter reach my wife's ears, her spirits are already too much agitated. [*Exit.*

Spruce. Zounds! we shall be paid home for the tricks we have play'd in other families. [*Exit.*

SCENE *changes to Capt.* SAVAGE's *Lodgings.*

Enter Captain SAVAGE.

Capt. The vehemence of my resentment against this abandon'd woman has certainly led me too far. I shou'dn't have acquainted her with my discovery of her baseness;—no, if I had acted properly, I should have conceal'd all knowledge of the transaction 'till the very moment of her guilt, and then burst upon her when she was solacing with her paramour, in all the fulness of security. Now, if she should either alter her mind, with respect to going to the masquerade, or go in a different habit to elude my observation, I not only lose the opportunity of exposing her, but give her time to plan some plausible excuse for her infamous letter to Belville.

Enter a Servant.

Ser. General Savage, and Mr. Torrington, Sir.

Capt. You blockhead, why did you let them wait a moment? What can be the meaning of this visit?

[*Exit Ser.*

Enter General SAVAGE, *and* TORRINGTON.

Gen. I come, Horace, to talk to you about Miss Walsingham.

Capt. She's the most worthless woman existing, Sir: I can convince you of it.

Gen. I have already chang'd my own opinion of her.

Capt. What you have found her out yourself, Sir?

Tor.

Tor. Yes, he has made a trifling discovery.

Gen. S'death, don't make me contemptible to my son. (*Aside to* Tor.

Capt. But, Sir, what instance of her precious behaviour has come to your knowledge? For an hour has scarcely elapsed, since you thought her a miracle of goodness.

Tor. Ay, he has thought her a miracle of goodness, within this quarter of an hour.

Gen. Why she has a manner that wou'd impose upon all the world.

Capt. Yes, but she has a manner also to undeceive the world thoroughly.

Tor. That we have found pretty recently; however, in this land of liberty, none are to be pronounced guilty, 'till they are positively convicted; I can't therefore find against Miss Walsingham, upon the bare strength of presumptive evidence.

Capt. Presumptive evidence! hav'nt I promis'd you ocular demonstration?

Tor. Ay, but 'till we receive this demonstration, my good friend, we cannot give judgment.

Capt. Then I'll tell you at once, who is the object of her honourable affections.

Gen. Who—who—

Capt. What would you think if they were plac'd on Belville?

Gen. Upon Belville! has she deserted to him from the corps of virtue?

Capt. Yes, she wrote to him, desiring to be taken from the masquerade to some convenient scene of privacy, and tho' I have seen the letter, she has the impudence to deny her own hand.

Gen. What a fiend is there then disguis'd under the uniform of an angel!

Tor. The delicate creature that was dying with confusion!

Capt. Only come with me to the masquerade, and you shall see Belville carry her off: 'Twas about the ſcandalous appointment with him, I was ſpeaking, when you conceiv'd I treated her ſo rudely.

Gen. And you were only anxious to ſhew her in her real character to me, when I was ſo exceedingly offended with you.

Capt. Nothing elſe in the world, Sir; I knew you would deſpiſe and deteſt her, the moment you were acquainted with her baſeneſs.

Gen. How ſhe brazen'd it out before my face, and what a regard ſhe affected for your intereſt! I was a madman not to liſten to your explanation.

Tor. Tho' you both talk this point well, I ſtill ſee nothing but ſtrong preſumption againſt Miſs Walſingham: Miſtakes have already happened, miſtakes may happen again; and I will not give up a lady's honour, upon an evidence that wou'd not caſt a common pickpocket at the Old Baily.

Capt. Come to the maſquerade then and be convinc'd.

Gen. Let us detach a party for dreſſes immediately. Yet remember, Torrington, that the punctuality of evidence which is neceſſary in a court of law, is by no means requiſite in a court of honour.

Tor. Perhaps it would be more to the honour of your honourable courts if it was. [*Exeunt.*

The Scene changes to an Apartment at Mrs. CRAYON'*s.*

Bel. (*Behind.*) My dear, you muſt excuſe me.

Maid. Indeed, Sir, you muſt not go up ſtairs.

Bel. Indeed but I will; the man is poſitive to the houſe, and I'll ſearch every room in it, from the cellar to the garret, if I don't find the lady. James, don't ſtir from the ſtreet door.

Enter BELVILLE *followed by a Maid.*

Maid. Sir, you are the ſtrangeſt gentleman I ever met with in all my born days:—I wiſh my miſtreſs was at home.

Bel. I am a ſtrange fellow, my dear—But if your miſtreſs was at home, I ſhou'd take the liberty of peeping into the apartments.

Maid.

Maid. Sir, there's company in that room, you can't go in there.

Bel. Now, that's the very reaſon I will go in.

Maid. This muſt be ſome great man, or he wou'dn't behave ſo obſtropolous.

Bel. Good manners, by your leave a little. (*Forcing the door.*) Whoever my gentleman is, I'll call him to a ſevere reckoning:—I have juſt been call'd to one myſelf, for making free with another man's ſiſter.

Enter LEESON *followed by* CONNOLLY.

Leeſ. Who is it that dares commit an outrage upon this apartment?

Con. An Engliſhman's very lodging, ay, and an Iriſhman's too, I hope, is his caſtle;—an Iriſhman is an Engliſhman all the world over.

Bel. Mr. Leeſon!

Maid. O we ſhall have murder. (*Running off.*

Con. Run into that room, my dear, and ſtay with the young lady. [*Exit Maid.*

Leeſ. And, Connolly, let nobody elſe into that room.

Con. Let me alone for that, honey, if this gentleman has fifty people.

Leeſ. Whence is it, Mr. Belville, that you perſecute me thus with injuries!

Bel. I am fill'd with aſtoniſhment!

Con. Faith, to ſpeak the truth, you do look a little ſurpris'd.

Leeſ. Anſwer me, Sir, what is the foundation of this new violence?

Bel. I am come, Mr. Leeſon, upon an affair, Sir—

Con. The devil burn me if he was half ſo much confounded a while ago, when there was a naked ſword at his breaſt.

Bel. I am come, Mr. Leeſon, upon an affair, Sir, that—How the devil ſhall I open it to him, ſince the tables are ſo fairly turn'd upon me?

Leeſ. Diſpatch, Sir, for I have company in the next room.

Bel. A lady, I ſuppoſe?

Leeſ.

Leeſ. Suppoſe it is, Sir?

Bel. And the lady's name is Moreland, isn't it, Sir?

Leeſ. I can't ſee what buſineſs you have with her name, Sir. You took away my ſiſter, and I hope you have no deſigns upon the lady in the next room.

Bel. Indeed but I have.

Leeſ. The devil you have!

Con. Well, this is the moſt unaccountable man I ever heard of, he'll have all the women in the town, I believe.

Leeſ. And pray, Sir, what pretenſions have you to the lady in the next room, even ſuppoſing her to be Miſs Moreland?

Bel. No other pretenſions than what a brother ſhould have to the defence of his ſiſter's honour: You thought yourſelf authoriſed to cut my throat a while ago in a ſimilar buſineſs.

Leeſ. And is Miſs Moreland your ſiſter?

Bel. Sir, there is inſolence in the queſtion; you know ſhe is.

Leeſ. By heaven, I did not know it till this moment; but I rejoice at the diſcovery: This is blow for blow!

Con. Devil burn me but they have fairly made a ſwop of it.

Bel. And you really didn't know that Miſs Moreland was my ſiſter?

Leeſ. I don't conceive myſelf under much neceſſity of apologizing to you, Sir; but I am incapable of a diſhonourable deſign upon any woman; and tho' Miſs Moreland, in our ſhort acquaintance, repeatedly mentioned her brother, ſhe never once told me that his name was Belville.

Con And he has had ſuch few opportunities of being in her company, unleſs by letters, honey, that he knew nothing more of her connections, than her being a ſweet pretty creater, and having thirty thouſand pounds.

Bel. The fortune, I dare ſay, no way leſſened the force of her attractions.

Leeſ.

Leeſ. I am above diſſimulation—It really did not.

Bel. Well, Mr. Leeſon, our families have ſhewn ſuch a very ſtrong inclination to come together, that it would really be a pity to diſappoint them.

Con. Upon my ſoul and ſo it would; though the dread of being forc'd to have a huſband, the young lady tells us, quicken'd her reſolution to marry this gentleman.

Bel. O ſhe had no violence of that kind to apprehend from her family; therefore, Mr. Leeſon, ſince you ſeem as neceſſary for the girl's happineſs as ſhe ſeems for your's, you ſhall marry her here in town, with the conſent of all her friends, and ſave yourſelf the trouble of an expedition to Scotland.

Leeſ. Can I believe you ſerious?

Bel. Zounds, Leeſon, that air of ſurprize is a ſad reproach! I didn't ſurpriſe you when I did a bad action, but I raiſe your aſtoniſhment, when I do a good one.

Con. And by my ſoul, Mr. Belville, if you knew how a good action becomes a man, you'd never do a bad one as long as you liv'd.

Leeſ. You have given me life and happineſs in one day, Mr. Belville! however, it is now time you ſhou'd ſee your ſiſter; I know you'll be gentle with her, tho' you have ſo much reaſon to condemn her choice, and generouſly remember that her elopement proceeded from the great improbability there was of a beggar's ever meeting with the approbation of her family.

Bel. Don't apologize for your circumſtances, Leeſon; a princeſs could do no more than make you happy, and if you make her ſo, you meet her upon terms of the moſt perfect equality.

Leeſ. This is a new way of thinking, Mr. Belville.

Bel. 'Tis only an honeſt way of thinking; and I conſider my ſiſter a gainer upon the occaſion; for a man of your merit is more difficult to be found, than a woman of her fortune. [*Exeunt Leeſon and Belville.*

Con. What's the reaſon now that I can't ſkip and

laugh, and rejoice, at this affair? Upon my ſoul my heart's as full as if I had met with ſome great misfortune. Well, pleaſure in the extreme is certainly a very painful thing: I am really aſham'd of theſe woman's drops, and yet I don't know but that I ought to bluſh for being aſham'd of them, for I am ſure nobody's eye ever looks half ſo well, as when it is diſfigured by a tear of humanity. [*Exit.*

A C T V.

S C E N E, *a Drawing-Room.*

Enter Belville.

Bel. WELL, happineſs is once more mine, and the women are all going in tip-top ſpirits to the maſquerade. Now, Mr. Belville, let me have a few words with you; Miſs Walſingham, the ripe, the luxurious Miſs Walſingham, expects to find you there burning with impatience:—But, my dear friend, after the occurrences of the day, can you be weak enough to plunge into freſh crimes? Can you be baſe enough to abuſe the goodneſs of that angel your wife; and wicked enough, not only to deſtroy the innocence which is ſhelter'd beneath your own roof, but to expoſe your family perhaps again, to the danger of loſing a ſon, a brother, a father, and a huſband? The poſſeſſion of the three Graces is ſurely too poor a recompence for the folly you muſt commit, for the ſhame you muſt feel, and the conſequence you muſt hazard. Upon my ſoul if I ſtruggle a little longer, I ſhall riſe in my own opinion, and be leſs a raſcal than I think myſelf:—Ay, but the object is bewitching;—the matter will be an eternal ſecret—and if it is known that

that I ſneak in this pitiful manner from a fine woman, when the whole elyſium of her perſon ſolicits me:—well, and am I afraid the world ſhould know that I have ſhrunk from an infamous action?—A thouſand bleſſings on you, dear conſcience, for that one argument;—I ſhall be an honeſt man after all—Suppoſe, however, that I gave her the meeting? that's dangerous;—that's dangerous:—and I am ſo little accuſtomed to do what is right, that I ſhall certainly do what is wrong, the moment I am in the way of temptation. Come, Belville, your reſolution is not ſo very ſlender a dependence, and you owe Miſs Walſingham reparation for the injury which you have done her principles. I'll give her the meeting—I'll take her to the houſe I intended—I'll—Zounds! what a fool I have been all this time, to look for precarious ſatisfaction in vice, when there is ſuch exquiſite pleaſure to be found at a certainty in virtue. [*Exit.*

Enter Lady RACHEL *and Mrs.* BELVILLE.

Lady Rach. For mirth ſake don't let him ſee us: There has been a warm debate between his paſſion and his conſcience.

Mrs. Bel. And the latter is the conqueror, my life for it.

Lady Rach. Dear Mrs. Belville, you are the beſt of women, and ought to have the beſt of huſbands.

Mrs. Bel. I *have* the beſt of huſbands.

Lady Rach. I have not time to diſpute the matter with you now; but I ſhall put you into my comedy to teach wives, that the beſt receipt for matrimonial happineſs, is to be deaf, dumb, and blind.

Mrs. Bel. Poh! poh! you are a ſatiriſt, Lady Rachel—But we are loſing time; ſhou'dn't we put on our dreſſes, and prepare for the grand ſcene?

Lady Rach. Don't you tremble at the trial?

Mrs. Bel. Not in the leaſt, I am ſure my heart has no occaſion.

Lady Rach. Have you let Miſs Walſingham into our little plot?

Mrs. Bel. You know ſhe cou'd not be inſenſible of Mr. Belville's deſign upon herſelf, and it is no farther than that deſign, we have any thing to carry into execution.

Lady Rach. Well, ſhe may ſerve to facilitate the matter, and therefore I am not ſorry that you have truſted her.

Mrs. Bel. We ſhall be too late, and then what ſignifies all your fine plotting.

Lady Rach. Is it not a little pang of jealouſy that wou'd fain now quicken our motions?

Mrs. Bel. No, Lady Rachel, it is a certainty of my huſband's love and generoſity, that makes me wiſh to come to the trial. I would not exchange my confidence in his affections for all the mines of Peru; ſo nothing you can ſay will make me miſerable.

Lady Rach. You are a moſt unaccountable woman; ſo away with you. [*Exeunt.*

S C E N E *continued.*

Enter SPRUCE *and* GHASTLY.

Spruce. Why, Ghaſtly, the old general your maſter is a greater fool than I ever thought he was: He wants to marry Miſs Walſingham?

Ghaſt. Mrs. Tempeſt ſuſpected that there was ſomething going forward, by all his hugger-mugger conſulting with Mr. Torrington; and ſo ſet me on to liſten.

Spruce. She's a good friend of your's, and that thing ſhe made the General give you the other day in the hoſpital, is I ſuppoſe a ſnug hundred a year.

Ghaſt. Better than two; I waſh for near four thouſand people: there was a major of horſe who put in for it, and pleaded a large family—

Spruce. With long ſervices, I ſuppoſe.

Ghaſt. Yes, but Mrs. Tempeſt inſiſted upon my long ſervices; ſo the major was ſet aſide—However, to keep the thing from the damn'd News-papers, I fancy he will ſucceed the barber, who died laſt night, poor wo-

 man,

man, of a lying-in fever, after being brought to bed of three children.—Places in public inſtitutions—

Spruce. Are often ſweetly diſpos'd: I think of aſking Belville for ſomething, one of theſe days.

Ghaſt. He has great intereſt.

Spruce. I might be a juſtice of peace, if I pleaſed, and in a ſhabby neighbourhood, where the mere ſwearing would bring in ſomething tolerable; but there are ſo many ſtrange people let into the commiſſion now a-days, that I ſhou'dn't like to have my name in the liſt.

Ghaſt. You are right.

Spruce. No, no, I leave that to paltry tradeſmen, and ſhall think of ſome little ſinecure, or a ſmall penſion on the Iriſh eſtabliſhment.

Ghaſt. Well, ſucceſs attend you. I muſt hobble home as faſt as I can, to know if Mrs. Tempeſt has any orders. O, there's a rare ſtorm brewing for our old goat of a General.

Spruce. When ſhall we crack a bottle together.

Ghaſt. O, I ſhan't touch a glaſs of claret theſe three weeks; for laſt night I gave nature a little fillip with a drunken bout, according to the doctor's directions; I have entirely left off bread, and I am in great hopes that I ſhall get rid of my gout by theſe means, eſpecially if I can learn to eat my meat quite raw like a cannibal.

Spruce. Ha, ha, ha!

Ghaſt. Look at me, Spruce, I was once as likely a young fellow as any under ground in the whole pariſh of St. James's:—but waiting on the General ſo many years.

Spruce. Ay, and following his example, Ghaſtly.

Ghaſt. 'Tis too true: has reduced me to what you ſee. Theſe miſerable ſpindles wou'd do very well for a lord or a duke, Spruce; but they are a ſad diſgrace to a poor valet de chambre. [*Exit.*

Spruce. Well, I don't believe there's a gentleman's gentleman, within the weekly bills, who joins a prudent ſollicitude for the main chance, to a ſtrict care of his conſtitution, better than myſelf. I have a little girl who ſtands me in about three guineas a week; I never bet more than a pound upon a rubber of whiſt; I always ſleep with my head very warm; and ſwallow a new laid egg every morning with my chocolate. [*Exit.*

SCENE *changes to the Street, two Chairs croſs the Stage, knock at a Door, and ſet down* BELVILLE *and a Lady.*

Bel. This way, my dear creature! [*Exeunt.*

Enter General SAVAGE, *Captain* SAVAGE, *and* TORRINGTON.

Capt. There! there they go in: You ſee the place is quite convenient, not twenty yards from the maſquerade.

Gen. How cloſely the fellow ſticks to her!

Tor. Like the great ſeal to the peerage patent of a chancellor. But, gentlemen, we have ſtill no more than proof preſumptive: —where is the ocular demonſtration which we were to have?

Capt. I'll ſwear to the blue domino; 'tis a very remarkable one, and ſo is Belville's.

Tor. You wou'd have rare cuſtom among the Newgate ſolicitors, if you'd venture an oath upon the identity of the party under it.

Gen. 'Tis the very ſize and ſhape of Miſs Walſingham.

Tor. And yet I have a ſtrange notion that there is a trifling *alibi* in this caſe.

Gen. It wou'd be a damn'd affair if we ſhou'd be countermin'd.

Capt. O, follow me, here's the door left luckily open, and I'll ſoon clear up the matter beyond a queſtion. [*Enters the houſe.*

Tor. Why your ſon is mad, General. This muſt produce a deadly breach with Belville. For heaven's ſake, let's go in and prevent any exceſſes of his raſhneſs.

Gen.

Gen. By all means, or the poor fellow's generous anxiety on my account may be productive of very fatal consequences. [*Exeunt.*

SCENE *changes to an Apartment,* BELVILLE *unmasked, and a lady in a blue domino mask'd.*

Bel. My dear Miss Walsingham, we are now perfectly safe, yet I will by no means intreat you to unmask, because I am convinc'd, from the propriety with which you repuls'd my addresses this morning, that you intend the present interview should make me still more deeply sensible of my presumption.—I never lied so aukwardly in all my life; if it was to make her comply, I should be at no loss for language. (*Aside.*) The situation in which I must appear before you, Madam, is certainly a very humiliating one; but I am persuaded that your generosity will be gratified to hear, that I have bid an everlasting adieu to my profligacy, and am now only alive to the virtues of Mrs. Belville.—She won't speak—I don't wonder at it, for brazen as I am my self, if I met so mortifying a rejection, I should be cursedly out of countenance.

(*Aside.*

Capt. (*behind.*) I will go in.

Gen. (*behind.*) I command you to desist.

Tor. (*behind.*) This will be an affair for the Old Bailey. (*The noise grows more violent, and continues.*

Bel. Why, what the devil is all this?—Don't be alarm'd, Miss Walsingham, be assur'd I'll protect you at the hazard of my life;—step into this closet,—you shan't be discover'd depend upon it; (*she goes in*): And now to find out the cause of this confusion. [*Unlocks the door.*

Enter General SAVAGE, *Captain* SAVAGE, *and* TORRINGTON.

Bel. Savage! what is the meaning of this strange behaviour?

Capt. Where is Miss Walsingham?

Bel.

Bel. So, then, Sir, this is a premeditated ſcheme, for which I am oblig'd to your friendſhip.

Capt. Where's Miſs Walſingham, Sir?

Gen. Dear Belville, he is out of his ſenſes; this ſtorm was entirely againſt my orders.

Tor. If he proceeds much longer in theſe vagaries, we muſt amuſe him with a commiſſion of lunacy.

Bel. This is neither a time nor place for argument, Mr. Torrington; but as you and the General ſeem to be in the poſſeſſion of your ſenſes, I ſhall be glad if you'll take this very friendly gentleman away; and depend upon it, I ſhan't die in his debt for the preſent obligation.

Capt. And depend upon it, Sir, pay the obligation when you will, I ſhan't ſtir 'till I ſee Miſs Walſingham.—Look'e, Belville, there are ſecret reaſons for my behaving in this manner; reaſons which you yourſelf will approve, when you know them;—my father here—

Gen. Diſavows your conduct in every particular, and would rejoice to ſee you at the halberds.

Tor. And, for my part, I told him previouſly 'twas a downright burglary.

Bel. Well, gentlemen, let your different motives for breaking in upon me in this agreeable manner, be what they may, I don't ſee that I am leſs annoy'd by my friends than my enemy. I muſt therefore again, requeſt that you will all walk down ſtairs.

Capt. I'll firſt walk into this room.

Bel. Really, I think you will not.

Gen. What phrenzy poſſeſſes the fellow to urge this matter farther?

Capt. While there's a ſingle doubt ſhe triumphs over juſtice, *(drawing.)* I will go into that room.

Bel. Then you muſt make your way thro' me.

Enter Mrs. Belville.

Mrs. Bel. Ah!

Capt. There, I knew ſhe was in the room:—there's the blue domino.

Gen.

Gen. Put up your ſword, if you don't deſire to be caſhier'd from my favour for ever.

Bel. Why, wou'd you come out, madam? But, you have nothing to apprehend.

Capt. Pray, madam, will you have the goodneſs to unmaſk?

Bel. She ſhan't unmaſk.

Capt. I ſay ſhe ſhall.

Bel. I ſay ſhe ſhall not.

Mrs. Bel. Pray, let me oblige the gentlemen?

Capt. Death and deſtruction, here's a diſcovery!

Gen. and Tor. Mrs. Belville!

Mrs. Bel. Yes, Mrs. Belville, gentlemen: Is conjugal fidelity ſo very terrible a thing now-a-days that a man is to ſuffer death for being found in company with his own wife?

Bel. My love, this is a ſurprize, indeed—But it is a moſt agreeable one; ſince you find me really aſham'd of my former follies, and cannot now doubt the ſincerity of my reformation.

Mrs. Bel. I am too happy! this ſingle moment wou'd overpay a whole life of anxiety.

Bel. Where ſhall I attend you? Will you return to the maſquerade?

Mrs. Bel. O no! Lady Rachel and Miſs Walſingham are by this time at our houſe, with Mr. Leeſon and the Iriſh gentleman whom you preſs'd into our party, impatiently expecting the reſult of this adventure.

Bel. Give me leave to conduct you home then from this ſcene of confuſion. To-morrow, Captain Savage, I ſhall beg the favour of your explanation; (*aſide to him as he goes out.*) Kind gentlemen, your moſt humble ſervant.

Mrs. Bel. And when you next diſturb a *tête à tête*, for pity to a poor wife, don't let it be ſo very uncuſtomary a party, as the matrimonial one.

[*Exeunt Bel. and Mrs. Bel.*

Gen. (*to the Capt.*) So, Sir, you have led us upon a bleſſed expedition here.

Tor.

Tor. Now don't you think that if your courts of honour, like our courts of law, ſearched a little minutely into evidence, it wou'd be equally to the credit of their underſtandings?

Capt. Tho' I am cover'd with confuſion at my miſtake (for you ſee Belville was miſtaken as well as myſelf,) I am overjoy'd at this diſcovery of Miſs Walſingham's innocence.

Gen. I ſhou'd exult in it too, with a *feu de joy*, if it didn't now ſhew the impoſſibility of her ever being Mrs. Savage.

Capt. Dear Sir, why ſhould you think that an impoſſibility? Tho' ſome miſtakes have occurr'd in conſequence, I ſuppoſe, of Mrs. Belville's little plot upon her huſband, I dare ſay Miſs Walſingham may yet be prevail'd upon to come into our family.

Tor. Take care of a new error in your proceedings, young gentleman.

Gen. Ay, another defeat would make us completely deſpicable.

Capt. Sir, I'll forfeit my life, if ſhe does not conſent to the marriage this very night.

Gen. Only bring this matter to bear, and I'll forgive you every thing.

Tor. The captain ſhou'd be inform'd, I think, General, that ſhe declin'd it peremptorily this evening.

Gen. Ay, do you hear that, Horace?

Capt. I am not at all ſurpris'd at it, conſidering the general miſconception we labour'd under. But I'll immediately to Belville's, explain the whole myſtery, and conclude every thing to your ſatisfaction. [*Exit.*

Gen. So, Torrington, we ſhall be able to take the field again, you ſee.

Tor. But how in the name of wonder has your ſon found out your intention of marrying Miſs Walſingham? I look'd upon myſelf as the only perſon acquainted with the ſecret.

Gen. That thought has march'd itſelf two or three times to my own recollection. For tho' I gave him

ſome

ſome diſtant hints of the affair, I took particular care to keep behind the works of a proper circumſpection.

Tor. O, if you give him any hints at all, I am not ſurpris'd at his diſcovering every thing.

Gen. I ſhall be all impatience 'till I hear of his interview with Miſs Walſingham: Suppoſe, my dear friend, we went to Belville's, 'tis but in the next ſtreet, and we ſhall be there in the lighting of a match.

Tor. Really this is a pretty buſineſs for a man of my age and profeſſion, trot here, trot there. But, as I have been weak enough to make myſelf a kind of party in the cauſe, I own that I have curioſity enough to be anxious about the determination.

Gen. Come along my old boy; and remember the ſong, " *Servile ſpirits,*" &c. [*Exeunt.*

SCENE *changes to* BELVILLE'*s*.

Enter Captain SAVAGE *and Miſs* WALSINGHAM.

Capt. Nay, but my deareſt Miſs Walſingham, the extenuation of my own conduct to Belville made it abſolutely neceſſary for me to diſcover my engagements with you; and as happineſs is now ſo fortunately in our reach, I flatter myſelf you will be prevail'd upon to forgive an error, which proceeded only from an extravagance of love.

Miſs Wal. To think me capable of ſuch an action, Captain Savage! I am terrified at the idea of a union with you; and it is better for a woman, at any time, to ſacrifice an inſolent lover, than to accept of a ſuſpicious huſband.

Capt. In the happieſt unions, my deareſt creature, there muſt be always ſomething to overlook on both ſides

Miſs Wal. Very civil, truly.

Capt. Pardon me, my life, for this frankneſs; and recollect, that if the lover has thro' miſconception been unhappily guilty, he brings a huſband altogether reform'd to your hands.

Miss Wal. Well, I see I must forgive you at last; so I may as well make a merit of necessity, you provoking creature.

Capt. And may I hope, indeed, for the blessing of this hand?

Miss Wal. Why, you wretch, would you have me force it upon you? I think, after what I have said, a soldier might have ventur'd to take it without farther ceremony.

Capt. Angelic creature! thus I seize it as my lawful prize.

Miss Wal. Well, but now you have obtained this inestimable prize, Captain, give me again leave to ask if you have had a certain explanation with the General?

Capt. How can you doubt it?

Miss Wal. And he is really impatient for our marriage?

Capt. 'Tis incredible how earnest he is.

Miss Wal. What, did he tell you of his interview with me this evening when he brought Mr. Torrington?

Capt. He did.

Miss Wal. O, then, I can have no doubt.

Capt. If a shadow of doubt remains, here he comes to remove it. Joy, my dear Sir! joy a thousand times.

Enter General SAVAGE *and* TORRINGTON.

Gen. What, my dear boy, have you carried the day?

Miss Wal. I have been weak enough to indulge him with a victory, indeed, General.

Gen. *None but the brave, none but the brave, &c.* (*Singing.*

Tor. I congratulate you heartily on this decree, General.

Gen. This had nearly proved a day of disappointment, but the stars have fortunately turn'd it in my favour, and now I reap the rich reward of my victory. (*Salutes her.*)

Capt.

Capt. And here I take her from you, as the greateſt good which heav'n can ſend me.

Miſs Wal. O, Captain!

Gen. You take her as the greateſt good which heav'n can ſend you, ſirrah; I take her as the greateſt good which heav'n can ſend me: And now what have you to ſay to her?

Miſs Wal. General Savage!

Tor. Here will be a freſh injunction to ſtop proceedings.

Miſs Wal. Are you never to have done with miſtakes?

Gen. What miſtakes can have happen'd now, my ſweeteſt? you deliver'd up your dear hand to me this moment?

Miſs Wal. True, Sir; but I thought you were going to beſtow my dear hand upon this dear gentleman.

Gen. How! that dear gentleman!

Capt. I am thunder-ſtruck!

Tor. General—*None but the brave, &c.* [*Sings.*

Gen. So the covert way is clear'd at laſt; and you have imagin'd that I was all along negociating for this fellow, when I was gravely ſoliciting for myſelf?

Miſs Wal. No other idea, Sir, ever once enter'd my imagination.

Tor. General—*Noble minds ſhould ne'er deſpair, &c.* [*Sings.*

Gen. Zounds! here's all the company pouring upon us in full gallop, and I ſhall be the laughing ſtock of the whole town.

Enter BELVILLE, *Mrs.* BELVILLE, *Lady* RACHEL, LEESON, *and* CONOLLY.

Bel. Well, General, we have left you a long time together. Shall I give you joy?

Gen. No; wiſh me demoliſh'd in the fortifications of Dunkirk.

Mrs. Bel. What's the matter?

Lady Rach. The General appears difconcerted.

Leef. The gentleman looks as if he had fought a hard battle.

Con. Ay, and gain'd nothing but a defeat, my dear.

Tor. I'll fhew caufe for his behaviour.

Gen. Death and Damnation! not for the world! I am taken by furprize here; let me confider a moment how to cut my way thro' the enemy.

Mifs Wal. How cou'd you be deceiv'd in this manner! [*To the Capt.*

Lady Rach. O, Mr. Torrington, we are much oblig'd to you; you have been in town ever fince laft night, and only fee us now by accident.

Tor. I have been very bufy, Madam; but you look fadly, very fadly indeed! your old diforder the jaundice, I fuppofe, has been very troublefome to you?

Lady Rach. Sir, you have a very extraordinary mode of complimenting your acquaintance.

Con. I don't believe for all that, that there's a word of a lie in the truth he fpeaks. (*Afide.*

Leef. Mr. Torrington, your moft obedient—You received my letter, I hope.

Tor. What, my young barrifter!—Have you any more traders from Dantzick to be naturalized?

Con Let us only fpeak to you in private; and we'll there clear up the affair before the whole company.

Tor. (*fpeaking apart to Leef. amd Con.*) This gentleman's letter has already cleared it up to my entire fatisfaction; and I don't know whether I am moft pleafed with his wit, or charmed with his probity.—However, Mr. Leefon, I ufed the bailiffs fadly.—Bailiffs are generally fad fellows to be fure; but we muft love juftice for our own fakes.

Leef. Unqueftionably, fir, and they fhall be amply recompenfed for the merit of their fufferings.

Con. And the merit of fuffering, I fancy, is the only merit that is ever likely to fall to the fhare of a fheriff's officer.

Tor.

Tor. One word—one word more, Mr. Leeſon.—I have enquired your character, and like it—like it much.—Forgive the forwardneſs of an old man.—You muſt not want money—you muſt not indeed—

Leeſ. Sir——

Tor. Pray, don't be offended—I mean to give my friends but little trouble about my affairs when I am gone.—I love to ſee the people happy that my fortune is to make ſo; and ſhall think it a treaſon againſt humanity, to leave a ſhilling more than the bare expences of my funeral.——Breakfaſt with me in the morning.

Leeſ. You overwhelm me with this generoſity; but a happy revolution in my fortunes, which you will ſoon know, renders it wholly unneceſſary for me to trouble you.

Con. (*wiping his eyes.*) Upon my ſoul, this is a moſt worthy old crater—to be his own executor. If I was to live any long time among ſuch people, they'd ſoon be the death of me, with their very goodneſs.

Mrs. Bel. Miſs Walſingham, Captain Savage has been telling Mr. Belville and me of a very extraordinary miſtake.

Miſs Wal. 'Tis very ſtrange indeed, miſtake on miſtake.

Bel. 'Tis no way ſtrange to find every body properly ſtruck with the merit of Miſs Walſingham.

Miſs Wal. A compliment from you now, Mr. Belville, is really worth accepting.

Gen. If I thought the affair cou'd be kept a ſecret, by making the town over to my ſon, ſince I am utterly ſhut out myſelf—

Capt. He ſeems exceedingly embarraſſed.

Gen. If I thought that;—why, mortified as I muſt be in giving it up, I think I cou'd reſolve upon the manœuvre, to ſave myſelf from univerſal ridicule: but it can't be;—it can't be; and I only double my own diſappointment in rewarding the diſobedience of the raſcal who has ſupplanted me. There!—there! they

they are all talking of it, all laughing at me, and I ſhall run mad.

Mrs. Temp. (Behind.) I ſay, you feather-headed puppy, he is in this houſe; my own ſervant ſaw him come in, and I will not ſtir till I find him.

Gen. She here!—then deliberation is over, and I am entirely blown up.

Lady Rach. I'll take notes of this affair.

Enter Mrs. TEMPEST.

Mrs. Temp. Mighty well, Sir. So you are in love it ſeems;—and you want to be married it ſeems?

Leeſ. My bleſſed aunt!—O how proud I am of the relation!

Gen. Dear Bab, give me quarter before all this company.

Mrs. Temp. You are in love, you old fool, are you? and you want to marry Miſs Walſingham, indeed!

Con. I never heard a pleaſanter ſpoken gentlewoman—O hone, if I had the taming of her, ſhe ſhou'd never be abuſive, without keeping a civil tongue in her head.

Mrs. Temp. Well, Sir, and when is the happy day to be fix'd?

Bel. What the devil, is this true, General?

Gen. True—Can you believe ſuch an abſurdity?

Mrs. Temp. Why, will you deny, you miſerable old mummy, that you made propoſals of marriage to her?

Gen. Yes I do—no I don't—propoſals of marriage!

Miſs Wal. In favour of your ſon—I'll help him out a little. [*Aſide.*

Gen. Yes, in favour of my ſon—what the devil ſhall I do?

Mrs. Bel. Shall I take a leſſon from this lady, Mr. Belville? Perhaps, if the women of virtue were to pluck up a little ſpirit, they might be ſoon as well treated as kept miſtreſſes.

Mrs. Temp. Harkee, General Savage, I believe you aſſert a falſhood; but if you ſpeak the truth, give your ſon this moment to Miſs Walſingham, and let me be fairly rid of my rival.

Gen. My ſon! Miſs Walſingham!—Miſs Walſingham, my ſon!

Bel. It will do, Horace; it will do.

Mrs. Temp. No prevarications, General Savage; do what I bid you inſtantly, or, by all the wrongs of an enraged woman, I'll ſo expoſe you——

Con. What a fine fellow this is to have the command of an army!

Gen. If Miſs Walſingham can be prevailed upon.

Tor. O, ſhe'll oblige you readily—but you muſt ſettle a good fortune upon your ſon.

Mrs. Temp. That he ſhall do.

Mrs. Bel. Miſs Walſingham, my dear—

Miſs Wal. I can refuſe nothing either to your requeſt, or to the requeſt of the General.

Gen. Oblige me with your hand then, Madam: come here you—come here, captain. There, there is Miſs Walſingham's hand for you.

Con. And as pretty a little fiſt it is as any in the three kingdoms.

Gen. Torrington ſhall ſettle the fortune.

Leeſ. I give you joy moſt heartily, Madam.

Bel. We all give her joy.

Capt. Mine is beyond the power of expreſſion.

Miſs Wal. (*aſide to the company*) And ſo is the General's, I believe.

Con. O faith, that may be eaſily ſeen by the ſweetneſs of his countenance.

Tor. Well, the cauſe being now at laſt determin'd, I think we may all retire from the court.

Gen. And without any great credit, I fear, to the General.

Con. By my ſoul, you may ſay that.——

Mrs. Temp. Do you murmur, Sir?--Come this moment home with me.

Gen.

Gen. I'll go any where to hide this miſerable head of mine: what a damn'd campaign have I made of it! [*Exeunt Gen. and Mrs. Temp.*

Con. Upon my ſoul, if I was in the General's place, I'd divide the houſe with this devil; I'd keep within doors myſelf, and make her take the outſide.

Lady Rach. Here's more food for a comedy.

Leeſ. So there is, Madam; and Mr. Torrington, to whoſe goodneſs I am infinitely oblig'd, could tell you ſome diverting anecdotes, that would enrich a comedy conſiderably.

Con. Ay, faith, and a tragedy too.

Tor. I can tell nothing but what will redound to the credit of your character, young man.

Bel. The day has been a buſy one, thanks to the communicative diſpoſition of the Captain.

Mrs. Bel. And the evening ſhould be chearful.

Bel. I ſhan't therefore part with one of you, 'till we have had a hearty laugh at our general adventures.

Miſs Wal. They have been very whimſical indeed; yet if repreſented on the ſtage, I hope they wou'd be found not only entertaining, but inſtructive.

Lady Rach. Inſtructive! why the modern critics ſay that the only buſineſs of comedy is to make people laugh.

Bel. That is degrading the dignity of letters exceedingly, as well as leſſening the utility of the ſtage. ---A good comedy is a capital effort of genius, and ſhould therefore be directed to the nobleſt purpoſes.

Miſs Wal. Very true; and unleſs we learn ſomething while we chuckle, the carpenter who nails a pantomime together, will be entitled to more applauſe than the beſt comic poet in the kingdom.

[*Exeunt omnes.*

FINIS.

THE ROMANCE OF AN HOUR

THE

ROMANCE OF AN HOUR,

A

COMEDY

OF TWO ACTS,

As it is performed, with UNIVERSAL APPLAUSE,

AT

The THEATRE ROYAL in COVENT-GARDEN,

WRITTEN BY

HUGH KELLY, Esq; of the MIDDLE TEMPLE,
Author of FALSE DELICACY, A WORD TO THE WISE, CLEMENTINA, THE SCHOOL FOR WIVES, &c. &c.

LONDON:
Printed for G. KEARSLEY, No. 46, Fleet-Street.
MDCCLXXIV.

THE ROMANCE OF AN HOUR

IS INSCRIBED

TO THOMAS HARRIS, ESQ;

AS A PUBLIC, THO' TRIFLING TESTIMONY,

OF THE VERY SINCERE ESTEEM

ENTERTAINED FOR HIM

BY THE AUTHOR.

Gough Square, December
16th, 1774.

ADVERTISEMENT.

AS the lovers of the drama are generally very desirous of dramatic anecdote, it will possibly please the reader to know, that the ROMANCE OF AN HOUR (be it what it may) owes its existence to Mrs. ABINGTON. This unrivalled daughter of comedy, in a conversation with me, once expressing a wish to perform a character of *perfect simplicity*, the interesting tale called the *Test of Friendship*, immediately struck upon my recollection, and Mrs. Abington concurred with me in thinking, that a native of the East, situated like Marmontel's heroine, might be advantageously introduced on our theatre.

The world, though perfectly acquainted with the professional excellence of Mrs. Abington, is perhaps to be informed, that there is scarcely a better judge of dramatic literature, than this great actress: flattered therefore by her opinion, I readily took up the pen, and sketched out the following scenes, with a view of exhibiting them at her benefit. The difficulty however of producing a new piece accurately, which is solely designed for the emolu-

 ment

ment even of the firſt performers, occuring to us both, Mrs. Abington generouſly refuſed to hazard any little reputation which I might poſſeſs, upon her account; and I took my trifle the more readily back, from a reflection that ſhe could only have, what ſhe always has on her night, an overflowing theatre. One of the many accidents attending the government of the ſtage, has now brought it to Covent Garden houſe, and though diſappointed in my purpoſe with reſpect to Mrs. Abington, the great juſtice done me by the managers, as well as by the performers, gives me abundant cauſe to be ſatisfied with my ſituation—But to the piece—

The circumſtance of a young lady's falling in love with the friend of a man whom ſhe was intended to marry, though the foundation of Marmontel's tale, has no novelty in it; thoſe who are converſant with the drama, will not only find it in many of our comedies, but in many of our tragedies alſo. On this account, I paid little attention to Marmontel's mode of advancing the cataſtrophe, and am ſolely indebted to him for the character of Zelida. Sir Hector Strangeways, Lady Di, Orſon, Pillage, and Buſſora, are entirely my own; and this acknowledgment is a juſtice indeſpenſibly due to the celebrated French novelliſt, becauſe thoſe who are unacquainted with the ſtory in the

the original, might otherwiſe think him anſwerable for many of my imperfections. Indeed, if the ſame indulgence ſhould accompany THE ROMANCE OF AN HOUR, to the cloſet, which diſtinguiſhed its appearance on the ſtage, Marmontel would not have much cauſe to tremble for his Gentle Eaſt Indian; nor ſhould I have any thing to apprehend from the animadverſion of criticiſm.

It has, I confeſs, been remarked by ſome of my warmeſt friends, that the manners neither of a Knight of the Bath, nor of an Engliſh admiral, are preſerved in Sir Hector Strangeways; I grant the objection in its fulleſt force, and have, in the character of Lady Di, myſelf made the obſervation; but it is for this very reaſon Sir Hector becomes an object of ridicule, and conſequently a fair object of comedy: the manners are frequently to comedy, what the paſſions are to tragedy. If people were to act with propriety in private life, or with juſtice in public, the chief ſources both of comedy and tragedy would be ſpeedily ſhut up. Sir John Falſtaff, Sir Francis Wronghead, and Sir John Brute, for inſtance, are ſo many diſgraces to their rank; yet, in the whole rounds of the ſock, where ſhall we find three ſuch admirable characters? In like manner, with regard to tragedy, we muſt admit that kings ſhould be juſt, liberal, and merciful;

 but

but if we are to condemn a poet for making them raſh, rapacious, or inhuman, what will become of thoſe three great works, which reflect ſuch honour on the Britiſh ſtage, Lear, Richard, and Macbeth?

Upon the whole, as there is no rank without its occaſional diſgrace, we muſt, to correct folly or vice, paint men as they *ſometimes are*, not as they *always ought to be*; and if in tragedy we terrify people into virtue, by exhibiting the conſequences reſulting from their crimes, we muſt in comedy, laugh them into correctneſs, by ſhewing the ridicule they neceſſarily incur when they act below the conſequence of their characters.

Had I held Sir Hector up as an object of *imitation*, there might be a juſt objection to him; but repreſenting him as an object of *ridicule*, he becomes, I hope, not only inoffenſive but inſtructive; and we may as well conceive ſociety to be degraded by the exhibition of a fool or a villain, as ſuppoſe either that the navy, or the order of the Bath is inſulted, by the character of Sir Hector Strangeways.———

HUGH KELLY.

PRO-

PROLOGUE

Written by Mr. KELLY.

Spoken by Mr. LEE.

TO-night, good folks, tho' led a little dance,
  Thro' the light mazes of an Hour's Romance,
No ſpells, no ſpectres have you cauſe to dread,
Not one poor thunder rumbles o'er your head;
Nor will the tempeſt howling thro' the trees,
Once rouſe your horror—with a ſtorm of peaſe.——
Between ourſelves, this poet was a fool,
To plan by common ſenſe, or build by rule;
When ev'n the mightieſt maſters of the ſtage,
Have gain'd ſo much from *trick*, in ev'ry age!
Shakeſpeare is great—is exquiſite—no doubt—
But then our carpenters muſt help him out;
The deep diſtreſſes of a mad'ning Lear,
In vain would aſk the tributary tear,
If, 'midſt the fury of the midnight ſky,
Our roſin light'nings did not aptly fly,
And pity warmly plead to be let in,
Thro' a ſmart-ſhower of heart-exploring tin.——
Let critics proudly form dramatic laws,
Give me, ſay I, what's ſure to meet applauſe;
Let them of time, and place, and action boaſt,
I'm for a devil, a dungeon, or a ghoſt——
When Hamlet weeping for a murder'd ſire,
Upbraids his mother with a guilty fire,
Tho' ev'ry line a plaudit ſhould command,
Not one god yonder will employ his hand.
But cas'd in canvaſs,l et the dead ſtalk in,
Then the loud pæans—then the claps begin——
And pit, box, gall'ry, eagerly contend.
Exalted ſtrife! who loudeſt ſhall commend
The frantic ha! The Bedlamite—" look there——
The ſtart—the heave—the ſtagger—and the ſtare!—
To dear Macbeath, the learned ladies all run——
What to enjoy?—the flaming of the cauldron.

Aſk

P R O L O G U E.

Ask Molly Dripping there, so sleek and mild,
(As good a cook as e'er drest roast or boil'd)
What in all *Juliet* makes her soonest *veep?*
She'll say the fun'ral—'Tis so *werry* deep!
Allur'd by sterling sentiment alone,
" Cato for me," (cries Darby Macahone)
" I never miss that play at any time,
" If 'tis but *added* to a pantomime."—
" Hoot,"—growls a bold North-*Bratton*, (taking snuff)
" A pantomime is *axacrable* stuff—
" Na bag-pipes in the bond—They donna play
" The Corn *Rags*, or the *Barks* of *Andermay*."—
In short, tho' all stage mummery despise,
All want a banquet for their ears or eyes;
And while at shews they take the most offence,
Still make them bladders to the shore of sense.
The name our author gives his piece to-night,
Wou'd well admit a supper for the sight;
A grand collection of dramatic dishes,
Of dragons, giants, forests, rivers, fishes;
Yet tho' he calls his trifle a romance,
He does not treat you with a single dance,
Nor use one hackney'd, one eccentric art,
To lull your judgment, or to cheat your heart—
He brings, indeed, a character to view,
From Indian climes, he trusts entirely new—
A poor Gentoo, compos'd of virtues all,
Tho' fresh from English nabobs at Bengal;
His face, perhaps, too swarthy you may find;
" Yet see Othello's visage in his mind—"
And 'till you've fairly tried our trembling Bays,
Forbear to blame—but do not fear to praise.

EPI-

E P I L O G U E.

Written by Mr. KELLY.

Spoken by Mrs. BULKLEY.

SOMEBODY ſays, but I forgot his name,
That howe'er faults or follies we may blame,
We're all in turn, tho' all extremely wiſe,
The very things we laugh at, or deſpiſe——
The bold fox-hunter juſt come up to town,
From—" Yoiks, hark forward," loves to ſeem a clown.
Thro' pride, tears up politeneſs by the roots——
Ne'er combs his hair—and viſits you in boots——
Milkſops alone, he thinks their forms ſhou'd deck,
And ſcorns the man that fears to break a neck——
In three months time, how alter'd is his note,
His head's all wings, or bak'd in papilotte——
The honeſt buckſkin which once clear'd the ditches,
Our modern Nimrod turns to ſattin breeches,
And grown half female, wondrous to relate!
He ſcreams in ſlumber at a five-bar'd gate.
The city buck, accuſtom'd long to bruiſe,
Who ſwears at France, and damns all " parley-voos ;"
If but one week from Margate led at moſt,
To ſwill and ſmuggle on the Flemiſh coaſt,
Returning bawls in ev'ry dowdy's face——
" Comment charmantè, quelle raviſſant grace!"
[*Spoken in the Engliſh accent.*
And in due courſe from Aldgate to the Strand,
Raves of a *cottilloon*, and *allemand.*
Monſieur, indeed, with cockney is quite even,
Tho' much to joke upon this nation given——
He calls a Briton—" Barbare, Unbelief!"
Yet leaves his frogs with rapture for roaſt beef;
And finds a ready fortune to be made is,
In rouge for men, and perriwigs for ladies.
At foul corruption, Surly tears his throat—
He ſcorns to give a ſhilling for a vote;
But mark the riot of the county round,
And every voice has coſt him twenty pound.
There ſome, who think our liberties divine,
Will eat them thro', in turkey, or in chine—
And other's, while at venal tools they rail,
Drown their poor country in a butt of ale.

E P I L O G U E.

But while our bards theſe gen'ral faults make known,
Pray let them hear a little of their own.
How many authors of our modern ſtage,
Affect to riſe the wonders of their age,
By bare tranſlations from Moliere, Corneïlle,
Racine, and numbers needleſs here to tell—
Yet each a jackdaw, dreſt in foreign plumes,
On his own beauty ſaucily preſumes;
Looks on the parent bird with haughty eyes,
From whom entirely he purloin'd his dyes;
Or ſolely tells us when he comes to print,
Tho' *all* is *ſtolen*—He *borrow'd* but a *hint*—
Ah that theſe daws were fortunately toſt on
Thy coaſts Connecticut, or thine O Boſton!
Their nobleſt flights thou might'ſt for ever mar,
And ſpoil their feathers, with a little tar.—
Whether by policy or juſtice led,
A diff'rent path our author means to tread;
And tho' a petty dealer, will not ſell
As his own goods, a thought of MARMONTEL—
The timid ZELIDA you ſaw to-night,
In that great maſter firſt beheld the light;
And if you hail her now dramatic morn,
I'll ever bleſs the moment ſhe was born.

DRAMATIS PERSONÆ.

M E N.

Sir Hector Strangeways,	Mr. SHUTER.
Colonel Ormſby,	Mr. CLARKE.
Brownlow,	Mr. BENSLEY.
Orſon,	Mr. QUICK.
Buſſora,	Mr. LEE LEWES.
Pillage,	Mr. DUNSTALL.
James,	Mr. BATES.

W O M E N.

Zelida,	Mrs. BULKLEY.
Lady Di Strangeways,	Mrs. GREEN.
Jenny,	Miſs PEARSE.

The SCENE LONDON.

Time, the Time of Repreſentation.

THE
ROMANCE OF AN HOUR,
A
C O M E D Y.

ACT I. SCENE I.

An Apartment at Sir Hector Strangeways.

Enter SIR HECTOR *and* LADY DI.

Sir Hector. AN impudent puppy, to pester me with his fees of honour. I thought that at court it was not honourable to pay any thing.

Lady D. But Sir Hector Strangeways—

Sir Hec. But Lady Di Strangeways, I tell you again, that if I had all the wealth of the Spanish galleons, I would not part with a single piece of eight upon this occasion.—I did not ask them to knight me, and they may unknight me again, if they like it; for I value the broad pendant on the Dreadnought mast-head, above any title which they can splice to all the red, or green, or blue rags in Christendom.

Lady D. Well, my dear, but though an admiral's uniform is a very pretty thing, there is something inexpressibly attracting in a star; and if I could only persuade you to wear a bag-wig, that red ribbon would give a world of brilliancy to your complexion.

Sir Hec. My complexion! Zounds, wife, don't make me mad! A weather-beaten sailor of fifty, ought to be mightily concerned about the brilliancy of his complexion.

Lady D. Lord, Sir Hector, you are not so old by half a year—and if you would follow my advice about the bag, you'd look as young as Billy Brownlow——

Sir Hec. Avast, Di—Avast—I have already suffered you to crowd too much canvass, and to make a puppy of me sufficiently.

Lady. D. I beg, Sir Hector, that you will soften the coarseness of your phraseology, and use a little less of the quarter-deck dialect.

Sir Hec. Zounds, madam, 'tis your own fault if the gale blows in your teeth—I might have been out with a squadron in the Mediterranean, hadn't I humoured your fancy, and foolishly staid to be pip'd in at the installation—However, there's some chance yet—the admiral appointed, is attended by three doctors, and if they heave him over, I have a promise of succeeding in the command – There's a cable of comfort for you to snatch at Lady Di.

Lady D. Yes, you cruel! and, for fear bad news should not reach me soon enough, you have ordered an express to be sent up directly from Portsmouth, the moment the poor admiral is gathered to his progenitors.

Sir

Sir Hec. Yes, the moment his anchor is a peak; and I'll take your ſon Orſon with me too, for I ſhall have him turn'd into a monkey if he ſtays much longer aſhore.

Lady D. Surely you won't be ſuch a brute, my love—The boy is quite a ſea-monſter already---and I muſt keep him cloſe under my own eye, to give him ſome little touches of humanity.

Sir Hec. Orſon is wild, I grant, but he is well-meaning; and therefore I forbid all leſſons of good breeding, that are likely to make a heel in his principles.

Enter ORSON.

Orſon. Huzza, father, huzza!

Sir Hec. What do you cheer at, lad?

Orſ. Here's an advice boat, that Colonel Ormſby has juſt made London, and will take a birth with us before the evening gun is fir'd!

Lady D. How often muſt I tell you, child, that it is exceedingly vulgar to appear either ſurprized or overjoyed at any thing.

Sir Hec. Don't deſire the boy to ſlacken his ſails in a chace of good nature.

Lady D. Why, what is the fool in raptures for? He never ſaw Colonel Ormſby ſince the moment of his exiſtence.

Orſ. No mother---but I know that he is my uncle Brownlow's friend---That he has weathered my uncle from many a bitter blaſt, and is to be married to the ſweet young lady my uncle lately brought us home from Bengal.

Sir Hec. And has any body carried the news to Zelida?

Lady D. The lady Zelida, my dear——you know that her father was an Indian Omrah, or nobleman of great authority!

Orſ. I ſent Buſſora aloft with the news, and the poor fellow was as much rejoic'd as a man of war at ſhort allowance would be in ſight of the Downs.

Sir Hec. I do love that Buſſora-- he's ſo faithful a creature, and has a heart as ſound as a biſcuit.

Lady D. I don't wonder that he's ſo great a favourite with his lady, for he's extremely intelligent, and would, I dare ſay, readily hazard his life in her ſervice.

Orſ. Zounds, I'd ſtand a broad-ſide for her myſelf at any time.

Sir. Hec. Damn you, ſirrah, do you ſwear? One would think that your ſhip was ſinking, and that you expected every moment to be launch'd into the next world, you young raſcal!

Lady D. Ay, this is your bleſſed ſyſtem of ſea-education.

Sir Hec. Hark'ee 'ſcapegrace, mind your hits, if you'd avoid a rope's end; and remember to keep your wickedneſs under hatches, 'till you come to years of diſcretion, you puppy!

Lady D. Mercy upon us! and is he then to let it appear above board—Fine doctrine, truly, that our vices are to be excus'd, in proportion as we acquire a conſciouſneſs of their enormity.—You ſhou'd ſtudy my mode of expreſſion, Sir Hector.

Orſ. Why, I meant no harm, tho' I've rais'd ſuch a ſquall. Every body loves Miſs Zelida, and many a heavy heart has it given me, ſince ſhe caſt anchor in this houſe, to ſee her ſo melancholy, poor ſoul!

Sir Hec. She's a delightful girl, that's the truth of it. And I hope that the arrival of Ormſby will prevent the worms of her ſorrow from eating into the planks of her conſtitution.

Lady D. Lord, my dear, do you think that a mind ſo delicate as her's, can be deſtitute of gratitude, or indifferent about a man, who not only repeatedly ſav'd her father's life in the commotions of the Eaſt, but what was ſtill more, preſerv'd the ladies of his family from violation.

Sir Hec. Come, come, Ormſby is a noble fellow.

Orſ. As ever ſtept from ſtem to ſtern, my uncle Brownlow ſays.

Sir Hec. And Zelida's father behav'd nobly to him, when his dead lights were hung out.

Lady D. I ſuppoſe you mean by bequeathing him this only daughter in his laſt moments, who is miſtreſs of ſo large a fortune.

Sir Hec. Why, is not ſhe an Acapulco veſſel in herſelf, to ſay nothing of her being ballaſted with rupees and pagodas?

Lady D. And cou'd her father, who lov'd the Engliſh extremely, who married her mother, an Engliſh woman, and who knew the Colonel's worth ſo well, act more prudently, in the diſtracted ſtate of his country, than in giving his child to a man, who was not only able to protect her againſt all dangers, but calculated beſides, to make her an admirable huſband.

Sir Hec. Why your brother tells me that Abdalla had none of his country ſuperſtition on board his mind.

Orſ. Wasn't he a heathen, father?

Sir Hec.

Sir. Hec. Yes, lad; but for all that he ſteer'd his courſe very ſenſibly, and knew that the chart of a good conſcience would bring a ſhip of any nation to ſafe moorings, in what our methodiſt boatſwain calls the river of Jordan.

Orſ. Lord, father, boatſwain ſays that river runs by ſome town call'd the New Jeruſalem, but I never cou'd find either of them in the map.

Lady D. You may eaſily judge the liberality of Abdalla's mind, by the accompliſhments of Zelida.

Sir Hec. Why ſhe ſpeaks Engliſh, French, and Italian.

Lady D. Like her vernacular tongue.

Orſ. Yes, ſhe has a rare knack at her tongue; and I don't believe that there's ever a foreign merchantman in the whole Thames, but ſhe's able to hail in her own lingo.

Sir Hec. Then ſhe ſings ſo ſweetly.

Orſ. Yes, father; but ſhe ſings always mournful, like the mad negro that died in love for the ale-houſe girl at Portſmouth.

Lady D. Like the mad negro! Mercy upon me, what a thing am I a mother to!

Sir Hec. Doesn't ſhe dance charmingly, Di?

Lady D. Divinely—I know but one woman in England who is her ſuperior in that accompliſhment.

Sir Hec. And ſhe is no more to be compar'd to that woman in any thing, than one of the royal yatchts to a bum-boat upon the Thames.

Lady D. I am always certain of a compliment from you, Sir Hector.

Orſ. Lord, mother, ſure it wasn't yourſelf that you were weighing up with Miſs Zelida.

Lady D.

Lady D. You odious ſea-calf—quit the room. Quit the room, you deteſtable porpoiſe!

Sir Hec. Who runs foul of politeneſs now, Di?

Orſ. We have beſt cut and run, father.

Lady D. And you, Sir Hector, to ſtand by and ſee me treated in this manner.

Sir Hec. Slip the cables, lad: this is damnable weather, and will ſpeedily blow a hurricane.

[*Exit Sir Hec. and Orſon.*

Lady D. The brutes—the abominable brutes! No woman, ſurely, had ever ſuch a huſband, or ſuch a ſon. But I deſerve it all, for having the leaſt connection with an element, where the utmoſt the very beſt can arrive at, is to be ſo many reſpectable Hottentots! My ſufferings ſhould teach ladies of beauty and birth not to throw their perſons away—Yet I ſhould not have been thrown away myſelf, if any lover had offered, of a more eligible character than this barbarian here.

[*Exit.*

The Scene changes to a Library.

BROWNLOW *and* BUSSORA *diſcover'd.*

Brown. Your lady burſt into tears, Buſſora, on hearing of Colonel Ormſby's arrival?

Buſſ. Yes, and not the tears of joy neither, Mr. Brownlow.

Brown. I am ſorry for it.

Buſſ. Ah! me wiſh ſhe have never leave Bengal—For tho' ſhe have no yet learn to teach the lie to her feelings, ſtill me fear that ſhe has learn

ſome

ſome other of the no good faſhions of this country.

Brown. What do you mean?

Buſſ. Me mean that ſhe is going to marry Colonel Ormſby, without having in my tink any regard for him.

Brown. You were born in her father's ſervice, Buſſora, are the only attendant ſhe has of her own country, and ſhe confides, I know, with great reaſon, in your attachment to her.

Buſſ. Me can die with pleaſure for her good---me muſt die with grief if her do wrong ting.

Brown. And would it be a wrong thing to fulfil her father's laſt commands, by marrying Colonel Ormſby?

Buſſ. Ah! Mr. Brownlow, wrong ting one place, right ting another. Wrong ting in India lady no to love huſband; very right ting for Engliſh lady to hate huſband heartily.

Brown. Why indeed, Buſſora, we never have any ladies here, deſirous of burning themſelves at the funeral of a huſband. But has your lady given you any reaſonable cauſe to ſuſpect an averſion to the marriage with Colonel Ormſby?

Buſſ. O, if ſhe love Colonel, why weep at him come to England?

Brown. (*aſide*) 'Tis as I fear'd.

Buſſ. Now for heaven love, Mr. Brownlow, as ſhe regard you much, adviſe her. You was all care, all goodneſs to her in paſſage from Bengal, and ſoon dried her tears for father and for country.

Brown. I think you ſaid, ſhe means to ſee me here in a few minutes.

Buſſ. Yes, yes, and pray tell, ſince her muſt marry Colonel, that though no love huſband is

very

very well among Chriſtians, him is very wicked mong Gentoos.

Brown. But you forget all this time that I am a Chriſtian, Buſſora.

Buſſ. Ah, no, you be too good; me ſaw you ſave black man's life, and no plunder in India. Beſides, you have behaved like brother to my lady, place her with your own ſiſter, and ſaid oftener, than a thouſand times, that there was no ſin in have copper complexion. [*Exit.*

Brown. Into what a diſtreſſing ſituation am I plung'd! Ormſby come, and Zelida, as I dreaded, upon my account; averſe to ratify her engagements. Little did I conceive that my very deſire to diſcharge my truſt like a true friend to poor Ormſby, would prove the ſource of his mortification, or that my endeavours, during the courſe of our paſſage from Bengal, to ſoften the anxiety of Zelida's mind at the death of her father, would be attended with ſuch unlucky conſequences. Let my ſentiments, however, in favour of this lovely infidel, be what they may, the obligations I owe my friend, as well as the truſt he has repoſed in my honour, would render it not only cruel, but infamous in me, to indulge a hope repugnant to his wiſhes. Since, therefore, ſhe can never be mine, I ſhall ſhew my regard for her in the beſt manner, by prevailing upon her to accept the only man on earth, who is moſt entitled to her affection, and who, if I had not unfortunately interven'd, would certainly have poſſeſſed it.

Enter ZELIDA.

Zel. So Mr. Brownlow.

Brown. Something has offended you, my deareſt Zelida.

Zel. I am not ſatisfied with myſelf, Mr. Brownlow.

Brown. Then I am afraid that you are not juſt to yourſelf; for when have you once committed an impropriety? You have heard that Colonel Ormſby is arrived?

Zel. It was upon this very buſineſs that I wanted to conſult you, Brownlow.

Brown. As your engagements with Colonel Ormſby are no ſecret, there can be no impropriety in ſpeaking upon the ſubject to his friend.

Zel. Engagements!—I am under no engagements.

Brown. No, Madam!

Zel. (with emphaſis) No, Sir! My father could not engage me to do an impoſſibility. I eſteem, I reverence, Colonel Ormſby: but my very gratitude for the ſervices which he has rendered my family, obliges me to deny him a hand which is not accompanied by a heart.

Brown. My deareſt creature, the Colonel's merit and your principles, will be ſufficient foundation for happineſs after marriage, tho' at the performance of the ceremony there ſhould not be as much paſſion as might be wiſh'd on your ſide.

Zel. The Colonel, as a man of merit, ſhould not be deceiv'd with an alienated heart—as a man of honour, he would deſpiſe it.

Brown. And have you no pity for the Colonel?

Zel. You have no pity for me, and indeed very little for your friend, when you want to give him a wiſe, who cannot be his without a falſhood.

Brown. Poor Ormſby, what muſt he feel?

Zel. He will feel like a man of honour; otherwiſe what he feels, is below conſideration.—In one word, therefore, I never will be his.

Brown.

Brown. Confider your father's laft commands.

Zel. I confider the fpirit of his intention, not the mere form of his words; he wanted to make me happy, and I will not difappoint him, if I can help it.

Brown. Excufe me for preffing this matter fo ftrongly.

Zel. I do excufe you. I know that you have obligations to Ormfby, as well as myfelf; but it is a falfe gratitude, a falfe generofity, which requires us to forego our happinefs, and if we muft repay a favour with our honour, or our peace of mind, it may often be the kindeft thing imaginable, to leave us finking under our misfortunes.

Brown. O, Zelida!

Zel. You tremble, Brownlow, a tear is ftanding in your eye, what's the matter with you?

Brown. Nothing. *(fighs.)*

Zel. And that figh fprings from nothing too, does it? Why do you torture me, Brownlow?

Brown. Torture you? I wifh you to be happy! I implore you to marry Ormfby.

Zel. And do you, Brownlow *really*, do you *fincerely*, do you *indeed* wifh that I fhould marry the Colonel?

Brown. Why do you afk fuch a queftion?

Zel. Why fhould you hefitate to anfwer it?

Brown. It is already anfwered in the advice I have given you.

Zel. Is it?

Brown. O, Zelida! You are as dear to me as---

Zel. As what, Brownlow?

Brown. What would I fay? As if you were actually my fifter.

Zel. However, if I *muſt* be your ſiſter, where is the neceſſity of my being married at all? I can live with you and Lady Di.

Brown. I muſt relinquiſh you to the guardianſhip of Ormſby.—My ſiſter, beſides, tho' a worthy woman, is a whimſical one, and my family is importunate with me——

Zel. To marry too—and perhaps your heart is already engag'd.

Brown. Spare me on this ſubject, Dear Zelida!

Zel. Why, you may tell me, you know, ſince I am your ſiſter.

Brown. If I muſt ſpeak, it is too deeply——

Zel. Ah! *(aſide)* And is the lady very handſome, Brownlow?

Brown. How ſhe wrings my heart! An angel!

Zel. But why do you ſigh? You don't deſpair of obtaining her?

Brown. I am totally hopeleſs! She muſt be married to another!

Zel. Oh! Brownlow, how I pity you! 'Tis a dreadful thing to loſe the object of one's heart!

Brown. I find it ſo, indeed, Zelida——but there is a fatality in love. Few, I fear, are happy enough to marry, where they really beſtow their affections. Your caſe, my deareſt girl, is far from ſingular; let me therefore again, conjure you, for all our ſakes, to give Ormſby the reception he expects at your hands: I will not treſpaſs any longer on your patience. To ſee you thus agitated, overwhelms me with affliction! Summon up your fortitude, my ſweet ſiſter, and be aſſur'd that if my life could purchaſe your tranquility, I ſhou'd chearfully reſign it.

[*Exit.*

(Zelida ſits and muſes ſome time, then rings a bell.)

Enter a Servant.

Ser. Did you ring, Madam?

Zel. Yes, James, ſend Buſſora to me.

Ser. I will, Madam. [*Exit.*

Zel. *(walking about ſome time in diſorder)* Where can this Buſſora be?

Enter BUSSORA.

You have been along time coming.

Buſſ. O dear lady, when mind is no eaſy—the lightning himſelf walk on crutches.

Zel. I have news that will rejoice you, Buſſora, *(ſighs)* I mean to leave England immediately.

Buſſ. And go again to land of our father's, lady?

Zel. I do.

Buſſ. How come him bleſſing about lady?

Zel. Not liking Colonel Ormſby——I am reſolv'd never to marry him.

Buſſ. Heav'n be tank lady.

Zel. We muſt, however, get away by ſtealth, Buſſora, for this is a nation of contradictions; and as the people are mighty lovers of liberty, we may not be ſuffered to follow our own inclinations.

Buſſ. Me thot that in this houſe you have all friends, lady.

Zel. Ah Buſſora, there is no living in this unaccountable place.—A father here, will break his daughter's heart to make her happy; and a woman may be a very excellent wife who has no regard whatever for her huſband!

Zel.

Buff. O dear!——Law too lady, him very vile here, of which 'em boaſt ſo much—Poor ſtarving devil he hang up, if he ſteal rupee for dinner—— But him good enough to be a lord, if he rob a hundred thouſand pounds.

Zel. Well Buſſora, we'll ſtay no longer in a place where the kindneſs of the beſt friends, is as dangerous as the malice of the worſt enemies—Yet, as I quit this houſe clandeſtinely, it will be proper to leave ſuch little preſents as I have accepted behind me, together with a letter accounting for my conduct, and making proper acknowledgments for the civilities I have received.

Buff. To be ſure, lady; ungrateful him only belong to chriſtian.

Zel. Here's a watch ſet with diamonds, given me by Colonel Ormſby.—This brilliant, *(heigh ho)* I had from Mr. Brownlow—and this is Lady Di's picture.

Buff. Yes, lady; me wonder how painter can make like of the lady's in England—um have ſo many complexion.—in morning um is yellow—in noon um is red—in evening um is red and white— and when em go to bed, um faces have fifty colours, juſt ſo as back of alligator upon Ganges.

Zel. I think I have recollected every thing.

Buff. No, lady: here is little paint of Mr. Brownlow for lady his ſiſter—You bid me borrow him this morning from limner, and me forgot him in other buſineſs.

Zel. This!—O—this I'll take with me.

Buff. Ah! lady—White man, him cou'd do no more worſe, as take what no his.

Zel. Why, to be ſure it is not mine, Buſſora, nor is it of any intrinſic value.

Buff.

Buff. So much lefs reafon for take him, lady—Then he flatter Mr. Brownlow fo much, that he no like at all.

Zel. Nay now I don't think it flatters him in the leaft.

Buff. Here is mout fo pretty.

Zel Why does not Mr. Brownlow fmile in this delightful manner?

Buff. Mr. Brownlow very good man—and grin very hanfome—but——

Zel. Then obferve thefe eyes.

Buff. Mr. Brownlow very good man—and ftare very well—but——

Zel. Here take the picture——I fee you know nothing of the matter—and yet Buffora, I have a ftrange fancy for the picture too—It will remind me of many interefting occurrences, and I would gladly give ten times its real value to take it along with me.

Buff. O then lady, leave him ten times his worth, and take him away——for greateft man in country here, he never quarrel with good bargain.

Zel. I'll follow your advice, my good Buffora—fo get a coach ready in the next ftreet, while I prepare a letter for Lady Di— I'am quite delighted that you have taught me a way of taking this trifle fo properly.

Buff. O lady, 'tis by do what him fhould not, in little ting, that Europe man learn trick of committing biggeft wickednefs——But we fhall foon again fee land of fore-fathers—and tank de kind Heav'n, that have no let our minds be worfend by live in England.

[*Exit exultingly.*

Zel.

Zel. Heigh ho!— Now Buffora is gone, my ſpirits ſink, and I tremble at the thought of executing my own reſolution——This houſe is very dear to me, tho' I am preparing to bid it an eternal farewel—How tenderly did Brownlow look at me!—And muſt I never ſee him again?——But why ſhould I deſire to ſee him; his heart is another's, and mine ſhall break before it entertains a wiſh which is either mean, or criminal.

[*Exit.*

Scene changes to another Room.

Enter ORSON *and* PILLAGE.

Orſ. Well Maſter Pillage, I am heartily glad to lie along ſide of you once more.——And how have you left all our old ſhip mates at Portſmouth?

Pil. Pure and well as to health, Maſter Orſon, but curſedly down in the mouth that there is no war.— Trade is damn'd dead in Portſmouth;—half the public houſes ſhut up—little or no playing at cards.

Orſ. And I ſuppoſe not a quarter of the girls at the back of the Point, that there uſed to be?

Pil. Nothing like it, Maſter Orſon— We did hope that the death of the French King would have kick'd up a duſt. But damn it, there's no ſpunk left in the nation now.

Orſ. No more there is, purſer—for even when they pipe all hands at the parliament houſe, they do nothing but refit the coin, or give a larger tier of cable to the papiſhes—Our ſhips are now rotting in peace, and we may as well have no navy at all, as not be at war with ſomebody you know!

Pil.

Pil. And I warrant now you have not half the pleaſure here that you have when you are down with the Dreadnought?

Orſ. Pleaſure! Lord help your head—I lead ten times a worſe life than a cabbin boy.

Pil. I feared as much.

Orſ. Mother is wanting me for ever to read fine books, and father, if I'm not at home before it's dark, is for ever threatning me with the bilboes—Then I'm oblig'd to go to church twice every Sunday.

Pil. You don't ſay ſo?

Orſ. Ay, but I do—father thinks me too young to be wicked—If I ſwear an oath, or get drunk now and then, he ſtorms as if a candle was left in the powder-room.

Pil. Why that's damn'd hard.

Orſ. *(Half crying.)* Iſn't it?—If there was a war, I could ſit up all night ſometimes at cards; and grapple now and then with a girl—Father loves a girl himſelf, tho' he is married.

Pil. Why I thought you had girls in plenty here.

Orſ. Yes, there's enough of 'em cruizing in every corner, at night—and for that matter, in the day time too—But they can't produce bills of health—— And there's no making 'em perform quarantine, you know.

Pil. Well I am come up poſt to London, to aſk your father a favour, and I'll beg of him to let you ſup with me this evening.

Orſ. Egad, and if you do, I'll take you on a little trip to Bagnigge Wells, where you'll ſee ſome tight ſloops very prettily rigg'd, tho' they moſtly fail under Jew commanders.

Pil. And if the Admiral——I beg his pardon, Sir Hector, ſtands my friend——You ſhan't want money, to keep a little pleaſure boat of your own, maſter Orſon.

Orſ. Zounds, you are the beſt friend I ever ſail'd with in all my life, and if I can help to tow you to your wiſhes, you need only make a ſignal.

Pil. Thank you kindly, maſter Orſon—— But where's your father?

Orſ. Aſleep in his great chair.

Pil. What, he got a little rocky or ſo, after dinner?

Orſ. Yes, he ſhipp'd a good deal of grog—— but he left ſtrict orders with me to wake him if any body came from Portſmouth.

Pil. Zounds that's lucky, for my buſineſs requires haſte—You muſt know the purſer of the Riſing Sun died laſt night.

Orſ. I wiſh you had his birth——She's a firſt rate.

Pil. And my preſent ſhip is only a ſeventy-four – I want a letter, therefore, from your father, to a certain great man—Sir Hector's intereſt is very good—and he promiſed to ſerve me at any time---- Beſides, I am a freeholder in five different counties.

Orſ. Ah! that won't do you much good now, as the elections are all over: tho' father ſays that above fifty thouſand pair of jaws have been wagging away theſe laſt three months, for the good of the kingdom. But come along with me to the ſhrouds, and I'll wake him directly.

Pil. He's above ſtairs then?

Orſ. Yes, mother and he had a tight engagement a while ago; and ſo to ſhew that he wan't afraid to keep the ſea, he ordered his pipe and his grog to be haul'd aloft into her dreſſing room.

Pil. Up with you then, I follow.

Orſ. Well, a good voyage to you, and then hey for the little pleaſure-boat, maſter Pillage.

[*Exeunt.*

Scene changes, and diſcovers Sir Hector *aſleep in a dreſſing-room. A punch-bowl, with pipes and tobacco on a toilet-table.*

Enter ORSON.

Orſ. Hip, father, holloa!

Sir Hec. Hey, what noiſe is all that? Can't you change the watch quietly and be damn'd to you? The timbers of my head are ſplitting.

Orſ. Maſter Pillage, the purſer, is come at the rate of nine knots an hour, from Portſmouth, father, and ſo I waked you according to orders.

Sir Hec. And how is the admiral? Has he ſtruck the flag of life?

Orſ. I didn't aſk, father.

Sir Hec. You blockhead—You are a fine one to keep a look out at the top-maſt—where is Pillage?

Orſ. Cloſe a-ſtern in the next room.

Sir Hec. Bid him come a-board here inſtantly.

Orſ. I will, father—Father lays a little gunnel to yet, but he'll be right upon his keel quickly—Zounds, if a match was ſet to him, now he's ſo hot, he'd go off like a ſky-rocket!

[*Exit.*

Sir Hec. My friend, the reſident commiſſioner, has certainly diſpatched Pillage to me, expreſs, with an account of the admiral's ſtriking—Well, there's there's a brave officer laid up for ever in dock—But death will yellow us all in turn, and ſo I ſhall only think of ſucceeding to the command.

Enter PILLAGE.

Pil. Sir Hector, your moſt obedient!

Sir Hec. Ha! honeſt Pillage—my old Heart of Oak, as I us'd to call you.

Pil. Ah! Sir Hector, you were always my good friend.

Sir Hec. And I always will be your friend, Pillage.

Pil. I know you never forget your word, Sir Hector.

Sir Hec. Never fail'd in the teeth of a promiſe, ſince I was firſt rated able on the books of creation—damn me—And ſo he is dead, Pillage?

Pil. Yes, Sir Hector, he's gone.

Sir Hec. And a worthy fellow he was!

Pil. As ever ſold a puncheon of rum, Sir Hector.

Sir Hec. Sold a puncheon of rum!—But what time did you leave Portſmouth, my good Pillage?

Pil. Within an hour after he died.

Sir Hec. And all the ſails in the harbour were lower'd

Pil. Not one, Sir Hector.

Sir Hec. Wasn't that behaving with too little reſpect to the ſervice, my dear friend?

Pil. He was not of rank enough, Sir Hector, tho' an excellent officer, and ſcarcely to be equalled in his ſtation by any in the navy.

Sir Hec. You are miſtaken, Pillage, 'tis a compliment always paid to an officer of his rank—How-

However, if my intereſt carries the weight of metal, I expect the navy will not ſuffer very much by the accident.

Pil. O you are too good, Sir Hector.

Sir Hec. Too good, man—for what? why 'tis the top-gallant object of my heart.

Pil. O Sir Hector—But as there may be other people puſhing, when ſhall I hope that you'll mention the matter at the Admiralty?

Sir Hec. I'll ſtretch for Chairing-croſs this very hour—the pinnace out there—Poh! I mean the chariot, you raſcals.

Pil. A thouſand thanks to you, Sir Hector.

Sir Hec. And a thouſand thanks to you for flying the ſtreamers of your ſatisfaction;---here's a little mark of friendſhip, I muſt beg you to wear as a keep-ſake. *(giving him a ring.)*

Pil. Dear Sir Hector, you quite diſtreſs me—Then you think there's no danger of refuſal?

Sir Hec. Refuſe me, Pillage!

Pil. Why, Sir Hector, I don't believe they'd venture to do that.—Your conſequence is too well known.

Sir Hec. Let me ſee which of them would open a port-hole of denial upon Hector Strangeways.

Pil. If they ſhou'd boggle, however, Sir Hector, you know I have ſome pretenſions.

Sir Hec. I don't underſtand you.

Pil. I have been thirty years in the navy, you know.

Sir. Hec. And what then, my dear friend?

Pil. Was wounded at Martinico.

Sir. Hec. I know your merit, my good Pillage—But what then?

Pil. Tho' I was not obliged to be on deck.

Sir Hec. Zounds! and what then?

Pil.

Pil. Nay, Sir Hector, I don't ſuppoſe that more regard will be paid to ſervice than uſual.

Sir Hec. Why which way does the wind blow?

Pil. Yet, if I ſhould have the good fortune to be appointed.

Sir Hec. You appointed, man! Why you have loſt the rudder of your underſtanding.

Pil. Why not, Sir Hector? For tho' a ſeventy-four is the largeſt ſhip I have ſerv'd in—

Sir Hec. We are ſailing here without compaſs.

Pil. Dear Sir Hector, didn't you ſay you'd be ſo good as to ſpeak for me at the admiralty.

Sir Hec. Zounds, for you! I coudn't be ſuch a madman.

Pil. O Sir Hector!

Sir Hec. Speak for you to ſucceed vice-admiral Grampus?

Pil. Vice-admiral Grampus! Why, Sir Hector, I'm not quite fit for Bedlam yet – I thought maſter Orſon had told you——

Sir Hec. What?

Pil. That I came to beg your intereſt to ſucceed honeſt Ralph Rapine.

Sir Hec. Who?

Pil. The purſer of the Riſing Sun.

Sir Hec. Damn Orſon—and damn you—and damn the purſer of the Riſing Sun.

Pil. Sir Hector.

Sir Hec. Why, harkee, ſirrah—Weren't you diſpatched by the commiſſioner, to acquaint me with the death of vice-admiral Grampus?

Pil. Not I indeed, Sir Hector.

Sir Hec. Not you indeed!—

Pil. For I left the admiral out of danger.

Sir Hec. You did?

Pil. Yes, Sir Hector, and never ſpoke to the commiſſioner in my life.

Sir Hec. Why then you are a moſt impudent raſcal, for ſuffering me to be diſturbed on your account, when I had turn'd in with a fire between decks, and a damnable ſmaſh in my round-top.

Pil. Sir Hector—

Sir Hec. Get out of my houſe this moment, you puppy.

Pil. Sir Hector—

Sir Hec. You deſerve a keel-hauling, you dog —or, damn me, if I was a deſpotic prince, I'd inſtantly hang you up at the yard-arm.

[*Exit Pillage driven off by Sir Hector.*

END OF THE FIRST ACT.

ACT II.

The Scene an Apartment.

Enter Lady DI *and* ORSON.

Lady Di. PART of Colonel Ormſby's baggage come already?

Orſ. Yes, mother, and he'll be here himſelf in a few minutes.

Lady D. Well, and where's your father, child?

Orſ. Lighting a freſh pipe, I believe, mother, over a little gin-grog, in the cabin above.

Lady D. Go, child, and tell him I wiſh to ſpeak to him this inſtant: this inſtant; do you hear, booby!—Mercy upon me, I am quite weary of this world.

Orſ. I wiſh you were landed upon a better, with all my heart then.

Lady D. Why, you wicked, unnatural reprobate.

Orſ. Lord, mother, is it wicked to wiſh you riding ſafe in the other world, if you are afraid of foundering in this? [*Exit.*

Lady D. Lighting a freſh pipe over a little gin-grog in the cabin above! A pretty employment for a Knight of the Bath, and my huſband. He'll breathe in flame, and ſpeak in ſulphur; yet I muſt throw myſelf into his atmoſphere, if he was as dangerous as an eruption from Veſuvius, for unleſs the bear is ſtroak'd into ſome conditions about beha-

behaviour, we ſhall appear downright ſavages to Colonel Ormſby.

Enter Sir HECTOR.

Sir Hec. Well, Di—I have bad news for you. The doctors have new ſheath'd Admiral Grampus—and I am to continue land-lock'd upon your hands perhaps, till the nation is indulg'd with another war.

Lady D. How can you, Sir Hector, do ſo much injuſtice to my feelings, as to think I ſhall conſider that bad news?

Sir Hec. Why how's this, Di?—The ſky's cleared up, and your temper as ſmooth as the Pacific in a trade wind!

Lady D. I have been thinking, my dear, how very ridiculous it is for us ever to have the ſmalleſt diſagreement.

Sir Hec. So it is, Di—The quarrel of a man and wife is like a fight between two privateers, where there is nothing but hard knocks to be got on either ſide.

Enter ORSON *and* ORMSBY.

Orſ. Here he is, father, here's Colonel Ormſby.

Lady D. What a bawling the blockhead keeps. Dear Colonel———

Ormſ. I rejoice to ſee your ladyſhip.

Sir Hec. What, my old boy! Here we are all, Hector, Aſtyanax, and Andromache!

Ormſ. You are too good to me in this kind reception, and I am already too much obliged in the protection which you have extended to my poor Eaſt Indian.

Orſ. Lord, father, neither ſhe nor Buſſora is come back yet.

Sir. Hec. Come back! I didn't know they were out of the houſe.

Ormſ. It was not altogether ſo kind of Zelida, to be abſent on this occaſion, as your brother informed me he had acquainted her with my arrival.

Sir Hec. That fellow there, might have kept an eye upon the harbour.

Orſ. Lord, father, as ſhe was not an enemy, what right had I to watch her ſailing in or out of port?

Lady D. She was our gueſt, not our priſoner, my dear Sir Hector.

Sir Hec. And therefore you ſhould have watch'd all her ſignals, my love.

Ormſ. Nay, Sir Hector, if Zelida would go out privately, how could Lady Di prevent it?

Lady D. I hope, my love, that I am not altogether deſtitute of breeding.

Sir Hec. My dear, you are the beſt bred woman alive, but, Zounds! what ſignifies your breeding, if this accident ſhou'd make us ſpring a-leak.

Lady D. My dear, don't loſe your temper—'tis ſo underbred, you know.

Ormſ. I am quite unhappy that ſo trifling a circumſtance ſhould occaſion the ſmalleſt difference between your ladyſhip and Sir Hector.

Lady D. You are very good, Colonel, and will make allowance for the manners of the forecaſtle.

Orſ. Now father———

Sir Hec.

Sir Hec. If he makes allowance for your manners, he'll be very good, indeed, Di.

Lady D. This is too much! Excuſe me Colonel Ormſby—Stand out of the way, you impudent puppy, *(to* ORSON*)* you ſeem quite delighted with your father's brutality! [*Exit.*

Ormſ. Sir Hector, let me requeſt that you will follow Lady Di, and make up this little difference.

Sir Hec. What, chace for the purpoſe of ſtriking to the enemy?

Ormſ. For my ſake do it, or I ſhall conſider myſelf a diſturber of the family union.

Sir Hec. Well, for your ſake, Colonel.—Tho' damme this begging a defeat, is very ſtrange ſervice for an Engliſh admiral. [*Exit Sir Hec.*

Orſ. Lord, Colonel, don't be concerned at this little bruſh between father and mother; they engage in the ſame manner twenty times a day.

Ormſ. I am ſorry for it, young gentleman.

Orſ. Why yeſterday it rained very hard, and father going out for a little pleaſure in an open boat—you muſt know—O here's my uncle—— I'll ſheer off: for two old meſſmates parted ſo long, may want ſome private jaw together.

[*Exit.*

Enter BROWNLOW.

Brown. My dear Ormſby! I aſk your pardon for not being immediately in the way to receive you; but after we parted at the India Houſe, I was unexpectedly detain'd on a very particular buſineſs.

Ormſ. Once more, Brownlow, let me expreſs my happineſs at ſeeing you, and my hopes that we are both now ſecurely fix'd for life in our country. We have each of us acquired a ſplendid fortune in the Eaſt, without incurring a ſtain upon our humanity.

(Enter JENNY *(with a letter.)*

Jenny (to Brownlow) Sir, my lady ordered me to deliver you this letter, which ſhe found directed to herſelf, in the young Eaſt India lady's dreſſing room.

Brown. Give it to me, Jenny. [*Exit* Jenny.

Ormſ. My dear Brownlow, excuſe my impertinence, but may I aſk if any thing in that letter relates to Zelida ?

Brown. There it is——'tis from herſelf—ſhe has abſolutely elop'd, and even ſays that my advice has determin'd her to purſue ſo extraordinary a meaſure.

Ormſ. (reads) " To Lady Di Strangeways.

" Madam,

" Tho' it is with infinite pain I tear myſelf
" from a family which has treated me with ſuch
" peculiar civility, neither my happineſs nor my
" honour, will allow me to receive the protec-
" tion of your hoſpitable roof any longer. 'Tis
" impoſſible for me to act as your brother wiſhes,
" and his advice, join'd to ſome other reaſons,
" determine me to leave England as ſpeedily as
" poſſible. In return for a miniature I have
" robb'd you of, I beg you will condeſcending-
" ly accept the diamond which lies on the toilet,
" and believe me, with the moſt perfect grati-
" tude for all your goodneſs, your ever devo-
" ted

" ZELIDA."

" Poſtſcript.

" The agitation of mind, under which I write, " is ſo great, that I have forgot to beg you will " preſent my beſt wiſhes, my beſt acknowledg- " ments, to Colonel Ormſby; your brother too " has my warmeſt regards, tho' he wants to make " me miſerable, and drives me from a country " in which I hop'd to end my days."

—Brownlow!——

Brown. Ormſby!

Ormſ. For heaven's ſake, explain this myſtery!

Brown. You know as much of it, my dear friend, as I do.

Ormſ. Why ſhe ſays poſitively here, that you wanted to make her miſerable, and have driven her from the kingdom.

Brown. Simply, Ormſby, you muſt either think that I am a man of honour, or that I am not.

Ormſ. I have ever found you a man of the niceſt honour, and as ſuch, I have priz'd your friendſhip among the peculiar bleſſings of my life. But, Brownlow, Zelida has exquiſite beauty, and you have a ſuſceptible heart.—What did you want her to do, which would have made her miſerable?

Brown. Nothing injurious to the friendſhip I profeſs'd for you, Ormſby.

Ormſ. Come, come, Brownlow, in the fulneſs of a generous friendſhip, I truſted you with the woman of my heart, and I muſt have a ſatisfactory account of her.

Brown. That menace, Ormſby, is very little calculated to anſwer your purpoſe, yet as I ſincerely ſympathize in your diſtreſs, and have no view but to reſcue you from farther anxiety, I again

again conjure you, not to inſiſt upon an explanation.

Ormſ. Don't inſult me, Mr. Brownlow, with your pity, while you are deliberately binding me upon the rack; but if you ever valued my peace, or regarded your own honour, be explicit and tell me.

Brown. You ſhall be obey'd, Ormsby—however reluctantly—what has driven Zelida from this houſe, was my adviſing her to marry you.

Ormſ. Adviſing her to marry me!—Why ſhould you adviſe her to marry me?—Where was the neceſſity of ſuch an advice?—She came from India for the purpoſe, and your interceſſion in my favour, was a friendly ſupererogation.

Brown. This ſneer, Mr. Ormsby, you will one day be ſorry for, becauſe you will one day know that it was not merited. However, inſtead of loſing our time in this fruitleſs altercation, let us exert ourſelves to recover the fair fugitive, and you will then know from her own lips, whether my conduct is entitled to your reſentment or your approbation.

Ormſ. O, doubtleſs, to my deepeſt gratitude—but, Sir, what right had you to tamper with her affections?—What right had you to think yourſelf of more importance to her than I was? You fancied, perhaps, that ſhe was ſmitten with that irreſiſtible form, and therefore coolly took ſnuff with a requeſt that ſhe would not quite kill the miſerable Ormsby.

Brown. Colonel, don't let us make this affair a war of words——you have more than once ſav'd my life, but you now attempt a murder on my honour. Let me ring for a ſervant to attend you to your apartment.

Ormſ. Will you be at leiſure at eight?

Brown. I ſhall certainly.

Ormſ. I'll beg to ſpeak with you.

Brown. You will particularly oblige me.

Ormſ. Your ſervant, Mr. Brownlow.

Brown. Your's, Colonel Ormſby.

[*Exeunt.*

The ſcene changes to an apartment.

Enter PILLAGE.

Pil. How lucky it was that ſo delicious a girl ſhould come, at this time, to lodge in my ſiſter's houſe.——She deſires to be very private—and I dare ſay ſhe has good reaſon for her deſire.—Yet demure as ſhe ſeems to be, it ſhall go hard if I do not get the purſerſhip of the Riſing Sun by her means. That hot-headed old fool, Sir Hector, will do any thing to obtain a pretty wench; and notwithſtanding he was lately in ſuch a paſſion with me, has, for anſwer to my note about the the new-comer here, promiſed to call upon me immediately. I can't ſay, indeed, that this way of gaining preferment is the moſt honourable; yet my betters are every day practiſing ways as bad, and not one of them is, in his own opinion, diſqualified for the firſt employment in the kingdom.

SIR HECTOR, *behind.*

In this cabbin, child, is he?

Pil. Here he comes———

Enter

Enter SIR HECTOR.

Sir Hec. Honeſt Pillage, I have a thouſand pardons to aſk for my late behaviour—but you are a true ſailor, and forget a friend's faults, where you can do him a favour.

Pil. O Sir Hector, it was a miſtake on both ſides.

Sir Hec. So it was—but I'll make amends—And now tell me, is the frigate you have brought me to look at, well built? Is ſhe likely to come to in a little time, or do you think ſhe'll ſtand out to ſea in expectation of a ſettlement?

Pil. Look at her firſt, Sir Hector, and ſee how you like her.

Sir Hec. I ſhould have made more way to you, but we are all in a damn'd buſtle about a wench at my own houſe—A wench that I ſhould have thought of myſelf, if ſhe had not claimed the protection of my own fort, and been brought in by my brother Brownlow.

Pil. In that caſe the laws of honour, Sir Hector—

Sir Hec. O intitled her to quarter, damme——Straight as a main maſt—none of your clumſy Dutch ſterns---her lanthorns bright as the ſun---and then ſomething divine about her bowſprit, (*feeling his noſe.*) But where's your girl all this time?

Pil. In the dining-room---My ſiſter's unluckily gone out---But if you'll walk into the next parlour a moment, Sir Hector, you'll find a new chart of Otaheite, which will amuſe you, while I ſtep up ſtairs myſelf, to ſee how the land lies.

[*Exit.*

Sir

Sir. Hec. Otaheite!---O that's Queen Oberea's country, heaven blefs her, who fent the failors in diftrefs, the fupply of women and hogs--- Zounds if ever I fhould be ftation'd there, I'll have a tender loaded with large nails, to prevent the honeft Johns from endangering his majefty's fleet a fecond time, in their prefents to the ladies.

[*Exit.*

Scene changes to a Stair Cafe, a Dining-Room in view, with a Landing Place.

Enter PILLAGE

Pil. Here's the door—The lady has been kept by one of the India captains, I fuppofe, and defigns to enter herfelf in the cargo of damag'd virginity, which, for the honour of Englifh delicacy now adays, makes fo confiderable an article in our exports to Bengal. [*Knocks at the door.*

Enter BUSSORA *from the Door.*

Buf. What you want, gentlemen?

Pil. I am brother to the miftrefs of the houfe.

Buf. And why you no ftay below with your fifter?

Pil. Come don't be furly, my honeft friend, here's half a crown for you.

Buf. Scorn your money, gentleman;—Buffora no do bad ting.

Pil. Why fhou'd you fuppofe I want you to do a bad thing.

Buf. Becaufe white man him never part with money but for fome to do—and good ting want no pay for.

Pil. That's not foolifhly thought for an Indian.

Buf. O Indian him no quite fool—tho' he no tink Englifhman right, when he choofe to take him life, or him fortune.

Pil. My fifter was telling me that your miftrefs wanted to know the proper method of taking a paffage to India.

Buf. Very true.

Pil. Now there's a friend of mine below, who knows every thing about it, and will be happy to tell her, if fhe will only give him leave to wait upon her.

Buf. Many tank in my lady name— me go afk if you only ftay one minute, gentleman. [*Exit.*

Pil. If the gentlewoman here condefcends to receive a vifit, I'll fend Sir Hector up by himfelf that he may have no interruption.

Enter BUSSORA *from the Door.*

Buf. Lady will be very glad to fee you friend gentleman.

Pil. I thought as much!

Buf. O you may depend—Indian man him always fpeak truth.

Pil. Indeed!

Buf. O indeed.

Pil. Well, I'll fend my friend— Who wou'd have thought this tawny rafcal fo well qualified to be either a pimp or a puritan. (*Afide.*)

[*Exit.*

Buf. He furprife at me for fpeak truth——me fure truth is all de treafure left to poor Gentoo – and no left poor Gentoo that, if truth he was worth any thing in England.

[*Exit thro' the door.*

Scene

Scene changes to an Apartment.

Enter ZELIDA.

Zel. This ſtranger's coming ſo opportunely is very fortunate, as Buſſora with all his fidelity might be unable to obtain the neceſſary information about our paſſage, without hazarding a diſcovery—Colonel Ormſby poſſible has emiſſaries in ſearch of me—or poſſibly Brownlow—— No, Brownlow's heart is occupied by other objects, and I muſt never expect to engage a moment of his recollection!

Enter Sir HECTOR.

Sir Hec. There ſhe is—a fine figure—and clear decks too.—Madam, I am your moſt——

Zel. (*turns about*) Sir Hector Strangeways!

Sir Hec. (*aſide*) Zounds, is it ſhe I have borne down upon?

Zel. For heaven ſake, Sir Hector, how did you know of my being here?

Sir Hec. 'Sdeath! I muſt tack about!

Zel. Speak, Sir.

Enter BUSSORA.

O Buſſora we are diſcover'd.

Buſ. Well, lady, we have do no harm.

Zel. True—but in a country where conſiſtency is abſurd, to be innocent may be criminal.

Sir Hec. Don't be alarm'd, madam.

Buſ. No lady--don't fear--me am come to protect you, or no live (*drawing his dagger*---) White

 man,

man, Gentoo he die more ſoon as ſpill blood-- But Buſſora he die two times more ſoon, as ſee danger offer him lady----- Go from room——

Sir Hec. Why you damn'd idiot!—— I'd die myſelf ſooner than do your lady the ſmalleſt hurt.

Zel. Put up your dagger, Buſſora, or I ſhall ſink with terror.

Buſ. There he ſtay 'till him wanted lady.

Sir Hect. Dear Madam, why ſhould you ſuppoſe me an enemy? you have hoiſted ſail from my houſe, and I am ſorry you did not like your moorings better, but I don't come to preſs you back; tho' quitting your former anchorage let me tell you, may perhaps endanger the lives of Ormſby and Brownlow.

Zel. Endanger the life of Brownlow!

Buſ. And Colonel Ormſby, him life too lady— Sir Hector he ſay.

Zel. But why ſhou'd they fight about me?

Sir Hec. I am afraid, Madam, that nothing but your marrying the Colonel, can prevent them from ſhattering one another's rigging a little.

Zel. Surely, Sir, the Colonel will hear reaſon.

Buſ. O Lady—— Engliſh gentleman when him in paſſion, ſcandalous for he to hear reaſon.

Zel. Heavens!— and can Ormſby, after the ſtricteſt intimacy of years with Brownlow, after receiving a thouſand proofs of his honour, believe him in a moment capable of being a villain.

Sir Hec. He muſt take care of his honour.

Buſ. And honour in here country, lady, oblige gentleman to kill friend without cauſe—— Poor man, he only give friend a black eye, or break him bones— It too grand for any but gentleman to make murder.

Zel.

Zel. What ſhall I do?

Sir Hec. Sling in the ſame hammock with the Colonel, if you wiſh to prevent miſchief, madam.

Zel. I'd do any thing to reſcue Mr. Brownlow from danger.

Buſ. (*aſide*) Mr. Brownlow! O me begin ſuſpect.

Sir Hec. Whatever you determine, madam, muſt be determined ſpeedily, for they will not be long drawing up in line of battle.

Zel. Then, Sir, I have determined, that Mr. Brownlow ſhall not loſe his life on my account— I am ready to marry Colonel Ormſby.

Sir Hec. Generouſly reſolv'd, and I'll ſteer you immediately to my houſe for the purpoſe, if you pleaſe.

Zel. I attend you, Sir Hector—Buſſora, follow me immediately.

Sir Hec. And be aſſur'd, my lad, you ſhan't have one worſe cheer for drawing your cutlaſs in defence of your miſtreſs— Come, madam.

(*Sings*,

" O the very next morning our engagement proved hot,
" And admiral Benbow receiv'd a chain ſhot.

[*Exit with Zelida.*

Buſ. O what fool me was, not to ſee lady how her love Mr. Brownlow!— ſhe take paint away-- Yet I ſo tick in head, I no ſuſpect—But love him ſtrange ting! When I was love at Tanjapour, me was ready to do thouſand mad action for Balſora— O ſhe was heaven hanſome— Fine high check bone— little grey eye — mout wide from ear to ear— and teeth more beautiful as brick duſt—— Then—Yet me am encourage fond idle thought-- when lady bid me follow at Sir Hector Strangeways——

ways —— And muſt ſhe marry him ſhe no love after all— I have a tink! [*Exit.*

The Scene changes to an Apartment at Brownlow's.

Enter BROWNLOW *and* ORMSBY.

Brown. Colonel Ormſby, you are very punctul, yet if reflection, ſince I laſt ſaw you, has made the ſame impreſſion upon your heart, that it has upon mine, I ſhall hope that this call is leſs hoſtile than you originally intended it.

Ormſ. Mr. Brownlow, you deſired that we ſhould have no war of words; I am not therefore come here to talk, but to requeſt your company a mile or two out of town.

Brown. Why ſhould I betray your confidence, when you ſee that I have deriv'd no advantage from the perfidy? Zelida is loſt to me, as well as to you, and unleſs you meant that I ſhould be her jailor, you have no juſt cauſe to be offended with me for her flight.

Ormſ. Mr. Brownlow, Mr. Brownlow! it is plain by the charge in Zelida's letter, of your having driven her away, it is plain by your own confeſſion of adviſing her to marry me, that ſhe has been temper'd with; perhaps you have not in direct, in poſitive words, ſolicited her affection, but there is an inſidious ſmoothneſs of behaviour, a cunning male coquetry, which is more perſuaſive with an innocent mind, than all the ſtudied modes of verbal ſollicitation.

Brown. Yet hear me.

Ormſ. I'll hear no more, Sir, come along with me.

Brown. When you conſider my obligations to you----

Ormſ. They aggravate the injury.

Brown. But they prevent me from drawing my ſword againſt you, and I will not attend you.

Ormſ. I'll brand you as a coward to the whole world.

Brown. What will the good opinion of the whole world ſignify, if I loſe my own?

Ormſ. Draw here, Sir.

Brown. Nay to defend my life--- (*Draws.*

Enter Sir HECTOR, ZELIDA, *Lady* DI, *and* ORSON.

Sir Hec. Hey! what the devil latitude are we in here?

Ormſ. My deareſt Zelida!

Zel. O there's my hand, Colonel Ormſby—You muſt not kill your beſt, your trueſt friend.

Brown. To what are we indebted for this happy revolution?

Lady D. Sir Hector will tell you, brother, when you are reconcil'd to the Colonel.

Brown. That, Madam, is eaſily done.—I ſincerely give you joy, my dear Ormſby.

Ormſ. Brownlow, I feel moſt ſenſibly the unworthineſs of my conduct. I feel alſo how wretched I muſt have been to loſe your friendſhip: can you, indeed, forgive me, and impute all my madneſs to the exceſs of my love?

Sir Hec. Poh man, of what uſe is friendſhip, if it does not teach us to forgive one another's tumbling on the ſea of abſurdity?

Zel. Mr. Brownlow, beſides, knows what it is to be himſelf in love.

Brown

Brown. I do indeed, Madam—know it deſpairingly.

Lady D. Lord, brother, and never conſult me?

Orſ. Nor me, uncle?

Sir Hec. You, you, puppy.—Well, madam, (*to* Zelida) I hope you'll now give me leave to ſalute you as Mrs. Ormſby.

Enter BUSSORA *abruptly.*

Buſſ. O heaven he forbid!

Brown. Why ſo, my honeſt fellow?

Ormſ. Buſſora, what's the matter?

Buſſ. Matter him enough. Lady no like—

Zel. Buſſora, retire this moment.

Ormſ. Permit him, madam, to ſtay; for his intelligence leads to a ſubject, upon which I was going to requeſt your own explanation.

Brown. Why, Buſſora, you are out of your ſenſes.

Sir Hec. Zounds, no interruption---We ſeem doubling the cape of a diſcovery here.

Ormſ. Buſſora, your lady, I much fear, has, from motives of generoſity, honour'd me with her hand, againſt the inclination of her heart.

Buſſ. O, fool ſo great as I ſee that---or why ſhe run away from you?

Zel. This mad-man will betray all!

Brown. But you ſee your lady is come back, you blockhead.

Buſſ. Yes, ſhe come for fear of you fight with Colonel.

Sir Hec. The wind is ſhifted here with a witneſs.

Orſ. And blows freſh againſt the Colonel, father.

Ormſ.

Ormſ. My happineſs, no leſs than my honour, is concern'd in this information.

Buſſ. O, if one of two, he muſt be unhappy---- me rather you unhappy great deal than lady.

Ormſ. Zelida, you are ſincerity itſelf, and you don't contradict Buſſora.

Zel. One cannot force one's inclinations.

Ormſ. I know it too ſenſibly.

Lady D. But if a lady is ready to marry, what more can a gentleman require?

Zel. O! I am ready to marry Colonel Ormſby.

Ormſ. Ah, Zelida! paſſionately as I admire you, neither my pride nor my reaſon can allow me to accept of your hand, if I am not in poſſeſſion of your heart.

Zel. How happy do you make me----O, Mr. Brownlow, did I not ſay, when you advis'd me this morning to marry the Colonel, that he wou'd nobly deſpiſe a reluctant heart?

Ormſ. My dear Brownlow, this is an unexpected ſtroke.

Orſ. Never mind it, Colonel; I'll marry her myſelf, with father's conſent, if ſhe'll lye up in harbour till I come of age.

Sir Hec. Damme, ſo you ſhall boy, if ſhe'll only turn Proteſtant.

Buſſ. Dear lady, make uneaſineſs him all end here.

Zel. What do you mean?

Buſſ. I mean that you ſhou'd no bluſh to be happy. Chriſtian, if him can make lady happy, here him is you know. (*Pointing to* Brownlow.

Zel. Buſſora, never ſee me more---O Lady Di!

Lady D. My own feelings to a tittle, at the firſt diſcovery of my affections for that dear deluder there.

Sir Hec. Me a deluder?

Ormſ. Then we have ſuſtain'd a freſh misfortune, Brownlow.---It wou'd have been ſome comfort to have ſeen Zelida your's, ſince I muſt reſign her for ever: but you are pre-engag'd, and my poor girl, like myſelf, is diſappointed in the firſt ſearch of her heart.

Brown. No, Ormſby, we have ſuſtained no new misfortune, if Buſſora is right in his conjectures; for after ſuch uncommon generoſity on your part, I need not heſitate to own that this angelic creature is the only object of my affections.

Zel. Heavens! is it poſſible!

Sir Hec. Zounds, will the wind never have done ſhifting?

Ormſ. I wou'd offer no violence to Zelida's inclination—Speak, my ſweeteſt girl.

Zel. I cannot ſpeak.

Buſſ. Oh lady, do no fear to tell true.

Brown. My lovely Zelida, look up.

Zel. Your affections are plac'd upon another.

Brown. It was neceſſary to make you think ſo, before I knew the peculiar nobleneſs of Ormsby's ſentiments.

Sir Hec. Come, come, don't let us waſte powder in idle ſalutes.

Zel. I am overwhelm'd with diſtreſs.

Brown. And you ſtill perſiſt in ſaying *no* to my ſolicitation?

Zel. What wou'd you have me ſay?

Brown. I'd have you ſay *yes.*

Zel. Why *no* often means *yes* among the ladies of England, does it not?

Brown. Bewitching creature! thus let me thank you (*kiſſing her hand*)

6 *Ormſ.*

Ormſ. 'Tis my turn to wiſh you joy, Brownlow, and I do it moſt heartily.

Sir Hec. So do we all.——This is a glorious voyage, indeed.

Orſ. And the ſhip may be paid off, father, for there ſeems to be an end on the ſervice.

Lady D. My deareſt ſiſter *(ſalutes Zelida)* this is a ſuperlative bleſſing—and I believe there are not two ſuch women as ourſelves in any one houſe of this kingdom.

Zel. O, Madam, I am too happy---but Buſſora! my faithful Buſſora!

Buſſ. Will you never ſee me more now, lady?

Zel. Mr. Brownlow, Colonel Ormſby, we are all indebted to my good Buſſora, and muſt all think of methods to reward him.

Buſſ. I am too reward in ſee you happy Lady. And Gentoo, you know, he ſcorn any other reward, than him own feelings, for behave like honeſt man.

Zel. What muſt I feel on this occaſion, then? My joy is ſo exceſſive, I think the whole a dream; yet if this company is but pleas'd, my dream will laſt for ever.

[*Exeunt Omnes.*

THE END.

THE REASONABLE LOVER

The Reasonable Lover.

Sir.

This Comedy, call'd The Reasonable Lover, is intended to be perform'd at the Theatre Royal Covent Garden, with the Permission of The Right Hon:^{b} Lord Hertford.

y^{r}. hum:^{b} Ser.^{t}

T. Harris

Feb:^{y} 5th 1776.

Prologue

Hard is his Task in this inconstant Age
Who writes for comic laurels from the Stage,
While public taste still changing like our Dress
Leaves no one sure criterion of success;
The parish 'prentice, when seven years are past,
Can make a shoe with certainty at last,
Can work securely without dread of blame,
To see his Trade and know your foot the same--
Not so the Bard--Tho' serving Twenty years--
He's still distracted by a thousand fears;
nd never sure your humour to discern,
ust still drudge on, and have his Trade to learn.
o day all charm'd with Sentiment wrought high,
ou think it mighty comical to cry.--
Lord Colonel Brag (drawls Lady Jane Spadille)
I'm almost dead . . . Indeed! . . . O monstrous ill--
I saw the fav'rite Comedy last night,

"'Tis a true Comedy--It kill'd me quite--
"So chaste--so polish'd--so extremely deep,
"I wept a Sea--and then fell fast asleep "--
Thrust out of doors poor Sentiment to morrow,
Has ample cause for all her sobs and sorrow;
The wits cry "Damn her with her sniv'ling stuff,
"The Comic Muse can never laugh enough;
"And these dull dogs, who strive to sieze our hearts,
"Are only mongrels of the lowest parts"--
The sober Cit, who leads a weary life,
Between high Taxes, and a scolding wife,
Thinks there's no need for misery to roam,
If pain be pleasure, he may stay at home;
And even the Gods now fond of some thing Funny!
Desire he! he! --a chuckle for their money--
To hit your fancy Gentle folks to night,
We're grave and gay--Pray heav'n we may be right--
For shou'd our Bard too much in dismals flow,
And turn he! he!--to Tragedy-- ho! ho!
You'll quickly crack his melancholy skull,
Tho' wisely cold, and classically dull--
Or shou'd he (thinking your last Winters passion
For downright laughing, still exists in fashion)
To raise a loud, an universal roar,
Take freedomns frequent with the wits of yore,
Your anger then from diff'rent springs may flow,
And mawl the fool as farcical or low;

Yonder he stews--Ay hide your recreant head,
Between ourselves [to the pit] there's room enough for dread.--
--But I've done tolling his dramatic knell,
So wish it bed time, and that all were well.

Epilogue.

Too much, ye fair, our Sex has been confest
The Scribbler's pastime, and the Coxcomb's Jest;
As if no flame of Sentiment refin'd
Cou'd ever blaze within the female mind--
Yet in this circle is there any Son,
Who'd save a father by the risques I run?--
And fly the Maid he fondly may adore
To wed some red fac'd Virgin of threescore.
Since Greece victorious set Old Troy on fire,
We've found but one Eneas to admire,
And he, perhaps, had never deign'd to pack
His poor Papa upon his pious back,
Unless it serv'd him with a decent blind,
To leave a Wife he sicken'd at, behind.
Among the men it seems a constant rule,
To treat each Woman as a pretty fool;
When Maids they scorn us, and when Wives they flout us,
et Wretches, say, what wou'd you be without us?
ur chat indeed is trifling oft perhaps,
e talk of Ribbands, laces, and of Caps;
ut is the Men's confin'd to wiser bounds,
o they ne'er talk of horses, or of hounds?
ften to one--Done first, my Lord--and done,
hose Colt was that?--mine, damn me--I have won--
here stands the bottle--push it round, my boys--
y no, I won't--I don't approve this noise--
u are drunk, Sir John--I am--draw--no pretences--

I'll have your life, to prove I'm in my Senses--
     When women war, they only fight with tongues,
And she must conquer, who's best off in lungs;
We part, incens'd, but quickly meet again,
To murder Friends belongs alone to men--
Out Sex no more, then mighty Sirs despise,
But learn to view us with respectful Eyes;
We're your Superiors in a great degree,
And he who doubts, may be convinc'd by me.

The

Reasonable Lover

A Comedy

Dramatis Personae

Sir James Clifford . . . .
Doctor Wilmington . . . .
Mr Freemore . . . .
Captain Cleveland . . . .
Mr Wyndham . . . .
Mr Lestock . . . .
Doctor Crisis . . . .
Doctor Ravage . . . .
Doctor Hemlock . . . .
Doctor System . . . .
Lady Winterly . . . .
M^{rs} . . . .
Mrs Freemore . . . .
Flavella Freemore . . . .
Urania Wilmington . . . .

The Scene London
Time, the time of Representation

The first Act

Scene and Apartment at Mrs Freemore's

P S ---Enter. Flavella followed by Captain Cleveland

Captn Clev

y dear Miss Freemore, you never can be serious, and this declaration is not he consequence of your real opinion, but the result of your agreeable ivacity--

Miss Free:

y real opinion positively--

Capt. Clev

What that a woman who wou'd be truly happy in marriage shou'd be utterly Indifferent about her husband?--

Miss Free

Nay shou'd have a hearty aversion for him--

Capt Clev

Indeed!--

Miss Free

Indeed! and I am astonish'd that you dont perceive the reason of the sentiment--

Capt Clev

I own it is entirely beyond my Comprehension

Miss Free

Why dont you see that where a woman really loves a husband, she is continually in Agonies about him?--If he is abroad she is miserable for his company; if he is at home she trembles lest he shou'd be weary of her's--If he is in health she shudders at the apprehension of accidents to make him ill, and if he is ill she is torn by a thousand terrors for his recovery--She participates in his very happiness with a secret dread, for fear it shou'd not be lasting And in short,--alive to nothing but the exquisite, feelings of her heart is the constant victim of her own sensibility--

Capt. Clev

And perhaps it is upon this account you determin'd to receive the addresses of Sir James Clifford--

Miss Freemore

Really Captain Cleveland, there is a great deal of modesty in that *perhaps,* considering how fully I have explain'd myself upon the subject of your addresses--

Capt Clev

My dearest Miss Freemore, you shou'd consider my very impertinence as a proof of my Affection--

Miss Free

And by the same mode of reasoning, whenever you are pleas'd to offend me, I am to think you the kindest creature in the universe--However, to leave this fooling, Captain, Cleveland, you are sensible of two things: first that I know but very little of you, and seconly that I have no will but my Fathers--

Capt. Clev

Your Mother's rather Madam; yet tho' our acquaintance has been but short, remember that by accidentially lodging in the same house with you I have been made as fully sensible of your merit in three weeks, as If I had the happiness of knowing you three hundred years--

Miss Free

And this very pretty speech you wou'd positively make to three hundred other women, if you had an equal opportunity of teizing them

Capt Clev

y heav'n, you are neither just to yourself nor me, Madam; and I will onvince you this moment of my sincerity

Miss Free

have no right to put your sincerity to the Test, Sir--

Capt. Clev

t I have a right to prove it Madam, where a doubt of it may affect the ole happiness of my life--Know then--

Miss Free

at--?

Capt Clev

That I am all a Cheat

Miss Free:

Sir!

Capt Clev,

That I have no more Titles to a Cockade than to a blue ribbon--

Miss Free:

Bless me--

Capt Clev:

That my name is not Cleveland!

Miss Free:

No--

Capt Clev:

No--But Wilminton--

Miss Free:

Wilmington!

Capt Clev:

Yes I am the son of that Doctor Wilmington! -- He introduc'd me by the name of Cleveland, and my passion for you is the sole cause of my present Transformation

Miss Free:

Very whimsical truly, and so all these Arguments of your artifice good Mr Wilmington, you wou'd have me receive as so many proofs of your Sincerity!

Capt Clev

And why not, my dearest creature, when you Consider the nature of my Situation--

Miss Free

What had your Situation to do in the case? You are an only Son, I have heard the Doctor say that you were bred up with a fond grandfather in Ireland, whose Estate you are to Inherit--

Capt Clev:

And have you not heard my father also say that, fearful the growing Indulgence of the Irish Grandfather would spoil his only Son, he had lately sent for him over with a view of marrying him to a woman of large fortune?--

Miss Free

I have--But what then--?

Capt Clev

When then, in one word, I had just arrived in London and was winging to my Fathers in Doctors Commons, the first time I had the happiness of seeing you--The Coach, in which you were with your mother, broke Down you know--

Miss Free

And were you but that moment came to Town?--

Capt Clev

That very moment You seem'd greatly terrified and to avoid the gathering of a crowd, your mother, at my entreaties, condescended to let me set you both down

Miss Free

Yes you provoking Creature; and when you found that we were only in lodgings here, I observ'd with what eagerness you agreed with the people of the house for the Second Floor--

Capt Clev

Consider that I had one woman to avoid; at whose idea my soul now sicken'd; nd another to sollicit, upon whom I had plac'd my everlasting happiness--

Miss Free:

Bravo!

Capt Clev

rigid Father expected my arrival every moment, and I must either have orefeited his favour entirely, or entirely relinquish'd all hope's of you-- hus circumstanc'd, I thought it prudent to change my name

Miss Free:

To conceal your being in Town?--

Capt Clev

Yes--

Miss Free:

And yet it was whimsical enough that the very father you wanted to avoid, shou'd be one of the first persons you became acquainted with, in our family--

Capt Clev

It was so--Yet when your father presented me to him, even in my assum'd name, I was terrified at the attention, with which he survey'd me, tho' the differemce between ten and twenty two; had luckily plac'd me beyond the reach of his recollection

Miss Free

And pray, may I ask you, how long you mean to continue in masquerade

Capt Clev

Till you consent to be mine, or till you bid me despair forever--

Miss Free

Poh! dont be ridiculous,--

Capt Clev--

Little I know is to be expected from my fathers Indulgence for with grief I own, his views are entirely bent on fortune but I am his inseparable Companion as Captain Cleveland, and the old Gentleman has let me in to so many secrets relative to his own Character that I fancy, in a short time, he will scarcely venture to deny me his forgiveness even where I act most repugnantly to his Inclination--

---

Mrs Freemore behind

---

walk in pray, Doctor Wilmington--Mr Freemore, persuade Doctor Wilmington to walk in--

Miss Free

As I live, my mother, and she has order'd me positively to converse no longer alone with you--

Capt Clev:

I'll say I stept down stairs to speak with your father

Miss Free:

No, for heav'ns sake, run up to your own apartment--My father, Tho' the best of men--

Capt Clev

Is like many another poor Man, no more than the second person in his own family

<u>[Exit Cleveland]</u>

<u>Enter</u> Mrs Freemore, Doctor Wilmington, and Mr Freemore

Mrs Free

Bless me, Flavella, what's the matter--You seem exceedingly confus'd

Miss Free

Confus'd Madam!

Mrs Free

Yes confus'd Madam!--Then see how frightfully your head is dress'd child--

Doctor Wilm

Nay, Madam I think Miss Freemores hair is dress'd with great elegance

Mr Freemore

I wish, my dear, you wou'd pay as much regard to your own dress, as Flavella does to hers

Mrs Free

And what business has a married woman to throw away her time in the fallals of dress and such trumpery

Doctor Wilm

But why, Madam if you despise dress yourself, shou'd you be so attentive about the appearance of Miss Freemore

Mrs Free

Because she is not yet married, Doctor Wilmington--when she is, she has my Free consent to be as indifferent as she pleases about her person--

Miss Free

Dear Madam

Mr Free

Her husband will be very much oblige to you my dear

Mrs Free

Go child, to your own room--and make yourself fit to be seen Sir James Clifford will be here presently

Miss Free

I obey your commands, Madam--What will become of me? [aside and <u>Exit</u>

Mr Free

Pray, Doctor, have you seen Sir James this morning?--

Doctor Wilm

Really Mr Freemore, tho I have the greatest regard in the world for Sir James, the growing peculiarilies of his disposition have not, of late, suffer'd me to see him with much satisfaction, except in concluding the treaty which is by Mr Lestock's means, to make an union between our Families.

Mrs Free

Sir James is, for all that, the best of Men, Doctor

Mr Free

And a Man of excellent sense too, tho' he sets up for a general reformer

Doctor Wilm

True--Yet--Rigidly attach'd to what is rationally right, he disdains to do many things, which custom has render'd absolutely necessary: and this humour grows upon him so strongly, that some people already begin to question the soundness of his Intellects

Enter a Servant

Servant

Lady Winterly Madam

Mrs Free

Shew her ladyship in you Booby--You shou'd always shew a lady up without asking--

Doctor Wim

This is an early visit for my Sister, Madam

Mr Free

And the Honour is encreas'd, as it is wholly unexpected--

Enter lady Winterly

Lady Winterly

My dear Mrs Freemore

Mrs Free

Your ladyships most devoted

Lady Win:

Mr Freemore I am overjoy'd to see you--

Lady Win

Brother good morning--Well , Mrs Freemore, tho' I take great shame to myself for not having call'd upon you these thousand years, I have more candour than to claim any merit from my visit--I was going to my Brother on some very particular business, when seeing his Chariot at your door, I judg'd he was here, and so took the Liberty of breaking in upon you--

Mrs Free:

I am always happy in any opportunity of seeing lady Winterly

Lady Win

You are too kind--I met Mr Lestock in my way to you Brother

Doctor Wilm

I have appointed him to call upon me here--Did you speak

Lady Win

Yes; and he obligingly told me that, hearing I was very fond of experimental Philosophy, he wou'd treat me, any morning I chose with the suffocation of some pigeons in the air-pump

Mr Free

Truly, a delicate kind of a Treat for a lady

Lady Win

Lord, Mr Freemore, did you never shoot a woodcock or a partridge for your diversion?--

Mr Free

I wou'd no more shoot a bird for diversion in the field, Madam than I wou'd put it to death for amusement in the cage

Doctor Wilm

You have been a hunter however in your time

Mr Free

Never: I am fool enough not to take a pleasure in wantonly torturing these humbler heirs of creation; and think that their slaughter shou'd be at least delay'd to the hour of necessity

Mrs Free

O I can't bear to torture any thing

Doctor Wilm

Unless her husband lady Winterly--

Lady Win

But where are you going Mr Freemore?--

Mr Free

No ceremony dear Madam--You have business with your Brother Exit

Doctor Wilm

But, Mrs Freemore, you are not likewise determin'd to rob us of your Company?--

Mrs Free

Only going to give a few directions about dinner--Will you eat a morsel with us?--We have Nothing but a couple of chickens reard by my own hand's, which I have just order'd to be kill'd, a pig Whipp'd to death, and dish of roasted Lobsters--Exit

Lady Win:

There's a woman of sensibility for you

Doctor Wilm:

Well, Sister, how have you left Urania?--

Lady Win:

In a thousand terrors--

Doctor Wilm

What, on Lestocks account?--

Lady Win:

Yes--and I beg you will think no more of this match, as she never can forget the other Nephew--

Doctor Wilm:

The other Nephew? what nonsense, when she knows, that he has been dead these ten days!--

Lady Win

Consider that you taught her yourself to look upon M[r] Wyndham as her husband, and that a Day was set apart for her marriage with him: I was in France at the time, and never saw Mr Wyndham if I had not immediately come over upon the receipt of your letter, and taken the poor Girl to live along with me, you wou'd have no daughter now, to exercise your tyranny upon

Doctor Wilm

And was I a tyrant when I gave her the Man of her heart in the fellow she pitifully whimpering after--

Lady Win:

Your indulgence proceeded from Wyndham's being the favourite Nephew of Sir James Clifford--Yet I hear that, with all his faults, he was neither destitute of good nature nor generosity

Doctor Wilm:

O! I admit that he had a very agreeable way of doing many things, which in strict justice, send a man to Tyburn--

Lady Win

If you had suffer'd Urania to open any of the letters, he sent from France perhaps he wou'd not have appear'd so much in fault--

Doctor Wilm

His Uncle, who lov'd him with a fathers fondness, thought him an abandon'd profligate, as well as myself--and you know, with all his singularities, Sir James is equally remakable for benevolence and Understanding--

Lady Win

And a fine proof he gave of both, when he not only refus'd to read a line which the poor young fellow sent over in his defence, but prevail'd upon you to be equally deaf to his justification---nay he carries his resentment beyond the grave, and has neither gone into mourning himself, nor suffers M[r] Lestock to pay that little tribute to the memory of his Cousin--

Doctor Wilm

'Sdeath, Madam, Wyndham's conduct was beyond the possiblity of justification--Did'nt he, on the day appointed for his marriage with your neice, instead of waiting upon her to church, fight a duel about another woman: and leave the heir of a noble family desperate wounded, because he wou'd'nt surrender up a Girl of the Town (perhaps) the proceeding evening? Did'nt he--

Lady Win:

If it is the same thing to you, Brother, to be in a passion sitting as standing I'll help you to a Chair: for your stamping about in this porterly manner quite distracts my head

Doctor Wilm:

Zounds what wou'd you have me do?--

Lady Win:

Not force your daughter into a marriage which must render her miserable--

Doctor Wilm

If you love me, Sister, don't oppose my views--But on the contrary prepare Urania to give M[r] Lestock every possible encouragement--He's a man after my own heart;--know's the world--

Lady Wilm

Really, brother, you pay your own heart no mighty compliment in the comparison

Wilm

And why so pray?

Lady Wiln:

Because in the Little I have seen in Lestock, he appears deep, designing and avaracious--

Wilm:

The three Qualities in the world which I wou'd soonest desire in a Son in law--

Lady Win:

You astonish me

Wilm

Ah! they are the best wear--&--tear accomplishments, a man can possess in these Times: for they will not only prevent him from running into any foolish Actions himself but enable him to profit by the follies of every body else--

Lady Win:

Give your daughter's feelings but a little respite; for there can be not doubt of her having as good an offer in point of fortune, at any time

Doctor Wilm

You dont reflect that all the great Estate, which Sir James Clifford possesses, will probably go to her children

Lady Win

Sir James is a going to be Married, you know, and may have Children himself--

Doctor Wilm

He is fool enough, with all his wisdom, to be violently in love with the Girl indeed, tho'--he has not known her above a month--But I think he shall not marry her--

Lady Win:

How can you prevent it?

Doctor Wilm

By getting a handsome, forward, brisk young fellow to supplant him--You have heard me talk of a Captain Cleveland--

Lady Win

Yes--That lodges in the second floor here

Doctor Wilm

This young Fellow is deeply Smitten with Flavella, and the Girl, I can easily see, returns his passion very Cordially

Enter Footman

Footman

Mr Lestock, Sir, Enquires for you

Doctor Wilm

Sister, will you give me leave--?

Lady Win

O', by all means--I'll step in to my friend's in the next room

Doctor Wilm

Desire Mr Lestock to walk up

Footman

Yes Sir--[Exit]

Lady Win

Ay follow your own plan, but, take my word, it is a very foolish thing [Exit]

Enter Lestock

Les't

Well, my dear Sir, have you spoke to Cleveland--?

Doctor Wilm:

No, but I intend it immediately--

Les

You know what expedition our little plot requires, to prevent Freemores rapacity from precipitating my Uncle into the marriage with Flavella

Doctor Wilm

To be sure I do--

Les:

Every moment is pregnant with danger, till Sir James is rescu'd from the fangs of this harpy

Doctor Wilm

Well well--I'll only speak one word to my Sister, and attend you directly to the Captain-- EXIT

Les

So, every thing succeeds to my utmost wish--The report, which I have caused to be circulated of Wyndahms death, is attended with all the delicious consequences I forsaw: and Sir James has not only chearful consented to give me the Estate design'd for my Rival, but I shall obtain the woman of my heart into the bargain--The sole circumstance which can now defeat my project, is the premature return of Wyndham yet he will scarcely venture back, while his antagonist is in danger, and I have given Dr Crisis, who attends this antagonist, as physician, a five hundred pound Bond to keep his patient confind for a fortnight longer; before the expiration of that period, Miss Wilmington must be mine: and I shall as well be rescu'd from all the miseries of a beggarly dependence, as from all the pangs of a disappointed love. It wou'd be lucky however, if I cou'd have trusted Wilmington with the secret of Wyndam's being alive, as he wou'd then see a reason for hastening the--celebration of the ceremony: but tho' I am such a favorite with him, his daughter has still stronger claims upon his Indulgence, and he might think of re-establishing his former son in law elect, especially as that wou'd equally promote the Interest of his family--

Enter Wilmington

Wilmington

Well I am now ready for the Captain

Les

That's right: he pays the highest regards to your opinion and, wont want much advising upon any point, which has your approbation

Doctor Wilm

Why it was from a view of making the fool answer our purpose with regard to Flavella, that I cultivated his acquaintance so intimately--There's judgmen & There's forecast for you

Les

Exquisite Sir, exsquisite: and Cleveland is admirably calculated to answer our ends.

Dr. Wilm

Ful of the ingenuous fire of youth--As they now a days politely phrase Extravagances

Les

A great despiser of money --ha ha ha--

Dr Wilm

And consequently the most proper son-in-law upon earth for our Friend Freemore--Zounds, if the Dog was mine, I wou'd nt leave him even a shilling to buy a halter

Les

I understand that his father is a man of fortune

Dr Wilm

Yes some prodigal puppy like himself, I suppose, who deserves to be punish'd in this manner for teaching his son no better principles EXEUNT

The Scene changes to Lady Winterly's

An Apartment

Miss Wilm

Wyndham--Wyndham--

Wyndham

My Angel--

Miss Wilm

Not so loud--My Aunt is gone out and will call at my fathers, to intercede for me as she promis'd

Wynd

I dread the Severity of his Temper--

Miss Wilm

So do I--But the more we endeavour to complete our wishes by proper measures, the less we shall have to reproach ourselves with, if we are ever driven to extremities

Wynd

You know my life, that, on my first coming from France in the capacity of a Footman with your Aunt, I propos'd to discover myself at once and avow my innocence to our families, as all my letters had been cruelly returnd unopen'd

Miss Wilm

But dear Wyndham, what poorfs have you of that innocence? a stern unrelenting father is not so soon to be appeas'd as a fond woman whose happiness depends upon believing you utterly unculpable

Wynd

My uncle, at least, knows that, tho I have been dissipated, I have never been despicable, Urania--

Miss Wilm:

But recollect the ill offices, which that Coxcomb Lestock has done you

Wynd

The Report, however, which he has circulated of my death, has been luckily of much service

Miss Wilm

In preventing any suspicion of your being in England

Wynd:

Yes: and Doctor Crisis, the only person, besides yourself, who knows of my return

Miss Wilm

And who is the best creature alive--

Wynd

Will not only keep an eye upon all Lestocks motions, but exert his utmost influence to re-establish me in the opinion of my Uncle

Miss Wilm

For the very reasons, there is no necessity to be precipitate in you discovery

Wynd:

Well, I am govern'd wholly by you: and acknowledge that we shall stand in need of more than justice, to have my story credited

Wilm

I have told you so all along--For your flying, the night before our intended marriage, to the assistance of a lady, who scream'd from a chair in the street--Your rescuing her from the violence of a Ruffan--Your being attack'd by this Ruffian early next morning, and your leaving him desperately wounded--I say, your doing all this thro' pure disinterested regard for virtue

Wynd

Do you doubt my story Urania?

Miss Wilm

My dear Wyndham; I want no justification of your conduct If I did not believe you a man of honour, I wou'd scorn to be your wife tho I lov'd you to distraction--The Barbarian, you wounded, indeed tells his tale, you know greatly in his own favour--

Wynd:

To what, my love, will not any man descend, who is capable of insulting a woman? Yet--if I was not devoted most passionately to you, what cou'd induce me to return from a secure assylum to encounter, mortification, to encounter danger and disgrace?--

Miss Wilm

No more, I beseech you--

Wynd

This habit is humiliating, Urania, to a man not meanly born and my adversary is still in danger: But neither death nor disgrace was painful to me as your Tears: and I came to dry them up, or to perish at your Feet

Miss Wilm

And did I, either with a mean resentment give way to reproaches when I saw you, or with a foolish jealousy, once question the sincerity of your heart? No I believed you true, the instant you told me so and I insist as a reward, that you will keep yourself concealed in your present Character, till your adversary, at least, is out of danger

Wynd:

Bewitching flatterer! to make the exercise of your authority a proof of your affection! But I promise implicit obedience--And yet, Urania you can little guess what a fordimable Rival you will have by enjoining my continuance in this Character

Miss Wilm

Pray explain yourself

Wynd.

Why woud you imagine that this fortunate figure of mine has kindled a flame in the bosom of the old house keeper

Miss Wilm

Mrs Glowworm--

Wynd

Tis scarcely credible to think how the poor woman persecutes me with proofs of her affection

Miss Wilm

I am glad you have got some amusement under-ground.

Wynd. If I stay but another week in your kitchen she'll absolutely kill me with kindness--she makes her approaches to my heart thro the larder

Miss Wilm

As I live, my rival is hobbling up stairs--Fall into your distance--

Enter M^{rs} gloworm

Mrs Glow

Madam my lady is Returnd

Miss Wilm

Where is my Aunt?

Mrs Glow

In the back parlour, Madam, with the arch deacon, putting seals upon the old Hock, that was brought home last night by the Dutch Smugglers--I hav'd sav'd a bottle for your drinking Mr William (aside

Wynd

I thank you Mrs Gloworm

Miss Wilm

Well, William, I have no more commands for you at present

Wynd

I shall pay the strictest attention to those you have been pleas'd honour me with Madam-- (EXIT)

Mrs Glow (aside

I dont believe the first dancer in the playhouse cou'd make a Genteeler bow

Miss Wilm

Tell my Aunt--that I shall wait upon her immediately EXIT

Mrs Glow

Poor Soul! she looks sadly--I dont wonder at it--Tis a Terrible thing to lose the man one love; and to be forc'd to take the man one hates I never saw Mr. Wyndham But I have heard the Servants say that he was the best natur'd creter in the world--And so fond of my sausages! But now to warm a Glass of the old Hock with a little sugar and to have a minutes chat with Mr William in my parlour EXIT

The End of the First Act

The Second Act

The Scene, Cleveland's Lodgings

Wilmington Lestock and Cleveland discover'd

Les

That's spirited my dear boy--

Wilm

So it is, and I heartily applaud your noble resolution of disregarding all pecuniary considerations, and flying off with Miss Freemore

Clev

What a couple of kind friends I have--and yet I fear you reckon too confidently upon Miss Freemore's consent Gentlemen

Les

Why so--?

Clev

She has an uncommon dignity of mind, you know, and solely consented upon her fathers account (whose affairs are greatly embarrass'd) to receive the addresses of Sir James

Wilm

What signifys that? she is in love, and I'll at any time stake the softness of such a woman's heart, against the dignity of her Mind my dear Captain

Clev

Well, it shan't be my fault if we are'nt on the road to Scotland this very Evening

Les

Bravo!--And since Sir James will be ultimatley as much oblig'd to you as Miss Freemore, the Doctor and I are bound to assist your expedition, to the utmost of our ability

Wilm

Doubtless--But our concern in this affair must a profound secret Cleveland

Clev

I see the necessity of your caution

Les

I am glad of it, for the world might say that we were actuated by illiberal motives--You understand me

Clev:

I do--I do--

Wilm

And it might be believed that instead of wishing to serve you to save poor Miss Freemore from am improper match, and finally to snatch Sir James from the Talons of a particular Vulture, we were meanly Desir'ous to prevent the honest baronet from marrying at all

Clev:

Very right--very right; and in this age of distraction men of honour cannot be too nice about the purity of their Character--they imagine me a precautions dupe, I fancy (aside--

Les [aside to Wilmington]

The fellow is a greater fool, than I, imagin'd him

Wilm

Zoundes, does'nt he disregard money and what farther proof wood you have of his stupidity--

Enter a Servant

Servant

Sir James Clifford is below at M^{r} freemores, sir, if you are disengag'd, will do himself the pleasure of waiting upon you

Clev

My Compliments to Sir James and I shall be very proud to receive the favour of his Visit

Servt

Very well Sir EXIT

Clev

Can you guess the reason of the honour intended me by Sir James?

Les

Yes he wants to speak to you about some reports which he has heard of Flavella's regard for you--

Wilm

Reports, which we have carefully circulated, Cleveland, tho' to his face we are oblig'd to express our highest approbation of the match

Clev

I wonder he has not spoken to Flavella on the subject

Les

Mrs Freemore has so firmly persuaded him of Flavella's passion, and he so firmly believes his Character an object of universal admiration, that he has hitherto treated the Reports in Question with the utmost ridicule

Clev

Something might surely be made out of this--and it is a matter of indifference by what means the match is broken off

Wilm

I am afraid not: unless we could work him up indeed to require some ridiculous proof of Miss Freemore's affection

Enter a Servant

Servant

Sir James Clifford Sir

Enter Sir James

Captain Cleveland, your most humble servant, Doctor, well met--well met, nephew Lestock--

Clev

Sir James, I am highly honour'd by your visit

Sir James

It is a visit of business, Captain Cleveland--

Les:

I have been giving the Captain a hint of the business, Sir James

Wilm

And he declares you the happy Lover, notwithstanding all the reports which you have heard to the contrary

Sir James

Be candid, Captain, for if Miss Freemore entertains any sentiments of a tender nature for you, I wou'd neither be barbarous enough to stand in the way of her wishes, nor foolish enough to think of marrying any woman who must consider me with aversion

Clev

It is impossible for me, Sir James, to give you proof of what you desire to know

Sir James

I thought as much

Wilm

But tell Sir James, whether you think Mrs Freemore has deceiv'd him in regard to her daughter's affections--

Clev

I do think she has deceiv'd him most egregiously--

Les

Impossible!--I know Miss Freemore's whole soul is my Uncles--Doctor, mind how I shall play upon this delightful instrument--

Sir James

Why I am vain enough to believe that she does not think me altogether contemptible nephew Lestock--

Wilm

And I dare say Sir James you are at all events determind to try the Justice of the Captains conjecture

Clev

By what means?

Sir James

A private conversation with Flavella on the subject

Clev

Flavella, in your interview, can do more than consent to marry you

Sir James

She shall do more--She shall satisfy my Judgment and declare in plain unequivocal Terms, that I am the object of her love

Les

Admirable my dear Sir, this will clear the fact beyond the Question

Wilm

A half declaration of love wou'd'nt serve me, if I was in Sir James's place--It will do Lestock

Clev

O Flavella will not stick at triffles, to remove the Distresses of her Father

Sir James

That's true

Les

Poh I am so convinc'd of her tenderness for my uncle, that I am sure he may have any proof he pleases of her love, consistent with her honour

Sir James

Without vanity I am persuaded I may--She is peculiarly amiable sets infintely greater store by the beauties of the mind than the circumstance of youth Captain Cleveland or the graces of the person.

Wilm

Very true--And therefore, besides a verbal declaration of her love, if I was Sir James, she sho'd honour me with a voluntary kiss, or some other such innocent mark of her affection--

Clev

But won't this be violating all decorum,--

Les

Right Sir--Common forms are for commen men--

Sir James

True, and a rational lover will be directed by nothing but reason

Wilm

Then Sir James, to put an end to all doubts, the sooner you proceed to the proof the better

Sir James

Well observ'd--And so confident am I of a triumph, that if you will all take the trouble to be in Mr Freemores Library, about a Quarter of an hour, you shall over hear our conversation--

Clev

It will be impossible to overhear you at such a distance, Sir James--

Sir James

I'll speak loud on purpose--Common forms for Comme Men Lestock

Les

True, Sir, true

Sir James

But rational Lovers are only regulated by Reason EXIT

Wilm

Zounds I never saw such a fool, as this fellow of superlative wisdom

Les

Why this exceeds my utmost hopes

Clev

And mine too--He'll alarm Flavella's delicacy in an instant

Wilm

And produce a repulse that must entirely disappoint his expectations--

Les

As She is an excellent Girl however, there is no knowing how much she will suffer for her fathers sake

Clev

My heart Bleeds for her situation

Wilm

Why then if the worst comes to the worst be prepar'd to press an elopement--Draw upon me for what money you will, if your agent is slack in Remittances

Clev

You woud'nt be oblig'd to any Body, who'd give this advice to your son, Doctor Wilmington

Les

And yet he has told me that his own son is as likely to take this advice, as any he in three kingdoms--?

Wilm

Poh! my Son is a drivellar, and must be kept tightly to the Bridle--He ought to have been here a fortnight ago, but his foolish Grandfather is spoiling him in Ireland

Clev

Suppose we now step down, and see how the land lies at Freemore's

Les

Twill be right but still remember the Elopement

Wilm

Your Father is your Father, and must forgive you in the End

Clev

Why I think so

Les

Nay he must be a damn'd old Scoundrel if he is angry with you at all EXEUNT

Clev

Was there ever so whimsical a confederacy as this in which I am joind with my father? I all along suspected the motive of his pretended friendship for me, in my assum'd name, but I little immagin'd that any combination of circumstances cou'd occur, which wou'd give him so complete an opportunity of counteracting his own purposes--by my Mother's Settlement, I am to have a thousand pound a year allow'd me, when ever I marry with my old Gentlemans consent--in my present pursuit therefore the very means, I am taking to obtain Flavella, furnishes me with the very means of giving her a comfortable establishment at least: and the fraud which my father is practising from the despicable views of Interest sufficiently excuses the stratagem which I have concerted from an Extravagance of love <u>EXIT</u>

<u>Scene</u> <u>An</u> Appartment at Lady Winterly's

Wyndham and Mrs Gloworm at opposite <u>doors</u>

Mrs Glow

O! Mr William, I was just looking for you--You must not mope like a Turkey all alone, as the man says in the play

Wynd

You are too good to me Madam

Mrs Glow

Lord love you! But it does not signify--You have had nothing to comfort you these two hours: and I have order'd the Cook to get a boild chicken with a few Mushrooms in my parlour

Wynd

I am infinitely oblig'd to you, Mrs Gloworm, but the state of my stomach requires no baiting, whatever, betweeen breakfast and dinner

Mrs Glow

Oblig'd to me!--Ah I wish it was in my power to oblige you to be sure I have endeavour'd to shew some regard for you Mr William and nothing has been wanting which my lady's cellar or kitchen cou'd bestow

Wynd

I feel the whole weight of my obligation with the greatest gratitude, Madam--But you have been long exercis'd in acts of goodness--

Mrs Glow

Long exercis'd! Perhaps I am not altogether so old, Sir, as you may imagine--

Wynd

You dont suppose I cou'd be ignorant enought to think of age, while I had the pleasure to view the beauties of that complexion

Mrs Glow

And yet perhaps I am not so young as you think one--What age woud you guess me at now? Come try--& speak honestly--

Wynd

Honestly then, I shou'd guess you to be about eight and twenty--you see I hate flattery

Mrs Glow

You are under the mark, I am almost two and thirty: and I am noway ashamd of my Age, that's what I am not

Wynd (aside

Nor of any thing else, I'll answer for you

Mrs Glow

No. I am no way asham'd of my age, nor have I any reason to be sorry for it either--For I have the best of proffers, I can assure you Mr William, if I was inclind to accept them

Wynd

Ah! Mrs Gloworm the fire of those eyes must do considerable execution

Glow

You are not mistaken--I might have a common Counsil man of London to morrow if I lik'd it as genteel a man as ever you saw--only he has the misfortune to stutter a little, and has got a wooden Leg--

Wynd

How the devil shall I get quit of this Hag-- (aside

Mrs Glow

But my heart is otherwise engaged, Mr William--Tis I confess--Lord my face is as red as scarlet now

Wynd

Your face is all sweetness, and sensibility Madam

Mrs Glow

Ah you are a coaxing creature!--And if you were not so distant

Wynd

Dont be offended with me, Madam, for behaving with proper respect

Mrs Glow

Respect! Lord that's so cold Mr William--You are not so cold to that broad fac'd blouze Molly,--the Housemaid--tho to my knowledge there is a woman in every degree above you, who O! Mr William!--[Seizing his hand

Wynd (aside

I must cry out for assistance

Mrs Glow

I protest you shant kiss me

ENTER Lady Winterly

Lady Win

Mrs Gloworm!

Mrs Glow

Madam!

Lady Win

What is the cause of this very extraordinary behaviour?--But leave the room--I'll talk with you presently--

Wynd

I'll sneak off before it comes to my turn

Lady Win

Stay you here, Sir--

Wynd

Yes, Madam,

Mrs Glow

Madam, I assure your Ladyship there was no harm in the matter. William was only struggling for an innocent salute, by way of joke

Lady Win

An innocent salute

Wynd

No more upon my honour Madam

Lady Win

Your honour! and and innocent salute! leave the room Mistress

Mrs Glow

Lord! what a fuss is here about no one earthly thing--I can easily guess the reason of it--She likes William herself & must not let him know it, for fear he should be taken with her fortune <u>EXIT</u>

Wynd (aside

So I am in a blessed situation--

Lady Win (aside

I must accellerate matters I see, or this Gentlewoman will prevent me--So Sir you are a man of great Gallantry

Wynd

I am sorry to have offended your ladyship--

Lady Win

I wonder where your confidence will stop, if you behave with familiarity to the principal Servant in my house

Wynd

If your lady ship will only pardon this offence you shall never again have reason to censure my presumption

Lady Win

Nay, William, I am not so angry at the presumption as I am fearful of the consequence; freedoms beget freedoms, you know and the passions are doubtless, as violent under a livery, as under a Ducal Coronet, William

Wynd

It is not for me to reason with your ladyship but to obey your Commands

Lady Win

Then let me command you for the future to avoid all familarities with Gloworm

Wynd

Your ladyship may be entirely satisfy'd that I shall--What the Devil does she mean to drive at?

Lady Win

Where are you going? For tho she is old enough to have more sense you are a very likely young Fellow, and theres no knowing how far she may be tempted

Wynd

Your ladyship is pleas'd to be merry with me--

Lady Win

Stay where you are, I tell you--I am not at all merry. I speak but an obvious truth, and I even know some women of fashion, who have married Footmen with less acomplishments

Wynd

She'll make love to me herself--Then they had great reason to blush for their condescension, Madam--

Lady Win

And why so, Sir? Suppose a lady of fashion was to entertain a partiality for yourself, wou'd she have reason to blush for her condescension--

Wynd (aside)

I must parry this thrust--

Lady Win

What do you say

Wynd

Really, Madam, it wou'd be very vain in me not to think so

Lady Win

Then you think like a Spiritless Fool--

Wynd

I hope, Madam, I shou'd never forget my due Distance

Lady Win

Not you blockhead, if the lady wou'd her superiority?--

Wynd

I don't see, Madam why, because the Lady shou'd chuse to do a mean action, that I shou'd commit an insolent one--

Lady Win

I have no patience

Wynd

I'll withdraw, Madam, if you please

Lady Win

Ah quit my sight this instant

Wynd

s, Madam

Lady Win

stay where you are, I did not, William, expect to find you so ignorant

Wynd [aside

dare be sworn, you did not

Lady Win

stinctions in rank are accidental

Wynd

ur ladyship, however, knows that they must be kept up

Lady Win

fools indeed, who prefer the opinion of the world to their own happiness-- ve you no ambition, William?--

Wynd

s Madam: to be a Butler

Lady Win

be a butler!--But suppose you were rais'd to a situation, which shou'd able you to keep a Butler of your own?

Wynd

an honest way, Madam--I shou'd like it greatly: but I'll not buy a ach and six, at the expence of my Character

Lady Win

the expence of your character!--At the expence of your character: y Ass! Ideot Lunatic!--I can support it no longer [Rings the Bell]

Wynd

unds I have gone too far

Lady Win

He cant be such a driveller, surely, as to misunderstand me--No the fellow is laughing at me--And he shall instantly be turned out of the house

ENTER Gloworm

Glow

Did your ladyship ring, Madam?--

Lady Win

Yes my ladyship did ring Madam--There is a Gentleman who trembles exceedingly for his Character, and consequently is not a fit companion for you in any house

Glow

Madam!

Wynd

Your ladyship does not mean to discharge me, I hope--

Lady Win

Yes, for a fool, or a hypocrite--Do you pay him his wages Madam and see that he is immediately dismiss'd from my family--An insensible--stupid--See that my orders are directly executed or prepare to follow that miracle of Character EXIT

Mrs Glow

Lord, Mr William what have you done?--

Wynd

What I ought to be turn'd out of any Widow-lady's house for

Glow

What's that pray--

Wynd

Nothing--

Glow

I dont understand you--But, since matters are, as they are this is no time to stand upon ceremony

Wynd

What do you mean?

Mrs Glow

I have sav'd 700 in my ladys Family, besides very good Cloathes, a little furniture, and a few pretty bits of plate.

Wynd

Well!

Mrs Glow

Spare my blushes dear Mr William--make these things lawfully yours, and we'll leave the family together--that's what we will

Wynd

You are too generous Mrs Glowworm

Mrs Glow

To be sure it wou'd have been better, if we were married, to have staid with my lady, because we could have liv'd upon the fat of the land, and cou'd have kept cribbing, and cribbing you understand me

Wynd

I do--I do

Mrs Glow

But as it is--Yet stay a thought strikes me, suppose I get Miss Wilmington to speak for you to my lady--She's the sweetest creature in the world

Wynd

And the most obliging

Mrs Glow

I'll to her this moment--and if the worst comes to the worst we can take a Country Teahouse in Marybone and have Shampetres of our own as well as the best of them--<u>EXIT</u>

Wynd

Generously concluded my dear Mrs Gloworm

The Scene changes to another Apartment

ENTER M^{r} and Mrs Freemore

Mr Free

How can you snap one up so perpetually? I protest before Company my dear you make me half afraid to open my mouth

Mrs Free

I suppose, you'd have me behave with the Turtle-like softness of Mrs Flimsy the Vicars wife, who was discover'd in an intrigue with the recruiting officer--I'd have you know that I am a woman of character Mr Freemore

Mr Free

I know your purity very well, my love, but does it necessarily follow that you must be always destroying the tranquility of your husband

Mrs Free

Yes, and you are angry at my appearance too? You want a virtuous woman to make a study of Dress, as if she was as if she was a Common customer of the Green Boxes at the play house

Mr Free

Heigh ho!

Mrs Free

What's that Heigh ho for? Is it because you think Captain Cleveland a much proper husband for your daughter than Sir James

Mr Free

Why, I must own my love, that from the similitude of their years, the Captain wou'd be more likely to make her happy than this man, who is half mad with the goodness of his understanding

Mrs Free

I dare say, you do--But will a Captains half-pay make your daughter's fortune, or extricate you out of your difficulties

Mr Free

I tremble to retrieve my Affairs, my dear, at the expence of my child's felicity--I am afraid she likes the Captain

Mrs Free

And for that very reason I wish the Cockaded Coxcomb fairly out of the house

Mr Free

Nay, my dear, dont distress the poor Girl unnessarily; you know it was a generous desire to remove our difficulties, which at first induc'd her to hear of Sir James's overtures--As she therefore sacrafices her feelings to our convenience

Mrs Free

You talk like an Ideot, as you generally do, Mr Freemore--Sacrifice indeed! --A mighty sacrifice, to get a good husband, a large Jointure a Coach and Six, and Title! --O that any body, when I was Flavella's age, had ask'd me to made such a Sacrifice

Mr Free

, that there had with all my soul, for then I shou'd not have been lagu'd with the greatest termagant in the Universe

Mrs Free

hat's that you say you barbarian?

Mr Free

say my dear, that I'll send Flavella to you, if you'll promise to be entle with her <u>EXIT</u>

Mrs Free

If this old fool, Sir James, shou'd want to <u>break</u> off the match after proceeding so far--he shall find-- <u>ENTER FLAVELLA</u>

Mrs Free

So Miss. . . why so melancholly? Meditating on Captain Cleveland I suppose--

Miss Free

Dear Madam, it is cruel to reproach me with sentiments, which I am determin'd to conquer, out of obedience to your commands

Mrs Free

I have told you, that Sir James suspects you have no affection for him

Miss

His suspicious shall never be justified by my conduct, Madam

Mrs Free

We'll he's now in the house, and means to have a private conversation with you--I believe, relative to your sentiments for him--Take care therefore, child--you understand me--

Miss Free

Madam why will you wring my heart? I know the distresses of my father's situation-- and if it necessary, can lay Down my life to remove them

Mrs Free

Why did'nt you put on a little rouge as I desir'd you?

Miss Free

Really Madam I dont think paint becomes a Modest Woman

Mrs Free

Not become a modest woman! Why child it is universally worn at Court, and the Boxes at the playhouse every night are quite a Gallery of pictures--You have a very fine Arm Flavella, and shou'd never have both your gloves on at a Time

Miss Free: I think I hear Sr James

Mrs Free

Well, I'll love you then: but recollect that much depend's upon your conduct in this Interview

Miss Free

I do Madam--I do--

Mrs Free

Throw out all your attractions now, to rivet him eternally, for, I fear he means to fly off

Miss Free

He's just at the door

Mrs Free

I am gone--your Timid eye upon the Ground--now and then a sigh with an irresolute stammer in the Accent--Your head some times pull'd so--

Miss Free

Here he is, Madam

Mrs Free

Ah I cou'd have done it once, but I never had the opportunity <u>EXIT</u>

Miss Free

Mercy upon me! a humiliating Scene am I to go thro'

ENTER Sir James

Sir James

My dear Miss Freemore your most obedient

Miss Free

Wont you please to be seated Sir James?--

Sir James

I will, and be seated near you my lovely creature: I want to have a little serious conversation with you

Miss Free (aside

This is very extraordinary--But this man is all peculiarity

Sir James

I have been told my dear Miss Freemore by Cleveland and others and by people who affect to be mighty wise (notwithstanding the ready acquiescence which you have shewn to be mine, in the treaty subsisting between us) that your compliance is rather an Act of Duty to your family, than a proof of your affection for the intended husband

Miss Free

You distress me exceedingly, Sir James

Sir James

Bewitching creature, I thought I shou'd distress you: dont tremble so-- For I give no credit whatever to the report, tho it was indeed added, that your affections were plac'd upon Captain Cleveland

Miss Free

This is a very disagreeable subject, Sir James--Yet I defy the world to prove that I have ever given the least encouragement to any addresses from Cleveland

Sir James

I believe it, my Angel!--I believe it sincerely--and have too high an Opinion of your good sense, not to think you see a greater probability of happiness with a Man of my turn, than with any young fellow in the Kingdom

Miss Free

It will always be my study, Sir James, to promote your happiness

Sir James

I know it will, my sweetest Girl--Yet, as this is a point of material consequence to the mutual welfare of our lives, you must generously do a violence to your delicacy, and answer me clearly to one particular Question--

Miss Free

What is your Question, Sir James--?

Sir James

There is some vanity in it Madam

Miss Free

Propose it however

Sir Jame's

Is not your consenting to marry me, as much the result of your choice as it is the consequence of your Judgement?--and wou'd'nt you, if I was divested of every advantage arising either from fortune or from birth, prefer me to all the men in the world--

Miss Free (aside

What shall I say to him?

Sir James (aside

How beautiful is her confusion! --and how her answer must mortify my friend the Captain

Miss Free

That proof indeed wou'd be conclusive Madam, if we had not daily instances of very good women, who give their hands in one place, while their hearts are engag'd in another

Miss Free

But what other proof can I give--

Sir James

Say in direct terms, that you love me--Tell me that you doat upon me and add that you wou'd be the most miserable creature on Earth if I was not to be your husband

Miss Free

I beg Sir James, that you will not tyrannize over my feeling's in this manner--

Sir James

Nay, my dearest creature, dont hesitate to speak the truth

Miss Free

Whatever I may think, Sir James, it is imposible for me to adopt this language.

Sir James

Then Madam candidly confess that I have no place whatever in you affections

Miss Free [aside]

If I do this, the match is broken off, and then what becomes of my father

Sir James

What do you say, Madam

Miss Free

I say Sir James, that as you have acknowledged your consciousness of my regard for you, there can be no occasion for your torturing me in this manner upon the rack of Examination

Sir James

And if you entertain that regard for me, which you insinuate, Madam, there can be no occasion for your hesitating to pronounce it in so many word's

Miss Free

have you no pity for my confusion, Sir James

Sir James

have you know compassion, Madam for what I must suffer, while I retain smallest doubt of your affection

Miss Free

Well then, dreadful as the conflict is, you must oblig'd

Sir James

Resistless loveliness, don't be terrified--I thought I shou'd bring her to at last

Miss Free

Know then, Sir James--

Sir James

Speak Audibly, my Angel

Miss Free

That if I was this moment Mistress of the world

Sir James [aside]

They'll never hear in the next room--

Miss Free

The Mistress of the world Sir James

Sr Jas. A little louder, my angel, a little louder.

Miss Free

My voice fails me--

Sir James

What a Misfortune at so Interresting a Moment

Miss Free

The task, which you have impos'd upon me is too great

Sir James

Madam--?

Miss Free

And let the consequence be what it may, it is impossible for me to obey your commands /<u>EXIT</u>

Sir James sits for sometime in a state of silent astonishment--*Then enter Wilmington, Lestock and* Cleveland

Wilm

overhearing Miss Freemore, retire, Sir James, we have ventur'd to make our appearance--

Les

I find, my dear Sir, that we have been a little mistaken in this matter

Clev

Pray Sir Jame what do you think of Decorum now?

Wilm

Well, I really look'd for nothing but compliance, when she declar'd that Sir James must be oblig'd

Les

And began to preface her harrangue with a Tragedy tone, that if she was Mistress of the world

Clev

Common form's for Commen Men, Sir James--Rational Lovers are only regulated by Reason

Sir James

I adhere to the sentiment Captain, and posess my temper unruffled under a disappointment, that wou'd make you perhaps seek the modern consolation of a pistol

Wilm

And what do you mean to do, my good friend

Sir James

What I told you I would do--Give her up Forever

Les

But dear Sir, she may love you very sincerely, notwithstanding the confusion just now created by her delicacy

Sir James

And she may not love me at all, Nephew Lestock--Therefore, I'll neither venture her happiness, nor my own, upon the fate of a Contingency

Clev

There is dignity in this Sentiment Sir James

Sir James

There is reason, at least--Besides I have some pride, if I am even destitute of common sense: and Scorn to play the legal Ruffian, by marrying any woman against her inclination <u>EXIT</u>

Wilm

Why really he carries it off with a better grace, than I thought he wou'd

Clev

His manner of bearing the disappointment gives me a very high opinion of his Character

Les

Come, come, tho' we have succeeded so far, we must not conclude the business finish'd--Mrs Freemore will stop at nothing to recover Sir James, and therefore till Flavella actually becomes Mrs Cleveland we are not to think our selves in port

Wilm

Very true--Therefore let us attend the issue of this business, and think with the wise man that nothing's done till all's done <u>EXIT</u>

<u>The End of the second Act</u>

The third Act

The Scene Lady Winterly

Enter Lady Winterly Miss Wilmington and Gloworm

Lady Win

Well, Urania, at your intercession he may stay

Miss Wilm

You are very obliging, Madam

Lady Win

But let me have no more pulling and hawling with that woman there

Lan

Pulling and hawling Madam!--

Miss Wilm

Hold your tongue Gloworm--

Lady Win

What does the worm turn upon me?

Lan

Why not, if you tread upon it, Madam?

Miss Will

Go down stairs Glow Worm

Lady Win

Or you shall instanly go out my house, Mistress

Glow

Lord! I wonder what some folks think we Servants are made of

EXIT:

Miss Wilm

Poor Glowworm is out of her wits, I believe

Lady Win

Yes, she is in love with that handsome young fellow, that you have just prevailed upon me to try a little longer

Miss Wilm

But her situation is not desperate, I suppose--

Lady Win

Nay I don't know that--Yet as our affections are not in our power, it is certainly a misfortune to love there is no likelyhood of a return Urània

Miss Wilm

As this is your ladyships opinion, I am in hopes, Notwithstanding my fathers severe Resolutions this Morning, that you will still kindly interest yourself, to prevent the odious match with Mr Lestock

Lady Win

Depend upon my utmost assistance, Urania: and remember besides I have fortune enough for us both, if your father shou'd think of proceeding to extremeties

Miss Wilm

I have no words to express my sense of this goodness--

Lady Win

My sweetest Girl--be compos'd--I know that there is no talking the heart out of its attachments, even where these attachments may be contrary to Reason

Miss Wilm [aside]

She's in an excellent humour--suppose I acquaint her with Wyndhams being in the house? it may serve to assist affairs greatly

Lady Win [aside

Yes having Secur'd her gratitude in this manner, I may safely trust her--She is besides, extreemly sensible, as well as delicate, and if she even cannot serve me, it will be no little consolation to have a confident, upon whose discretion I can reckon with Security

Miss Wilm

You are Meditating, Madam,

Lady Win

I am thinking, Urania, whether, warmly concern'd as I am for your happiness, you wou'd feel equally for mine If I shou'd by any fatality be involv'd in a like struggle of the heart

Miss Wilm

You are not cruel enough to doubt me seriously Madam--

Lady Win

No my dearest Girl, and to convince you how perfect a reliance I have both upon your honour and your good sense, I shall repose the whole happiness of my life this moment in your hands--

Miss Wilm

And I shall consider it as my own

Lady Win

I believe you--Know then that this heart of mine, which was frost to all the fire of your poor Uncle, Sir Walter Winterly and adamant to all the world besides, is at last engag'd

Miss Wilm

Indeed.

Lady Win

Transfix'd beyond the posibility of a recovery--and yet I blush, Urania; I almost despise myself while I make this acknowledgment

Miss

Why so Madam. The passion of love is a generous one--

Lady Win:

True--But mine is so utterly misplaced, that I shall stand in need of all my philosophy to support the ridicule of the world, if I give a Scope to my Affections

Miss Wilm

You have too much understanding, Madam, to let your happiness depend upon the opinion of fools--

Lady Win

But you cant think how very humble the situation of the man is who has unfortunately engag'd my inclinations

Miss Wilm

I must suppose him a man of merit, because he is honourd with your Ladyship's approbation--and in that case he is self-enobled to your hands

Lady Win

My dear Girl, let me embrace you--Your mind is in perfect unison with my own, I see--and a Woman has more happiness to expect in a marriage with a Footman of feeling, than in a union with a Duke of ten descents, who is either a fool or a libertine

Miss Wilm

Very true Madam: and the footman for whom I have just now interceeded with you, has a person and a manner, that wou'd do credit to the first order of Nobility

Lady Win

Embrace me again, my dearest creature--You reconcile me to myself

Miss Wilm

Madam!--

Lady Win

That footman is the object I die for

Miss Wilm

Who, William

Lady Win

Yes and you must assist me in the proper manner of making him acquainted with my Sentiments

Miss Wilm [aside]

I shall sink into the earth--

Lady Wilm

You tremble my dear

Miss Wilm

An excess of concern for you, Madam

Lady Win

Generous Girl!--But the service, which you have just render'd this Jupiter in a livery, enables you to do me another

Miss Wilm

How, Madam--?--

Lady Win

Send for William--talk to him about the danger you have sav'd him from--hint to him the necessity of a proper ambition; and tell him, at last that a lady of fortune has commission'd you to say she wou'd not disdain him for a husband

Miss Wilm

Woud'nt it be better, if you spoke to him yourself Madam--?

Lady Win

I have spoke to him--But my delicacy wou'd not suffer me to go the necessary lengths: and he was perhaps afraid of understanding me

Miss Wilm

If he is so dear to you, Madam, how cou'd you think of discharging him

Lady Win

There is no describing the conflict here Urania, between the impulsive of my weakness, and the arguments of my pride--One moment I cou'd die for the fellow --And the next I cou'd devote him to death, for plunging me into so humiliating a state of Embarrassment--

Miss Wilm

In what manner shall I conduct so critical a conversation with a footman--

Lady Win

There is the mortification, as well as the Dificulty, my dear I have been myself with a thousand different Methods of making him acquainted with my sentiments: but this way appears to me the shortest, as well a well as the surest and I beg you'll undertake it immediately

Miss Wilm

I will at any rate, attempt it, Madam

Lady Win

Take care of my delicacy, however, dear Girl: and don't reveal my name, till you are certain he will accept of the proposal

Miss Wilm

Can there be any doubt of that, Madam?

Lady Win

I don't know--He seems a very extraordinary young fellow, and if you had not been prepossess'd I shou'd have wonder'd at your seeing him without partiality

Miss Wilm

Alas, Madam, my heart is devoted to the memory of Wyndham--

Lady W

Go down stairs then, my dear, and do as I requested

Miss Wilm

I will--

Lady Win

And do you hear, my dear, send Gloworm up to my dressing Room--Something must be done to this head--And that dawdle has lately got a method of making me look most hideously

Miss Wilm

What an unexpected misfortune! EXEUNT severally

Lady Winterly Miss Wilm

The Scene Changes to Freemores

An Apartment

ENTER Mrs Freemore, Freemore, and Sir Jame Clifford

Mrs Free

Never tell me Sir James--I say again that if your supposition was even founded on Fact, Time wou'd have render'd the Girl fond enough of you--

Sir James

Really, Madam, I see no reason why time which often lessens a lady's affection for the young and the handsome, should overcome her disgust to the old and the ugly--In one word therefore I love your Daughter too well to marry her--

Mr Free

And very much I commend your determination--

Mrs Free

Indeed, and what do you mean to do, Sir James? I need not tell you that a capricious breach of contract where a young lady's honour is concern'd must be thought a very serious circumstance

Sir James

You need not threaten me with a suit-at-law, Madam--No man of reason will ever have any thing to do with Westminster Hall--

Mr Free

Very true Sir James

Sir James

I say therefore, to shew how much Miss Freemore's happiness is necessary to my own

Mrs Free

Well!

Sir James

I'll immediately settle five thousand pounds upon her--

Mr Free

Dear Sir James, this is extremely generous

Sir James

But it must be on this express condition, Mrs Freemore

Mrs Free

What condition

Sir James

That she is never contrain'd in the choice of her husband: but left wholly to follow the course of her own inclination--other old blockheads may be as foolish as myself--but they may not possess altogether so much humanity

Mr Free

Sir James, I shall be as much oblig'd to you, for the proviso, as for the sum contain'd in the Settlement

Mrs Free

You will--will you?--But I must consult my lawyer upon this proposal--before I can consent to accept of it--

Sir James

You have my hearty consent to consult with whom you pleas, Madam

Mrs Free

I'll step this moment to my attorney. Mr Vulture of Grays Inn, and be back in half an hour: if you favour me with a call about that time--Sir James you will have an Answer from me-- (Going

Mr Free

shall I attend you, my dear

Mrs Free

You! what good can you do? No stay at home with your dead Company as you call them, in the Library--It is not likely that Sir James wou'd offer so large a sum as five thousand pounds, if he did not think the law wou'd make him pay a great deal more (aside & <u>EXIT</u>

Sir James

Why, my dear friend, you seem not much attended to by your lady, in this business

Mr Free

No nor in any other, I must needs acknowledge, Sir James: yet there was a time in which I stickled stoutly for my conjugal prerogative

Sir James

And how have you lost it pray

Mr Free

In the arms of victory, Sir James--I was wearied out with conquest and now find even the Slavery you see me in, more tollerable than an everlasting war

Sir James

O! if an Englishman runs into Voluntary Slavery, I shall never feel for the heaviness of his chains

Mr Free

In the days of domestic hostility, Sir James, my quarrels wou'd not let me mind my books--for tho the foe was hourly vanquish'd still there was no prospect whatever of a peace: I therefore determin'd

Sir James

Like another Socrates

Mr Free

Ay--To let her have her own humour, since she wou'd not submit to mine and custom has long render'd her scolding so familiar to me

Sir James

That now like a Boy's whipping Top, the more you are lashed, the sounder you sleep

Mr Free

Just so, Sir James, and I find a great convenience in being a henpeck'd husband, for not a single error committed in my Family is ever attribute to me--My friends all know that I have no will of my own, and therefore when any thing happens amiss, the whole blame is thrown upon Miss Freemore

Sir James

Well really I did not think so much cou'd be said in favour of a Submission to Petticoat Government--However my dear Friend, I must now leave you to give directions about this Deed of Gift to Miss Freemore

Free

You are very good, Sir James, and I rejoice to see you bear your disappointment so chearfully

Sir James

See what it to be a Man of reason, Mr Freemore--The Disappointment I own is not without its mortifications--But it might have been much worse, if I had implicity listen'd to Mrs Freemores Account of things, and believ'd that becaus Flavella was all sentiment herself, she wou'd therefore marry a patriarch of principle--

Free

I said from the first the disparity of your ages made the match extremely improper

Sir James

You did, and I might have found the Justice of your observation in the feelings of my own heart, for I never shou'd have thought of Flavella, if she had either been carbuncled in the nose like myself or ten years older than my Grandmother--

EXIT

Mr Free

So every thing is in a fair train, and my Angle girl will not be sacraficed to my difficulties--Where is she? Flavella Flavella

---

ENTER Miss Freemore

Miss Free

Your commands Sir

Mr Free

Well my dear has your mother told you how generously, Sir James behaved

Miss Free

She has, Sir, but she is by no means satisfied at the failure of the Match

Mr Free

But you are satisfied, I hope--You are overjoy'd: say you are and make me happy--

Miss Free

here is but one condition, which can make me happy Sir!

Mr Free

hat is it my love--?

Miss Free

hat you will kindly apply the money accruing from this disagreeable ransaction to the removal of your difficulties

Mr Free

hat, and have you again exposed to the danger of being miserable--Never lavella;

Miss Free

ou are fearful of making me miserable

Mr Free

ll other calamaties, my child, are triffling compard to that

Miss Free

et can I ever be otherwise, if you shou'd continue surrounded by misfortunes?--onsider, my dearest father, that it is the --expectation of this marriage with ir James, which has restrained the merciless hands of your Creditors

Mr Free

ell here's my body for them

Miss Free

Prison, Sir,--

Mr Free

s a palace to a contented mind, and a palace but a prison to the mind that s otherwise [Besides I can yet go to France--The Liberty which is denied me n a land of freedom--I can find among a nation of slaves

Miss Free

nd fly your Country

Mr Free

Who wou'd stay in a Country, where crimes are punishd with less severity than Misfortunes

Miss

You affect me exceedingly

Mr Free

If I had committed a Highway-Robbery, broke open a house at midnight, or murder'd my Friend, I might have some hope of pardon but the crime of being in debt is never to be forgiven. and I must be made a prisoner for life, because I am guilty of wanting bread for my unfortunate family]

Miss Free

The money in Question, Sir will more than discharge all your debts and leave your little estate unincumberd--If you will not gratify my tenderness, at least indulge my pride: and let me have the glory of saving the most generous of fathers

Mr Free

The father that cou'd be sav'd at the expence of his child, does not merit so exalted an instance of affection--You don't know what I suffer'd when in complyance with your tears (for your mother's reproaches wou'd never have subdu'd me) I consented to the match with Sir James Clifford

---

ENTER a Servant

Servant

Captain Cleveland, Sir--EXIT

Mr Free

Shew him in--Flavella, my dear, receive him, my Eyes are not at present unfit to see Company EXIT

Miss Free

And do you think mine are dry Sir--

ENTER Cleveland

Capt Clev

My dear Miss Freemore--I did not expect to see you alone, tho' I rejo at my good fortune in finding you so

Miss Free

You wou'd have found me at all, If I had not staid to receive to you by my fathers commands

Capt Clev

How unkindly said! Yet I come to congratulate you on your happy escape from a match, which, I knew was disagreeable--

Miss Free

Pray, Sir, how do you know that it was disagreeable

Captn Cleve

Sir James Clifford told me so within these ten Minutes

Miss Free

Then you know that has pass'd?

Capt Clev

Everything Madam--and shall, upon the foundation of one particular circumstance, give you a still stronger proof of the Sincerity, with which I adore you, than the discovery of my real Character this Morning

Miss Free

Sir

Capt Clev

I know Madam, that your fathers present situation is by no means equal to his virtues

Miss Free

Perhaps you are Mistaken Sir

Capt Clev

Wou'd to heav'n that I was--However Madam, be his situation what it may here upon my knees I beseech you to accept a faithful hand together with an honest heart and implore you also, to dedicate the five thousand pounds which James will pay, to the uses of your worthy father

Miss Free

Captain Cleveland--

Capt Clev

I have numberless apologies to make, Madam, for daring to take this liberty: But my Motive must be my excuse: I know the dignity of virtue, when it is unhappily embarrass'd by pecuniary causes, and feel a Double veneration for it here, [striking his bosom] whenever I behold it attended by misfortune

Miss Free

I cannot speak

Capt Clev

You need not speak, my Angelic, Miss Freemore! Let me only gently seize this hand and once-for all tell you, that tho' I shall possess more than the wealth of worlds if I can obtain your approbation, we shall have no great occasion to be uneasy with respect to fortune

Miss Free

O Cleveland--!

Capt Clev

What does my charmer say?

Miss Free in a tender tone

Let my hand go

Capt Clev

dont bid me part with my first felicity

Miss Free

You wont resign it then

Capt Clev

I'd sooner resign my life--

Miss Free:

Then you must keep it you provoking Creature

Capt Clev

Eternal blessings on the lips which tell me so!--

Miss Free

You must however obtain my father consent

Cap Clev

As your mother is luckily gone out, I'll to him instantly

Miss Free

I fancy you'll find him in his library: and when you have finish'd your conversation, you may, if you please, let me know the result of it

Capt Clev

Remember however, my dearest Creature, that I am still Capt Cleveland

Miss Free

I'll remember what-ever you desire I shou'd <u>EXEUNT severally</u>

The Scene changes to an Apartment at Lady Winterlys

ENTER Gloworm

Glow

My mind missgives me mightily--William I see plainly slights my lady but he slights me also. tho' is no comparison, I flatter myself between the two women: and if her large fortune is not a sufficient bait for him, it is not likely that he will be tempted by my seven hundred pounds--My lady says, that nothing can happen without a cause and I have been thinking what can cause this behavior in William--Miss Wilmington, to be sure, is younger than I am if she is not all to gether so genteel--and notwithstanding she pretends to take on wonderfully for Wyndhams death she is for ever speaking in private to this dear hard hearter monster of mine--Today, when my lady was going to discharge him, she was terrified out of her wits and she has now been shut up with him in that Room this half hour. I wish I knew what they were talking about--Ay--and I will know too Here's a Closet that open's into the room, from which I can hear every thing And slip down stairs without being discover'd by anybody--EXIT

The Scene changes to an appartment

Miss Wilmington and Wyndham discoverd

Miss Wilm

Why did'nt you tell me that you suspected my Aunt entertaind these sentiments for you?

Glow, (peeping--

O ho! as I thought

Wynd

ecause if had been mistaken in my suspicions, you miht have very easonably charged me with a most consummate vanity

Miss Wilm

can assure you, tho! that this unnecessary refinement was likely to have een attend with very disagreeable Consequence

Wynd

ow so, my love

Glow

is love, indeed!--But I'll be reveng'd

Miss Wilm

hy when my aunt made me the confidant of her passion, I was going to tell er every thing about you, and had actually made some progress in my reparations

Glow

, I'll tell her every thing depend upon it

Wynd

onsidering the favourable light, thro which she is pleas'd to view me hat indeed might have been a lucky communication

Glow

ighty fine!

Miss Wilm

! exceedingly so!--For, tho I am now in high favour with her if she once onceiv'd that I stood in the way of her wishes, she wou'd naturally be the irst for having me sacrific'd to Lestock

Glow

'll talk to her about M[r] Lestock presently--EXIT

Wynd

But suppose you were to acquaint Lady Winterly, in this exigence with my real Character? she will have just reason to be offended if we endeavor to impose upon her--

Miss Wilm

True and there is besides a littleness even in any kind of fraud, which must be painful to a mind of the least sensibility--Yet

Wynd

Yet what my Angel?

Miss Wilm

My Aunt has a violence of temper, which wou'd make it highly improper to trust her with our secret, while your adversary is in any danger--

Wynd

O her scene with me, tho, at first, wore all the gentleness of the Lamb, did not conclude without a little of the Tigress

Miss Wilm

I can easily suppose so--And if she was acquainted with your real character, her passion for you is so strong, that we shou'd have much less to accept from the generosity than to dread from her disappointment--

Wynd

I see the force of your reasoning

Miss Wilm

I am persuaded she wou'd not hesitate at any thing, to gain you herself, or to seperate us for ever: and therefore I will not incur the very posiblitiy of losing you--

Wynd

Thus let me speak my gratitude, adorable urania [embracing her

---

Enter Gloworm and Lady Winterly from the Closet

Glow

There, Madam, you see I am not the only one, he pulls and hawls about in the family

Miss Wilm

Undone undone!

Lady Win

So. Madam, your heart is entirely devoted to the memory of Wyndham and you, Sir, I find, have lost all terror on account of your Character

Wynd

I hope your ladyship will not be offended with Miss Wilmington, I was only returning her my humble thanks for her great goodness to me

Glow

O! I dare say she has been verry good to you

Lady Win

What, Sir, and you always embrace, a Lady when you return humble thanks, and call her your adorable Urania

Glow

O fie upon you Mr William! ---Is this your way of thanking me for all my kindnesses

Wynd

It was extreemly presumptious, I must confess. Madam, to express my gratitude with so much familiarity--Yet I am the only person in fault, and if

Lady Win

I see you are the only person in fault--for this lady appears quite shock'd at the excess of your presumption--What, Madam, guilt makes you dumb--

Miss Wilm

No, Madam but the fear of your displeasure--I cou'd easily prove my innocence if you wou'd but listen to my justification--

Lady Win

Innocence?--I shall run mad--did'nt I see you in the fellow's arm's

Glow

And did'nt I hear you cry out, undone undone--

Wynd

Be pacified my dear Mrs Gloworm--

Glow

Dear me no dears, you ungrateful Monster, there's your dear--

Lady Win

Ay Gloworm and let him take his last look of her--

Miss Wilm

What does your ladyship mean to do

Lady Win

To lock you up immediately, Madam, till I send for your father--Gloworm desire that modest Gentleman to prepare for immediate dismission

Glow

with the greatest pleasure, my lady--Perhaps, Mr William, you may condescend to think of your equals, when you are out of this house

Wynd (aside

What shall I do?

Lady Win

Come, my hopeful Miss

Miss Wilm

Your ladyship must pardon me, if I do not choose to be lock'd up

Wynd

Miss Wilmington is a visiter here, I humbly apprehend Madam, and therefore your ladyship can have no right to confine her

Lady Win

Indeed--!

Wynd

And if she gives me leave to call a chair, I'll attend her to Doctor Wilmington's

Lady Win

That is, in plain English, you'll carry her off by force--But hark ye Sir Amadis from the kitchen, it is now open day, and there are three or four fellow's as lusty as yourself in the hall, who shall instantly drag you to Bridewell, if you perform any feats of Knight errantry here--

Miss Wilm

For heavn's sake, William, don't attempt any thing despearate

Wynd

You shall be obey'd, Madam--It is impossible to rescue her now

Glow

See, Madam, how fondly she looks at him--But young ladies are asham'd of nothing now a days

Lady Win

I attend you to your Chamber Madam

Miss Wilm

Leave this place directly, William, you know my Reason

Glow

O! she's jealous of Me--

Wynd

Immediately Madam

Lady Win

Upstairs, Madam, immediately with you

Glow

And down stairs Sir with you EXEUNT

The End of the third Act 58

The fourth Act

The Scene changes to an Appartment at Freemores

ENTER Freemore & Mrs Freemore

Mrs Free

Why really I can't deny that Cleveland's proposal is a very generous one but still the match with Sir James Clifford is so desirable, upon a thousand accounts, that I am determin'd, if possible to bring it about, especially, as Mr Vulture tells me a Jury might not give so much as five thousand pound damages

Free

I thought--my dear, that you had determin'd to consult the poor Girls inclinations

Mrs Free

Consult her inclination--I have told you of my accidental conversation with Sir James on my way home from Mr Vultures

Free

You said indeed, that, not dreaming of this liberal offer from Cleveland, you had endeavour'd to persuade Sir James that he was very unjust in his doubts of Flavella's affection

Mrs Free

And I said moreover, that Sir James was so very easily persuaded to believe, what he very eagerly wish'd to be true, that, I gave what colour I pleas'd to Flavella's conduct in the interview this Morning

Free

And is he then determin'd to renew his addressses, my dear

M^{rs}

Immediately, to my very great Satisfaction

Free

My poor Flavella! what a disappointment. at the very moment she exultingly flatter'd herself with obtaining the man of her heart

Mrs Free

The man of her heart Quotha--I am surpris'd you should talk so Mr Freemore when you have been so long intimate with people of Quality

Free

I do not want to make my daughter a woman of Quality, Madam--and therefore request

Mrs Free

But I do--And therefore request that you will leave the matter entire to my Management--

Free

Consider that Sir James--

Mrs Free

May safely refuse to pay a shilling, if the match is broken off on our side, and I wont trust to the result of his singularity--I have told Flavella this, and she sees the necessity of humouring the old fool in the ridiculous proofs, which he has requir'd of her affection

Free

Surely of all Tyrants a female Tyrant is the worst

Mrs Free

What's that you say

Mr Free

I say that a cruel mind is doubly detestable in those bosoms nature intended to string with a peculiar share of sensibility <u>EXIT</u>--

Mrs Free

Hey day what a language he begins to use but he is the errant'st ideot in the universe--Here has he, by becoming security for one needy fellow, and giving large sums to relieve another, brought himself to the very door of a Jail, and still he is at his feelings, tho' there is so noble an opportunity of making the fortune of his family--For my part I dont see but we are much better without these fine feelings, of which people talk so much--I am sure they only serv'd to make this fool of mine Miserable Every body's distresses brings tears into his Eye Now I never cry'd but once in all my life; and that when my mother in her last will, left her, Jewells to my youngest Sister

---

ENTER Miss Freemore

Miss Free

Sir James Clifford, Madam, is in the next room

Mrs Free

Well, Child and are you determind to receive him in the manner I advis'd you

Miss Free

I am, Madam, since you say there is no other way left of saving my father with certainty

Mrs Free

There is no other way, my dear--Had I known of Cleveland's offer time enough, why, perhaps, I shou'd not have oppos'd your inclinations: but ignorant of that, and depending upon your attachment to your father, I have promis'd what I told you to Sir James

Miss Free

And if I fail in the performance

Mrs Free

The match is broken off upon our part, and Sir James is not oblig'd to pay a Shilling to any body

Miss Free

Poor Cleveland

Enter Mr Freemore and Sir James Clifford

Mrs Free

Sir James your Servant--Mr Freemore we dont want your Company here

Sir James

Pardon me madam his presence is very necessary

Mrs Free

I have acquainted my Daughter with your mistake, Sir James, and she is prepared not only to forget it, but to accept of your hand whenever you think proper

Sir James

I am for ever indebted to her Goodness and thus Seal my Gratitude on her lovely Cheek

Miss Free

Sir James

Sir James

No, no reproaches, my dearest creature--Had I once conceiv'd to what a degree you lov'd me--or remembrd that the Business of love is not regulated by reason among the ladies

Mr Free

Sir James do not be dup'd a second Time

Mrs Free

Mr Freemore leave the Room this Moment

Mr Freemore

No, relentless woman, I will not leave my child to be sacrificed to your Avarice or your Vanity

Mrs Free

Dont you tremble at my resentment Monstor

Mr Free

No, Madam--but you shall Shudder at mine--Here your Tyranny shall End for ever--what my own Sufferings cou'd not effect the barbarities exercised upon my Child have produced; and now let me see who shall dare to touch her hand without the consent of her father

Miss Free

O Sir!--But I will save him from the Danger of his own generosity (aside)

Sir James

Soft and fair good Mr Freemore--you have no reason to suppose That I am a friend to Compulsion or that I would stoop to accept even this Ladys Hand against her Inclination

Mr Free

Yet you are going to do it, believe me, Sir James

Sir James

Miss Freemore to avoid the possibility of any farther Mistakes give one leave to ask you a few Questions

Miss Free

If you please Sir James

Sir James

In the first place Madam may I intreat to know if you are willing to accept of me for a Husband

Miss Free

I am

Mr Free

Flavella

Sir James

with your whole heart and soul

Miss Free

Yes

Mrs Free

You hear that Sir James

Sir James

In preference to any other man on Earth

Miss Free

I am

Sir James

Why, Mr Freemore, you really want somebody to take care of you

Mrs Free

I'll take care of him, depend on it

Mr Free

Flavella, I see your motive for this act of elevated falsehood

Sir Jame

Silence, Mr Freemore!

Mr Free

Stop your Examination one moment, and I'll bring a witness that shall wake you to conviction Sir James <u>EXIT</u>

Sir James

And yet, I see no Reason why Mr Freemore shou'd oppose the happiness of his own Daughter

Mrs Free

And do you see any Reason why Flavellla shou'd make herself Voluntary Miserable, Sir James?--she has her fathers free consent and mine to marry Captain Cleveland if she chooses it

Sir James

Indeed

Mrs Free

Ask her--

Sir James

It wou'd now be offering an insult to her sincerity

Enter Freemore and Captain Cleveland

Capt Clev

My dearest Miss Freemore, your father has overwhelm'd me with distress and astonishment

Miss Free

I am overwhelmd with distress myself Captain Cleveland--

Sir James

But what can this mean

Mr Free

Nothing more, than that Flavella, who is now so ready to marry you consented not an hour ago to marry this Gentleman

Sir James

Is this true Mrs Freemore

Mrs Free

Very true--But my wise husband does not tell you that Flavella's consent was additional and given even after you withdrew your addresses Sir James

Mr Free

Conditional, Madam

Mrs Free

Yes, conditional--and given solely upon the Captain promising to apply the five thousand pounds which Sir James offer'd to pay to the re-establishment of your affairs, Mr Freemore

Sir James

O this alters the case and proves not the want of a tender regard for me, but the extent of affection for her father

Capt Clev

Sir James, this point may be very soon decided--I love Miss Freemore passionately--But I love my honour more

Miss Free

Go on, Sir

Capt Clev

And I scorn to urge any clain to a lady's hand, who is unwilling to fulfill her engagements--Miserable she may make me--But shall never make me mean: and in the hour of her very perfidity, her heart shall secretly consider me with approbation

Mr Free

Well said, Captain

Sir James

Ay and rationally said--too Mr Freemore

Miss Free (aside

What a task is mine!

Mrs Free aside

So my views are promoted, I dont care whether they are advanced by the vanity of the old fool, or the pride of the young one

Capt Clev

Madam there is no necessity for expostulation upon this Subject: and I disdain the littleness of reproach--If you wish to be releas'd from your engagements with me, you are instantly absolv'd--Yet as I am willing to believe any thing, sooner than the possibility of your forgetting these Engagements, I shall still consider this hand to be mine till a declaration from your own lips has clearely remov'd my delusion

Miss Free

This hand Captain Cleveland, I have just dispos'd of to Sir James Clifford

Sir James

And convinced my reason that it was accompanied by a heart, Captain

Cleve

You gave it to him unforc'd, uninfluenc'd, Madam

Miss Free--I did

Ja^{s}--Have you any more questions to ask, my dear Captain?

Cleve---No, Sir James, I am perfectly satisfied, and shall only wish that the title for which Miss Freemore has sacrificed me, may not in the end by purchas'd at the expence of her own tranquility EXIT

Free----- And here, Flavella, I solemnly swear by all the tender feelings of a father, that if you do not renounce Sir James, I never will hold commerce with you more--Never will I owe an obligation to the Child, that strikes at the most essential object of my happiness, and plunges me into the deepest Calamity I can possibly experience, to save me at the worst, from a trifling misfortune EXIT

Mrs Free--There let him go--what are you in tears for Child?

Miss Free--Can you ask Madam, after such a parting from my Father.

Sir James--Nay, my lovely girl, don't weep, or you'll make me weep too

Mrs Free--Well, Sir James, what do you think now?

Sir James--That I am the happiest man upon Earth, in this proof of Miss Freemore's love--Not only to spurn this handsome young fel[low] before my face, but even to give up her father for me-- I sha[ll] run wild with the excess of my own felicity.

Miss Free--I suppose, Madam, I have now your permission to retire

Mrs Free--Yes, you may go, my Dear, and I am extremely pleas'd w[ith] you.

Sir James--One kiss, my Angel--nay, dry your eyes--I can have no more doubts of your tenderness, and to make you perfectly happy, I'll apply instantly, thro' Doctor Wilmington, for a special licence, and be married to you this very Evening EXEUNT

The Scene changes to lady Winterly's

Enter Lady Winterly, and Doctor Wilmington

Lady Win

Well, have you seen Lestock

Wilm

No, but I have written to him, and in, pursuance of your advice, have fix'd five o Clock this afternoon for his marriage with this hopeful Daughter of mine

Lady Win

That's right Brother, there is no other way to preserve the honour of our family--But you took care, I hope, to assign some probably cause as an excuse for this precipitancy

Wilm

Let me alone for a stroke of policy--I assign'd Mrs Freemores having Sir James a second time in her Toils as an excuse: and said I coud not take any open steps with propriety in his affairs, till he was become a part of my family, hey Sister

Lady Win

Excellent!--And as the writings are all sign'd between Sir James and you there is nothing to apprehend from his Resentment, when he finds that the marriage has been thus hastily celebrated without his knowlege

Wilm

If the case had been otherwise, I shou'd scarcely venture to be so precipitate--However I still mean to ask Sir James to the Wedding and the excess of his Nephew's passion for Urania must excuse this unexpected hurry in the celebration of the ceremony

Lady Win

Surely, Brother, you don't see the danger of asking Sir James

Wilm

Why where is it pray

Lady Win

Sir James has feelings, and shou'd Urania struggle, or shew any obstinate opposition to the ceremony, he might be for breaking off the match

Wilm

Very true, Sister, and I am Infinitely oblig'd to you for the caution

Lady Win

Nay indeed, I am almost afraid of Lestock's seeing her aversion

Wilming

O you need not fear him--His feelings are entirely under the direction of his judgement, and the very treaty, now subsisting between him and this profligate Neice of yours, is a convincing proof that he is not the slave of any ridiculous Delicacy

Lady Win

Well then be punctually here at five, with the Clergyman and the special Licence

Wilm

To the second of a second, and much joy shall I wish my friend Lestock of his delicate bargain-- EXIT

Lady Win

So I have effectually fix'd the fate of this perfidious little hypocrite: and if I am even wretched myself, it will be some consolation to know that she is equally miserable--EXIT

The Scene changes to Sir James Cliffords

Enter Lestock and Crisis

Les

Yes there are three physicians, at this moment, in the house beside yourself my dear Crisis

Crisis

Indeed

Les

Yes but let us be sure that we are not overheard by any body

Cri

shall I shut this door?--

Les

If you please and I'll fasten this

Cri

So all's safe

Les

You must know my dear friend, that from the first moment my Uncle commenc'd a man of Reason, and profess'd an open Defiance to the authority of custom it struck me that some opportunity might occur to take out a commission of lunacy against him

Cri

What has the thought been so long revolving in your mind

Les

It has, and in order to advance my schemes the more effectually I constantly humor'd the singularity of Sir James's turn ha! ha! ha!

Cri

With a view of driving him upon some Extravagances

Les

You have hit it and the time is, at last arriv'd, my Boy, to make a golden harvest of my labours

Cri

How so pray--?

Les

You know Sir James intends to be married this Evening

Crís

I do

Les

The moment he had determind upon this wise affair, he came home quite delighted to consult me about a wedding suit, and what dress wou'd you think the old fool has seriously resolvd to wear upon my suggestion

Cri

Something, I suppose, as peculiar as his disposition

Les

Tis too ridiculous upon my soul-- ha! ha! ha! It is infinitely too ridiculous to be credited

Cri

O! there is nothing so ridiculous, with which the wiset men will not readily do if they are attack'd upon the side of any favourite singularity

Les

Why then to keep you no longer in suspense I have play'd so successfull upon Sir James foible that he has resold to be married in the turkish dress which he wore at the last Masquerade, and which he made up at the particular recommendation of Miss Freemore

Cri

ha ha ha--And every body besides yourself, I suppose think's him out of his senses?--

Les

Nay so seriously is every body of this opinion, that I have been applied too by several of his friends, to have him Confind and therefore mean to seize the opportunity of locking him up within this hour

Cri

While he is proudly exalting in the superiority of his understanding Really this is doing things very expeditiously

Les

Zounds no other way to prevent the precipitate marriage with Miss Freemore

Cri

And this will prevent it effectually--

Les

Ay and effectually prevent his cateroauling in any other family--The charge of insanity is almost as dangerous as the proof Crisis--

Cri

Very just--Besides the whole race of woman does not center in Flavella

Les

True and where ever he picks up his goose she may supply him plentifully with goslings--If he marries, tis ten to one that neither Wyndham nor I ever get an Acre of the Unsettled Estate where as if the madhouse-scheme succeeds, we shall come in for the whole as heirs at law

Cri

so that everything is to gain'd upon the one hand

Les

and nothing to be risqu'd on the other, my boy, for say that Sr James shou'd be prov'd in possession of his senses still what I have done ha! ha! ha!

Cri

only listen'd to the solicitations of his friends

Les--

Right and lock'd my Worthy Uncle up, from a principle of downright Affection

Cri

And may I ask in what you expect my assistance

Les

Why you must know that, to give this matter every air of plausality and to make security doubly secure, I have call'd a Consultation of physicians--

Cri

That their report may furnish a ground for an application to chancery--

Les

Yes--and, as you have attended Sir James so long professionally you can do me infinite service by giving the other physicians a proper impression of the case, and pronouncing doubtfully upon his singularities--You understand me--

Cri

I do--I do--And since the pigeon must be pluck'd

Les

The feathers may as well continue in his own family boy

Cri

Very true--But we phisicians do not even kill people without being paid--You understand me

Les

I do, and a life-charge of 500 a year which is just executed, (on condition I succeed) instead of a paltry Bond, shall speak my graditude my dear Crisis

Cri

This indeed is making the Obligation reciprocal--But where are the other physicians

Les

I'll ring for a Servant to shew you to them directly, as I wou'd not have them suppose we had any private conversation [Rings

---

ENTER a Servant

Shew Doctor Crisis to the gentleman below stairs

Servant

Yes Sir

Cri

Farewell, you may rely implicity upon me if you only remember the annuity

Les

A thousand thanks to you, my friend-- EXIT Crisis] what a pitty it is that a Man of spirit cant execute his own schemes without the assistance of these Mercenary Rascals? And now let me think a little--I suppose I was to let Wilmington into this business--He must be astonished when he hears that Sir James is confin'd.--But I know he will be pleas'd at bottom even if he shou'd entertain suspicions, and it wou'd be ridiculous to divulge a secret of this consequence, where I can derive no benefit whatever from the communication This old Blockhead is completely in my power at last Wyndham was his favourite and till the flight of this favourite, I was only an object of secondary consideration--I ask'd leave to pay my addresses to Urania before Wyndham applied, and was indignantly refused tho' he knew she was the absolute Mistress of my Heart--I smild because I cou'd not strike but now the opportunity affords I am determind upon ample revenge--[EXIT]

The Scene Changes to an Apartment at Sir James's Cliffords

Discovered A Consulatation of physicians. Crisis Ravage Hemlock and System Sir James

Dr Cri

Well Gentlemen Mr Lestock has been acquainting you with the nature of Sir James's Case

Rav

And a very Alarming case it is according to his Account of it--A man to regulate himself by nothing but reason

Dr Sys

I wonder he did not apply sooner for the Opinion of the Faculty

Dr Hem

Ah! veniento occurito morbo--

Dr Rav

an Excellent rule--But where is Sir James--I have thirteen clients to visit before seven oClock--

Dr Sys

Thirteen patients, Dr Ravage:--A good number for a Single Evening

Dr Cri

Why the parliament is sitting you know and we have a fresh Supply of strong substantial diseases from the Country-- hahaha

Dr Hem

And yet at present I have not above three fevers, two gouts, and a bilious Complaint to my back for the Support of a large Family ha ha

Dr Rav

I am very sorry for it my dear Friend--but I hope you had a Comfortable share of the late Influenza

Dr Sys

Ah such good things dont happen every day

Dr Rav

I dont wonder that people complain about the Times

Dr Sys

Nor I either you talk'd of the Parliament Just now--why of late years the folks at Westminster have seem'd determin'd to destroy our business

Dr Cris

So they have, Dr System--What with rendring the Town more Airy and healthful

Dr Hem

This Precaution against the Jail Distemper

Dr Rav

And a Thousand other scandalous Actions--But here comes our Patient--to business Gentlemen--and let us if possible engage him in conversation

Enter Sir James

Sir James

Gentlemen your most Obedient--pray be seated--[Sir James sits with two physicians on each hand

Dr System whispers Crisis

He looks well

Sir James

May I beg to know Gentlemen, what has procured me the Honor of this Visit

Dr Crisis to Sys:

And speaks civilly

Sir James

For tho I am very proud to see you all, I should as soon look for a Visit from the whole College as from four of the Faculty at a time

Dr Hem

You need not be much Alarm'd Sir James at our Numbers for we come as friends

Dr Rav

And hearing that you was a little indisposed wish to ask you a few Questions upon the Nature of your complaint

Sir James

You are extreamly Obliging Gentleman--Yet I have no complaint upon earth but what you can remove

Dr Sys.

By what means, pray

Sir James

By making your visit as short as possible

Dr Cri

Tis a bad Symptom Doctor System when the patient wants to send the Physician away

Sir James

But it is a much worse when he wants the physician to continue his Attendance--However Gentlemen you must excuse me at present for I have very Urgent Business on my hands

Dr Hem

So we hear Sir James, no less than a Wedding to be celebrated this Evening

Sir James

You hear what is very true, and I was just preparing to dress when your Names were announced to me Gentlemen

Dr Rav

Well Sir James and what Dress do you propose to wear upon this happy occasion--? This is the Main point to go upon

Sir James

A very strange kind of a Question, Doctor Ravage

Sys

White and Silver I suppose, Sir James, the customary emblems of matrimonial Felicity

Sir James

I have as little business with custom Gentlemen as you can possibly have with me

Cri

We know your Sentiments in this respect perfectly Sir James, yet we hear that you are carrying your Philosophy to an unusual length and intend to have a Turkish Habit for your Wedding Suit

Sir James

And what then--A Turkish Dress is highly preferable to an English one

Sys

In what respect Sir James

Sir James

Why a fine Muslin Turban is much cleaner than a greasy Wig

Dr Hem

You see how it is with him

Sir James

A loose flowing Robe is much more convenient than one of those ridiculous Coats

Dr Rav

Ay Sir James with fantastical Skirts, and tight Sleeves

Sir James

That keep a Mans Arm continually skewer'd down like the pinnions of a Truss'd Turkey

Dr Cri

Undoubtedly--Besides everybody now a days, follows his own fancy in dress

Sir James

Very true--You Gentlemen have discharg'd the deep professional tye which formerly render'd the most wizen faces among you--so venerable--some of our Lawyers begin to plead in Bag Wigs and even the   of our dignified Clergy are now a days so closely crop'd and so carefully powdered that if you only covered their face with a Cabbage Leaf yo might easily mistake them for a parcel of Walking Caulisflowers

Sys:

You shou'd not humour him Doctor Crisis

Sir James

Nay the very ladies indulge the utmost latitude in Dress and appear in all public places like so many American Savages--Their Cheeks are as Deeply daub'd and their heads as highly Feather'd and want not but Simplicity of Manners to make Admirable Wifes for a Nation of Carpenters

Hem

Do you hear him

Rav

Wild

Cri

Very Wild

Hem

Yet it seems rather reasonable

Dr Rav

O when the disorder is at the very worst it will wear an appearance of great plausibility--

Sir James

What is the matter Gentlemen

Dr Sys

Pray, Sir James will you give me leave to feel your pulse

Sir James

For what Doctor System

Dr Cri

Suppose you look at his tongue first

Sir James

Why at his tong Doctor Crisis

Dr Hem

Sir James give me leave to ask a Question

Sir James

What is the meaning of this Whimsical behaivour

Dr Hem

How long do you generally lye in bed Sir James

Sir James

Till the very Minute I get up--Did any body every hear such rudeness

Dr Rav

And you Sleep all the Time Sir James

Sir James

Yes if I am not awake

Dr Sys

Poor Man--And when do you generally eat Sir James--

Sir James

Most commonly when I am hungry

Dr Cri

And you Drink I suppose

Sir James

Most commonly when I am dry

Dr Hem

I dont know what to think

Dr Rav

I think he is very far gone

Sir James

And I'll be gone entirely Gentlemen--Do you come into my house to insult me

Dr Sys

You are all Agreed Gentlemen--

Sir James

Murder me are you--who waits there

Dr Hem

We only mean to prescribe a few things

Sir James

I knew they wanted to destroy me--But I won't take any of your prescriptions; and beg you will get about your business for I want to go about mine

Dr Cri.

Mariage is a foolish business Sir James

Sir James

Perhaps so--But I am nevertheless determin'd on Matrimony Dr Crisis

Dr Rav

If thats the Case call in the Attendants

ENTER KEEPERS

Sir James

Where are all my servants--where's my Nephew,--why you concieve Gentlemen That I am out of my senses perhaps

Dr Sys

Take great care of that gentleman and convey him with as little Noise as possible to Your House

Keeper:

I will Sir

Sir James

I who am remarkable for the Clear possession of my understanding--Ishall dearly pay for this outrage--but let me not loose my reason because I am rob'd of every thing else

Keepers

Come along Sir

Dr Hem

You have best go quickly Sir James

Sir James

Have I no Friend--no Servant

Dr Rav

Well Genleman, I suppose we may now retire and sign our general Opinion

Dr Sys

With all our Hearts

Dr Hem

Move him off

Dr Cri

But dont hurt hurt him for your lives [exeunt Doctors]

Sir James

This is a General Conspiracy against me--but it is what a Man of Superior Wisdom deserves for living in a Country of fools [exeunt]

The End of the fourth Act

Act 5th.

Captain Cleveland's Lodgings

Enter Cleveland & Dr Wilmington

Dr Wilm

But consider the generosity of the poor Girls motive, Cleveland

Cleve

I have told you the whole particulars of the Transactions; and my own behavior, I may say, without vanity, was not despicable

Dr Wilm

Miss Freemore however conceives that her first duty is to preserve her Father-- And Sir James being now persuaded that she is seriously in love with him, there's no expectation of his again offering five thousand pounds to break of the match

Cleve

You forget that I told you how nobly the old Gentleman has resolv'd never to receive an Obligation from her, if she commits this murder upon her own tranquility

D^{r}. Wilm

And you forget that she has as nobly resolv'd to call all his Creditors by public advertisement, the moment she is married to Sr James and to pay off every Demand upon her Father's fortune--Mr Freemore may perhaps beleive like a Simpleton, but beleive me, the people he is indebted to, will not be equally ready to play the fool

Cleve.

But what is there to be done, my Dr Sir? The lovely Tyrant is inflexible, and even disobeys the very Supplications of her father, from an excess of filial affection

D^{r}. Wilm

Leave that to me--Freemore and his wife have each of them been soliciting me to assist in a Plot against each other.

Cleve

How?

D^{r}. Wil.

He will neither suffer Sir James to come here, not let his Daughter stir out of the house, unless to marry you

Clev

I wish he had recovered the Dominion of his family a little sooner

D^{r}. Wil

'Twou'd have sav'd us a good deal of trouble--now the mother wants me, if possible, to remove the Girl, depending upon her filial piety, for a readiness to marry Sir James

Cleve

Well?

Dr Wilm.

And the father wants to practise a friendly artifice, a pious fraud, to prevail upon Flavella to marry you

Cleve.

Ay! there's the difficulty

D^{r}. Wil.

Which is not insurmountable--I am to see Flavella, and to represent you as the heir of a very large fortune.

Cleve

I begin to conceive you

Dr. Wil.

And, I am moreover, to say, that your father, provided she consents to receive your hand is so charm'd with her generosity, that he will immediately extricate Mr Freemore out of all his difficulties

Cleve.

I am afraid, Sir, that this will never do.

Dr Wil.

Never do! Zounds, man, rather than you shou'd be disappointed, in the first wish of your heart, I'd swear that I was your Father, myself and pass you upon her for that fellow I have in Ireland.

Cleve

Dear Sir, how shall I thank you?

Dr. Wil.

Thank me thus, my dear boy (embrace)

Enter Miss Freemore.

Miss Free.

What do I see, and hear--I wait upon you by my mother's commands, Dr. Wilmington.

Dr. Wil.

My dear Madam, you come in a fortunate moment

Cleve

I hope so.--and tho' you have deaf to my Sollicitations, I trust you will listen to this Advocate

Miss Free

Then you have told the Doctor every thing, Sir?

Cleve

Every thing, Madam.

Dr Wil.

O! he has no secrets whatever from me, Madam.

Miss Free.

Why can you, Sir, approve his Sentiments, for an object so unworthy, as the person who stands before you.

Dr Wil

What the Devil does she mean? --but I must yes.

Cleve

He does, Madam, in the warmest manner.

Dr. Wilm

Yes, in the warmest manner.

Miss Free.

Your Goodness, Sir, is too much for me.

Dr. Wil. (to Cleveland)

My Goodness, Madam--Mind, Cleveland, what a sudden reverence she entertains for me, because I furnish her with an opportunity of following her own inclinations

Cleve

I do, Sir, I do.

Dr. Wil.

Zounds! the women are all alike, I know that even this Paragon cou'dn't hold her resolution half an hour, against the man of her heart--But, Miss Freemore--

Miss Free.

Sir.

Dr. Wil.

As you do not seem displeasd at my interception in his favour, let me frankly ask, whether under colour of complying with your Mother's views, you have any objection to make against escaping with me, and to bestow that hand, which she designs for Sir James, upon the man, who is really honour'd with your affection

Miss Free.

I have a father, Sir, and you know his unhappy Situation

Cleve

And do you think that your Lover's father will suffer yours to remain a moment in embarrass'd circumstances?

D^{r}. Wilm

If he did, he ought to be hunted from the earth, as a disgrace to humanity.

Miss Free.

Satisfy me but of that, and I'll shew my Gratitude by an instant compliance with you wishes.

Cleve

You'll pledge your Honour, Sir!

D^{r}. Wil.

Most readily, that every thing in my power shall be done to serve M^{r}. Freemore-- Are you satisfied now?

Miss Free

Yes, dearest Sir, and shall eternally bless you for this generosity

D^{r}. Wil.

Don't let us lose a moment then--my Coach is at the door, Madam, and if M^{r}. Freemore, and your Lover here will but follow us to next Street, we can take them up, without creating the least disturbance in the family

Miss Free.

'Twill doubtless be the best way, and I wou'd spare my poor Mother as much moritification as possible,--tho' there is some thing extremely humiliating in dissimulation

Cleve.

I'll fly to communicate the happy intelligence to your father.

Dr. Wil.

Did you ever see any thing so easily manag'd? (to Cleveland)

Cleve.

Never

Dr Wilm

O this precious! precious sex!--But, away with you to Freemore, that he may strike while this pretty ideot is so compleatly warm'd up to our purposes.

Cleve.

I will--for a few minutes adieu my Charmer, when we meet next, you are mine for ever. EXIT

Dr. Wilm. (aside)

Now I have all the fools securely in my Toils.

Miss Free

What do you say, Sir?

Dr. Wilm.

That I am ready to attend you, Madam--I have a thousand things to do--and I must again observe that we have not a moment to lose in the present business.

Miss Free

We shall surely have the pleasure of your Company at the Ceremony, Sir.

Dr. Wil.

Mr. Freemore's presence will be sufficient, my sweetest Girl-- and I am so singularly engag'd, that I cannot enjoy that happiness; after the Ceremony is perform'd, however, I shall expect you to sup with another new married couple, at my Sister's. EXEUNT

Scene, Lady Winterly's

Enter Lady Winterly, and Glow worm

Glow.

Yes, Madam, William was so flush of money, that he gave one of the maids two guineas to slip the letter to Miss Wilmington

L^{y} Wint

And the honest Creature gave it immediately to you.

Glow

She did, Madam, and I desired her to tell William, that she wou'd contrive a way for Miss Wilminton's escape, about this time, if he'd only wait at the little garden door, which opens into the Park

L^{y}. Wint

Well, and have you sent the Girl up with the key to let her out of her room?

Glow.

I have, my lady, and she is to pretend that she stole it off your Ladyship's dressing table.

L^{y}. Wilm.

That's right! perhaps we may discover something.

Glow

Hush! Madam, I hear a foot.

L^{y}. Wint

Hold your tongue then. (Retires)

Enter Miss Wilmington

Miss W.

Well! thus far I am safe.

L^{y} Wint

'Tis she.

Miss W.

And I shall be speedily beyond the reach of danger (*opens a door*) Yet, I pity my Aunt--For surely the greatest of all misfortunes is to place our hearts, where we can never hope for a return of affection

Glow

Do you hear that, Madam?

L^{y}. Wint. (*seizing Miss Wilmington*)

I'll hear no more--Come back, my pretty dutiful run away.

Miss Wil.

O heavens! what shall I do?

L^{y}. Wint.

So, Madam, this is a new proof of your regard for the memory of Wyndham

Glow

And your gratitude for my lady's goodness, to run away with the man she loves

L^{y}. Wint.

The man I love! Insolence! how dare you give your tongue that freedom.

Doctor Wilmington behind.

And the moment M^{r}. Lestock comes, shew him up.

Miss W.

My father's voice!--Then my fate will be speedily decided

Enter Doctor Wilmington

D^{r}. Wil.

What is the matter? you talk almost loud enought to be heard in the Street.

L^{y}. Wint.

See the matter there.

D^{r}. Wil.

Urania!

L^{y}. Wint.

Just going to elope with a footman.

D^{r}. Wil

I don't wonder at it.--She has been kept too long unmarried--and to make her amends, instead of a footman, She shall marry a man of rank and fortune, within this very hour.

(<u>a loud rapping</u>) Glow

There he is, Sir.

Miss W.

To M^{r}. Lestock himself then I must appeal.

D^{r}. Wil.

Do, Child, and see how much he will regard it.

Miss W.

If he is either Prudence or Pride, he will not marry a woman who considers him with horror.

D^{r}. Wil.

And, where was either your pride, or your prudence, Madam, when you wanted to scamper away with a footman?--what wou'd you say to your Aunt, if she was to fall in love with a Scoundrel in livery?

Glow. (<u>aside</u>)

My Lady has it there on both sides of her face.

Ly. Wint.

Don't waste the time in talking with her, Brother, every thing is ready above Stairs

Miss W

Yet spare me, Sir, and I'll convince you--

Dr. Wil

Nay, Miss, if you struggle--

Miss W.

That footman you upbraid me with.

Lady Win

Why don't they shew Mr. Lestock in?

Miss W.

But no word.

Enter Wyndham

Where is my Life! my Love?

Miss W.

O! Wyndham! (*sinks into his arms*)

Dr. Wil.

Wyndham!

Lady Wint

I am Thunder struck

Glow

Is this William after all

Wynd.

For whom you wou'd keep cribbing from your Lady

Glow

I shall never be able to survive it. EXIT

Lady Wint

This the footman!

Wynd

For whom you wou'd have kindly kept a Butler, Madam--I acknowledge my reproach to be a little ungenerous, but your behavior to Urania, has cancell'd all obligations.

Lady Wint.

You shall repent your insolence severely--Here Glow worm, order some body to go instantly for the officers of Justice

Miss W.

O, Wyndham! this is what I dreaded

Wynd.

Banish your amiable terrors, my Charmer; for tho' I have been condemn'd unheard, I can now safely deny the utmost exertions of injustice--My Adversary is happily out of danger, and nothing forbids me to proclaim, in the face of the world, how much I glory in my passion for you.

Miss W.

Gracious Heaven! Then we shall be happy after all

Enter Lestock

Lest.

What, at Prayers, my lovely Miss Wilmington? but so much the better--There's a Chaplain ready to assist you--Your friend the Parson is come, Doctor.

Dr. Wil.

Ay! and he may take himself away again.

Lest. (taking hold of Miss Wilmington)

Why so? The beautiful Urania will surely be prevail'd on to bless the most ardent of her Adorers.

Wynd. (twirling him away)

I hope so, for that title belongs to me, Mr. Lestock.

Lest.

Really, Sir, I can't say that I was prepar'd for the pleasure of seeing you.

Wynd.

I beleive not--Nor for the pleasure of seeing this Bond, Mr. Lestock.

Lest.

Then all's discover'd --Perdition on that villain Crisis.

Dr. Wilm.

What's discover'd man?

Lest

Let me out of this infernal house

Miss W.

Why, Mr. Lestock, you seem to want the assistance of the Chaplain too.

Lest.

Hell and Damnation!--I cannot support it--and now see that Genius is a very foolish thing, when it is opposed to common honesty. RUNS OFF

Dr. Wilm.

Why, what is the meaning of all this?

Wynd.

I have my Uncle's commands, Sir, to request the honour of your Company immediately at his house--as we go along, I shall acquaint you with the particulars, of Mr. Lestock's Conduct, and enter into such a defence of my own, as will, I trust, induce you to hear once more of my union with Miss Wilmington.

Dr. Wil.

I attend with Impatience, and am so rejoiced to find Urania innocent, where I thought her beyond measure culpable, that I shall readily listen to your Justification

---

Enter Glow worm

Glow worm, where's your Lady?

Glow.

Very ill in her own room, Sir.

Dr. Wilm.

What's the matter with her?

Glow

Miss there can tell Sir.

Miss W.

I'll go to her.

Glow

You may spare yourself that trouble, Madam, she won't see you, and as for Mr. Wyndham, she desires he may--may instantly leave the house (*sobbing*)

Wynd

I shall obey her Ladyships Commands.

Dr. Wil

O! I begin to see the matter now!--Why, Wyndham, you have made a pretty piece of business here, and I fancy we had best take Urania with us, from the resentment of her Rivals.

Miss W.

As my Aunt will not see me, Sir, I shall not wish to remain in her house.

D^{r}. Wil.

Come along then, Child--and, Glow worm, as I expected some Company here to Supper, you'll tell them, that on account of your Lady's illness, I beg they will adjourn to my own house.

Glow.

Yes, Sir.

Wynd.

Won't it be better, Sir, if they call on you a S^{r}. James's?

D^{r}. Wil.

It will, it is in the direct road--and upon recollection, their calling there, may be necessary to undeceive S^{r}. James upon a very particular business.

Miss W.

You hear, Glow worm! --nay, don't look so cross, we must be friends, and you may very honourably receive this trifle, now you see I don't rob you of your Sweet heart.

Glow

My heart's too full.

Wynd

And, Glow worm, you must accept my acknowledgements too, for all the kindnesses you have shewn me.

Glow.

O that ever I was born. <u>EXEUNT</u>

Scene, Sir James Clifford's

Enter Sir James, and Crisis

Sir Jas.

What a Monster, to send me to a Mad house! my Singularity how ever has materially assisted his Manoevres, but he has cured me of that foible, and since it is so dangerous to teach the world what is proper, I'll endeavour to put up with the World's improprieties

Crisis

I hope, at least, that my desires to shew you the Virtures of one Nephew, and to discover the deepest designs of the other, will apologize for the ludicrous part which I have acted in this business.

Sr. Jas.

My dear Doctor, don't apologize for overwhelming me with obligations--I owe you, as well as Wyndham, more than ever I can pay, but you shall both see, that I do not want the will to be properly grateful, tho' I may not possess the Ability.

ENTER a Servant.

Servt.

Mrs. Freemore, Sir. EXIT & Enter Mrs. Freemore

Mrs. Free

Ah! my dear Sir James, I have been so terrified upon your account, that I must have a Salute.

Sr. Jas.

And, I suppose, my Dear Flavella has been terrified on my account also

Mrs. Free

I fancy she has not yet heard of your hopeful Nephew's behavior, since I don't find her here with Dr. Wilmington

Crisis

Here comes the Doctor.

Enter Dr. and Miss Wilmington & Wyndham.

Dr. Wil

My dear Sir James, your Nephew here has been telling me a most extraordinary affair.

Sr. Jas.

You must assist me, Doctor, to reward his worth, and make attonement for the Injuries I have done him.

Dr. Wil.

Most readily, Sir James--I have treated him severely myself, but, I trust, he will consider this hand as some little reparation.(*gives him Miss Wilmington's hand*)

Wynd.

It is an ample reparation for an age of misfortunes, Sir.

Miss W.

Take care that you don't find this ample reparation a new source of Inquietudes, Mr. Wyndham!

Crisis

It must be his own fault if he does, Madam.

Miss W.

There is no end to your goodness, Doctor,--yet tho' you have done so much for us, I must beg another favour of you.

Crisis.

I am always happy when you honour me with your commands, Madam.

Miss W.

Why then, I command you to call upon my Aunt immediately, whe is taken suddenly ill, and will, I am sure, consider your visit as a great obligation.

Crisis

I'll attend her instantly, Madam.

Wynd.

Wou'dn't it be right, Urania, to give the Doctor some little hint of her disorder, that he may know at a certainty what to prescribe?

Miss W.

It will, but we must go into another room, for it cannot be talk'd of with delicacy, before company.

Wynd.

Let me shew you then into another Apartment. EXEUNT Wynd: Crisis & Miss Wilm. (D^{r}. Wil. & M^{rs}. Freemore converse apart)

M^{rs}. Free.

Took her from you in the Street, Doctor Wilmington?

D^{r}. Wil

Yes, Madam, and I had no power to oppose the exertions of parental authority.

S^{r}. James

Did father ever so barbarously oppose his child's affections?

D^{r}. Wil.

My dear Sir James,--You are a man of excellent Sense, but you know little of the world, and are therefore liable to be deceiv'd.

S^{r}. James

And are you never apt to deceive yourself, my good friend?

D^{r}Wil.

Not often, I hope--And, on the present occasion, I can tell you truly, that Cleveland has been all along the man of Miss Freemore's heart

M^{rs}. Freemore

The Doctor has play'd us both false, I fear, Sir James, it was not for the Interest of his family, that you shou'd marry any body.

D^{r}. Wil.

Madam, you know what I say to be fact, tho' you would cruelly force your Daughter's inclinations.

S^{r}. James

Force her inclination! Why Miss Freemore voluntarily rejected Cleveland before my face, and acknowledg'd that she rejected him on my account, Dr. Wilmington-- Do you think I would persevere, if my reason was not entirely satisfied.

ENTER a Servant.

Servt.

M^{r}. Freemore.

EXIT--and Enter M^{r}. Freemore

Free.

Sir James, your Servant--Doctor, I was directed by a Servant of yours to find you here.

D^{r}. Wil.

And, I am glad you are come so opportunely to settle a little dispute, I had with Sir James, about your Daughter.

Free

You are very kind to trouble yourself about my Family Doctor, but I shall soon return the Compliment, by talking about your Son.

D^{r}. Wil.

Why, what of my Son, Sir?

Free.

He is come from Ireland.

Dr. Wil.

And where is he?

Free.

Below stairs.

Sir James.

Why wou'd you suffer him to remain a moment below Mr. Freemore?

Free.

Because he first stands in need of forgiveness from his father.

Dr. Wil.

What the devil has he done?

Free.

Married.

Dr. Wil.

Zounds! he dare not do it.

Sir James

You see, with all your knowledge of the world, you may be deciev'd yourself, Doctor.

Free

And what's still worse, he has married a girl without a Groat

Dr. Wil.

I'll never see the Scoundrel's face.

Mrs. Free.

Why surely, you wou'd not be so cruel, as to force his affection

Dr. Wil

He shall perish--he shall rot.

Sr. James.

What, for doing a Action necessary to his own happiness?

Dr. Wil.

What right had the dog to be happy against my consent?

Sr. James.

Come, come, you have no cause to punish youself for the misbehavior of others: and your worldly wisdom shou'd recollect that, in repining at evils, which you cannot prevent, you double the measure of your own misfortunes.

Dr. Wil.

Well, I will see the fellow, but let him keep out of my reach.

Free.

I'll bring him to you, immediately. EXIT

Sr. James

I suppose Mr. Wilmington has married an Irish Lady?

Dr. Wil.

O! no doubt of it, with a brogue as broad as St. Giles's--but the world shall never prevail upon me to suffer her in my sight

Sr. James.

That's right Doctor, always sacrifice your humanity, to prove your Understanding.

Mrs. Free.

How I hate these hard hearts.

Enter Freemore and Cleveland

Dr. Wil.

So, Cleveland, my Scoundrel of a Son is return'd from Ireland, and has married a bog trotter, without a Groat.

Cleve

At your feet, Sir, behold that Son.

D^{r}. Wil.

What?

Cleve

On my knees, I beg you will receive you.

D^{r}. Wil.

Impossible! you can never be my Son.

Cleve

This letter will remove the possibility of doubt, and prove my claim to that Title, if I must even despair of your pardon.

D^{r}. Wil.

From Sir Robert Dillon, my father in law, and the Truth is too evident.

S^{r}. Jame's

Why, Doctor, your Son is a pleasant young Gentlemen, to think of Miss Freemore, when he was previously married in Ireland?

D^{r}. Wil.

Death and Damnation! to be the dupe of my own designs.

M^{rs}. Free.

To dig a pit for others, and to tumble in yourself.

S^{r}. James.

But where is my adorable Flavella, all this time?

Free.

She's at home, Sir James.

S^{r}. James.

Will you give me leave to order my Chair for the dear Girl?

Free.

With all my heart, Sir James, for I have now relinquished my authority over her.

Sr. James.

Then the soft authority of love shall commence immediately--I hope, Doctor, this little circumstance will shew you the folly of being too positive. *EXIT*

Dr. Wil.

Sdeath, don't distract me--to toil, to drudge, for the defeat of my own Purposes.

ENTER Flavella.

Mrs. Free.

So, Madam, you have play'd me a pretty trick, and assisted your foolish father to ruin himself.

Flav.

No, Madam, this best of men-- (*turning to Dr. Wilmington*) has kindly promis'd to extricate him from all his difficulties

Dr. Wil.

I shall grow frantic.

Flav.

Yes, in the most generous, the most noble manner.

Dr. Wil.

I was deceiv'd!--impos'd upon.

Free.

Yes, Sir. By your own desire to impose upon others.

Flav.

Surely, Sir, I practis'd no imposition on you.

Dr. Wil.

No, but that fellow there did.

Flav.

You know, Sir, your Honour is pledg'd to me.

Mrs. Free.

And, if it is, the Law shall oblige him to redeem it.

Flav.

When you interceeded for your Son, you know.

Dr. Wil.

I have no son.

Flav.

You were so anxious for his happiness--

Dr. Wil.

O damn his happiness--Yet what signifies tormenting myself the thing is done, and by my own curs'd contrivance too.

Mrs. Free.

Sir James will have his disappointment to encounter as well as yourself, Doctor.

Dr. Wil.

That's poor Consolation, tho' he has been laughing at me so unmercifully.

Cleve.

Remember, however, Sir, that the marriage of your Son may be the means of keeping the Clifford estate to your Daughter's family.

Dr. Wil.

That's true--And therefore since what is lost upon the one hand, will probably be gain'd upon the other, take my forgiveness freely.

Cleve

It will make me happy upon any terms, Sir,--My dear Flavella

Flav.

How cou'd you deceive me, Mr. Wilmington--But as the Doctor is reconciled, I forgive you, and thank him with the deepest gratitude.

Free.

This is as it shou'd be.

Mrs. Free.

Ay, if the Doctor will stick to what he promised Mr. Freemore.

Cleve

Don't be uneasy about Mr. Freemore, Madam; he has made me happy, and I will make him so. Nay, my dear Sir, no acknowledgments, I only pay a debt, where you generously think I confer an obligation

---

ENTER Sr. James, Wyndham, & Miss Wilmington.

Sir James

My dearest Creature, this is unspeakably kind, to come of your own accord.

Miss Free.

You are very good in excusing the liberty, Sir James, but not being able to accompany my father, I was directed here from Lady Winterly's.

Sr. James.

In a fortunate moment, for I was just ordering my Chair for you.

Miss Free.

Pray, Sir James, who Is that Gentlement? (*pointing to Wyndham*)

Sr. James.

Give me leave to present him, Madam--Mr. Wyndham, my Nephew! who will be ambitious to cultivate your good opinion.

Wynd.

You consider me attentively, Madam.

Miss Free.

Pray, Sir, didn't you rescue a Lady from a ruffian about six weeks ago?

Wynd.

One night in a Chair, Madam?

Miss Free.

Yes.

Wynd.

I did

Miss Free.

I was the person you generously protected; and tho' I was then too much terrified to think of thanking you, being solely attentive to my escape, my heart shall ever retain a just sense of the obligation.

Wynd.

Providence of heaven!--Did you hear her, Urania?

Miss Wil.

I did, with Joy, tho' I wanted no confirmation of your innocence.

Free.

You never told us of being attck'd in a Chair, my dear.

Miss Free.

'Tis true, Sir, but I did not think it proper to alarm you needlessly, Sir.

Miss Wil.

Yet, Madam, if you knew the Consequesnces of that night--

Dr. Wil.

Ay, if you did, Flavella, they wou'd alarm you exceedingly.

Mrs. Free.

Yes, but at that time we were not acquainted with any of the present Company.

S^{r}. James

And neither Doctor Wilmington, nor myself, chose to mention an affair, which we then considered no less the misfortune than the disgrace of the families.

Cleve

Your having once obliged this lady, makes me eternally your Debtor, M^{r}. Wyndham.

S^{r}. James

It has made me eternally his Debtor, if you please, Sir--This Lady, my dear Wyndham, is your Aunt elect, the Angel that is so speedily to make me the happiest of mankind.

D^{r}. Wil.

Now George!

Cleve.

Not so speedily as you may imagine, Sir James.

S^{r}. James.

Why, really, young Gentlemen, you must have a comfortable share of modesty, if you will persevere in your pretensions to this Lady, when we have so lately discover'd that you are already married.

Cleve.

And, really, Sir James, you will have a superior degree of modesty, if you still insist upon being married to my wife.

S^{r}. James

Your Wife! it is not reconcileable to reason.

M^{rs}. Free.

'Tis too true for all that, Sir James.

S^{r}. James.

Too true--why then, into what a fools Paradise had I been flattering myself all this time

Free.

It was not my fault, Sir James; and I hope this little circumstance will shew you the folly of being too positive.

Dr. Wil.

Ay! and I hope, you will now see, my good friend, that your all sufficient reason, is as liable to err, as my worldly wisdom.

Sr. James.

I do see that it is not all together an infallible guide, where the Ladies are concern'd, yet it teaches me to look upon that as a piece of great good fortune, which wou'd make your worldly wisdom, a Candidate for Bedlam.

Wynd.

I rejoice, Sir, to find you can bear so great a disappointment with such a degree of fortutude.

Sr. James

A disappointment, man! It is a miraculous Escape, I was on the verge of becoming wretched for life, myself, by marrying where I was detested, and, what was still worse, of making a deserving young creature for ever miserable.

Cleve

The light, in which Sr. James sees this matter is unspeakingly pleasing to me, as it removes the only alloy which could have lessen'd the excess of my present felicity.

Miss W.

That's politely said, Brother.

Sr. James.

It is so, Madam--Yet, I own, I cou'd have wish'd that things had been as I thought they were--But since things are as they are, my reason is satisfied once for all, and I heartily congratulate you on your mutual happiness.

Enter a Servt. who whispers Wyndham, & EXIT

Miss Free.

You ever had my Esteem, Sir James, and ever shall have my Gratitude.

Wynd.

Doctor Crisis, Sir James, and some other Company, are already assembled in the Drawing room

S^{r}. James.

Very well, we'll wait upon them, and dedicate the Evening to Festivity-- Nay, M^{rs}. Freemore, you must not wear that cloud upon your brow

M^{rs}.

Ah, Sir James, how can I help it, when--

S^{r}. James.

Silence, my dear Madam--Don't wound the Sensibility of your Husband, by a public mention of his Embarrassments. There is no reason because I have been rescued from a foolish action that I am to be discharg'd from the performance of an honourable one.

M^{rs}. Free

You are the best of men, and shall have an other.

S^{r}. James.

You have been already too bountiful to me, Madam.

Free.

Hey, Sir James, what have you done to render my Lamb so frolicksome?

S^{r}. James.

You shall know at a proper time, M^{r}. Freemore--For the present, let us join the Company, and unite the hands of another couple.

D^{r}. Wil.

Why this is being a man of the world again.

S^{r}. James

From this day I bid adieu to Singularity; and shall allow myself really a lunatic, if I ever again make love to a young woman, or attempt to give Society Customs, instead of receiving Customs from Society.

FINIS

"PROLOGUE" AND "EPILOGUE"

PROLOGUE.

Spoken at Drury-Lane, for the Benefit of the INFANT POOR.

THOUGH famed in arms, in commerce though renown'd,
Though great in arts, with liberty though crown'd,
Though wherefoe'er her mighty flag's unfurl'd
Britannia rifes emprefs of the world,
Still when array'd in meek-eyed Pity's robe
She looks more great than when fhe rules the globe,
And all the glories which her crowns can dart,
Are poor, if balanced with her feeling heart—
When late wild war provoked her Lions' roar,
And fpread her victories from fhore to fhore,
How did your bofoms exquifitely glow,
To mark her godlike conduct to the foe?
The hoftile bands in triumph as fhe led,
She warm'd with rayment, and fhe cheer'd with bread:
That needful fuccour their own ftate denied
Her gracious hand exultingly fupplied;
And fnatching every captive from the grave,
Proved it much lefs to conquer, than to fave—

While

While this bleſt ſtory melts along your ear,
What *native* woe can ever want a tear?
At Britiſh pangs a Britiſh heart muſt ſigh,
When foreign griefs can deluge every eye;
When even we weep for enemies o'erthrown,
And ſooth'd the breaſt that arm'd againſt our own:
To-night we ſee you, in ſupport of thoſe
Too young to ſpeak, though not to feel their woes;
The humble, helpleſs family of pain,
Without your favour, brought to light in vain;
Nay, doom'd to miſery e'er they ſaw the morn,
And here, unfriended, wretched to be born.——
From this hour's bounty many a hapleſs ſire,
Who fought your battles with heroic fire,
His drooping innocent reſtored ſhall view,
And be repaid the blood he ſhed for you.
How many a mother too, whoſe ſoul-fetch'd cries
Had elſe torn wildly through the echoing ſkies,
From madneſs reſcued, while her life endures,
Shall beg down bleſſings upon you and yours:
Nay, more exalted objects ſtrike the ſight
Through the kind viſto of this generous night;
Your grateful country in your virtue draws
New ſwords to guard her liberty, her laws,
And, with delight unſpeakable, muſt ſee,
That even your tears are arms to keep you free.

EPILOGUE,

Intended to have been ſpoken by Mr. MOODY, *at Drury-Lane Theatre, in the Character of Sir* CALLAGHAN O'BRALLAGHAN, *in Macklin's Farce of* LOVE-A-LA-MODE.

TOO dully juſt to literary rules,
Our bards conduct their pieces by the ſchools;
Warm, without fire, the motley ſcenes appear,
Juſt ſpun to drawl or ſleep upon the ear:

Too nicely wrote from precept to depart,
They pleaſe the fancy but neglect the heart.
Hibernia too, in this politer age,
Has long been only laugh'd at on the ſtage;
Her harmleſs follies have been painted forth,
Without the ſmalleſt mention of her worth;
And every genius would his wit employ,
To joke with *Paddy*, or to banter *Joy:*
Her very *accent* ſwell'd the comic ſong,
And every phraſe was nationally wrong.
As if *Britannia* could herſelf conceal,
Her thoughtleſs ſlips of *winegar* and *weal.*
For *breakfaſtis* had ne'er prepared the *toaſtis,*
Or bruiſed her *theſe here fiſtis* with the *poſtis.*
Ye ſons of Ireland, whereſoe'er ye ſit,
For once take off the manacles from wit;
And let theſe Lords of beef and pudding know,
That merit ſprings in *every* ſoil below.
Some native ſpark of heavenly fire confeſt,
Glows to divine within the *Indian*'s breaſt,
Swells unconfined from Briton to the Pole,
Expands, exalts, and dignifies the ſoul;
While *every* clime, by ſubtlety's trepannings,
Has *Bottle-Conjurers* and *Betty Cannings;*
Peculiar follies mark'd on every coaſt,
A *human Rabbit* or a *Cock-Lane Ghoſt.*
Yet *others* errors move their mirth alone,
Too blindly dull, or partial to their own.
Opinion lifts ſelf-conſciouſneſs to pride,
And ſhews *their* actions on the faireſt ſide;
Or elſe too vain from habit to deſcend,
They ſee their faults, but never ſtrive to mend.
For once here *Iriſh* excellence diſplay'd is,
That they can *love*—they leave it to the ladies;
That they can *fight*, each honeſt Briton knows,
And bravely too—they leave it to their foes.

Fair

Fair *Science* long has led them to explore,
The deep refearches of her myftic ftore.
Their *Genius* too, impartial truth declares,
If BACON's yours, an USHER has been theirs;
And SWIFT or STEELE the facred beam fecures,
Though deathlefs POPE and ADDISON were yours.
Then, nobly juft, O ratify their claim,
The equal heirs of liberty and fame:
Their warmeft hopes no higher can afcend,
Than calling *Britain*—Sifter—Guardian—Friend.
By your example generoufly fired,
They rife refpected, and they live admired.
This glorious ifle with gratitude they view,
And foar to *virtue*—for they copy you.
By you infpired, to *liberty* they fing,
And love the name of BRITON—like their KING.
Then fcorn each mean or defpicable art,
That would deprive a SISTER of your heart;
The facred paths of *amity* purfue,
And *fmile* on THEM, who *die* with *pride* for YOU.

Textual Notes

Textual Notes

Preparing a facsimile edition is not at all like preparing even the most conservative eclectic edition. Working on principles enunciated by W. W. Greg, the eclectic editor looks for the earliest state of the text on the assumption that, in the earliest text, the accidentals will have been least tampered with by compositors and publishers. He then supplies variants from later texts and emendations as he sees fit. Since this procedure is impossible in a photographic facsimile, it has seemed simplest to choose as the copy-texts the latest versions revised by the author. The collation after each play's note includes only substantive variants, since a full collation would go beyond the scope of this volume.

Because *The Works of Hugh Kelly* (London, 1778) was reset posthumously, it has no textual authority and has not been included in the collations.

FALSE DELICACY

CBEL lists four editions of *False Delicacy* in 1768. Alice E. Crozier, superceding *CBEL* ("An Old-Spelling Edition of *False Delicacy* [1768] by Hugh Kelly," Diss. Catholic University of America 1974), identifies five issues. There is clear evidence that all were impressions of the same setting of type and, moreover, of the sequence in which they were issued. Crozier (p. 83) identifies the issues 1768 *a* through *e* as follows:

1768a	No edition designation
1768b	No edition designation
1768c	"The Fourth Edition"
1768d	"The Fifth Edition"
1768e	"A New Edition" (text identical with 1768*d*)

For full bibliographical discussion and collation see Crozier. The "Fifth Edition" has corrected several minor errors found in earlier impressions. The University of Texas does not own a copy of the first impression (1768a), which can easily be distinguished from the second (1768b) by the omission of the words "By His Majesty's Servants" from the title page of the former; thus only three of the four extant texts appear in the collation.

Copy-text: *False Delicacy: A Comedy.* "The Fifth Edition." (London, 1768); collated with 1768b and 1768c.

Collation:

Act I	
1.6	that] but 1768b,c
3.14	passionately I] I passionately 1768b
3.26–27	funeral-sermon face] funeral sermon-face 1768b,c
7.13	of] about 1768b
9.30	I wish] wish 1768b
11.20	upon] for 1768b
Act III	
35.33	your] you 1768b
41.29	for her happiness] for happiness 1768b
47.11–12	of family] of a family 1768b
Act IV	
55.2	You] your 1768b,c
66.29	is a security] are notes 1768b,c
71.28	fault] faults 1768b,c
Act V	
73.2	that it is] that is 1768b,c

A WORD TO THE WISE

CBEL shows three editions of *A Word to the Wise*; the copy-text used here is that of the first edition, 1770. There are two other "editions," both, according to William B. Todd's criteria ("Recurrent Printing," *SB* XII, 1959), impressions of the original edition. The 1773 edition is evidently made up of leftover sheets of the first (subscription) edition, the only one which contains Kelly's "Preface" and the list of subscribers. The lack of variants, substantive or accidental (only one, in fact: "regents" for "tenants" in line nine of the Epilogue), and especially the identical press figures lead to the conclusion that at least some copies of 1773 are made up of unsold sheets of 1770. Of the four other United States libraries holding 1773, three have copies identical with the University of Texas copy; one reports an additional press figure.

Copy-Text: *A Word to the Wise, A Comedy*. (London, 1770); collated with 1775.

Collation:

Act I

10.8–9	what unaccountable coxcombery] *om*. 1775

Act II

30.23–24	—So the Captain thought I shou'dn't succeed with her. [*aside*] *om*. 1775
34.35	Jack] my brother 1775

Act IV

66.39–67.1	with her own consent] willingly 1775
72.20	nevertheless] *om*. 1775
73.24	he] they 1775

Act V

77.20	that I may] *om*. 1775
85.15	vices,] vices with death 1775

CLEMENTINA

According to *CBEL* there were two editions of *Clementina* in 1771; in fact, there were three issues. One has no edition designation, and two are both called "A New Edition." The first will be called 1771a, the second 1771b, and the third 1771c. The two latter can be distinguished most easily by the fact that in 1771b the text begins on page 1, while in 1771c the text begins on page 13. A second distinguishing feature is the pagination of 1771c: [i– ix], x, [xi– xii], 13– 60, 49– 56, 69– 78. This third issue, selected as copy-text, contains a number of clearly authorial variants and is almost certainly later than 1771b.

Copy-text: *Clementina, a Tragedy.* (London, 1771); collated with 1771a and 1771b.

Collation:

Act I

23.23	soul's] heart's 1771a,b

Act II

25.9	Yet, lovely maid, take heed] Yet oh take heed, sweet maid, 1771a,b
27.4	wretched] weeping 1771a,b

Act III

39.23	a father, like Anselmo] like me, a father 1771a,b
44.17	Where shall I turn] What shall I say 1771a,b

Act IV

50.6	tyranny and France] France 1771a,b
57.5	*Enter . . . &c.*] *Enter* Anselmo *attended.* 1771a,b
71	following line 22, 1771a,b have two lines not in copy-text: Our hearts were just united, when the fatal/Quarrel, between his sire and you, took place;

THE SCHOOL FOR WIVES

CBEL notes four 1774 editions of *The School for Wives*, and one in 1775. Examination of the texts, however, shows that the first three "editions" are a first edition and two others, called "second" and "third" editions, identical with the first down to their press figures, except for the title pages. The "Fourth Edition," 1774, thus rightly may be regarded as the second edition, and "A New Edition," 1775, as the third. The first edition and the two following impressions will be identified as 1774a,b,c, the "Fourth Edition" (actually the second) as 1774d. The third edition has been chosen as copy-text because it contains presumably authorial substantive variants not in previous texts.

Copy-text: *The School for Wives. A Comedy.* A New Edition. (London, 1775); collated with 1774a, 1774b, 1774c.

Collation:

Dramatis Personae

Leech, Mr. Bransby.] *om*. 1774a,b,c
Crow, Mr. Wright.] *om*. 1774a,b,c
Wolf, Mr. Ackman.] *om*. 1774a,b,c

Act II

16.23	in] of 1774a,b,c
25.28	*om*.] [*Exit*. 1774a,b,c
32.21	communicative] communicate 1774a,b,c

Act III

33.16	forte] fort 1774a,b,c
35.6	shine] stream 1774a,b,c
35.28	and] that 1774a,b,c
38.25	*om*.] [*Exeunt*. 1774a,b,c
42.17–31	and . . . *Exeunt*.] *om*. 1774a,b,c
43.1	SCENE . . . *Temple*.] *om*. 1774a,b,c

43.2 *Enter . . . other.*] *Enter* Connolly, *at the opposite side.* 1774a,b,c

43.4 after me] in sight 1774a,b,c

43.6 neither] *om.* 1774a,b,c

43.9 —however . . . well.] However, I see no more than three people, and think we could beat them to their hearts content in three minutes. *Lees.* What! and fly in the face of the law? *Con.* To be sure you have a great regard for the law, when you are going to fight a duel! 1774a,b,c

43.10–13 True . . . will] S'death! is this a time to talk? Stay here, and throw every possible impediment in the way of these execrable rascals. (*going.*) 1774a,b,c

43 (following line 13, 1774a,b,c have twenty-seven lines not in copy-text): *Con.* Halloa! honey come back: These execrable rascals are very worthy people, I fancy, for they are quietly turning down the next court. *Lees.* Their appearance alarm'd me beyond measure. *Con.* O you shou'dn't judge by outside show, my dear; for there is no being a complete rogue, without the appearance of an honest man. *Lees.* Circumstanced as I am at present, every thing terrifies me; for should I be arrested, the consequence would possibly be fatal, both to my honour and my love.—Belville would proclaim me publicly a coward; and Emily set me down as a base, a mercenary adventurer, who was solely attracted by her fortune. *Con.* Why faith, honey, like yourself, they might be apt to judge by appearances. *Lees.* O, Connolly, a man of spirit should learn prudence from his very pride, and consider every unnecessary debt he contracts as a wanton diminution of his character! The moment he makes another his

	creditor—he makes himself a slave! He runs the hazard of insults, which he never can resent, and of disgraces which are seldom to be mitigated! He incurs the danger of being dragg'd, like the vilest felon to the felon's prison! and, such is the depravity of the world, that guilt is even more likely to meet with advocates, than misfortune! [*Exit Leeson.*
43.14–48.14	*Enter* . . . [*Exit*.] *om*. 1774a,b,c
	(following line 15, 1774a,b,c, have two and one-half lines not in copy-text): wish I had any thing besides my carcase to venture for you, for that's nothing; yet you are as welcome to it as the flowers in May. Poor lad!
48.17	at your being] that he is so much 1774a,b,c
48.17–18	'Tis to be sure] to be sure it is 1774a,b,c
48	(following line 18, 1774a,b,c, have two and one-half lines not in copy-text): and a blessed law it must be, which coops a man up from every chance of getting money, by way of making him pay his debts—
48.18	And not] But now 1774a,b,c
48.19	there's any way] there is any method 1774a,b,c
48.20	peace] pace 1774a,b,c
48.21	gentleman] gintleman 1774a,b,c
48.21	peace] pace 1774a,b,c
48.27	quality] fashion 1774a,b,c
48.27	creature] creter 1774a,b,c
48.30	but] only 1774a,b,c
49.31	*om*.] [*Exit*. 1774a,b,c
50.13	on] of 1774a,b,c
58.1–61.10	Scene . . . Thames.] *om*. 1774a,b,c,
Act IV	
64.4	*om*.] me 1774a,b,c,

67.17– 18	will be] are at present 1774a,b,c,d
67.18– 19	till . . . Torrington] *om*. 1774a,b,c
67.27– 32	I . . . face] *om*. 1774a,b,c,d
67.33	Yet] Tho' 1774a,b,c
68.1	*om*.] the 1774a,b,c
69.2	intended] intend 1774a,b,c
Act V	
83.26	especially] specially 1774a,b,c
84.7	*om*.] The 1774a,b,c
85.4	*om*.] The 1774a,b,c
88.13	in] *om*. 1774a,b,c
89.16	*om*.] The 1774a,b,c
92.22– 93.20	*Lees* . . . goodness.] *om*. 1774a,b,c
92.22– 23	You . . . hope.] *om*. 1774a,b,c; Give me leave to speak to you— 1774d
92.26– 27	Let . . . company] *om*. 1774a,b,c; If you'll give us leave to explain the thing to you in private, we'll clear it up to you before all the company. 1774d
92.28– 93.20	*Tor* . . . goodness] *om*. 1774d
96.7– 14	*Lady* . . . man.] *om*. 1774a,b,c

THE ROMANCE OF AN HOUR

CBEL indicates two 1774 editions of *The Romance of an Hour*, but only one appears to be extant and thus is used as copy-text in this edition. The Larpent MS subtitle for this two-act comedy is "The Innocent Incendiary"; no hint of such a subtitle is found in the one edition I have seen.

Copy-text: *The Romance of an Hour, A Comedy of Two Acts*. (London, 1774).

THE MAN OF REASON

The text of *The Man of Reason* comes from Larpent MS 401, where it has the title "The Reasonable Lover. A Comedy," and is here printed for the first time with the permission of the Huntington Library, San Marino, California. The MS contains ninety-seven pages of text, copied by three scribes. The first also copied the "Prologue" and the "Epilogue." The first scribe wrote nearly to the bottom of page fifty-seven (IV.81); the second to the end of page seventy-four (IV.650); the third from page seventy-five to page ninety-seven (V.1–733). These scribes differ in handwriting, in the treatment of accidentals, and in accuracy. Scribe One corrects errors or omissions seventy-seven times in 1,960 typed lines; Scribe Two twenty-nine times in 530 lines; Scribe Three once in 733 lines. A list of these corrections appears below.

I have tried, within the limitations of typewriting, to duplicate the manuscript. I have followed spelling, punctuation, and capitalization even when they are inconsistent, and I have also followed the scribes in underlining, in sporadically enclosing stage directions in horizontal lines, in using brackets, parentheses, and straight lines indiscriminately, and in raising final letters of abbreviated titles; I have not expanded any speech prefixes. When the scribe has squeezed a speech prefix into the margin, I have put it on the same line as the speech (see II.534 for an example). I have not been able to duplicate the larger letters in which entrances and exits are written, but otherwise the typescript is a faithful rendition of the manuscript.

According to Genest (V, 517) the following cast acted in this play's single performance:

Sir James Clifford . . . . .Woodward
Freeman . . . . .Clarke
Lestock . . . . .Lee Lewes
Dr. Wilmington . . . . .Aiken
Wilmington . . . . .Wroughton

Wyndham	Lewis
Flavella	Mrs. Bulkley
Miss Wilmington	Mrs. Mattocks
Lady Winterley	Mrs. Hunter
Mrs. Glowworm	Mrs. Green
Mrs. Greeman	Mrs. Pitt

Copy-text: The Reasonable Lover. A Comedy. (Larpent MS 401). ⋀ indicates that the word (or words) enclosed in quotation marks immediately after the symbol has been inserted with a caret.

Scribal Corrections:

I. 61	"you are sensible" lined through
I. 106	⋀"my"
I. 125	⋀"a"
I. 230	⋀"Honour"
I. 370	⋀"think"
I. 420	⋀"be"
I. 446	"upon" lined through; ⋀ "for"
I. 478	⋀"have never"
I. 503	⋀"a"
I. 504	⋀"ruffian" over "morning," which is lined out
I. 547	⋀"week"
I. 550	⋀"to"
I. 574	⋀"the"
I. 575	⋀"in"
II. 15	⋀"and"
II. 73	⋀"treated"
II. 141	⋀"than the"
II. 158	⋀"r" in "Quarter"
II. 175	⋀"l" in "repulse"
II. 214	⋀"from"
II. 234	⋀"i" in "William"

II. 290 "leave" written in margin
II. 454 "generally" lined through last syllables, ∧ "rously"
II. 466 ∧"must"
II. 468 ∧"at"
II. 474 ∧"for"
II. 487 ∧"the"
II. 530 ∧"it"
II. 563 ∧"or" in "extraordinary"
II. 565 ∧"By"; ∧ "and" over a lined-through "by"
II. 580 ∧"is" crossed out after "it"
II. 613 ∧"I was"
II. 628 "h" lined through before "as"
II. 629 ∧"torturing" over "hesitating," which is lined through
II. 671 ∧"been"
II. 689 "Les" marked through, "Sir James" substituted
II. 691–93 put in at bottom of page, marked with asterisk
II. 692 "But dear Sir" lined through; ∧ "and"
II. 715 ∧"all's"
III. 36 ∧"As" over "and," which is lined through
III. 50 "I" lined through before "suppose"
III. 55 ∧"e" in "whose"
III. 96 "union" lined through; ∧ "unison"
III. 123 ∧"to"
III. 181 illegible word lined through
III. 210 ∧"r" in "course"
III. 219 ∧"consent"
III. 238 ∧"how" and "you"
III. 267 ∧"good"
III. 279 illegible word lined through
III. 311 ∧"it"
III. 336 ∧ "of"
III. 347 ∧"un" of "unfit"

III. 349 ∧“you”

III. 386 ∧“it”

III. 394 ∧“who” lined through; ∧ “we”

III. 409 ∧“n” in “Then”

III. 426 illegible word lined through between “me” and “mightily”

III. 430 ∧“I”

III. 431 “cause this” lined through

III. 434 ∧“hard”

III. 435 ∧“has”

III. 458 ∧“me”

III. 469 “he” lined through before “she”

III. 475 ∧“suppose”

III. 508 “head” lined through; ∧ “heart”

III. 517 ∧“her”

III. 525 ∧“the”

III. 546 “my” lined through; ∧ “the”

III. 573 ∧“nothing”

IV. 24 ∧“is”

IV. 29 ∧“herself”

IV. 45 ∧“he”

IV. 52 “(aside” erased or scraped away

IV. 54 ∧“but he is the”

IV. 69 “sure” lined through; ∧ “since”

IV. 73 “bid” lined through; ∧ “but”

IV. 168 ∧“It”

IV. 192 ∧“and”

IV. 195 “dedicated” lined through; ∧ “decided”

IV. 202 superfluous “very” lined through

IV. 219 ∧“a” in “clearly”

IV. 222–251 is an inserted page marked with ⊙

IV. 244 “from” lined through; ∧ “for”

IV. 255 ∧“seen”

IV. 259 ∧“of”

IV. 261	∧"no"
IV. 271	∧"there"
IV. 275	∧"his"
IV. 291	∧"the"
IV. 295	∧"be"
IV. 297	∧"a"
IV. 321	∧"a"
IV. 329	"of" lined through; ∧ "upon"
IV. 349	"which" lined through; ∧ "with"; ∧ "il" in "readily"
IV. 365	∧"things"
IV. 367	∧illegible word
IV. 372	"instantly" lined through; ∧ "insanity"; "and" lined through; ∧ "as"; "it" lined through
IV. 383	∧"on the other, my boy, for say that S[r] James should"
IV. 392	"aire" lined through; ∧ "air"
IV. 395	"there" lined through; ∧ "their"
IV. 409	∧"I"
IV. 420	"arnuity" lined through; ∧ "annuity"
IV. 423	∧"c" in "schemes"
IV. 496	illegible word between "can" and "remove"
IV. 513	"un" before "happy" erased or scraped away
IV. 546	"even" lined through; ∧ "wizen" (?)
IV. 547	illegible word between "the" and "of"
IV. 557	illegible word between "of" and "Carpenters"
V. 10	∧"is"

"Prologue . . . for the Benefit of the Infant Poor."

The "Prologue" was probably given December 21, 1773. See Stone, *London Stage* IV, Appendix B and p. 1772.

Copy-text: *The Works of Hugh Kelly* (London, 1778), pp. 420– 21.

"Epilogue . . . Macklin's Farce of LOVE-A-LA-MODE."

Copy-text: *The Works of Hugh Kelly* (London, 1778), pp. 421–23.

Mary J. H. Gross
University of Texas, Austin

THE LIST OF TITLES

1. **Restoration Adaptations.** Edited with an introduction by Edward A. Langhans.

2. **The State and the Licensing Act, 1729–1739.** Edited with an introduction by Vincent J. Liesenfeld.

3. **The Performers and Their Plays.** Edited with an introduction by Shirley Strum Kenny.

4. **The Plays of Isaac Bickerstaff.** Edited with an introduction by Peter A. Tasch. *Three volumes.*

5. **The Plays of James Boaden.** Edited with an introduction by Steven Cohan.

6. **The Plays of Henry Carey.** Edited with an introduction by Samuel L. Macey.

7. **The Plays of Susanna Centlivre.** Edited with an introduction by Richard C. Frushell. *Three volumes.*

8. **The Plays of Colley Cibber.** Edited with an introduction by Rodney L. Hayley.

9. **The Plays of Theophilus and Susanna Cibber.** Edited with an introduction by David Mann.

10. **The Plays of George Colman, The Elder.** Edited with an introduction by Kalman Burnim. *Two volumes.*

11. **The Plays of George Colman, The Younger.** Edited with an introduction by Peter A. Tasch. *Two volumes.*

12. **The Plays of Hannah Cowley.** Edited with an introduction by Frederick M. Link. *Two volumes.*

13. **The Plays of Richard Cumberland.** Edited with an introduction by Roberta F.S. Borkat. *Three volumes.*

14. **The Plays of John Dennis.** Edited with an introduction by J.W. Johnson.
15. **The Plays of Samuel Foote.** Edited with an introduction by Paula R. Backscheider. *Two volumes.*
16. **The Plays of David Garrick.** Edited with an introduction by Gerald Berkowitz. *Four volumes.*
17. **The Plays of Charles Gildon.** Edited with an introduction by Paula R. Backscheider.
18. **The Plays of Eliza Haywood.** Edited with an introduction by Valerie C. Rudolph.
19. **The Plays of Aaron Hill.** Edited with an introduction by Calhoun Winton.
20. **The Plays of Thomas Holcroft.** Edited with an introduction by Joseph Rosenblum. *Two volumes.*
21. **The Plays of John Hoole.** Edited with an introduction by Donald T. Siebert, Jr.
22. **The Plays of John Home.** Edited with an introduction by James S. Malek.
23. **The Plays of Elizabeth Inchbald.** Edited with an introduction by Paula R. Backscheider. *Two volumes.*
24. **The Plays of Robert Jephson.** Edited with an introduction by Temple Maynard.
25. **The Plays of Samuel Johnson of Cheshire.** Edited with an introduction by Valerie C. Rudolph.
26. **The Plays of Hugh Kelly.** Edited with an introduction by Larry Carver and with textual notes by Mary Jean Gross.
27. **The Plays of George Lillo.** Edited with an introduction by Trudy Drucker.
28. **The Plays of David Mallet.** Edited with an introduction by Felicity Nussbaum.
29. **The Plays of Edward Moore.** Edited with an introduction by J. Paul Hunter.
30. **The Plays of Arthur Murphy.** Edited with an introduction by Richard B. Schwartz. *Four volumes.*

31. **The Plays of John O'Keeffe.** Edited with an introduction by Frederick M. Link. *Four volumes.*

32. **The Plays of Mary Pix and Catherine Trotter.** Edited with an introduction by Edna L. Steeves. *Two volumes.*

33. **The Plays of Frederick Reynolds.** Edited with an introduction by Stanley W. Lindberg. *Two volumes.*

34. **The Plays of Edward Thompson.** Edited with an introduction by Catherine Neal Parke.

35. **The Plays of James Thomson.** Edited with an introduction by Percy G. Adams.

LIBRARY OF DAVIDSON COLLEGE

ʼᵃʳ loan ma·ʼ ʼᵉ checked oʼ